THE USE OF TECHNOLOGY
IN MENTAL HEALTH

ABOUT THE EDITORS

Kate Anthony, MSc, FBACP, is a psychotherapist, consultant and international expert regarding online therapy and the impact of technology on mental health. She is cofounder of the Online Therapy Institute. She is widely published on such topics as the use of email, bulletin boards, IRC, videoconferencing, stand-alone software, and more radical innovative use of technology within therapeutic practice, such as virtual reality. She coedited *Technology in Counselling and Psychotherapy: A Practitioner's Guide* with Stephen Goss in 2003, coauthored *Therapy Online [a practical guide]* with DeeAnna Merz Nagel in 2010, and coauthored all three editions of the British Association for Counselling and Psychotherapy's *Guidelines for Online Counselling and Psychotherapy.*

DeeAnna Merz Nagel, LPC, DCC, is a psychotherapist, consultant and international expert regarding online counseling and the impact of technology on mental health. She specializes in text-based counseling and supervision via chat and email. Her expertise extends to assisting individuals and families in understanding the impact of technology in their lives from normalizing the use of technology and social media to overcoming Internet and cybersex addictions. Her presentations and publications include ethical considerations for the mental healh practitioner with regard to online counseling, social networking, mixed reality, and virtual world environments. She is cofounder of the Online Therapy Institute.

Stephen Goss, PhD, MBACP, is an independent consultant in counselling technology, research and evaluation and a counselling practitioner and supervisor. He coedited *Technology in Counselling and Psychotherapy: A Practitioner's Guide* with Kate Anthony and coauthored the first and third editions of the British Association for Counselling and Psychotherapy's *Guidelines for Online Counselling and Psychotherapy.* He also coedited *Evidence Based Practice for Counselling and Psychotherapy* and is the author of over 70 other reports and publications and sits on the Editorial Board of the *British Journal of Guidance and Counselling.*

THE USE OF TECHNOLOGY IN MENTAL HEALTH

Applications, Ethics and Practice

Edited by

KATE ANTHONY, MSc, FBACP

Online Therapy Institute

DEEANNA MERZ NAGEL, LPC, DCC

Online Therapy Institute

STEPHEN GOSS, Ph.D., MBACP

*Independent Consultant in Counseling, Research,
Supervision and Technology in Mental Health*

CHARLES C THOMAS • PUBLISHER, LTD.
Springfield • Illinois • U.S.A.

Published and Distributed Throughout the World by

CHARLES C THOMAS • PUBLISHER, LTD.
2600 South First Street
Springfield, Illinois 62794-9265

© 2010 by CHARLES C THOMAS • PUBLISHER, LTD.

ISBN 978-0-398-07953-6 (hard)
ISBN 978-0-398-07954-3 (paper)

Library of Congress Catalog Card Number: 2010018410

With **THOMAS BOOKS** *careful attention is given to all details of manufacturing
and design. It is the Publisher's desire to present books that are satisfactory as to their
physical qualities and artistic possibilities and appropriate for their particular use.*
THOMAS BOOKS *will be true to those laws of quality that assure a good name
and good will.*

Printed in the United States of America
MM-R-3

Library of Congress Cataloging in Publication Data

The use of technology in mental health : applications, ethics and practice /
edited by Kate Anthony. DeeAnna Merz Nagel, and Stephen Goss.
    p. cm.
    Includes biographical references and index.
    ISBN 978-0-398-07953-6 (hard) – ISBN 978-0-398-07954-3 (pbk.)
    1. Mental health services. 2. Communication in medicine. 3. Medical infor-
matics. I. Anthony, Kate. II. Nagel, DeeAnna Merz. III. Goss, Stephen,
1966–. IV. Title.
    [DNLM: 1. Counseling–methods. 2. Telecommunications. 3. Internet. 4.
Professional-Patient Relations–ethics. 5. Psychotherapy–methods. WM 55
U84 2010]

RA790.5 U84 2010
362.196'893–dc22   2010018410

For Julie, ATWABA; and for my nephew Oscar, my Legend of Zelda hero. Also for P, for making space for me in his shed and his life. ˆ_ˆ

Oh Captain! My Captain! . . . For my dear Pete whose boat rides helped to inspire this work! Love, DA.

For Catriona, Andrew, and for E, working hard through the night. Together. ˆ ˆ
* ‿*

CONTRIBUTORS

Azy Barak , PhD, is a professor of psychology in the Departments of Counseling and Human Development and Learning, Instruction, and Supervision at the University of Haifa, Israel. He is Fellow of the International Society for Mental Health Online (ISMHO), and an active member of the International Society for Research on Internet Interventions (ISRII) and other professional organizations. His research interests include the psychological impact of the Internet on individuals, groups, couples, families, and communities, as well as exploitation of the Internet to promote various psychological applications.

Meyran Boniel-Nissim, MA, is an advanced doctoral student in the Department of Counseling and Human Development at the University of Haifa, Israel. She received a BA degree in education and in Hebrew literature, and an MA degree in counseling. Her research interests are in the psychology of the Internet, including online writing therapy, teenagers' blogs, virtual communities, online support groups, and online risk behavior such as Pro-Ana communities.

Linnea Carlson-Sabelli, PhD, is Professor of Psychiatric Nursing at Rush University College of Nursing, Chicago, where she has been a faculty member since 1978. She is nationally certified both as a clinical nurse specialist in Adult Psychiatric Nursing and as a trainer, educator, and practitioner of psychodrama, sociometry, and group psychotherapy. She has received grants totalling more than one million dollars from the U.S. Department of Health and Human Services to develop and implement creative online methods to provide faculty clinical supervision to distant Psychiatric Mental Health Nurse Practitioner students.

Kate Cavanagh is a Senior Lecturer in Psychology at the University of Sussex and Honorary Clinical Psychologist in Sussex Partnership NHS Trust. Her research interests include increasing access to evidence-based psychological therapies for common mental health problems and she has been involved in the research, development, and implementation of Computerised Cognitive Behavioural Therapy programmes over the past 10 years.

Ginger Clark is an Associate Professor of Clinical Education and Program Lead in the Marriage and Family Therapy program at the University of Southern California. In addition to her academic position, she is a licensed psychologist and part of a group practice in Long Beach, California. Ginger has been infusing technology into her academic work, requiring students to utilize common online platforms and websites to further enhance their learning process.

Diane H. Coursol, PhD, is a Professor in Counselor Education at Minnesota State University, Mankato. She currently teaches Technology in Counseling, Assessment, Treatment Planning, Counseling Procedures and Skills, Practicum, and Internship.

David Coyle, PhD, is a postdoctoral Research Fellow at Trinity College Dublin. He currently holds a Marie Curie Mobility Research Fellowship, based jointly with Trinity College Dublin and the University of Cambridge. His research focuses on the application of Human Computer Interaction methods to the design of technologies for the mental health care domain. In particular, this research focuses on investigating sustainable approaches to the development of technologies to improve the effectiveness of mental health interventions.

Kathleene Derrig-Palumbo, PhD, is a leading figure and international speaker in the world of online mental health services. She is a lead consultant and expert for the Dr. Phil Show. She is a recent recipient of a Stevie Award for "Best Woman Entrepreneur–Service Business." In addition to many published articles in magazines and journals as well as authored chapters in books, she is well-known for her book, *Online Therapy: A Therapist's Guide to Expanding Your Practice.*

Mark Dombeck, PhD, directs Mental Help Net (www.mentalhelp.net), a leading online mental health consumer education and community resource since 1995. He is a partner in CenterSite, LLC (www.centersite.net), a provider of web content and hosting services to community mental health and employee assistance organizations. A licensed psychologist, he received his doctorate in Clinical Psychology from the UCSD/SDSU Joint Doctoral Program.

Joe Ferns is Deputy Director of Policy and Projects at Samaritans. He is a media spokesperson and has worked on several national and international advisory groups on suicide prevention. Prior to Samaritans, he worked for the Institute of Psychiatry on a project running psychoeducational workshops for people with depression and anxiety problems. Joe has over 14 years experience in mental health in settings including residential services, community outreach, day services, advocacy, and 1:1 support work.

Nicole Gehl is an experienced existential-integrative psychotherapist based in North West London. She is a member of the Priory Healthcare Team and currently sees patients at their acute hospitals in Roehampton and North London. In private practice, her work includes online therapy through chat and videoconferencing software at www.hereandnowtherapy.co.uk. She previously held positions as a psychotherapist with the National Health Service and Westminster Drug Project.

John M. Grohol, PsyD, has been writing, researching, and publishing in the area of online mental health, psychology and human behavior since 1992. He sits on the editorial board of *CyberPsychology & Behavior,* and is a founding member of the Society for Participatory Medicine. Since 1995, he has been overseeing the leading mental health network online today, Psych Central.com, named one of the 50 Best Websites in 2008 by *TIME.*

Melissa Groman is a Licensed Clinical Social Worker with a private practice in Nutley, New Jersey. She is the founder and director of the Good Practice Institute for Professional Psychotherapists (www.goodpracticeinstitute.com), a clinical resource and learning center for psychotherapists. The Good Practice Institute offers individual and group clinical supervision and consultation and classes via telephone, bringing together clinicians from around the world to consult, learn, study, and advance their practice.

Samara (Rainey) Harms is a freelance research consultant based in the northeast United States. Published in the areas of mental health, technology, and the law, she frequently collaborates with Dr. Patricia Recupero and her colleagues at Butler Hospital. A major research and teaching psychiatric hospital in Providence, Rhode Island, Butler is affiliated with The Warren Alpert Medical School of Brown University.

Tristram Hooley is the Head of the International Centre for Guidance Studies at the University of Derby. He is interested in the interface between research, policy, and practice and has particular interests in career education, e-learning, and Web 2.0. He has been very involved in the training of researchers in research and transferable skills and has taught extensively on online research methods. He maintains an academic blog entitled *Adventures in Career Development* at http://adventuresincareerdevelopment.posterous.com/.

Eva Kaltenthaler, PhD, is a Senior Research Fellow at the University of Sheffield working in the field of health technology assessment. She has a special interest in mental health issues, especially patient acceptability of technologies. She has completed two comprehensive systematic reviews of Computerised Cognitive Behaviour Therapy for the National Institute for Health and Clinical Excellence and is currently involved in a review of group cognitive behaviour therapy for postnatal depression.

Thomas J. Kim, MD, received his BA in Philosophy from Georgetown and MD, MPH from Tulane University. He continued at Tulane to complete a combined residency in Internal Medicine and Psychiatry and a General Medicine fellowship in health services research. At present, he serves as Physician Advisor for Government Affairs at athenahealth, an integrated web-based practice management company.

Reid Klion, PhD, is the Chief Science Officer of pan-A TALX Company (www.panpowered.com). He is an expert in web-based assessment and is actively involved in scientific, regulatory and industry issues related to testing. He has published extensively and presents regularly at international professional conferences. A licensed psychologist, he is a graduate of Hobart College and received his doctorate in Clinical Psychology from Miami University.

Jacqueline Lewis is a Professor in the Department of Counseling and Student Personnel at Minnesota State University, Mankato. Her research areas include technology in counseling and student affairs, career development, and diversity in counseling and student affairs.

Clare Madge is a Senior Lecturer in Human Geography at the University of Leicester. She is a feminist geographer with interests in Africa and cyberspace. Clare led the development of the "Exploring Online Research Methods" website (www.geog.le.ac.uk) and has published on online research methods and on the impact that the internet is having on social relations. She is also on the editorial board of ACME, an e-journal of critical geography and sits on the advisory board of the National Centre for Research Methods ReStore project looking at the sustainability of online resources.

Mark Matthews, PhD, is a computer scientist and researcher at Trinity College Dublin. He is an expert in the design and evaluation of therapeutic technologies including mobile support systems, computer games, and virtual environments. He has developed many clinical systems including Mobile Mood Diary, which uses clients' personal mobile phones for symptom tracking and Personal Investigator, a 3-D computer game. His research interests include the use of technology to assist behaviour change and to develop therapeutic alliances.

Paul McCrone, PhD, is a Reader in Health Economics at the Institute of Psychiatry (King's College London), where he has worked for 13 years after having previously worked at the University of Kent. He has worked on a large number of economic studies in health and social care. Currently he is involved in evaluations in psychiatry, neurology, and palliative care. He teaches health economics to Masters level students and has published widely in peer-reviewed journals.

Thomas A. Merz, LPC, DCC, is currently in private practice, providing clinical and forensic evaluations as well as online counseling and psychotherapy. Tom holds a BA in Sociology from Georgia State University and an MEd in Rehabilitation Counseling from the University of Georgia. He is a Georgia Licensed Professional Counselor as well as a National Certified Counselor and Distance Credentialed Counselor. Tom has been an advocate of online therapy and mental health strategies supported by the internet for over 10 years.

Emma Morrow, PhD, is a Chartered Clinical Psychologist in Grampian, Scotland, working within the public and private sectors. She completed her undergraduate degree in psychology at Aberdeen University in 2000. She was awarded a Doctorate in Clinical Psychology from Glasgow University and returned to Aberdeen in 2005. Dr. Morrow is an Honorary Research Fellow with the Centre for Obesity Research and Epidemiology, at Robert Gordon University. She has a special interest in obesity, particularly working with those patients undergoing weight loss surgery.

Gregory Palumbo is a pioneer in online mental health services technology. He has overseen the project management of enterprise-level software systems designed for use by mental healthcare providers. He is currently overseeing the development of a suite of Web 2.0 solutions adapted for use by mental healthcare providers. Previous to this work, he served as CEO of Galilay Entertainment, COO of Innerlight Entertainment and CTO for Magic Image Films, a subsidiary of Digital Magic, now Todd AO West.

Daniel M. Paredes, PhD, is a clinical counselor in the North Carolina Agricultural and Technical State University's Counseling Services. A member of national and state professional associations, he has been inducted into the Chi Sigma Iota Counseling Academic and Professional Honor Society. He is a graduate of the University of California at San Diego and of the University of North Carolina at Greensboro.

Marcos A. Quinones is a staff therapist at The Albert Ellis Institute for Cognitive and Rational Emotive Behavioral Therapy, Adjunct Professor at the New York

University School of Social Work, and President and Founder of The Jove Institute, an online portal distributing self-help cognitive behavioral therapeutic techniques using technologies such as Podcasts, Pencasts, Electronic Newsletters, Skype, and Smart Phone Applications. Currently, he lives in New Jersey and treats local and international clients from his New York City office.

Sara Riley earned a BSc in Psychology and Business Administration from University of Maryland, Asian Division, while living in Misawa, Japan. Upon returning to the United States she attended Alaska Pacific University in Anchorage, Alaska, where she received her Masters of Science Counseling Psychology. She is a Licensed Professional Counselor (LPC) in Georgia, a Nationally Certified Counselor (NCC), and a Distance Credentialed Counselor (DCC). She has obtained extensive clinical, assessment and forensic experience while serving a multitude of culturally diverse populations.

Giuseppe Riva, PhD, is Associate Professor of Communication Psychology and Director of the Communication and Ergonomics of New Technologies Lab.–ICE NET Lab.–at the Catholic University of Milan, Italy. He also serves as Head Researcher at the the Applied Technology for Neuro-Psychology Laboratory–ATN-P Lab., Istituto Auxologico Italiano, Milan, Italy. He is Editor in Chief for the *Emerging Communication* book series and for the online journals *Annual Review of Cybertherapy and Telemedicine* and *Psychnology,* European Editor for the *CyberPsychology & Behavior* journal and Associate Editor of the *Journal of CyberTherapy & Rehabilitation.*

Patricia Ryan Recupero, JD, MD, is the President and CEO of Butler Hospital, a private psychiatric hospital in Providence, Rhode Island, and she also serves as Clinical Professor of Psychiatry in the Department of Psychiatry and Human Behavior at the Warren Alpert Medical School of Brown University. She holds board certification in Forensic Psychiatry and Addiction Psychiatry and is especially interested in legal aspects of the role of information technology in medical practice.

Denise E. Saunders, PhD, maintains a private practice in Chapel Hill, North Carolina, providing psychotherapy, counseling, and consultation services to her clients. In addition to work with individual clients, she has consulted with higher educational organizations, small businesses, and state and federal government agencies. She engages in distance counseling services as a counselor and trainer with ReadyMinds, a provider of distance career counseling services. She is a Licensed Psychologist in the state of North Carolina, a National Certified Counselor and a Distanced Credentialed Counselor.

John W. Seymour, PhD, LMFT, is an Associate Professor in Counseling at Minnesota State University, Mankato. He is an Approved Supervisor with the American Association of Marriage and Family Therapy and a Registered Play Therapist-Supervisor with the Association for Play Therapy. He currently teaches the Supervision in Counselor Education course in the doctoral program at Michigan State University. Prior to teaching graduate supervision, family therapy, and play therapy courses at the University, he worked in a variety of settings, including hospital, agency, and residential treatment.

Susan Simpson is an Australian Clinical Psychologist based in Aberdeen,

Scotland. She set up the video therapy service between Aberdeen and remote and rural parts of northeast Scotland and Shetland and Orkney islands for people with psychological problems in the mid 1990s. She mainly works in the NHS Grampian Eating Disorder service which provides specialist psychological therapies by videolink over a large geographical area. She completed her doctoral research on the treatment of bulimic disorders by video therapy and has published widely in the area.

Cedric Speyer, MA, MEd, helped design and develop Shepell·fgi's groundbreaking E-Counselling service and conducted their first 2000 Canadian EAP cases online. He currently recruits, trains and supervises an "E-team" of almost 50 online counsellors. He holds Master degrees in Education, Counselling Psychology, and Creative Writing. He conceived and teaches a therapeutic approach to solution-focused E-Counselling called InnerView.

Jean-Anne Sutherland, PhD, is assistant professor of sociology at University of North Carolina, Wilmington, and focuses on two areas of research: the sociology of mothering, guilt, and shame and sociology through film. Her chapter, entitled Ideal Mama, Ideal Worker: Negotiating Guilt and Shame in Academe" appears in, *Mama PhD., Women Write About Motherhood and the Academy.* Her textbook, edited with Kathryn Feltey, is entitled *Cinematic Sociology: Social Life in Film.*

Leon Tan, PhD, MHSc, is a psychotherapist and art historian based in the United Kingdom and Sweden. His research interests include schizoanalysis, art, and social media. He consults and provides online therapy privately and is a member of the British Association for Counselling and Psychotherapy.

Allison Thompson is an Outpatient Counselor for St. Aloysius Orphanage, and works with children, adolescents and families. She is a graduate from Xavier University's Master of Arts program in Counseling (2008) and earned a Bachelor of Science from Ohio University (2004). She was published in the August 2008 issue of *Counseling Today.* She looks forward to future writing opportunities as well as continuing to serve children and families.

Jane Wellens is the Head of Researcher Development at the University of Nottingham where she leads the University's research training programme for early career research staff. She is a member of the Careers in Research Online Survey Steering Group and contributed to the revised CROS 2009 survey. She has considerable experience of using online research methods and has been an investigator on two ESRC-funded projects addressing this theme.

John Wilson, PG Dip, MBACP, is a counsellor in private practice working with individuals and couples face-to-face, on the telephone, and online using email, chat, and virtual environments. He is a lecturer in counselling skills at Stevenson College, Edinburgh. He also runs onlinevents.co.uk which streams events live to the Internet and records for future distribution with the express purpose of making professional development for mental health professionals more affordable and accessible.

John Yaphe, MD, CM (McGill University), MClSc (Western Ontario) is a family physician and associate professor in community health in the School of Health Sciences of the University of Minho, Portugal. He has been an active online counsellor with Shepell-FGI since 2004, contributing to the development of the theory and practice of online counselling and the training and supervision of new E-counsellors.

FOREWORD

AUDREY JUNG, ISMHO PRESIDENT 2010–2011

I used my first text messaging system in 1986.
Impossible, you say? Digital cell phones didn't introduce texting capabilities until the late '90s? Wrong. This was a large keyboard attached to an acoustic coupler, a two-inch digital screen, and a thermal paper printer. Known as a TeleTYpewriter, or TTY, I used that machine to text a deaf friend through my telephone landline. At that time, the TTY cost over $400, was not portable, and had many incompatibility issues with other machines. Despite it all, the TTY enabled its users to establish relationships with each other from remote settings using only text. Nine years later, my graduate school professors and classmates used this same modality to discuss mental health related concepts, to provide clinical supervision and, naturally, simply to stay in touch with each other during off-campus internships.

Web browsing, texting, im'ing, emoticoning—all gave birth to a new language development in the 2000s which enhanced the ability of an individual to express himself thoroughly and deeply without needing to travel for face-to-face meetings or to call or to send a letter. Similar to the American Sign Language used by deaf individuals in the United States, this new form of written communication appears to have its own grammar and syntax—utilizing obscure abbreviations, punctuation symbols, and pace to convey emotional content. Commercials reflect this shift in modern culture as a young child retorts to her mother, "IDK, my BFF Jill?" Pop songs are currently using the abbreviated language of texting in their refrains "I let my fingers do the talk, talk, talkin, They say lolololol, they say lololololololol, they say lololololol yeah" (Sinai Rose, Kidz Bop 16, 2009). People are using online dating sites to meet their soulmates.

The virtual realm is not based in any one country. It exists in the ether and is crossing political territories. International businesses are capitalizing on the virtual gold they can earn in MMORPGs by selling it back to the gamers for a very real price. And very real people are reaching out for psychological help online. Websites have emerged that have offered psychoeducational literature, hypnosis, and self-help merchandise and finally—counseling in synchronous or asynchronous modalities. Regardless of the localized reservations of a vocal minority, the global socio-cultural response for the provision of mental health services online has been resoundingly positive.

The International Society for Mental Health Online and the Online Therapy Institute have been instrumental in establishing best practice criteria and ethical codes for clinicians who have extended their practices to the virtual realm. Both entities have established wiki compendiums for professionals to use to better understand the cultures, psychosocial values and legal concerns of individuals in remote locales. But there is so much more work to be done.

Thankfully, Kate Anthony, DeeAnna Merz Nagel and Stephen Goss have been instrumental in responding to the call for increased resources in training and supervision of international clinicians. Whether you have been a therapist for eons, or are a student new to the field, *The Use of Technology in Mental Health, Applications, Ethics and Practice* is an important tool for better understanding the psychological struggles of our clients and the impact that technology will have on our practices.

INTRODUCTION

KATE ANTHONY

As our authors can testify, this book has been a long time in preparation. The sheer scale of the different uses of technology in the mental health professions is now vast and as each cycle of manuscript preparation came about, we decided to extend our reach and include as many up to the minute technologies as possible. It is testament to the profession that we are now accepting these technologies as the way forward rather than the avoidant attitudes that were apparent just ten years ago, although caution is still rightly exercised, for the most part, when employing technology.

The range of technologies now apparent in the profession—from the simple use of a website to advertise and promote offline services to full immersion in online virtual worlds to conduct therapy—shows that this is no longer a new field in mental health. We have empirical research to back up the use of technologies, training programmes dedicated to their use and a growing ethical base from which to develop services and practice. Each technology has its own benefits and limitations, as evidenced in these chapters, but no one can deny it is a fascinating and exciting field to be in. As new generations of clients and mental health practitioners emerge into a world where the Internet and mobile technology—to name just two facets of the field—have always existed, reliance on, and acceptance of, technologies as melded into everyday life indicates that using technology is unlikely to disappear from the profession.

OVERVIEW

It is the intention of this book to give the reader a wide range of chapters that may be read in isolation depending on the needs of any service provision, or as a complete study of as many technologies as are available at the time of writing. We, as editors, are aware that new technologies will emerge even as it is in production and look forward to including these in future editions of the book.

It should be noted that each author may have a different view of how these technologies are best implemented. As example, the editors conclude that the use of encryption is paramount and nonnegotiable, but the legal implications of what service, product or platform to utilize is not within the purvue of this book. The editors advise practitioners to seek legal counsel regarding such matters, particularly concerning terms of use and privacy issues.

What you will also find in the book is a wide range of styles, from the individual practitioner exploring a new technology and writing anecdotally about their personal experience, to medical practitioners writing an academic overview of a technology and its uses in the profession.

Within each chapter, you will find reference to definitions of the technology, application to the therapeutic intervention being discussed, case material and illustrations, ethical examination and concluding thoughts on the future impact of the technology on the profession. All case illustrations are fictionalized, although all are based on the authors' direct, practical experience. This book is an extensive body of work on the topic and we hope you find it of use professionally and personally in your online and offline life.

In Chapter 1, "Using Email to Conduct a Therapeutic Relationship," Patricia Ryan Recupero and Samara Harms look at the impact of the use of email for therapeutic use, its application and ethical issues such as risks to confidentiality, appropriateness for client work, standards of care and administrative issues before turning to the cases of clients "Sheila" and "John" by way of illustration. They conclude, as do many other authors in the book, that further research is still needed to be able to provide an ethical, practical and beneficial service via the technology discussed in the chapter.

In Chapter 2, "Using Chat and Instant Messaging (IM) to Conduct a Therapeutic Relationship," Kathleene Derrig-Palumbo considers how to conduct a therapeutic relationship via chat rooms and instant messaging. She discusses issues such as identity, how the therapeutic relationship is formulated and maintained, practical strategies for encouraging progress of the work via text and some theoretical orientations that successfully underpin the work. She then gives a chat room session with a client "Joshua," who was unable to communicate face-to-face, but through chat rooms developed an ability to open up and therefore communicate better with his parents. She concludes that in the future, online therapy may well be regarded as no different than in-person therapy.

In Chapter 3, "Using Cell/Mobile Phone SMS for Therapeutic Intervention," Thomas A. Merz looks at the use of mobile or cell phone texting (SMS or "Short Message Service") and how this has emerged and developed from casual communication to a vehicle utilized for targeted therapeutic interventions and support in clinical settings. He describes it within a medical setting as well as a therapeutic support setting, before going on to consider the ethical implications of using text. Case study material includes a client texting her therapist within a face-to-face session. He concludes that SMS has become a bridge between service providers and clients and as such its use is likely to expand.

Chapter 4, "Using Social Networks and Implications for the Mental Health Profession," is by Allison Thompson and studies the impact of online communities and their role in impacting on mental health. Her extensive description of this focuses on MySpace.com. She examines the dangers of dual relationships and the importance of boundaries and gives two clear examples of when this can impact negatively on therapeutic or professional work. Ethical consideration looks at the attitude of professional organisations, in particular the American Counseling Association (ACA) and the British Association for Counselling and Psychotherapy (BACP), and the lack of clear guidance elsewhere on using social and professional networks. She concludes with the need for research in this topic, which is much underestimated by the profession in the opinion of the editors.

In Chapter 5, "Using Forums to Enhance Client Peer Support," the book shifts towards looking at technologies for peer support with Azy Barak's work. He describes and defines online support groups and points out the differences between them and conducting therapy online. Procedures and the practice of providing online support groups are looked at, before examination of the psychological processes that occur within these online groups and the importance of facilitation. He discusses the research into the field and concludes that the advent of online support groups has significantly positively changed the mental condition of many people suffering from various types of personal distress.

Chapter 6, "Using Cell/Mobile Phone SMS to Enhance Client Crisis and Peer Support," by Stephen Goss and Joe Ferns, examines SMS Crisis Support and Peer Support, based on a presentation given at the first Online Counselling and Therapy In Action (OCTIA) conference in the UK in 2009. They explore the development process and use of SMS text messaging systems in counselling and support services, in particular The Samaritans in the UK. They include case material–text messages sent and responded to–to illustrate the chapter and conclude that as in the case of many of the technologies examined in this book, the initial fears and doubts about the use of SMS in mental health services are steadily being dispelled.

Chapter 7, "Using Websites, Blogs and Wikis Mental Health," is by John M. Grohol, who offers an examination of websites, blogs (covered further in Chapter 8) and wikis. He defines the latter two in relation to Web 2.0 technologies, a theme you will find runs through the book. He discusses the application of these technologies and also the ethical implications and issues that are inherent in them. For example, wikis can be a huge source of *mis*information as well as information and blogs "can provide people with all sorts of potentially harmful (or at the very least, useless) personal opinions that carry some legitimacy if the blog is popular." The case example of "Jane" describes her journey in exploring options to treat her depression via websites and blogs on the topic, before finally taking the plunge to seek professional help from an individual. He concludes with thoughts on the role of the Internet in lessening isolation and the stigma around seeking help for mental health issues.

In Chapter 8, "The Role of Blogging in Mental Health," DeeAnna Merz Nagel and Gregory Palumbo take a look at blogging in detail, noting how the Internet brought change not only to how people could distribute their writings, but also to how those writings could remain dynamic and alive. The most popular example of technologies that support this interactivity is blogging. The authors examine the business applications of blogging as well as the use of blogs in mental health for disseminating information and education and also as a form of journaling for clients. They also visit microblogging sites such as Twitter. They conclude that "whether for professional or personal pursuits, when used responsibly, blogging can make a substantial and positive impact on the counseling profession and the world at large."

At Chapter 9, "Using the Telephone for Conducting a Therapeutic Relationship," the book again shifts towards nontext-based technological interventions with Denise E. Saunders' chapter on using the telephone for mental health services. She defines "telephone counseling," examines the state of it in practice via evidence-based findings, the benefits and limitations, the ethical considerations of telephone use such as security and confidentiality and the practical applications. She offers the case examples "May" and "John," describing their experience working by telephone. She concludes with thoughts on the possibility that "one day it will be commonplace for counselors to provide distance services to clients exclusively" and states the prominent role the telephone will have in this.

Continuing the theme of voice-based interactions, Chapter 10, "Using Videoconferencing for Conducting a Therapeutic Relationship," is by Susan Simpson and Emma Morrow, who look at the role of videoconferencing. They discuss how the therapeutic alliance works over video links and the role of the available visual clues while still working at a distance. Their extensive case study, "Angela," provides an illustration of a complex case using schema-focused therapy to treat Bulimia Nervosa, depression and chronic low self-esteem. They examine legal and ethical issues of videoconferencing and also the benefits with particular regard to breaking down geographical barriers. They conclude with thoughts for future research.

In Chapter 11, "Using Virtual Reality to Conduct a Therapeutic Relationship," John Wilson discusses his experiences of working therapeutically with clients in virtual environments, specifically Second Life. He describes the growth of Massively Multiplayer Online (MMO) environments and games and what it is like to exist in a virtual space. He then goes on to apply this to conducting therapy inworld and compares its opportunities in relation to the limitations of offline therapy sessions. He also describes the applications of theories such as outdoor and wilderness therapy and how these can easily be applied inworld. This is extended to discussion of Virtual Reality (VR) Exposure Therapy (discussed in Chapter 13) and further implications for potentially damaging psychological issues such as acting out and different sub personalities. Wilson closes with ethical implications and points out the importance of seeing virtual environments as an extension of the offline world rather than a substitute.

Extending the theme of virtual environments, in Chapter 12, "Using Virtual Reality Immersion Therapeutically," Guiseppe Riva examines immersion in four virtual environments: full, CAVE, augmented and desktop. He gives an examination of the role of virtual reality (VR) in clinical psychology in relation to conditions such as phobias, posttraumatic stress and anxiety disorders. He also notes, however, that VR has further implications for treatment beyond desensitisation and exposure therapy, such as being immersed in the environment with the practitioner in such a way that is indistinguishable from the nonvirtual world via the role of "presence." Riva identifies four major issues that limit the use of VR in practice and how he and colleagues have addressed this.

In Chapter 13, "The Use of Computer-Aided Cognitive Behavioural Therapy (CCBT) in Therapeutic Settings," Kate Cavanagh gives a history of the evolution of Cognitive Behavioural theories into providing these interventions via Computerised Cognitive Behavioural Therapy (CCBT). She introduces various software packages before focusing down on Beating the Blues and FearFighter and the evidence of outcomes for such programmes. Ethical consideration is given to their use and the importance of balancing this with in-person intervention. She concludes with showing how CCBT is important as a hands on early option for effective self-help in a growing number of mental health problems. CCBT is further discussed in Chapter 25.

Chapter 14, "The Role of Gaming in Mental Health," by Mark Matthews and David Coyle, discusses the use of games to engage adolescents–a client group notoriously reluctant to access counselling–in the therapeutic process. He shows how appropriately designed games (in contrast to the other types that receive so much negative media coverage) can be used for this purpose and to help adolescents get the mental health assistance they need. Matthews starts with ethical discussion before giving a history of the limited previous research and noting some of the benefits defined by such research, advocating caution in trusting results without further examination. He describes *Personal Investigator,* a 3D computer game based on Solution Focused Therapy, its use in clinical settings and by way of a case study, the opinions of a therapist who has used the game with clients, before looking to the future of the genre.

In Chapter 15, "Web-based Clinical Assessment," Reid Klion considers web-based clinical assessment, including its history, application in relation to therapeutic intervention and ethics. He goes on to discuss the case of "Robert," before concluding with a look to the future, where he postulates that tests will be developed specifically for Internet-based delivery and that we are at the edge of the revolution when it comes to web-based assessment.

In Chapter 16, "The Role of Behavioral Telehealth in Mental Health," Thomas J. Kim discusses behavioural telehealth, showing how technology has transformed healthcare and defining its role through historic examination, looking at the current landscape and offering opinions based on clinical and program development experience. Kim starts with a case study to illustrate postdisaster intervention via psychiatric telehealth, before offering a telehealth model. He goes on to show the challenges the profession faces in this field such as licensure and malpractice suits, some future directions and a call for meaningful healthcare reform.

At this point, the book takes a turn towards using nontext-based interventions, as in the previous eight chapters, and applies similar technologies to peer support. In Chapter 17, "The Use of Virtual Reality for Peer Support," Leon Tan takes a look at the use of Virtual Reality for this purpose. He describes both in-vivo exposure therapy (IVET) and Virtual Reality exposure therapy (VRET) before discussing mental health affordances, defined as the "opportunities and risks provided by a social environment to affect the mental health of individuals" and its application to VR, in this case Second Life (SL). He illustrates his chapter with reports from CBS news about a woman, "Patricia," who suffered from agoraphobia but overcame her difficulties through SL. Tan discusses some of the psychological processes a client can undergo in such environments and in which peers can assist. He concludes with pointing out the powerful impact such environments can have on an individuals' mental health.

In Chapter 18, "The Use of Podcasting in Mental Health," Marcos A. Quinones describes his work with podcasting in helping clients improving their mental and physical health by downloading MP3 (or similar) files on various topics. He also defines best practice for testing in Mental Health and gives anecdotal evidence to support the success this method of communicating to clients. He recommends structures for content and the hardware and software required, before examining the ethical considerations needed when planning to podcast.

Chapter 19, "The Use of Online Psychological Testing for Self-Help," is a study of online psychological testing, by Mark Dombeck, as it applies to self-help efforts. Dombeck reviews how online testing supports mental health self-help efforts, discusses problems and concerns associated with online testing and self-help practices and offers informed speculation concerning the ways in which online psychological testing and self-help technologies are likely to develop in the future. He also examines in detail the downsides of this technology.

The book takes another turn with Chapter 20, "Using Email to Enrich Counselor Training and Supervision," by John Yaphe and Cedric Speyer, towards using text-based technologies to enrich counsellor training and supervision. Yaphe and Speyer examine the use of email for supervision, using their own model—InnerView—and describe how e-counsellors within an Employee Assistance Program (EAP) setting receive supervision online. They discuss some of the challenges of this method and illustrate their work with several case vignettes, before concluding with the need for more research into the topic.

In Chapter 21, "Using Chat and Instant Messaging (IM) to Enrich Counselor Training and Supervision," DeeAnna Merz Nagel and Sara Riley discuss the use of chat and instant messaging for online supervision and illustrate this with their own experience of working together in an agency setting that offered in-home counseling and evaluation services to clients in rural locations. They define chat, clinical supervision, peer supervision, and field supervision and conclude that chat supervision can be used as a stand-alone method of delivery or it can be combined with other technology and face-to-face supervision, enriching any supervisory experience.

Chapter 22, "Using Forums to Enrich Counselor Training and Supervision," is by Linnea Carlson-Sabelli. Her goals are to provide definitions, applications, ethical considerations, illustrations of supervision techniques and speculation on the future of online text-based clinical supervision based on extensive experience supervising graduate level Psychiatric Mental Health Nurse Practitioner students at a major medical university located in the Midwest United States. She also looks at future applications of technologies using virtual reality environments and how they may best be implemented in the future to enrich counsellor training and supervision.

In Chapter 23, "Text-Based Credentialing in Mental Health," Daniel M. Paredes examines how text-based continuing education (CE) in the USA and continuing professional development (CPD) in the UK can meet the requirements imposed by credentialing bodies for the profession. He defines what text-based CE/CPD is and examines some of the issues inherent in it. He also examines the ethical considerations needed and a framework to classify

CE activities according to general content area, including research into the topic to illustrate it.

The book takes a final turn towards using other, nontext-based technologies to enrich counsellor training and supervision, starting with Chapter 24, "Online Research Methods for Mental Health," by Tristram Hooley, Jane Wellens, Clare Madge and Stephen Goss. The chapter focuses on online methods for counselling and psychotherapy research, including a brief history and considering the ethical issues in inherent in conducting research in this way. They conclude that although online research should not be seen as a replacement for traditional onsite methods, they will continue to be an essential part of the researchers' toolkit.

Chapter 25, "Evaluating the Role of CCBT in Mental Health," returns to the subject of Computerised CBT (CCBT) from Eva Kaltenthaler, Kate Cavanagh and Paul McCrone. They give an evaluation of stand-alone computer software programmes for depression and anxiety, with attention to issues of trial design and the components of CCBT packages. Program and client considerations are taken into account, as well as logistical and ethical balances.

In Chapter 26, "Traditional Uses of Technology in Counseling Trainee Supervision," Ginger Clark gives an overview of the traditional use of technology in counseling education and supervision. She defines various types of technologies used for this purpose and examines the ethical issues in each, the effect on the trainee practitioner, the client and the therapeutic process itself, illustrated with case vignettes. She concludes that it is unlikely that any of these technologies will disappear in the near future but that their implementation will change and develop.

In Chapter 27, "The Use of Telephone to Enrich Counselor Training and Supervision," Mellissa Groman gives an analysis of the use of the telephone for supervision and consultation. Among the questions she considers are how the relationship between consultant and therapist gets established and develops, whether the benefits of clinical consultation and supervision can apply across the airways and whether the goals of supervision can be met without visual cues and sight induced transferences. She concludes that "phone supervision's appeal will likely continue to grow as technology continues to dissolve geographic limitations."

Chapter 28, "The Use of Videoconferencing to Enrich Counselor Training and Supervision," by Diane H. Coursol, Jacqueline Lewis, and John W. Seymour, considers the same field but in relation to the use of videoconferencing software and hardware. They discuss the concept of what they name "cybersupervision," its implementation and the process, illustrating these with two case examples. They give an overview of the ethical implications of cybersupervision, before concluding that there is increasing evidence for its viability and the likelihood of this perception growing.

In Chapter 29, "Online Training for Online Mental Health," Nicole Gehl and two of the coeditors of this book, Kate Anthony and DeeAnna Merz Nagel, turn to issues of experiential training using technology, defining the types of online learning environments and their benefits and limitations. The chapter is illustrated by the lead author's Personal Learning Statement–the final piece of coursework from her online training to apply her counselling experience to online work at OnlineCounsellors. co.uk. The authors conclude that although online learning environments are established, caution should be exercised in "making sure the training offered does not attempt or imply that it can train people to have skills that are not actually provided."

In Chapter 30, "The Role of Film and Media in Mental Health," Jean-Anne Sutherland turns the reader's attention to the use of films and media in educating counsellors and supervisors by noting how they provide an opportunity for clients in a therapeutic setting to recognize, struggle and potentially identify with deep-seated conflicts. She reviews the literature and notes cautions and considerations before concluding that films can be an ideal tool for illustrating life and how it is the work of the therapist is to frame those representations in such as way as to provide meaningful analysis for the client.

The book concludes with two essays by two of the editors which were published at The Future of Innovation project at www.thefutureofinnovation. com. We also include an introduction to the work and mission of the Online Therapy Institute, which we hope will be of value to readers as a useful resource in bringing mental health and technology together.

NOTE ON THE SCOPE OF THE TEXT AND THE LANGUAGE USED

The collaboration of the editors from both sides of the Atlantic is deliberate, as addressing an audience that is international is appropriate when discussing a topic that provides therapeutic, peer support and education services globally, regardless of geographical limitations. Our range of authors reflect that international spread.

The scope and language of the book has been kept as internationally applicable as possible, while US and non-US spellings (e.g., of "counselor" or "counsellor") have generally been retained to reflect each author's original use in their own country. However, some language has been edited for the sake of consistency, such as using "therapy" to indicate counselling/counseling and psychotherapy, which are also used interchangeably (McLeod, 1994) only using the more specific terms where they are clearly applicable. Also, we have adopted "therapists" or "practitioners" in a similar vein and used the term "mental health" to indicate that much of the material here is applicable to different tiers of the profession. Although sometimes the term "patient" may be applicable to the person seeking therapeutic help, the authors, for the most part, use the term "client" throughout. The editors recognise that many of the technologies and their applications from chapter to chapter may overlap and be applicable to other technologies. Duplication of some basic information in chapters is deliberate to allow for each chapter to be read in isolation if preferred.

We hope you enjoy this collection of chapters on technology and mental health.

REFERENCE

McLeod, J. (1994). The research agenda for counselling. *Counselling,* 5(1), 41–3.

ACKNOWLEDGMENTS

We would like to thank the authors who have contributed to this volume for their wide-ranging expertise and their patience, the team at Charles C Thomas, likewise, Audrey Jung for contributing the foreword, and our friends, family and the many colleagues from the online and offline world, too numerous to mention, but particularly the members and friends of the Online Therapy Institute.

CONTENTS

THE USE OF TECHNOLOGY IN MENTAL HEALTH

Chapter 1

USING EMAIL TO CONDUCT
A THERAPEUTIC RELATIONSHIP

Patricia Ryan Recupero & Samara Harms

INTRODUCTION

Written communication between therapists and clients dates back to the origins of psychotherapy. Sigmund Freud corresponded with his patients (Pergament, 1998) and electronic mail (email) has been available for nearly two decades. Unfortunately, there are relatively few studies that evaluate email applications in psychotherapy. This chapter defines email as asynchronous electronic communication. Email offers the benefit of eliminating "telephone tag" difficulties. However, delays in replies may be problematic for clients needing a quick response.

Email may be conducted in any of several formats. Emails may be sent directly through a server to recipients within that server; from a server and routed to a recipient through another server; or through a password-protected connection on a secure website (secure, web-based messaging, sometimes referred to as a web board). Emails sent through servers rather than directly through a secure website may be com-posed and directed online in an Internet browser window, or they may be sent through an email client such as MS Outlook or Eudora. Emails may also be sent through cellular-phone or personal digital assistant (PDA) based messaging ("mobile email").

In the clinical practice of psychotherapy and mental health counseling, the use of email ranges from incidental e-mails for prescription refills and appointment setting to therapeutic emails (Anthony, 2004). Incidental emails may be analogous to routine telephone calls. Therapeutic emails range from brief follow-up emails (e.g., brief motivational tips for exercise or quitting smoking, food diaries for eating disorders, etc.) to therapy or treatment conducted, at least in part, via email. Risks associated with the use of email tend to increase as the communication moves away from inci-dental matters and toward therapeutic uses, just as providing psychotherapy in one's office arguably involves greater risks than confirming or rescheduling a client's appointment.

Email has numerous potential therapeutic uses and in some situations may be especially helpful to clients. A Deloitte study reports that 75% of patients want their physicians to provide online services including email and 25% say they would be willing to pay more for such services (Deloitte, 2008). This replicates a 2006 Harris Interactive poll finding that 74% of adults would like to be able to email their doctors directly (Harris, 2006). Email has been shown to improve communication between clinicians and patients and to improve patient satisfaction scores in family medicine (Leong et al., 2005). However,

physicians have been slow to adopt regular email communication with patients (Brooks & Menachemi, 2006). Therapists and mental health professionals seem to have been earlier adopters of the technology. Some psychotherapy clients may be even more receptive to communicating with providers via email, particularly for issues that may be difficult to discuss in person. People with low self-esteem generally prefer email to face-to-face communications, particularly when communications involve an element of risk. This chapter discusses some relevant applications of the use of email as well as some important ethical considerations.

APPLICATION

The use of email by psychotherapists and counselors varies considerably. Even providers who do not communicate with clients through email may address email-related concerns in therapy. Malater writes of clients for whom email becomes an important element of issues explored in therapy (2007). Email may occupy such an important part of the client's life that he may bring in copies of emails with third parties, such as family members, to discuss in therapy. Therapists should be aware of the role of email in a patient's life and should be aware of the patient's use of email as a potential area to explore during sessions. The clinical use of email may be adjunctive (Peterson & Beck, 2003) or offered as a sole form of treatment. Therapists should have a well-thought-out email policy that should be communicated to clients, just as one has a policy for telephone calls. The policy should clarify expectations about the use of email, when it is and when it is

not appropriate, as well as the various risks associated with email and the available safeguards; this chapter details additional suggestions for email policies in the section on Ethical Considerations.

Adjunctive applications of email may be among the most common. Yager, an early adopter of the technology, uses email with his clients for both administrative and clinical purposes. He has written extensively about his experience using email with adolescents in treatment for eating disorders (Yager, 2003) and his observations and recommendations will be helpful to many clinicians who use email or who are contemplating it. He notes the utility of email for encouraging clients to report daily food diaries, which enhances accountability and self-awareness.

Eating disorders are among the most studied indications for the clinical use of email (Robinson & Serfaty, 2007; Yager, 2003). There is some evidence that automated email messaging may help to improve outcomes in smoking cessation (Lenert et al., 2004) and, interestingly, that email CBT with minimal therapist contact may be helpful for social phobia (Carlbring et al., 2006). Email has shown some potential for helping abuse victims in increasing rates of abuse disclosure and facilitating communication among parents, children and treatment providers; these applications were originally suggested by women in domestic violence shelters (Constantino et al., 2007). Self-directed writing exercises with therapist email were found to be helpful for posttraumatic stress and grief (Lange et al., 2001). Conditions for which email may be helpful range from clinical disorders such as depression to subclinical, "worried well" difficulties, such as work stress (Ruwaard et al., 2007). Email has been proven effective for weight-loss counseling, even when using automated, computer-tailored feedback instead of email counseling by a therapist (Tate et al., 2006).

Email may elicit more honest information about a client's conditions. The Samaritans, a UK-based charity best known for its work with suicide hotlines, noted that their email contacts describe suicidal feelings more frequently than phone contacts (Armson, 1997). Turkle (1999, p. 643) notes: "The relative anonymity of life on the screen . . . gives people the chance to express often unexplored aspects of the self. Additionally, multiple aspects of self can be explored in parallel." As email communication between therapist and client delves more deeply into clinical matters and psychological difficulties, ethical considerations abound.

Practically speaking, emails offer numerous benefits, including the ability to compose and send communications at any time, even from numerous different locations. Many consider email's automatic documentation a benefit, although having a complete and literal record carries some risks as well (Recupero, 2005). Email can be used in conjunction with other forms of electronic technology for therapeutic purposes. Tate and Zabinski (2004) provide a helpful review of technological applications that may be useful adjuncts to therapy, such as online support groups.

ETHICAL CONSIDERATIONS

Most of the important ethical considerations for email are merely extensions of existing ethical standards and problems in the practice of psychotherapy in general. Among the central ethical concerns for the use of email are:

- confidentiality and privacy;
- the appropriateness of email communication in a particular clinical situation;
- the implications of email for professionalism and the standard of

care and
- administrative issues, such as licensure and reimbursement.

Because clinical scenarios vary significantly among different clients, it is impossible to address every potential ethical concern that may confront the therapist who uses email. This chapter aims, instead, to offer some starting points for reflection and to encourage the reader to seek out additional resources, such as existing ethical guidelines for therapists and counselors on the use of email (e.g., Anthony & Goss, 2009; Nagel & Anthony, 2009).

CONFIDENTIALITY AND PRIVACY

Client confidentiality and privacy concerns arise frequently in connection with Internet-based communications, including email. In some countries, communications between therapists and clients are normally subject to therapist-client privilege, a legal principle that protects confidentiality, with some exceptions. Therapists everywhere, in any case, also have an ethical duty to protect clients' confidentiality that arguably transcends legal obligations. Psychotherapists can be held liable for breach of confidentiality even where no law was broken (Grabois, 1997). Because email carries risks to client confidentiality and privacy, the decision to communicate with clients via email should not be made without involving the patient in a full discussion of the risks and available safeguards.

Emails may be analogous to tape-recorded therapy sessions. They both contain a literal transcript of the client's and therapist's words, unlike summaries in chart notes or even process notes. Even emails deleted by both parties are often retained in storage by third parties such as Internet service providers (ISPs) or on individual parties' hard drives and are typically recoverable by information technology (IT) professionals (Fitzgerald, 2005). The exact words of therapist and client are preserved in email communications, so it is important to be mindful of potential future readers when writing (Recupero, 2008). Clients should be fully informed about this risk and the therapist should make sure that the client has understood before agreeing to communi-

cate by email.

Laws that apply to medical records in general apply to emails as well. In the USA, emails are covered by the Health Insurance Portability and Accountability Act (HIPAA), as well as potentially more restrictive state laws regarding the privacy of protected health information (PHI). Like any medical record, emails are subject to subpoena and although therapists in most cases should decline to release client emails without the client's consent, courts and legal professionals may still be able to obtain the emails from third parties, such as ISPs, who often retain emails on their servers for a specified period of time. HIPAA requires providers to develop a security policy and to notify clients of privacy practices. An established security policy and open discussion of privacy practices are good risk management practices to help protect clients and therapists.

Security issues are an important consideration. While many have expressed concern about risks posed by hackers and high-tech threats, Sands (2004) notes that "the biggest threats to security are low-tech ones: failure to log off or use a screen saver, misaddressing email messages, sharing email accounts and using employer-owned email systems" (p. 268). Although space constraints do not allow us to address all possible security-enhancing measures in this chapter, the following list offers some suggestions:

- Use secure, web-based messaging systems instead of sending emails through multiple servers; these systems can be configured so that clients only receive a notification email alerting them to log in to the website in order to retrieve your message. These sites are secure and password-protected and they may offer the strongest (although not perfect) security protection for therapist-client email.

- If you work in a multiprovider facility or if you have office staff, additional security measures may be appropriate. Some technological tools to increase security are encryption, authentication, electronic signatures, password-protected screen savers, automatic logouts, audit trails, return receipts for email, password protection for email accounts, firewalls and virus protection.

- If you have staff, or if you work with others, develop a policy regarding staff/others' access to client emails; be sure that clients are fully informed of these practices and consent to them in advance.

- If it is necessary to use traditional email (as opposed to secure, web-based messaging), keep track of clients' email addresses so that you do not confuse two clients' email addresses and send confidential communications to the wrong person.

- Instruct clients not to compose or send emails through workplace computers or networks. Many employers routinely screen and monitor emails sent or received by employees (Tam et al., 2005). Warn clients about the risk of others reading their emails, particularly if they will be using a shared computer at home. If clients are not technology-aware, it is appropriate to help them learn how to protect their emails from family members who may have a vested interest—or just curiousity—in accessing the sessions.

- An email retention and confidentiality policy will help to clarify client and therapist expectations of email confidentiality (or lack thereof). The policy may address, for example, which ISP the therapist will use, whether the therapist will save or delete emails, how long emails may be retained after therapy has concluded and policies for protecting the security of email communications. There are several questions to address when formulating such a policy. Will you retain all emails in the client's medical record? If so, the client should be aware of this. Will you retain no emails, but instead keep just a record of the content of sessions? If so, what will be your policy for deleting emails? Some commentators (Sands, 2004) believe that deleting or destroying entire or portions of emails ". . . is tantamount to destroying or altering medical records." If you do delete emails, be sure to keep at least a record of what was communicated, in essence. Even if you will delete emails and keep session notes instead, clients may decide to keep emails, so it may not be possible to guarantee that no permanent record is maintained. There are software packages that help to completely delete emails from hard drives, but clients may not be able to afford these programs and, furthermore, ISPs and other networks may retain emails; clients should be forewarned that even if you delete emails, it is no guarantee that they will be completely erased. Articles and reports from technology news can be helpful sources for tips on increasing data security, software to help remove old files and so forth (Fitzgerald, 2005).

- Concerns about email privacy should not defeat otherwise sound plans to communicate with clients online. In the US, in the case of Warshak v. United States, the Sixth Circuit upheld a district court's opinion that emails should not be subjected to search and seizure without a valid warrant.

APPROPRIATENESS OF EMAIL FOR THE CLINICAL SITUATION

There is an almost infinite variation in clinical situations. In some cases, email will not be an appropriate medium for therapist-client communication. Therapists must consider the needs of the particular client. Demographic and clinical factors alike can affect the advisability of using email. When treating children and adolescents, an email record could be problematic for the young client if the parent requests access to the emails. Generally speaking, parents often have the legal right to view their children's medical records until the child has reached the age of majority. Since courts may consider emails part of the medical record, parents could demand to view the young person's emails, which could have a detrimental effect on the client's progress as well as the therapeutic relationship. Furthermore, parents may own the account and the hardware through which the email were composed; this risk should be recognized and discussed. Numerous legal and ethical issues related to documents and records must be considered when treating children and adolescents (Recupero, 2008).

The therapist should also consider questions of accessibility. People unfa-miliar with email and computers may need help ensuring they know how to hide messages from family members on shared computers and those who do not have Internet access at home might not have appropriate locations to compose or read therapeutic emails. If the patient must use a public terminal (e.g., library or internet café) for email, his or her privacy may be compromised and s/he may not be able to openly discuss important, but sensitive, issues. Clients should be strongly discouraged from using workplace computers or email addresses/networks for therapy-related emails. Therapists may decline to use email with clients who intend to email from work.

Finally, different diagnoses can have vast implications for correspondence via email. ISPs can review emails and certain phrases or key words (e.g., political delusions) may be "red flags" that trigger increased monitoring or, possibly, surveillance by law enforcement agencies. Email may not be the best option for clients with psychotic symptoms. The case illustration section below provides an example to help guide reflection on these concerns.

PROFESSIONALISM AND STANDARD OF CARE

Among the potential problems cited with using email for psychotherapy is the inability to detect nonverbal cues such as crying or alcohol on a client's breath. While this is admittedly a drawback to the medium, there are also benefits. Clients can describe problems in more detail and can write *when* they are upset instead of waiting until they are calm so may be and better able to recall details. Similarly, the therapist can respond carefully, editing her reply to contain thoughtful reflection instead of "canned" responses or first impressions. Email can have positive or negative implications for the standard of care.

Communication via the Internet may affect transference and counter transference in therapy. Inaccurate first impressions and stereotypes are more likely to persist over email than when communication occurs by voice transmission (Epley and Kruger, 2005). People often overestimate their ability to communicate effectively via email (Kruger et al., 2005), believing that others will "hear" the same intent and context that they feel when composing a message. The overall tone of an email is very important in determining how the message will be perceived (Turnage, 2008) and therapist and client alike may need to work on clarifying meaning and affect in emails until they have developed more skill at conveying tone. Subtle humor and sarcasm, for example, may be easily misun-

derstood by email recipients and may need clarification (for example, a "just kidding" or "jk" after a joke). Murphy and Mitchell (1998) have developed a technique to help communicate emotions through email. They write:

> For example, we might write the following to a client: "it has been several weeks since I have heard from you John (concern, worry) and I would very much appreciate it if you could at least acknowledge this email (feeling pushy, demanding)." This gives John a better idea of the emotional context and intent of the email. We call this technique "emotional bracketing". . . (p. 24)

Such techniques may help to clarify meaning in potentially messages otherwise open to misinterpretation.

An oft-cited characteristic of email is its tendency to elicit disinhibited communication (Suler, 2004). Depending on the situation, this may result in candor, honesty and openness; in other situations, it may lead to lying, dishonesty and deception. Conversely, the asynchronous, distant nature of Internet communication may also prompt excessive, self-conscious control of one's behavior or self-image. Researchers refer to this phenomenon as impression management and it is common in cyberspace (Rosenbloom, 2008).

ADMINISTRATIVE ISSUES

There are many administrative issues, which have a bearing on ethical aspects of counseling by email. Although they are too numerous to detail here, several

issues are important to mention. Licensure and regulatory issues may emerge, particularly if the therapist and the patient reside in different states or

countries. Some areas require the therapist to be licensed in the patient's state in
order to provide any type of therapy,
including e-therapy. Furthermore, some
states and countries have laws regulating
telemedicine and cybermedicine, including therapy via email–it is severely
restricted in Germany, for example.
Therapists should investigate the relevant state laws prior to beginning a
course of email therapy and one should
develop a system for finding out when
laws have changed, preferably through
an evolving trusted wiki. Malpractice
insurance providers are often helpful
with such questions.

Reimbursement is another issue that
has provoked much debate. Many providers express concern that using email
will require an excessive time commitment without adequate financial reimbursement. Initial reports, however,
have not supported this fear. On the contrary, email has been credited with
improving practice efficiency (Rosen and
Kwoh, 2007), by reducing both telephone workload and unnecessary office
visits. The question, then, becomes one
of what fees, if any, will be charged for
email and how fees will be set. Clients
and therapists should agree upon the fee
structure prior to beginning a course of
therapy.

Communications with third parties
and "prospective clients" can be problematic. Therapists must decide how to
respond to those clients who send unso-
licited email requests for advice or
appointments. Baur (2000) suggests that
one address these contacts in the same
way that one would respond to equivalent contacts via telephone calls.
Although this chapter is primarily concerned with email between therapists
and clients, additional ethical concerns
apply to the use of email with colleagues
and other third parties. Standards of
"netiquette" are typically higher for professionals such as therapists than for the
general population; Cleary and Freeman
(2005) offer email suggestions for mental
health nurses that are applicable to
numerous other professionals in the
mental health field.

CASE EXAMPLES

Example 1

Suppose that Sheila, a fictional client,
forwards the following email from her
therapist to her husband, who then forwards it to his mother:

Sheila,
From what you have told me about
your father-in-law, it sounds as if he
may suffer from a psychiatric disorder.
I know at times it must seem as though
he is being unreasonable, but I would
urge you to consider that the way he
acts sometimes might be beyond his
control.
Hang in there.
Dr. Cyberpsych

Such communications may be common in the context of media psychology,
advice columnists, or radio personalities
who are offering advice for entertainment purposes, but may be unethical in
the context of an established therapist-
client relationship. While the therapist
can decide to whom she forwards or
sends email, whether to delete the email
and so forth, she cannot control what her
client does with email once it has been

sent. Being mindful of this, communications should be "sanitized" to some degree in the same way that progress notes and comments during therapy sessions may be censored. While verbal statements similar to those in Dr. Cyberpsych's email, above, may be commonplace in face-to-face therapy sessions, different implications arise when such thoughts are put into writing. Dr. Cyberpsych's response, above, could be tactfully revised as follows:

> Sheila,
> It must be very difficult for you to face these family struggles so often. While every family goes through its ups and downs, there are some things we could talk about in our next session at my office that might help you to understand a little better why you are feeling so frustrated and why it seems so hard for you and your father-in-law to communicate.
> Hang in there,
> Dr. Cyberpsych

Example 2

The following example illustrates some of the difficulties and ethical questions raised by different clinical scenarios and symptom-specific problems:

John A., a young man who operates a forklift at a distribution center, is referred for therapy following an altercation with a coworker at the warehouse. Mr. A. reports that he has previously been disciplined for similar incidents and conflicts with his coworkers. You observe that Mr. A. avoids eye contact, mumbles and often responds inappropriately to subtle social cues, such as humor and sarcasm. You suspect that Mr. A. may suffer from Asperger's Syndrome and you recommend psychotherapy directed at developing stronger interpersonal communications skills to reduce the incidence of workplace misunderstandings. Mr. A. says that he will not be able to attend weekly therapy appointments and he inquires about the possibility of conducting the appointments online, via email.

In this example, email communications may not adequately address Mr. A's difficulties with face-to-face, nonverbal communication. As a general rule, if a client's difficulties cannot be addressed in somewhat generalized, cautious language, with the limited capabilities of email communication, then it may be prudent to question whether email is the appropriate medium for the particular discussion. A patient struggling with anxiety and stress related to corporate fraud at work, for example, may not be the best candidate for email therapy, as courts would be interested in the content of the emails a criminal investigation is involved. Similarly, a manic client may be unable to recognize appropriate boundaries and may not hesitate before including the therapist's email address in a list of recipients for a chain-letter type of mass email. The decision whether, and how, to use email communications in therapy should be made on a case-by-case basis.

CONCLUSION

Rates of adoption of email are still low and many therapists who use email with clients either do so for incidental or adjunctive, symptom-tracking uses, or rely on clients who can afford to pay out of pocket for this option. Recently, there have been some efforts at reimbursement through major insurance companies allowing reimbursement for "web visits," i.e., clinician-patient communication via online, secure messaging. If these options are well received by clinicians and clients, they are likely to spur reimbursement for other forms of electronic communication, including email. Tate and Zabinski (2004) note the current lack of studies investigating asynchronous communications between therapists and clients. Further research is needed to help elucidate the benefits, pitfalls and safeguards to help ensure that clients and therapists alike are able to use email to their benefit. In the mean time, in the absence of many published research studies, providers should develop policies to help guide decisions and procedures related to the clinical use of email. In formulating such policies, therapists may refer to existing published guidelines promulgated by professional organizations.

REFERENCES

Anthony, K. (2004). Therapy Online–The Therapeutic Relationship in Typed Text. In G. Bolton, S. Howlett, C. Lago & J. Wright (Eds.), *Writing cures*. Hove: Brunner-Routledge.

Anthony, K., & Goss, S. (2009). *Guidelines for online counselling and psychotherapy including guidelines for online supervision* (3rd ed.). Lutterworth: BACP.

Armson, S. (1997). Suicide and cyberspace: Befriending by email. *Crisis, 18*(3), 103–105.

Brooks, R. G., & Menachemi, N. (2006). Physicians' use of email with patients: Factors influencing electronic communication and adherence to best practices. *Journal of Medical Internet Research* [online], 8(1) e2 [Accessed May 5, 2009]. Available from: http://www.jmir.org/2006/1/e2/.

Baur, C. (2000). Limiting factors on the transformative powers of email in patient-physician relationships: A critical analysis. *Health Communication, 12*(3), 239–259.

Carlbring, P., Furmark, T., Steczkó, J., Ekselius, L., & Andersson, G. (2006). An open study of Internet-based bibliotherapy with minimal therapist contact via e-mail for social phobia. *Clinical Psychologist, 10*(1), 30–38.

Cleary, M., & Freeman, A. (2005). Email etiquette: Guidelines for mental health nurses. *International Journal of Mental Health Nursing, 14*(1), 62–65.

Constantino, R., Crane, P. A., Noll, B. S., Doswell, W. M., & Braxter, B. (2007). Exploring the feasibility of email-mediated interaction in survivors of abuse. *Journal of Psychiatric and Mental Health Nursing, 14*(3), 291–301.

Deloitte (2008). *2008 Deloitte Survey of Health Care Consumers*. Washington, DC: Deloitte Center for Health Solutions.

Epley, N., & Kruger, J. (2005). When what you type isn't what they read: The perseverance of stereotypes and expectancies over email. *Journal of Experimental Social Psychology, 41*(4), 414–422.

Fitzgerald, T. J. (2005). Deleted but not gone. *The New York Times* [online], 3 November. [Accessed May 5, 2009]. Available from: http://www.nytimes.com/2005/11/03/technology/circuits/03basics.html.

Grabois, E. W. (1997) The liability of psychotherapists for breach of confidentiality. *Journal of Law and Health, 12*(1), 39–84.

Harris. (2006). *Few patients use or have access to online services for communicating with their doctors, but most would like to* [online]. [Accessed January 28, 2010]. Available from: http://www.harrisinteractive.com/NEWS/allnewsbydate.asp?NewsID=109.

Kruger, J., Epley, N., Parker, J., & Zhi-Wen,

N. (2005). Egocentrism over email: Can we communicate as well as we think? *Journal of Personality and Social Psychology, 89*(6), 925–936.

Lange, A., van de Ven, J. P., Schrieken, B., & Emmelkamp, P. M. G. (2001). Interapy: Treatment of posttraumatic stress through the Internet: A controlled trial. *Journal of Behavior Therapy and Experimental Psychiatry, 32*(2), 73–90.

Lenert L., Muñoz R. F., Perez J. E., & Aditya Banson, B. S. (2004). Automated email messaging as a tool for improving quit rates in an Internet smoking cessation intervention. *Journal of the American Medical Informatics Association, 11*(4), 235–240.

Leong, S. L., Gingrich, D., Lewis, P. R., Mauger, D. T., & George, J. H. (2005). Enhancing doctor-patient communication using email: A pilot study. *Journal of the American Board of Family Medicine, 18*(3), 180–188.

Malater, E. (2007). Introduction: Special issue on the Internet. *The Psychoanalytic Review, 94*(1), 3–6.

Murphy, L. J., & Mitchell, D. L. (1998). When writing helps to heal: Email as therapy. *British Journal of Guidance and Counselling, 26*(1), 21–32.

Nagel, D. M., & Anthony, K. (2009). *Ethical framework for the use of technology in mental health* [online]. [Accessed May 5, 2009]. Available from: http://www.onlinetherapy institute.com/id43.html.

Pergament, D. (1998) Internet psychology: Current status and future regulation. *Journal of Law Medicine, 8*(2), 233–279.

Recupero, P. R. (2005). Email and the psychiatrist-patient relationship. *Journal of the American Academy of Psychiatry and the Law, 33*(4), 465–475.

Recupero, P. R. (2008). Ethics of medical records and professional communications. *Child Adolescent Psychiatric Clinics of North America, 17*(1), 37–51.

Robinson, P., & Serfaty, M. (2007). Getting better byte-by-byte: A pilot randomised controlled trial of email therapy for bulimia nervosa and binge eating disorder. *European Eating Disorders Review, 16*(2), 84–

93.

Rosen, P., & Kwoh, C. K. (2007). Patient-physician email: An opportunity to transform pediatric health care delivery. *Pediatrics, 120*(4), 701–706.

Rosenbloom, S. (2008). Putting your best cyberface forward. *The New York Times* [online]. 3 January. [Accessed May 29, 2008]. Available from: http://www.ny times.com/2008/01/03/fashion/03impres sion.html.

Ruwaard, J., Lange, A., Bouwman, M., Broeksteeg, J., & Schrieken, B. (2007). Emailed standardized cognitive behavioural treatment of work-related stress: A randomized controlled trial. *Cognitive Behaviour Therapy, 36*(3), 179–192.

Peterson, M. R., & Beck, R. L. (2003). E-mail as an adjunctive tool in psychotherapy: Response and responsibility. *American Journal of Psychotherapy, 57*(2), 167–181.

Sands, D. Z. (2004). Help for physicians contemplating use of email with patients. *Journal of the American Medical Informatics Association, 11*(4), 268–269.

Suler, J. (2004). The online disinhibition effect. *CyberPsychology and Behavior, 7*(3), 321–326.

Tam, P. W., White, E., Wingfield, N., & Maher, K. (2005). Snooping email by software is now a workplace norm. *The Wall Street Journal* [online]. [Accessed May 5, 2009]. Available from: http://www.work rights.org/in_the_news/in_the_news_wall streetjournal.html.

Tate, D. F., & Zabinski, M. F. (2004). Computer and Internet applications for psychological treatment: Update for clinicians. *Journal of Clinical Psychology, 60*(2), 209–220.

Tate, D. F., Jackvony, E. H., & Wing, R. R. (2006). A randomized trial comparing human email counseling, computer-automated tailored counseling and no counseling in an Internet weight loss program. *Archives of Internal Medicine, 166*(15), 1620–1625.

Turkle, S. (1999). Cyberspace and identity. *Contemporary Sociology, 28*(6), 643–648.

Turnage, A. K. (2008). Email flaming behaviors and organizational conflict. *Journal of Computer-Mediated Communication, 13*(1), 43–59.

Yager, J. (2003). Email therapy for anorexia nervosa: Prospects and limitations. *European Eating Disorders Review, 11*(3), 198–209.

Chapter 2

USING CHAT AND INSTANT MESSAGING (IM) TO CONDUCT A THERAPEUTIC RELATIONSHIP

Kathleene Derrig-Palumbo

INTRODUCTION

The term online therapy is a broad-reaching term that describes any means of delivering mental health services via the Internet. It includes video conferencing, audio conferencing, chatroom or instant messaging and secure email dialogues between client and therapist among the many other modalities described in the following chapters. This chapter discusses one of the frequent definitions of online therapy: chat–real-time, text-based online communications using the Internet.

There are three separate terms that refer to the same type of communications delivery–chat, chat room and instant messaging. All three indicate real-time communications between client and therapist. The distinction between chat and instant messaging is that chat rooms are usually open "rooms" in which any number of individuals may come and go as they please and communicate with any or all of the attendees of the chat room. Instant messaging is usually a private dialogue, occurring between two or more people in a secure chat room to which no one other than the invitees is able to enter. Therefore, "chat" therapy utilizes instant messaging technology for the delivery of mental health services.

Chat therapy involves the exchange of dialogue using the written word. People who utilize chat will often abbreviate words and use "emoticons" to express their feelings, such as being happy, sad, or angry. Emoticons can be actual facial expressions that the chat room technology renders ☺, or they may be keyboard characters strung together to resemble facial expressions. For example, happy is :), sad is :(. Therapists who work online must be aware of their client's predisposition toward abbreviation and emoticons prior to utilizing them. It is important to observe how the client makes use of the medium and to then mirror that usage as appropriate.

Chat therapy has received its share of scrutiny over the years. There have been a series of concerns surrounding the use of chat in therapy that have been discussed and debated rigorously since the medium was first used for the provision of mental health services. The concerns that were voiced are highly important points to consider carefully, as they all speak to the efficacy of the medium and to the best interests of the clients seeking therapy in this fashion. As of this writing, although many therapists have come to realize the benefits to be had from using chat, online therapy is still being used primarily by early adopters. Many of the original arguments against chat therapy still persist. It is important for therapists new to this medium to realize that much study and analysis has gone into examining chat therapy and many of the concerns that have been voiced have been thoroughly deliberated and addressed.

IDENTITY

The discussion surrounding chat therapy begins with identity, with regard to the identity of the therapist as well as concern about the identity of the client.

The primary concern regarding the identity of the therapist is centered on how the consumer can be certain that he or she is meeting with an actual licensed mental health provider. Because chat does not utilize physical facial expression, theoretically a person who is not a therapist could pose as one by simply researching and assuming the credentials of a real therapist. Typically the names and license numbers of therapists are listed on the websites of the state regulatory boards that license the therapists in the United States and other countries list membership of professional organizations. This is where it may be sensible for therapists to use a credible clearinghouse to vet their information and present them to consumers. Some websites, such as www.MyTherapyNet.com, research every therapist that applies, require multiple forms of identification, conduct interviews, check for malpractice insurance and check that their professional licenses are in good standing with no outstanding complaints. These websites then present therapists to the public who can be relied upon as legitimate, qualified mental health providers who have been trained in the techniques and the legal and ethical issues of online therapy

There is equally a good deal of discussion regarding determining the identity of the client who engages in online therapy. The one perspective from which client identity is not analyzed is in regards to health insurance coverage. As of this writing (July 2009), online therapy is now beginning to be looked at by insurance companies in the United States and elsewhere. Some insurance companies are conducting pilot studies and/or are actively providing insurance for their members for online therapy. This is still very new to insurance companies. As a result, many forms of identification are needed as well as additional paperwork in order for online sessions to be covered. At this point, there is no concern that an uninsured client may be assuming the identity of a covered member. However, it is likely that the health insurance industry will lean towards covering online therapy regularly in the United States soon, as with other countries (MyTherapyNet, 2009).

There is also concern amongst providers that by not knowing the identity of their client, there could be legal and ethical ramifications. For instance, if a client is presenting as a child abuser, therapists in the United States, the United Kingdom and many other countries have mandatory responsibilities to report child abuse. Be sure to identify if this law exists in your country of practice and if the therapist has no idea where the client lives and what the client's real name is, the therapist is unable to make their mandatory report. However, the person using online therapy needs to use a credit card to purchase the session, unless it is provided free of charge. The credit card must have a correct name and correct address attached to it or the charge will not go through. As a result, you will have some information to begin a report. Since child abuse laws exist in most countries it is imperative legally and ethically that you follow through with a report. We are mandated to report suspected child abuse. Be sure to report all the information that you have to your local child protection services. It is then up to them to investigate the report or to refer it out to the state/region in which the suspected child abuse exists. There are many permutations of this, all leading to the necessity of having some information on whom the client is and where they live. However, it is interesting to note that in traditional face-to-face private practice, most providers do not ask for identification from their clients and many clients pay in cash. Therefore, it is also possible that a client in face-to-face therapy is using an assumed name and false contact information on their intake form.

As it turns out, by its very nature, online therapy tends to make it more difficult for a client to be seen anonymously, because the cash pay alternative is removed. Online clients pay for services using a credit card or other electronic means, meaning that the credit card

billing address as well as the name of the person on the credit card is provided by the client. By utilizing an established online therapy service, these details are addressed in the proper fashion. In addition to billing information, the online therapy service is able to track the I.P. address of the client, which although on its own does not provide a precise geographical location, in the case of an emergency the Internet Service Provider can relay that information.

Another point that is raised frequently regarding client identity is how is it possible to know that it is actually the client who signed up that is using the service? For example, what if someone signs up to the service who is having issues with domestic violence and subsequently, their partner finds out. What prevents the partner from signing on as the victim? When there is no face to go along with the dialogue, it can be near impossible to know with certainty that the person is on the other end. This is where once again it may be important to consider utilizing established, credible online therapy clinics, because they will utilize the appropriate security authentication protocols that maximize identity security. However, the responsibility does not end with the service; it ultimately rests on the client. The client must take appropriate measures to protect his or her password, changing it often and utilizing letters, numbers and capitalization schemes that become impossible to guess. If the client takes these precautions and a credible online therapy service is utilized, this issue is mitigated (Derrig-Palumbo, 2005).

So in summary, the question of "how do I know I'm speaking to a real therapist" is answered in one way by accessing therapists only from established online therapy services. The question of "how do I know the identity of my client" is answered the same way. Additionally, both parties need to protect their login information and change their passwords regularly in order to reduce the potential for identity theft. Therapists in private practice may ask for copies of a driver's license or passport and/or ask for some sessions to be done in person if possible or ask the client to engage in a video-conferencing session. By following this protocol, people utilizing the Internet to provide and access mental health services can be confident that the issue of identity is addressed.

THE THERAPEUTIC RELATIONSHIP

Quickly following on the heels of the question of identity is the issue of efficacy. There is much captivating debate as to the efficacy of chat therapy. This question is typically broached in a general fashion by asking whether the use of the written word can adequately establish the therapeutic relationship. To answer this, we must take a step back and ask if the written word can adequately communicate the depth and breadth of human experience. For the last few thousand years, the written word has been used to convey a rich palette of human experience with great success. More specific to the case of chat therapy, personal relationships are known to commonly flourish through the exclusive use of the written word. Some pen pals, who have never met in person or spoken by telephone, develop the strongest of bonds. This has carried over to the use of email and chat rooms where, again, people who have never met nor spoken form lasting friendships and business partnerships, resulting in love affairs, marriages and successful business ventures. It is illuminating to look at why these bonds are often so strong because these are the same underlying reasons that can make chat therapy effective.

Relationships that make use of the written word for communication eliminate some of the inherent barriers to honest self-disclosure in a face-to-face setting. Many people who feel inhibited in sharing aspects of their lives in a face-to-face situation lose that inhibition when putting those thoughts and feelings to paper. Disclosing intimate details of one's life while face-to-face with someone often carries a fear of the possibility of judgment. Sometimes the judgment is only perceived. For instance, one person may speak of a personal indiscretion, while the listener grimaces because of a momentary flash of pain. The grimace had nothing to do with the disclosure, but to the person speaking, it appears to be a reaction to what has been said. Even when no outward sign of judgment is perceived, being in intimate proximity with the listener creates a greater sense of anxiety. Therefore, especially with regard to disclosing intimate personal details, using the written word can often free the person to disclose thoroughly. This is advantageous when such communication is used to build a personal relationship and perhaps even more so when in a therapeutic relationship. In general, clients report that chat therapy frees them to get to their root issues much more quickly than if they had been face-to-face with their therapist. In fact, some individuals have reported that after having spent months in face-to-face therapy without getting to their real issues, the switch to chat therapy led them to divulging these issues within the first few sentences of discourse with their therapists.

Since the client and the therapist are not in the same room, the compassionate, caring, collaborative, nonjudgmental and accepting attitude needs to carry across through written words and can thus be made even more apparent to the client.

The following are samples of questions and statements that can be used to elicit a certain response from the online client. Most are short and are easy to incorporate into the session (Meichenbaum, 2000; Wachtel, 1993).

Expressing empathy

- "How sad."
- "How tragic."
- "That is terrible."
- "What an incredible ordeal."

Permission-gathering statements

- "Is it okay if I ask you some questions about . . . ?"
- "Are you up to some questions now?"
- "Only tell me about what you feel comfortable with."

Normalizing statements

- "Often it is hard to . . ."
- "Often it is hard not to . . ."
- "It is okay if you . . . This is a lot to go through."

Nuture collaboration

- "Do you think it would be advisable to . . . ?"
- "As we have both seen. . . . "
- "If you can't have what you want, at least you can feel that you are. . . ."

Columbo-like statements

- "Correct me if I am wrong."
- "I get the impression that . . ."
- "You seem rather . . . and seem to expect . . ."
- "I have the sense that you . . ."
- "I think you are trying to . . . Am I correct?"

Comments that pull for patient's "strengths" and nurture hope

- "All this weighs on you so heavily and yet you somehow go on!"
- "What has allowed you to . . . in spite of . . ."
- "So, somehow you were able to get past the obstacle of . . . Is that correct?"
- "How did you do that?"

Initial behavior analytic interview questions

- "In order to understand your situation, I would like to ask you some questions."
- "Can you take a few moments and describe the situation you are in now?"
- "What are the problems as you see them?"
- "How would you describe the specific (problem) behavior?"
- "How serious a problem is this as far as you are concerned?"
- "How often does this behavior happen?"
- "Where do the problem behavior usually occur?"
- "How long does it go on for?"

Questions that focus on expectations

- "What else do you think I should find out about you and your situation to help you with this problem?"

- "What questions have I not asked that I should ask in order to learn more about you and your situation?"
- "What *other* questions *should* I ask in order to better understand your situation and what we can do to help you?"
- "Do you have any questions you want to ask me?"

Questions to consider in the goal-setting process

- "Why is it important to think about goals before beginning an activity?"
- "Does your goal seem realistic? Should you establish sub goals?"
- "Of these goals, which one should you begin with? How should you choose?"
- "How can you go about achieving these goals?"
- "Do you have a plan? Do you need help?"

Questions designed to enhance motivation to change

- "What is different when the problem is absent or managable?"
- "How would you like for things to be different?"
- "If you were completely successful in accomplishing what you want, what would be changed?"
- "How would things be different if you followed this idea and did X?"

Questions designed to assess and bolster confidence

- "How confident do you need to feel to be able to do X?"
- "How sure are you, say on a 1 to 10 scale, that you can keep doing what

you are doing?"
- "What things might get in the way of your being able to follow through on this?"
- "What can you do (or do with the help of others) about this problem?"

Questions designed to elicit commitment statements

- "What are one or two things you should do first?"
- "How would you know if the effort was worth it?"
- "So, are you saying that you are willing to try doing Y?"
- "Are you saying, and I want to make sure that I get this straight, that you would be able to . . ."

Questions designed to highlight situational variability

- "Are there some times that you can handle it better than at other times?"
- "What is different when things are not as bad or when you are not experiencing X?"
- "For now don't change anything; just keep track (notice) when things are better."

Questions designed to elicit self-motivational statements

- "I don't know if this would be too difficult for you, but . . ."
- "Maybe this is asking too much of you."
- "Of the things we have discussed, which are the most important reasons to change?"
- "How are you going to do that in spite of . . . ?"
- "Of these different options, which one would you choose? How did

you select that one?"

Questions designed to help individuals notice changes that they have been able to bring about

- "How will you/others be able to tell?"
- "What would be different?"
- "How will we know when the goals have been achieved?"
- "How will you feel about such changes?"

Questions designed to help the individual take credit for change or improvements

- "How did it go?"
- "How were things different this time as compared to the last time?"
- "What do you think accounts for the change?"
- "What, if anything, did you do differently this time?"
- "How did your 'game plan' work? Were you able to follow your game plan?"

It is apparent that once identity and the ability to create the therapeutic relationship are addressed, the idea of chat therapy becomes plausible. However, chat still must pass muster with the legal and ethical mandates of the profession. There are certainly some overlying legal and ethical questions, such as practicing outside your own region and mandated reporting, but for the purpose of this discussion, the focus will be on those mandates that apply directly to chat therapy.

From the legal perspective, first and foremost there is the question of confidentiality. As opposed to being together in an office where, barring someone listening in outside the door, the words spoken between client and therapist leave no record, using chat via the Internet has the potential of being overheard. The issue of confidentiality provides the blueprint for how security must be handled for systems that enable the process of online therapy. In fact, this issue originates with the intake, transfer and storage of client personal information. In the US, HIPAA (Health Insurance Portability and Accountability Act) compliance lays out underlying requirements for the structure of the online therapy service's company, the software systems that are employed and the data management protocols that are employed. Indeed, most countries have legislation governing these matters, such as the Data Protection Act in the UK. These systems and protocols generally mandate a secure chat environment that not only meets industry standard security protocols for the handling of personal data, but also takes the special needs of therapy into consideration. Some large online therapy service providers employ a proprietary chat system that follows very specific mandates regarding encrypting chat stream identifiers, storage of chat session details and emergency procedures for locating a client's local police and hospitals.

The overriding ethical principle regarding confidentiality and the safekeeping of any sensitive information is that the practitioner must be assured of adequate protection for their clients. In some cases, this will mean that the best option is for the practitioner to be the only keeper of records pertaining to treatment or of, for example, transcripts of therapy chat sessions. Back-up to the practitioner's computer can be provided by storing copies of data on a removable storage device (like a pen/flash drive or removable hard drive) and that can then be stored securely. Where a practitioner decides to have data stored by a third party–such as when records of chat sessions are kept by the chat service provider–it is always the responsibility of the therapist to verify that those records are kept in a safe, encrypted manner and will be treated with appropriate regard to confidentiality, almost certainly requiring a written agreement laying out how the information will be treated. In the US, this requires that the service provider is, at least, contracted with the practitioner as a HIPAA compliant business associate, although even this may be insufficient in some areas where additional safeguards may apply. In the UK, it would require the practitioner to be assured of compliance with the Data Protection Act plus the requirements of good practice and the relevant ethical codes. Most countries, states or regions have their own rules on proper protection of sensitive client information and it is recommended that practitioners seek legal and professional advice on how to proceed in their own practice. In any event, data should always be encrypted and properly stored.

From the ethical perspective, a therapist must be certain that treating a particular client using chat therapy is an appropriate treatment plan for that client. If a client is being considered for chat therapy, the therapist should take care to screen the client and determine the appropriateness of that particular choice of treatment. Is the client a proficient typist? Does typing frustrate the client? Is chat therapy appropriate considering the severity of the client's disorder? Does the client live in a rural area with no other access to a therapist? If the first contact between client and therapist occurs online, the therapist should consider if the client is searching for and interviewing therapists. Has the client ever been in traditional and/or online therapy before? Is this just an experiment of whether the client is committed to the process of therapy? Does the client want a one-time educational and counseling session? Is the client interested in the minimization of symptoms or in long-term therapy? Chat therapy may also serve as a bridge to traditional, in-person therapy, where such interaction is preferred. Consider hypothetically a victim of domestic violence who is virtually held captive in the home. His or her only means of reaching out may be through the computer and working online with a therapist to create a plan may be the only viable first step. Therapists must carefully consider all the presenting factors prior to making a judgment on the appropriateness of online therapy for any particular client.

This brings us to the question of who is best served by chat therapy. As always, there are exceptions to every rule, but adolescents and young adults who have grown up on the Internet tend to do very well with chat therapy. They are very used to communicating via the written word, predominantly by using mobile texting, computer instant messaging, chat rooms, blogs and social networks. Many therapists report that when adolescents are "forced" to go to therapy, they tend to sit through the session in silence. However, that same child may type prolifically and discuss every intimate detail of their life when using chat therapy. Online therapy for the younger generation shapes up to be a natural assumption in that they figure that they do nearly every other thing imaginable online, so why not therapy?

Those who live in rural areas also benefit from chat therapy. Often, small rural communities are places where mental health issues carry great stigma. Even if there is a therapist nearby, this is likely to be someone that is well known in the community, which causes great reluctance when considering making an appointment. Although web-cam or audio is an option available to someone living in a rural community, a first venture toward getting help is likely to be quite stressful. For many people, eliminating the face-to-face presence reduces their anxiety levels and chat therapy is likely to be the online therapy method of choice for many rural clients.

Chat therapy can also be quite useful in couple therapy. Using chat forces the other party to stop talking, to stop thinking about what to say next and to just read what their partner is saying. For those couples who function poorly when in the same room, particularly in cases of divorce, chat therapy can be effective. For couples who may not be able to meet in person due to work or any host of reasons, chat therapy can get them into couple's therapy despite geographical challenges.

Chat therapy is also well suited for use by people who lack a private area in their home or office in which they would be comfortable speaking out loud to their therapist, say, by telephone. It is well suited for busy workers who can benefit from short stress interventions or coaching sessions. Businesses are beginning to recognize the financial benefit to providing early interventions for mental health issues, especially in the areas of stress, depression and relationships. These three areas are the biggest causes of loss of productivity in the workplace and the cost of treatment is far outweighed by the direct and indirect savings.

Some therapeutic approaches are better suited to chat therapy than others. Client-directed Outcome-Informed Clinical Work, Cognitive Behavioral Ther-

apy, Family Brief Therapy, Imago Relationship Therapy, Narrative Therapy, Rational Emotive Behavior Therapy, and Solution-Focused Brief Therapy all work very well when utilized online (Derrig-Palumbo, 2005).

Client-directed Outcome-informed Clinical Work was founded by Dr. Scott Miller. This theory is based on score generated outcomes at the beginning, during and at the end of each session. Since this form of therapy has been largely studied through a telephonic EAP setting, it can easily be transferred online. All the forms that are used for this type of treatment can be turned into a web-based program. This form of treatment can be used with adults as well as children (Miller et al., 2004).

Cognitive Behavioral Therapy is a theory that focuses on the connection between thoughts and feeling and how our perceptions influence our feelings (Beck, 1979). It has a large number of interventions that can easily be done online through chat, audio or video-conferencing. Those interventions that require written feedback from the client can easily be transformed into a web-based document that can be shared online between client and therapist. Your chat room interface must have document share capabilities to share the document.

Family Brief Therapy is best conducted online when all family members log into a group chat room setting (or group video-conferencing session). Each family member can reflect on what is being said by other members as well as the responses from the therapist. Most adolescents chat online and/or through text messaging. This is a natural part of their everyday life. Adolescents may even initially relate better online than face-to-face with their parents due to outward power struggles. Sessions can be conducted online with the intention to bring the sessions face-to-face (Derrig-Palumbo, 2005).

Narrative Therapy is based on the retelling and rewriting of people's stories in their lives. The key is to understanding these stories and assisting the client to re-author their own life story in order to separate their problems from who they are as a person. The writing of one's stories can be a cathartic release. Narrative Therapy relies on the written word of the client's stories; chat is an ideal way to achieve this type of process.

The focus of Rational Emotive Behavioral Therapy (REBT) is to replace irrational beliefs, thoughts and feelings with rational and more effective ones. Using this theory within the chat room setting is ideal because REBT deals with the present and challenges thoughts with rational short statements to uncover the client's set of beliefs (Ellis, 1994: 1957).

Solution Focused Behavioral Therapy (SFBT) focuses on promoting solution behavior rather than studying the changing of problematic behavior. SFBT also focuses on the language client's use. This is ideal to use in a chat setting. Chat allows the client to look back and see what exactly was said in order to uncover patterns of language. The success of SFBT is to focus on clear paths towards solution. The most common intervention is "The Miracle Question," keeping the client focused on what they want and the steps necessary to achieve it (deShazer, 1985).

Client Scenario–Joshua

This is a session with a 16-year-old boy who had a difficult time communicating face-to-face. Half of his sessions were conducted online and the rest were carried out face-to-face. Joshua was fearful of relating to other people. His father was always working and his mother suffered from addiction to pain medication and was diagnosed with depression. He felt as though his thoughts and opinions were not important and had severe problems meeting others due to his lack of communication skills and self-confidence. However, he was able to communicate online with others through chat and games. Chatting online with him gave him the opportunity to open up in an environment that was comfortable and which ultimately lead him to feel comfortable face-to-face. Using both types of session allowed him to communicate better with others as well as his parents.

Kathleene:	Hello
Joshua:	*Hi*
Kathleene:	how are you?
Joshua:	*good and you?*
Kathleene:	pretty good thanks
Kathleene:	How are things going
Joshua:	*things are going well*
Kathleene:	Tell me details about school
Joshua:	*school is going well*
Joshua:	*i am doing good in all my classes*
Joshua:	*i am happy with my homework and quiz scores*
Kathleene:	What type of grades are you getting?
Joshua:	*A's, B+*
Joshua:	*B's*
Kathleene:	GREAT!!!!
Joshua:	*Yes*
Kathleene:	What is your favorite class?
Joshua:	*Hmm*
Joshua:	*i really don't have a favorite class*
Joshua:	*history is a joke this year*
Kathleene:	why is that
Joshua:	*our teacher gets her*

	notes from Google, but then she copies and pastes them to Microsoft word and then states that they are her lecture notes	Kathleene:	*washington for 10 days*
		Kathleene:	Are you spending time with your dad?
Kathleene:	that sucks	Joshua:	*so we are all savouring each minute*
Kathleene:	how do you know?	Kathleene:	Really
Joshua:	*there are little links in blue on most sites that lead to other sites*	Kathleene:	I bet you are
		Joshua:	*yes*
Joshua:	*they are in brackets most of the time*	Kathleene:	It must be so quiet there
		Joshua:	*yes it is*
Kathleene:	I see.. great detective work	Kathleene:	does everyoone seem more relaxed?
Joshua:	*then we typed in the specific topic on Google and we found her exact notes on it*	Joshua:	*yes, i believe so*
		Kathleene:	SO . . . I hear that you wil be moving into your new house in January or so
Kathleene:	Well are they good notes		
Joshua:	*of course, they aren't hers, someone else wrote them*	Joshua:	*my mom gets to sleep in now and she doesn't have to worry about picking daniel up from school*
Kathleene:	But are they good		
Joshua:	*yes they are good and then she goes on to read almost the whole things, at a fast pase, which we have to write down on paper for notes*	Joshua:	*yes*
		Joshua:	*i a very excited*
		Joshua:	*i am looking foward to my big room*
		Kathleene:	what color are you going to paint it?
Joshua:	*pace**	Joshua:	*i am not quite sure what they are painting the house, maybe just white for now and some thing else later*
Kathleene:	Then maybe that is the best that she uses them.. but that is not good that she just reads them		
		Joshua:	*really not sure, going to have to ask them*
Joshua:	*so, myself and other people said, "screw this" and we find the notes on Google and read them over*	Kathleene:	Do you want it a specific color?
		Joshua:	*nah, i really don't care what color they paint it, its all up to them, what ever they get is fine*
Kathleene:	Good idea		
Kathleene:	How things going with your parents and you?	Kathleene:	ok
		Kathleene:	So how much bigger is the new room than the room you are in now?
Joshua:	*they are going well*		
Joshua:	*daniel went away to*	Joshua:	*100x bigger*

Joshua:	*even the closet is big*
Kathleene:	that is great
Kathleene:	Do you still have someone living with you guys?
Joshua:	*well . . . dave moved out, but now unvle wayne is here with us*
Joshua:	*uncle**
Kathleene:	How do you feel about that?
Kathleene:	Tell me how you really feel
Joshua:	*I'm fine, at least he's better than dave*
Joshua:	*uncle wayne leaves early for work, cleans up nicely and doesn't ever use the computer here at home*
Joshua:	*never comes home at 1:00 or 2:00 in the morning*
Kathleene:	that is good
Kathleene:	But I know you had problems with him before
Kathleene:	Are you concerned?
Joshua:	*not as much*
Kathleene:	Good
Kathleene:	do you have any concerns
Joshua:	*no, not really, just as long as he doesn't stay for a prolonged amount of time*
Kathleene:	What is a prolong amount of time?
Kathleene:	prolonged*
Kathleene:	2 months?
Joshua:	*more like 3–4 months*
Kathleene:	I got ya
Joshua:	*thats just way too long, i mean, he really needs to get his life on track*
Kathleene:	SO did you ask ow long he is staying?

Kathleene:	You are so right
Joshua:	*i don't want to ask how long he is staying for because, that is just implying "when will you leave and find your own place?"*
Kathleene:	No I meant . . . ask your parents
Kathleene:	What they had in mind
Kathleene:	Do you want him moving with you guys to the new house?
Joshua:	*i am pretty sure they don't have an answer either, they would probably say, "as long as he needs to"*
Joshua:	*i would really rather not anyone live with us in the new house*
Kathleene:	then it might be agood idea to share your feelings with them
Kathleene:	Maybe talk to your Mom first
Kathleene:	What do you think?
Joshua:	*maybe, not quite sure yet*
Kathleene:	OK
Kathleene:	Let me know if you need some help with this
Kathleene:	So how are things going socially?
Joshua:	*ok, i w ill*
Joshua:	*will**
Joshua:	*Good*
Joshua:	*my friends and I go to our weekly lunch and movies*
Joshua:	*on Fridays*
Kathleene:	That is great
Kathleene:	Do you feel good about this?
Joshua:	*yes, it was a wise idea from the start*

Kathleene: Really . . .

Joshua: *now we have set a precedent for the rest of the year*

Kathleene: very good

Kathleene: DO you like having social plans?

Joshua: *Yes*

Joshua: *I feel it is good to have plans like these*

Kathleene: Why is it good?

Joshua: *It is good because we meet each other out of school, away from the working environment, then we just have a fun relaxing time together*

Joshua: *the weight of the week has been lifted because its Friday*

Kathleene: Yes exactly

Kathleene: great . . . I am glad that you see the importance of being social on a regular basis.

Kathleene: It is vital for us

Kathleene: So who goes out with you on Fridays?

Joshua: *alex, linden, micah*

Joshua: *thats mainly it*

Joshua: *we eat then go see a movie*

Kathleene: whi is Micah?

Kathleene: who*

Joshua: *micah is an 11th grader, we have know him for a while now*

Kathleene: Is he a good friend

Joshua: *Yes*

Kathleene: You have never mentioned him before

Joshua: *hmm, i thought i have*

Kathleene: no . . . when did you become friends with him?

Joshua: *last year*

Kathleene: Oh

Kathleene: Joshua . . . you seem to appear more confident

Kathleene: Do you feel more confident?

Joshua: *Possible*

Joshua: *Possibly*

Kathleene: and even more comfortable in this conversation

Kathleene: Why do you think?

Joshua: *Yes*

Joshua: *i am really not sure*

Kathleene: Do you feel differnt?

Kathleene: Have other poeple noticed?

Kathleene: People

Joshua: *i think so, not sure though*

Kathleene: What about others?

Joshua: *not sure, they wont just come up to me and say, "you seem different"*

Kathleene: No but I thought maybe in comments to you

Joshua: *oh, well, no comments*

Kathleene: Anyway it seems like you are really starting to take some responsibility and you are evolving

Joshua: *thank you*

Kathleene: Stay focused on this track

Kathleene: I was really concerned after our last session

Joshua: *ok, i will*

Kathleene: Good

Kathleene: Two weeks?

Joshua: *OK*

Joshua: *30th?*

Kathleene: Monday or Wednesday at 7:30

Kathleene: What is better?

Joshua: *Monday*

Kathleene: OK . . . Go ahead and book it. If there is a problem, please call Paul

	tomorrow. Thanks	Joshua:	*ok thanks, bye*
Kathleene:	Keep up the good work	Kathleene:	Bye

CONCLUSION

It is obvious that with the twenty-first century, communicating with anyone, anywhere in the world is a mere mouse-click away. It is inevitable that in greater numbers, therapists will practice online as the profession comes to accept its efficacy and more and more consumers demand online services. Someday in the not-so-distant future, online therapy may very well be regarded no differently than in-person therapy. It is the responsibility of the current generation of providers to navigate these new waters intelligently and always with the primary consideration being the best interest of the clients they serve.

REFERENCES

Beck, A. T. (1979). *Cognitive therapy and the emotional disorders.* New York: Meridian Books.

Derrig-Palumbo, K. (2005). *Online therapy: A therapist's guide to expanding your practice.* New York: W. W. Norton.

DeShazer, S. (1985). *Miracle question* [online]. [Accessed June 14, 2009]. Available from: http://www.brief-therapy.org.

Ellis, A. (1994: originally published 1957). *How to live with a neurotic.* North Hollywood, CA: Wilshire Book Company.

Meichenbaum, D. (2000). *A clinical handbook for Donald Meichenbaum's presentation at The Evolution of Psychotherapy Conference.* Miami, FL: Melissa Institute Press.

Miller, S. D., Duncan, B. L., & Hubble, M. (2004). Beyond integration: The triumph of outcome over process in clinical practice. *Psychotherapy in Australia, 10*(2), 2–3.

MyTherapyNet (2009). *Homepage* [online]. [Accessed December 2, 2009]. Available from: www.MyTherapyNet.com.

National Board for Certified Counselors. (2004). *Standards for the ethical practice of web counseling* [online]. [Accessed December 2, 2009]. Available from: www.nbcc.org/ethics/wcstandards.htm.

TherapyHosting (2009). *Homepage* [online]. [Accessed December 2, 2009]. Available from: www.TherapyHosting.com.

Wachtel, P. L. (1993). *Therapeutic communication.* New York: Guilford Press.

Chapter 3

USING CELL/MOBILE PHONE SMS FOR THERAPEUTIC INTERVENTION

Thomas A. Merz

INTRODUCTION

The use of Short Message Service (SMS) has evolved over the years from a casual application in the general population to a vehicle utilized for targeted therapeutic intervention and support in clinical settings. SMS is a technology that facilitates the sending and receiving of text messages, more popularly known as "text messaging" or "texting." This process most often occurs between cell phones but also includes the use of landlines and other networks to generate text. While the technological details are not relevant to the current discussion, it is important to note that the amount of data transmitted in a text message is limited. The data contained in a message is often described in terms of "bytes" or "bits" with a corresponding number of encoded characters. The quantity of bits and characters can vary, but one most commonly encounters 7-bit, 160 character or 16-bit Unicode, 70 character limits. The former accommodates Latin based characters typical of English alphabets, while the latter is suitable for non-Latin characters, including the Chinese, Japanese, Korean, and Arabic languages. There are adaptations, such as "concatenated SMS" and Enhanced Messaging Service (EMS) that permit more and richer data to be transmitted, but have the drawback of not being universally well supported at this time (HarmoniousTech, 2008a).

SMS DEVELOPMENT

One of the earliest examples of text messaging was the use of alphanumeric pagers, in which the paging company utilized its network to deliver a brief message to a specific pager. SMS, as it is known now, was developed in the early

1980s by Finnish telecom worker Matti Makkonen and initially utilized by government and commercial interests. On December 3rd, 1992, telecommunications engineer Neil Papworth sent the text message "Merry Christmas" to a colleague, thus initiating the first recognized consumer use of SMS. However, texting remained rather limited until SMS communication between different networks became a reality in 1999. SMS is now the most widely utilized mobile data service on the planet with well over two billion users, accounting for approximately 75 percent of cell phone users (Turrettini, 2009). While the most common perception of SMS transmission is cell phone to cell phone, text messaging can also be generated through the use of desktop software or websites, such as NotePage or Upside Wireless. In fact, there are a number of SMS related applications including:

- the provision of information or content such as sports, news, weather, etc.
- the downloading of ringtones, pictures, etc.
- alerts and notifications, including remote system monitoring (for example, a program that "pings" a server regularly and notifies the system administrator if there is a problem); email, fax, and voice mail notifications; e-commerce and credit card transaction alerts; and stock market alerts
- marketing purposes, such as sending out discounts and product information and allowing for the individual to text back comments or questions

- two-way interactive text messaging between wireless devices and servers (for example, texting to a search engine to obtain information that is then sent back in one or more messages (HarmoniousTech, 2008b)
- two-way interactive text messaging supplied by a live individual at the supplier end to answer questions put by the user.

SMS has evolved from the fringes of technological development to a component of everyday life in a number of ways. Perhaps one of the most interesting illustrations of this movement is the approach utilized by a high school English teacher. By injecting SMS into the learning environment, she demonstrated how a familiar technology captured the interest of junior level students in a positive way. In addition to composing poetry through text, the students transcribed lines from Shakespeare's Macbeth into text language to increase their comprehension of the subject matter. The teacher commented, "This is something they love doing and their success rate is far greater" (NZPA, 2004, p. 1). Aside from learning, SMS can provide students with a sense of community and connection to others. Horstmanshof (2004) contends that the use of SMS among first year university students allows them to have better contact with tutors, lecturers and other faculty members thereby reducing anxiety and better engaging them in the academic process. The preceding examples portend the expanding acceptance and utility of SMS with this and future generations.

SMS: A MEDICAL TOOL

Given the multitude of texting applications, it is not surprising that SMS has become an increasingly relevant tool in providing services and support for patients and clients in various settings. As is often the case, communication related technological advances in the mental health profession parallel or follow those in the medical field. This relationship is beneficial as developments in the medical profession tend to gain public, professional and service user credibility at a relatively rapid pace. Within the realm of medical treatment, SMS is utilized to prompt or remind patients to take a specific action, to provide support to patients and to stimulate interactive information sharing. These approaches are designed to increase compliance with a specific treatment regimen and thereby positively influence desired outcomes. The advantages of SMS within this context include the widespread nature and acceptance of SMS, ease of use for data entry, the ability to integrate information into a database and real-time monitoring.

Neville et al. (2002) recruited 30 patients with asthma to help illustrate the usefulness of prompting behaviors using a texting medium. The authors note that young patients try to make the disease comply with their lifestyle rather than focusing on adherence to treatment objectives. The participants received text messages in contemporary language from a virtual friend with asthma named "Max." While the sample size is very limited and outcomes are not subject to quantitative analysis, the authors report that participants developed rapport with Max and favorably responded to reminders such as "Yo dude, its Max reminding U2 take ur inhaler." One participant commented, "I used to forget [my inhaler] two to three times each week. . . . I haven't missed once this month" (p. 600). Another variation of the same concept is to use SMS reminders to increase the rate of appointment compliance (Price et al., 2009).

One study (Franklin et al., 2008) involving diabetes patients shows how the provision of information can support and reinforce favorable patient behavior. An intervention called "Sweet Talk" was implemented among 64 subjects over a twelve month period to provide support between clinic visits. Content of the text messages consisted of individualized scheduled messages, generic "newsletters" and anonymized tips from other patients. Over the span of one year, a total of 1180 messages were generated from patients in response to the program. It was found that subjects not only responded to news items, but provided personal experiences and tips, as well as unprompted blood glucose levels. The authors concluded that text messaging successfully engaged young people with diabetes. The level of response helped to establish a sense of community among the participants and highlighted the potential for "passive support" derived from reading messages. It is postulated that this model could be adapted to serve other populations of varying ages with chronic diseases.

Another study (Shapiro et al., in press) involving children and adolescents with obesity illustrates how transmitting clinical information via SMS can lead to improvements in health. In this case, the researchers recruited 31 subject families involved with University of North Carolina hospitals who tracked pedometer readouts, minutes of television time and number of sugar-sweetened beverages consumed per day. The population was divided between three self-monitoring groups: those reporting results using text messaging, those recording results utilizing a paper diary and those in a no-monitoring control group. The subjects in the SMS group received positive feedback messages each time data were submitted. The results showed that the individuals in the text messaging group had a lower attrition rate (28%) compared to the paper diary (61%) and control group (50%) and that adherence to the self-monitoring regimen was significantly greater for the SMS group (43%) than the paper diary group (19%). The authors conclude that text messaging is a useful tool in monitoring one's health and can play a role in improving health. In summary, implementing SMS in treatment protocol capitalizes on a popular and accepted communication medium to achieve positive health outcomes in a brief, cost effective and noninvasive manner.

SMS will continue to evolve within the medical field as commercial interests find utility in its application. Companies such as iPlato Healthcare have developed SMS products that allow organizations to perform an array of functions, including access to healthcare information, interactive messaging, health promotions and supportive texts for individuals with such issues as smoking cessation, weight management and methadone treatment compliance. A service called HealthLine developed by Grameenphone provides access to medical care for people living in Bangladesh. The remote areas and paucity of doctors combined with an ever increasing cell phone subscriber base creates the opportunity to use cellular technology to link patients with medical professionals, including the use of SMS in issuing prescriptions (Ivatury, Moore & Bloch, 2009). Finally, in an interesting union of medical care, mental health, and SMS, a pilot project was conducted at a hospital in which text messages were sent from the operating room to the patient's family in the waiting area. The overwhelming majority of families reported that the two to five messages helped to relieve their waiting anxiety (Huang et al., 2006).

APPLYING SMS TO THERAPEUTIC INTERVENTIONS

As previously noted, SMS application within the therapeutic realm in many respects mirrors its usage in the medical field. Data collected in real time can be utilized to assess patterns of client functioning, to develop treatment protocol and to ultimately influence choices, behaviors and experiences. SMS intervention is not restricted to use with individuals who have relatively innocuous disorders, but rather can be helpful in treating major life disrupting symptoms associated with such diagnoses as eating disorders, schizophrenia and bipolar disorder. It is important to understand that whether SMS is used for basic data collection or a more nuanced exchange of information, its efficacy depends on a variety of factors related to the client and the treatment characteristics. For example, a study by Robinson et al. (2006) examined the role of SMS as part of an outpatient treatment "step-down" or aftercare program for clients with bulimia nervosa. Over a six month span and on a weekly basis, participants were instructed to text their responses to five questions regarding their symptomology and mood states. In contrast to a prior similar study conducted in Germany with clients discharged from inpatient bulimia nervosa treatment (Bauer et al. 2003), the results indicated only marginal acceptance of SMS as a treatment resource. The authors postulated that the high participant acceptance rate in the German study (approximately 80%) was reflective of several client and treatment differences, including a greater client investment in the therapeutic process, as they had already been in a lengthy, more intensive treatment setting, an introduction to the SMS program prior to being discharged from the inpatient setting and the involvement of a more homogeneous population in terms of symptoms and treatment. The researchers also concluded that their program might have been more efficacious had clients first been screened for their willingness to respond to therapist-aided treatment.

Recent research indicates that the treatment of schizophrenic related cognitive impairments can be enhanced through the use of text messaging. A study conducted by Pijnenborg et al. (2007), involving eight males diagnosed with schizophrenia, centered on the hypothesis that SMS messages could be used to prompt relevant behaviors, thereby increasing the number of desirable goals achieved in daily living. It was also assumed that the removal of SMS prompts would lead to a decrease in functional gains. Although three men were withdrawn from the study because of an exacerbation of symptoms during the evaluative period, the remainder completed the process and generally showed improvements in completing such tasks as taking medication on time, complying with scheduled appointments and attending training and therapy sessions. After the text messaging was withdrawn, the participants largely returned to baseline functioning. While the authors note the study was limited by the number of participants, a somewhat unstable baseline and large interpersonal variability, they conclude that SMS was "the effective component in improving performance and improvement was not simply a reflection of time, medication, or participation in a cognitive rehabilitation program in general" (p. 239).

Simply stating that SMS can be used to monitor symptoms does not fully capture its capability from an objective and subjective standpoint. The BBC News (Elliott, 2008) profiled a 23-year-old client under the fictitious name "Joe" who had bipolar disorder. Each morning Joe received a text from his treatment team prompting him to enter numeric values describing his mood. The data, collected on an ongoing basis, was used to plot mood swings, assess medication efficacy and determine when the next face-to-face appointment should be scheduled. Joe was part of at least 150 clients being monitored via SMS in a collaborative project in the United Kingdom, headed up in part by John Geddes. Geddes noted that SMS is ideal because it is widely available, easy to use and charts moods in real time rather than trying to reconstruct them after the fact. A bipolar advocate added that, "to have a mood mapping text messaging service to a health professional will provide a window into your illness. This could lead to early intervention and potentially head off serious episodes of this mood disorder" (Elliott, 2008, p. 1). From Joe's point of view, the SMS intervention has made a significant impact in life functioning. He described participation in the program as a way to inject structure in his life, a means to reassure him "things are being processed" and a benefit in face to face sessions as archived data is readily available for discussion. With respect to the impact SMS had on his ability to function with bipolar disorder, Joe stated, "It has been a massive support to me. It has made recovery relatively painless" (Elliott, 2008, p. 1). Joe's intervention was so successful, he returned to college to finish his degree.

Because of the data transmission limitations involved in using SMS, its current application often more resembles an adjunct to or enrichment of therapy rather than a therapeutic modality. However, that is not to say that 160 characters cannot at times take on a more substantial role within therapeutic interventions. Hazelwood (2008), a nursing professional who specializes in treating clients with eating disorders, states that for more than three years, she has utilized SMS as an integral part of therapy. She began using text messaging as a way of maintaining therapeutic contact, but realized over time that SMS had some other important qualities, not the least of which was acceptance and ease of use. Hazelwood notes that clients can send a text message at any time, creating a sense of connection to the therapist and allowing for the expression of thoughts or feelings in real time. Before composing a response, the therapist has time to evaluate the message in terms of concrete, abstract or emotional expression; sentence structure and vocabulary; length of communication; and use of emoticons. These clues provide insight into a client's type of eating disorder, their mood, cognitive/personality style and how client and therapist will react to each other. In addition to having time to compose messages and gaining clues to a client's state of mind, Hazelwood describes several therapeutic benefits inherent to SMS: it serves as an outlet for clients who are not confident in their verbal skills or who have social anxiety, it encourages trust and self-expression within the therapeutic relationship and it allows for saved messages to be reviewed at various points in the therapeutic process. Hazelwood even describes how she successfully managed suicidal clients after they alerted her of their condition via SMS. Of the three clients, two were monitored through text messaging at regular intervals until they stabilized. In the case of the third client, she was able to use the text messages to demonstrate active suicidality to a local crisis team, while keeping the client occupied until the police arrived. Hazelwood concludes, "The use of texting as part of the therapeutic process will become very significant in developing practice in the 21st century" (p. 29).

ETHICAL CONSIDERATIONS

One of the primary concerns related to SMS technology is the security of the transmitted and/or stored information. Although in the USA, HIPAA (the Health Insurance Portability and Accountability Act, which sets the rules on the storage and transmission of health information) does not specifically address SMS and cell phone use, it is incumbent on the therapist to take reasonable measures to protect sensitive data and to encourage their clients to do the same. The National Institute of Standards and Technology (NIST), an agency of the United States Department of Commerce, has issued a set of guidelines related to cell phone and PDA security (Jansen and Scarfone, 2008). The NIST identified several security risks that need to be managed when using SMS for therapeutic contact. The Subscriber Identity Module, often referred to as the SIM card, not only identifies the user to the cell phone network, but stores phone book entries and text messages. Therefore, physical security of the device is paramount and password access is recommended whether text messages are generated by phone or computer software. When disposing of an SMS generating device, the user should always take measures to wipe out data through resetting or reformatting. The device screen should be shielded from the view of others through strategic location and/or the use of privacy filters. Devices used to transmit text messages should have virus and spyware monitoring as well as firewall protection to prevent unauthorized access to data. These functions can be supplied as an option to the subscriber or installed separately by the user.

Finally, text messaging encryption measures should be used to ensure the integrity of the data. Text messages can be intercepted at several points during the transmission process. Individuals with the desire, a little research and some basic electronics gear can potentially gain access to transmitted text messages. Cell phone providers and a number of services such as CellTrust, Kryptext, TextEncrypt and PhoneCrypt offer encryption solutions for individuals and organizations. In addition to the encryption feature, users are able to confirm receipt of messages and in some cases expand the message size. It is possible for someone with sophisticated equipment and software to decipher some encryption codes, but this is not a significant concern at this time. Although not a data

breach issue, it is possible for law enforcement to use cell tower triangulation or Global Positioning System (GPS) to locate a cell phone and its user. This capability can be an asset in certain client suicide threat situations.

While using SMS to support therapy or as a part of the therapeutic process might seem fairly innocuous because of its brevity and commonplace nature, there are ethical considerations to bear in mind. First and foremost, therapists should assess their knowledge of SMS technical capabilities and level of comfort in using SMS. McEnery West and Mulvena (2008) discuss an initial reluctance to text clients because it might seem unprofessional or too personal. However, this fear was allayed after realizing other therapists were successfully integrating this form of communication into their practice. They also point out that as simple as it might sound, at every point an SMS contact is made, the therapist should be especially cognizant that he or she is not mixing up different clients or using the wrong client cell phone number.

Professionals need to understand the proper context and methods for making client contact. As previously noted, text messages can provide information regarding a client's mood, state of mind, expressiveness and boundaries. Whether the client makes the initial SMS contact or it is jointly decided to utilize SMS, the therapist should begin using communications in and out of session to help correctly determine what would benefit the therapeutic process. If texting is used, should it be reserved for occasional housekeeping such as appointment changes or does it have a more substantive role with a specific client? For instance, in the case of the latter does the additional option of text messaging help bring needed comfort and connection or does it potentially cause harm for individuals who need to develop stronger boundaries and autonomy? When appropriate, these types of issues can be discussed in session before and after SMS communication has occurred. If a professional does not give sufficient thought to SMS meaning and affect, there is a risk of disrupting the therapeutic process, damaging trust with the client and damaging professional status. Anthony and Nagel (2010) cite an example of a therapist who was removed from membership in the British Association for Counselling and Psychotherapy (BACP) in part for using inappropriate text messaging language with clients. They also note that text messages serve as a date and time stamped verbatim account of therapeutic exchanges that can be admissible in legal proceedings. However, as with all types of therapeutic endeavors, the clinician can greatly reduce risk to self and others by obtaining training, thinking through interventions, utilizing peer support and setting protocol and expectations with the client initially and as needed.

CONCLUSION

The use of Short Message Service (SMS) has evolved greatly over the last few years and is now a widely accepted and useful form of communication for personal and professional use. As is the case in the medical field, SMS has become a bridge between service providers and clients. Text messaging allows for the convenient and rapid transmission of data, the ability to offer support and information and to a limited extent, the opportunity to engage in therapeutic interventions. SMS has proven to be effective in monitoring symptoms, prompting behaviors and providing feedback in the treatment of eating disorders, schizophrenia and bipolar disorder. Within the therapeutic process, the exchange of text messages in real time allows the therapist check for clues related to the client's state of mind and to better understand the client's communication style, thought processes and emotional expressiveness. SMS has even been used to manage suicidal clients with and without law enforcement involvement.

As with any form of therapeutic intervention, interactions must be considered within an ethical context. To ensure confidentiality and privacy, security measures should be in place, such as ensuring possession of the communication device, using password access, concealing screen views and adding transmission encryption. With respect to the latter, there are a growing number of communication service providers and software companies offering complete solutions. It is incumbent upon therapists who utilize SMS to understand how the process works and to gain a certain level of proficiency. Therapists should always bear in mind the consequences of using SMS as a therapeutic tool. They need to understand their clients' issues and determine whether texting should be reserved for such functions as appointment changes transmitting data or whether it can play a larger role, such as developing a sense of connection and support outside of sessions or perhaps providing real time feedback in handling a situation or reaction. In the final analysis, the therapist is responsible for taking all reasonable steps to ensure SMS interventions are secure, safe and potentially beneficial for the client.

So what does the future hold for SMS? From a technological standpoint, it is very likely that the standard message size (number of characters) will continue to expand, keyboard layouts will continue to be refined and voice activated texting will be an expected feature. In addition, individuals and businesses will become increasingly aware of the need for security precautions, as they have in other areas of technology, such as personal computer use.

Text messaging will continue to grow in popularity as the number of users and devices increases and, as younger generations mature, they will bring with them a sense of acceptance, savvy and enthusiasm related to SMS as a communication device with widespread applicability. It will be quite advantageous for therapists and other professionals to embrace the use of SMS in some capacity within their practices. At the very least, they will need to develop enough SMS proficien-cy to discuss the issue with clients as needed. While SMS has proven its merit for therapeutic monitoring and basic feedback, it will become increasingly interactive in and out of sessions. Cooper (2008) hints to the future direction of SMS in a scenario posed by a therapist at Seton Hall University. The therapist described an adolescent client who in the middle of a therapy session took out her cell phone and began texting. The therapist stated that at one time she might have considered this to be resistance or lack of focus. However, her own phone rang and the client had texted, "u r not getting what im saying." This type of interaction represents a fusion of digital technology and human interaction that will become increasingly commonplace in the realm of therapeutic interventions. As with chat, video and virtual realities, SMS will shift over time from being an occasional tool to support or augment therapy to a recognized and accepted ingredient in the process of meaningful change.

REFERENCES

Anthony, K., & Nagel, D. M. (2010). *Therapy online [A practical guide]*. London: Sage.

Bauer, S., Percevic, R., Okon, E., Meerman, R., & Kordy, H. (2003). The use of text messaging in the aftercare of patients with bulimia nervosa. *European Eating Disorders Review, 11*(3), 279–290.

Cooper, G. (2008). Therapy and global warming. *Psychotherapy Networker,* July/August [online]. [Acessed August 10, 2009]. Available from: http://www.psycho therapynetworker.com/magazine/recent issues/125-clinicians-digest?start=1.

Elliott, J. (2008). Monitoring mental health by text. BBC WorldNews America (December 31 2008) [online]. [Accessed August 10, 2009]. Available from: http://news. bbc.co.uk/2/hi/health/7797155.stm.

Franklin, V. L., Greene, A., Waller, A., Greene, S. A. and Pagliari, C. (2008). Patients' engagement with "Sweet Talk"–a text messaging support system for young people with diabetes. *Journal of Medical Internet Research, 10*(2): e20. [online]. [Accessed August 10, 2009]. Available from: http://www.jmir.org/2008/2/e20/ HTML.

HarmoniousTech (2008a). Introduction to SMS messaging. *Developers' Home* [online]. [Accessed August 10, 2009]. Available from: http://www.developershome.com/ sms/smsIntro.asp.

HarmoniousTech (2008b). Example applications of SMS messaging. *Developers' Home* [online]. [Accessed August 10, 2009]. Available from: http://www.developers home.com/sms/sms_tutorial.asp?page=eg Apps.

Hazelwood, A. (2008). Using text messaging in the treatment of eating disorders. *Nursing Times, 104*(40), 28–29.

Horstmanshof, L. (2004). Using SMS as a way of providing connection and community for first year students. In R. Atkinson, C. McBeath, D. Jonas-Dwyer, & R. Phillips (Eds.), *Beyond the comfort zone: Proceedings of the 21st ASCILITE Conference. Perth, 5–8 December* [online]. [Accessed August 10, 2009]. Available from: http://www.ascilite.org.au/conferences/perth04/procs/horstmanshof.html.

Huang, F., Liu, S. C., Shih, S. M., Tao, Y. H., Wu, J. Y., Jeng, S. Y., & Chang, P. (2006). Reducing the anxiety of surgical patient's families access short message service. In *AMIA Annual Symposium Proceedings 2006.*

Ivatury, G., Moore, J., & Bloch, A. (2009). *A doctor in your pocket: Health hotlines in developing countries* [online]. [Accessed August 10, 2009]. Available from: http://www.g smworld.com/documents/a_doctor_in_your_pocket.pdf.

Jansen, W., & Scarfone, K. (2008). *Guidelines on cell phone and PDA security: Recommendations of the National Institute of Standards and Technology.* Washington, DC: U.S. Government Printing Office.

McEnery West, C., & Mulvena, T. (2008). Text speak. *Therapy Today, 19*(8), 21–28.

Neville, R., Greene, A., McLeod, J., Tracy, A., & Surie, J. (2002). Mobile phone text messaging can help young people manage asthma. *British Medical Journal. 325*(7364), 600.

NZPA (2004). Teacher finds novel way to use texting. *The New Zealand Herald.* (June 25) [online]. [Accessed August 10, 2009]. Available from: http://www.nzherald.co.nz/nz/news/article.cfm?c_id=1&object id=3574815.

Pijnenborg, G. H., Withaar, F. K., Evans, J. J., van den Bosch, R. J., & Brouwer, W. H. (2007). SMS text messages as a prosthetic aid in the cognitive rehabilitation of schizophrenia. *Rehabilitation Psychology, 52*(2), 236–240.

Price, H., Waters, A. M., Mighty, D., Nixon, J., Burton, N., Picket, J., & Sullivan, A. K. (2009). Texting appointment reminders reduces 'did not attend' rates, is popular with patients and is cost-effective. *International Journal of STD and AIDS, 20*(2), 142–143.

Robinson, S., Perkins, S., Bauer, S., Hammond, N., Treasure, J., & Schmidt, U. (2006). Aftercare intervention through text messaging in the treatment of bulimia nervosa–feasibility pilot. *International Journal of Eating Disorders, 39*(8), 633–638.

Shapiro, J. R., Bauer, S., Hamer, R. M., Kordy, H., Ward, D., & Bulik, C. M. (in press) Text messaging to increase healthy eating and physical activity in children. *Journal of Nutrition Education and Behavior.*

Turrettini, E. (2009). SMS, A little history. *Textually.org* [online]. [Accessed August 10, 2009]. Available from: http://www.text ually.org/textually/archives/cat_sms_a_little_history.htm.

Chapter 4

USING SOCIAL NETWORKS AND IMPLICATIONS FOR THE MENTAL HEALTH PROFESSION

ALLISON THOMPSON

INTRODUCTION

Online communities, or profile sites, as discussed in this chapter, are Internet sites where the goal is for members to keep contact with friends and/or allow members to meet new people. There are several sites available online with different target populations (e.g., college students, singles, animal lovers and so on). Each site offers different communication tools, such as e-mail, instant messaging, chat rooms, discussion boards and/or blogs (on-line public or private diaries). Many sites provide different levels of privacy to protect members from unwanted attention; however, members' user name and picture may still be available to public viewing.

Given the popularity of online communities, one can assume that some counseling professionals have personal profile sites. If an active counseling professional posts private information to a public domain, one can assume that there may be potential issues related to the integrity of the counselor and client relationship. While online communities can be used as a great communication tool in terms of one's personal life, they can also potentially blur professional boundaries. In order to understand how online communities could affect the counseling relationship, this article will describe myspace.com, relevant boundary and ethical issues and the benefits and risks associated with belonging to online communities. In addition, this chapter will apply the American Counseling Association and the British Association for Counselling and Psychotherapy codes of ethics to a potential problem and offer suggestions for future consideration by the counseling profession.

DESCRIPTION OF MYSPACE.COM

Myspace.com is an online community where individuals can join to stay in contact with friends, meet new people and/or network with professionals. The site offers blogs, pictures, videos, e-mail and a search engine to find classmates, friends or new people for its members. The site has two settings: private and public. The private setting allows a member to keep information hidden (except the user's picture, username, age and state or country) from members other than friends the person has accepted from myspace.com. Around 150,000 new members register for myspace.com each day and over 80 percent of its registered members fall into the age demographic of 16–34 year olds (Sullivan and Millunchick, 2006). With the dramatic addition of daily memberships, it is more likely members will know at least one person on myspace.com when he or she joins. With a new generation of counselors emerging into the profession, it is more likely that these counselors will have an online profile with some type of online community.

Members registered with myspace.com can acquire a large quantity of information about other members. Listed on profiles are the age, location, ethnicity, sex, education level, relationship status, sexual orientation, purpose of joining myspace.com (i.e., dating, friends and networking), pictures and work experience as well as other information. To communicate with members on the site, members can send e-mail, an instant message, or a request to be friends to anyone on myspace.com with a profile. Again, members can choose to be public or private, which limits the communication and information sharing from members who have not been approved as friends.

Already, the mental health profession is using online-communities as a tool to network with other mental health profession as well as potential clients. Using the search engine provided on the site, myspace.com members or random web browsers can either type in the name of the desired profile or type in a general search for counseling related profile pages. When searching msypace.com, the following amount of counseling profiles exist (February 25, 2009, www.myspace.com):

- 63 profiles found when searching under the word counseling or counselling.
- 157 profiles found when searching under the word counselor
- 17 profiles found when searching under the phrase mental health.

Online-communities can offer convenience for both the counselor and client in case of conflicts in scheduling and/or mental health professionals wanting to broaden their professional and social networks with other mental health professionals and potential clients. Erasing possible discomfort with face-to-face contact, some clients reveal more about themselves electronically than they would in person. However, amongst the benefits, numerous potential issues regarding boundaries, confidentiality and other ethical issues could result in serious consequences for mental health professionals that do not take into consideration the potential risks.

BOUNDARIES AND DUAL RELATIONSHIPS

A study by Neukrug, Milliken and Walden (2001) examining ethical complaints against credentialed counselors concluded the top complaint was because of inappropriate dual relationships. When disciplinary action was taken, 36 percent of counselors had their credentials revoked and 19 percent had their licenses suspended. Because of the severity of potential disciplinary action, counselors need to be aware of potential outcomes and effects of engaging in a relationship with a client through an online profile site like Myspace.com. Dual relationships can cross boundaries by allowing counselors to engage in conversation and/or behavior that are deemed inappropriate for the therapeutic relationship. Because dual relationships are a major complaint made against counselors, counselors need to be aware of their actions inside and outside the therapeutic relationship with their clients (Thompson, 2008).

In order to understand how a simple profile on myspace.com could lead to a potential ethical issue for counselors, it is important to review the literature regarding professional boundaries in counseling. When developing a therapeutic relationship, "boundaries provide a flexible set of conditions that . . . establish rules and role expectations that the patient may rely upon for the safety required for treatment" (Glass, 2003, p. 429).

Boundaries create an atmosphere of predictability and safety for the client while creating a guideline for counselors when interacting with their client. The difference between counselors violating a boundary versus crossing a boundary depends on the intent of the action. If the counselor reacts to what he or she believes is in the best interest of the client, it is a boundary crossing. However, if the

counselor is acting towards her or his own needs, then the action is a boundary violation (Glass, 2003, p. 433–436).

Example

Having a profile on a site such as Myspace.com can lead to potential ethical dilemmas with the therapeutic relationship with clients who search on myspace.com and find the profile of their counselor. The client could try to communicate with the counselor through the site or try to add the counselor as her/his friend. This could lead to boundary crossings for counselors if they believe this could harm their client by not communicating with the client on the site. However, once a counselor adds a client onto their profile site, their private information is not private to their client anymore; thus, the counselor would be inadvertently self-disclosing information about themselves to their client. The information that could be exposed to a client might evolve into an ethical "slippery slope."

Because of the "slippery slope" effect with crossing or violating boundaries, it is important for counselors to handle clients finding their profiles on myspace.com or themselves finding clients on myspace.com professionally. For example, tools such as blogs or comments on myspace.com could end up harming a client if a counselor discusses work on his profile site without having a private setting. The client could read information about the counselor's work and it may or may not be about the client, but could make the client paranoid and/or mistrustful of the counselor. This could lead to damage in the therapeutic relationship or cause the client to avoid scheduled sessions.

CONFIDENTIALITY

Online-communities can offer feelings of safety for the client and an increase in accessibility for the counselor. Unfortunately, potential issues of confidentiality can arise with mental health professionals who create and monitor online-communities as well as their clients. Even with safety precautions, passwords and other privacy settings, hard drives, e-mail messages and other component parts of an online community, information from your hard drive can still be vulnerable to hackers. In addition to hackers, family members or coworkers could stumble upon confidential information if a monitor of a community forgets to sign-out of his or her online community. A mental health professional creating and monitoring a profile site's privacy is also at risk, since clients can record telephone conversations and save e-mail messages (HPSO, 2008). As well as human error, technology can result in ethical dilemmas. All records or messages of crisis could be lost or destroyed and the monitor of the online community may not have any control of the situation. Although it can be helpful to create a tool to increase a client's trust and safety when disclosing information, this feeling of safety could backfire and can invite abuse of the therapeutic relationship (HPSO, 2008). Clients or mental health professionals could send a monitor of a profile site, or a counselor who uses an online-community to counsel an individual could have a client that sends messages to them many times a day. These actions create a string of questions regarding boundary issues as well as how to handle the situation.

ACA CODE OF ETHICS

When the American Counseling Association revises its ethical codes in 2010 online profile sites may need to be taken into consideration. The American Counseling Association's (ACA) *Code of Ethics* currently does not provide guidelines pertaining to counselors belonging to online-communities. Section A.2a. of the ACA *Code of Ethics,* states, "counselors act to avoid harming their clients . . . to minimize or to remedy unavoidable or unanticipated harm" (2005, p. 4). Another relevant code is A.5.c, which deals with nonprofessional interactions or relationships (this does not cover sexual or romantic relationships with clients). The code states that, "counselor-client nonprofessional relationship with clients, former clients, their romantic partners, or their family members should be avoided, except when the interaction is potentially beneficial to the client (p. 5). These codes do not provide clear decision-making guidelines for counselors facing a decision as to whether to interact with clients through their online-community. This is definitely a gray area of boundary crossings and violations. Adding a client onto a counselor's profile site could be possibly beneficial to the client (increase in self-esteem, worthiness, trust); however, the counselor would be self-disclosing personal information about him or herself, which could threaten the therapeutic relationship, blur boundaries and could cause the counselor to cross other boundaries and in the end violate boundaries. As previously discussed, crossing or violating boundaries can cause a "slippery slope" effect for the counselor.

When addressing potential ethical dilemmas, answers vary state to state and country to country; therefore, it is difficult to know how to handle a client that lives in another state or country than the counselor. When examining the structure of the online community as well as examining decision-making steps for monitors, many questions arise as to how to handle ethics. When deciding action, which laws would the monitor of the online communities follow when handling a crisis? If a counselor were sued over his/her actions, what state or country would hear the case? In general, for a US-based practitioner, for example, it would be wise for any mental health professional interested in developing an online community to first review the ACA's *Code of Ethics*, consult with an attorney, professional associations, licensing boards and other mental health professionals in order to develop an awareness of potential risks in developing a site.

ACA is starting to recognize the increase and rise of technology in the mental health profession by developing ethical codes to assist counseling professionals. In the ACA's *Code of Ethics* (2005, p. 6), section A.12 discusses technology applications. A.12.a discusses counselors informing clients the benefits and risks to engaging in technology applications. It may be wise for future monitors to explore and spend time developing thorough informed consents on the site in order to provide those seeking communication or other tools provided on the profile to be fully aware of risks, benefits, the purpose of the online-profile and other information to develop knowledge as to whether the online-community would be appropriate. Other parts of A.12 address issues addressed elsewhere in this volume, such as providing additional contact if there is computer failure. With more time and research, ACA and other professional associations around the world are likely to create additional codes to assist counselors in making ethical and safe decisions when using technology, where they have not already done so.

BACP ETHICAL FRAMEWORK AND GUIDELINES FOR ONLINE WORK

The British Association for Counselling and Psychotherapy (BACP) offers a different approach than the ACA *Code of Ethics*, preferring the term "Ethical Framework" (http://www.bacp.co.uk/ethical_framework/). The BACP Ethical Framework recognizes that most work is undertaken face-to-face but that there are also a growing number of telephone and online services. Some practitioners are moving between these different settings and modes of delivery during the course of their work and are therefore required to consider what constitutes good practice in different settings. All practitioners encounter the challenge of responding to the diversity of their clients and finding ways of working effectively with them. This statement therefore responds to the complexity of delivering counselling and psychotherapy services in contemporary society by directing attention to essential issues that practitioners ought to consider and resolve in the specific circumstances of their work.

In addition to the statements within the Ethical Framework, the BACP offer guidelines specifically for online counselling and psychotherapy, including guidelines for online supervision, now in their third edition (Anthony & Goss, 2009). Although these guidelines focus specifically on text based (email, chat and forum communication), the third edition acknowledges that guidelines are appropriate for other technologies, including social networking and online communities.

IMPLICATIONS FOR FUTURE RESEARCH

Online-communities are starting to get more research after their rise in popularity, the increase in participation and increased discussion of online-communities in the media. Presentations at the 2008 ACA Annual Conference and Exhibition (Mascari & Webber, 2008) indicated a need for counselors to become educated as to current technology and encouraged working professionals to gain a better understanding by creating profiles with online communities in order to develop competence in such sites as well as learning how clients are connecting and communicating with one another through online communities. Mascari and Webber also pointed out how developing competence with online communities can assist counselors with understanding relationship dynamics with clients who use online communities as well as help address potential dangers when participating with online communities.

New research related to counseling and online communities focuses on using online communities as tools and techniques in the counseling session. Wilson (2009) used online profiles from clients in the session to explore identity, personal relationships, communications skills, examining relational patterns online versus in person, developing problem-solving skills with conflict triggering from online community communications and so on. The goal for the counselor is to use creativity and online communities in order to engage with the client and build a therapeutic relationship using a medium the client enjoys outside of the session. Wilson also suggests using online communities to develop coping skills, such as using the blog (to which the client can make an entry private or public) and developing social supports with online friends to help reach out during disturbed moods or conflict. Last, Wilson suggests encouraging the client to self-explore personal traits by developing an online profile that expresses themselves creatively and through different meda, such as choosing certain songs to list on their profile, developing layouts with a variety of colors and pictures, and/or communicating about themselves through how they describe personal interests on their profile. This article helps encourage mental health professionals to take online communities, that currently seem controversial due to the lack of research and concerns regarding dual relationships, and turn them into a positive therapy tool.

However, in general, there is a lack of research with regards to online communities and the effects on the counselor-client relationship. With the current increase in participation in membership of online communities, research is needed to become aware of the possible outcomes of such communities for the counselor and addressing the nature of these relationships for counselors. Researching this topic area is not intended to prohibit or promote membership to online communities, but to examine the potential risks and benefits for professional counselors in belonging to an online community. The issue at hand could be one that affects all types of counselors in the field: private practice, agency, counseling educators, school counselors, supervisors and so forth. Professional organizations and new emerging generations of professionals need to examine a new medium of communicating private and public information outside of the counseling relationship and look at possible questions or ethical issues that could arise before problems emerge.

Possible questions to examine are:

- What percentages of counselors belong to online-communities?
- What problems have been reported as a result of clients contacting counselors through these sites?
- How do counselors balance their personal life with their professional life?
- What is the research on current online counseling communities?
- Does membership of an online community jeopardize a counselor's integrity?
- Is it the right of a professional organization to place limits or boundaries on the personal lives of counselors in or outside of the membership?
- How many counselors and/or agencies are using social networks as a tool to build clientele or reach those in need of counseling?
- In what ways are counselors, agencies and professional counseling organizations currently using social networks?
- Studies of the effectiveness of counselors who are using social networks as tools in counseling and determining if the tool is helpful or harmful in developing therapeutic relationships and achieving treatment goals.

CONCLUSION

Research addressing the above questions could benefit the counseling profession in future ethical decision-making as well as having an influence on how organizations around the world may monitor the private lives of counselors who belong to online-communities. Again, without credible research on online communities and counselors who participate on these sites, it is hard to predict the effects of these sites and how professional bodies will need to react to the potential boundary issues resulting from interaction on online communities.

REFERENCES

American Counseling Association. (2005). *ACA code of ethics.* Alexandria, VA: American Counseling Association.

Anthony, K., & Goss, S. (2009). *Guidelines for online counselling and psychotherapy including guidelines for online supervision* (3rd ed.).

Lutterworth: BACP.

Glass, L.L. (2003). The gray areas of boundary crossings and violations. *American Journal of Psychotherapy, 57*(4), 429–444.

Healthcare Providers Service Organization (HPSO). (2008). *Should you counsel patients electronically?* [online]. [Accessed May 5, 2009]. Available from: http://www.hpso.com/resources/article/61.jsp.

Mascari, J. B., & Webber, J. (2008). Keeping up with the facebook and myspace generation: What counselors can do [online]. *ACA Annual Conference and Exhibition, March 26–30, 2008, Honolulu, HI* [online]. [Accessed May 6, 2009]. Available from: http://counselingoutfitters.com/vistas/vistas08/Mascari.htm.

Myspace.com. (2008). *MySpace.com* [online]. [Accessed October 20, 2008]. Available from: www.myspace.com.

Neukrug, E., Milliken, T., & Walden, S. (2001). Ethical complaints made against credentialed counselors: An updated survey of state licensing boards. *Counselor Education and Supervision, 41*(1), 57–66.

Sullivan, J., & Millunchick, M. (2006). Outside the box–using myspace.com as a recruiting tool. *Ere.net* [online]. [Accessed May 6, 2009]. Available from: http://www.ere.net/2006/03/27/outside-the-box-recruiting-151-using-myspacecom-as-a-recruiting-tool/.

Thompson, A. (2008). Counselor's right to privacy: Potential boundary crossings through membership in online communities. *Counseling Today, 51*(2): 44–45.

Wilson, A. (2009). How to use myspace in counseling: Social networking sites provide tool for mental health professionals. *Suite101.com* [online]. [Accessed May 6, 2009]. Available from: http://counseling.suite101.com/article.cfm/how_to_use_myspace_in_counseling.

Chapter 5

USING FORUMS TO ENHANCE
CLIENT PEER SUPPORT

AZY BARAK AND MEYRAN BONIEL-NISSIM

INTRODUCTION

Support groups operated through the Internet have existed since the middle of the 1990s, exploiting modern technology in continuation of traditional, face-to-face support groups (aka self-help or mutual-aid groups), which have been employed since the 1930s. The Internet has provided a special platform for operating these groups, which are able to take advantage of the unique features of virtual communication: convenience; anonymity and privacy; asynchronicity; textuality and saved history; optional use of external links, pictures, movies and sound; availability almost anywhere, anytime; relative inexpensiveness; and broad social acceptability. Moreover, the Internet more readily enables the matching of group participants who possess similar needs; for many, this is apparently a unique opportunity to communicate and associate with people who share one's interests.

Initially online support groups were constructed through e-mail lists and relatively primitive server-based software that created newsgroup sites. Technological developments, as well as users' experiences and desires, contributed to more advanced web-based platforms that created highly dynamic support communities characterized by advanced and rich design. The result is that today hundreds of thousands of online support groups are active worldwide, trying to meet users' expectations and provide some relief to human difficulties.

DEFINITION AND DESCRIPTION OF ONLINE SUPPORT GROUPS

An online support group connects people who share a common problem, difficulty or area of distress. Most such groups are operated through an Internet

47

forum ("bulletin board") platform, which provides anonymous, invisible, text-based, usually asynchronous, normally open and generally free virtual social environment. In this environment–typically run by means of server-based software (meaning that participants access a website by using a regular Internet browser)–people share information and personal experiences, communicate with one another and form interpersonal interactions with the purpose of obtaining emotional relief, on the one hand, and supporting others in need, on the other. A smaller number of groups take place through an e-mail list–which is another way of creating asynchronous group communication online. Although forum-based groups are more advantageous from the perspective of both technology and usability, some people prefer joining an e-mail-based group because it saves the necessity of accessing a website in order to read messages. Online support groups sometimes take place in chat rooms, too, as this format allows real-time (synchronous) communication and offers the advantages of immediacy and spontaneity of interactions, though it does present the disadvantage of having to be connected at specific, nonflexible times.

Online support groups allow people in need to receive help in numerous areas of distress: physical medical conditions, such as a certain disease or syndromes (e.g., diabetes, breast cancer, tinnitus, epilepsy); emotional difficulties (related to various issues, such as bereavement, divorce, being fired, school failure, sexual assault); coping difficulties (e.g., smoking cessation, diet and weight loss, immigration); living with disabilities (e.g., hearing impairment, dwarfism, limb amputation); and relatives of people with certain difficulties (e.g., parents of children with autism, children of Alzheimer patients). People in need usually locate appropriate, relevant groups through online indices and search engines, but also through referrals by professionals, links on various websites, the media and recommendations from friends or relatives.

In most cases, online participants use nicknames in order to retain full privacy and secrecy unless they choose to identify themselves or disclose personal information. The degree and type of participation in a group is usually a matter of choice, the participants themselves deciding how often to participate, how deep their writing is to be and to what degree to support others. However, intimate disclosures are quite normative as is both asking for and providing help and advice to others in the group.

DISTINCTION BETWEEN THERAPY AND SUPPORT GROUPS

There is much confusion between therapy and support groups, whether online or offline. This misunderstanding has developed apparently because these two forms of providing psychological help to people in need have certain common denominators. However, it is important to emphasize that despite several similarities, they are two different entities, they have different goals and they expose clients to different procedures and protocols. Four of their major distinctions are as follows: first, an online support group is fundamentally based on mutual-help among its participants, not on dedicated professional intervention (by one or another psychotherapeutic approach). Second, an online support group is neither necessarily managed nor supervised by a trained professional. Third, the procedures and policies of most online support groups seldom adhere to standards of professionalism and ethics or to legal obligations. Fourth, unlike therapy groups, practically all online support groups are open to anyone and no pre-screening is conducted; similarly, members can leave and return at will.

PROCEDURES AND PRACTICE OF ONLINE SUPPORT GROUPS

There are various types of online infrastructure that enable group communication. Synchronized communication allows all online participants to take part in the communication at the same time through chat rooms. Asynchronous communication provides a vehicle for participants to communicate without the necessity of simultaneous participation as through email lists and forums, which enable delayed reading and responding. While a forum is operated through a website and is usually open to anyone, an email list involves more concealed communication, since only members of the list can receive or send messages.

In many ways, synchronized communication is similar to face-to-face communication in terms of instantaneous response, because the responses of other participants are immediately presented on the chat window and associated with the name of the participant who posted them. This form of online communication, which enhances spontaneity and authenticity of people conversing, may become an obstacle as participants are dependent on the presence of other group members in the chat room at a given time. Setting appointments in advance, as is done for offline support group meetings, may help overcome this obstacle. In addition, the size of a synchronous group must be taken into consideration: it is difficult to hold a chat discussion with more than a few participants because of the lack of visibility and nonverbal communication cues. In contrast, a forum may in principle successfully serve a very large group of participants (Hsiung, 2000, 2007). The immediacy of communication and the need to write down a response, as opposed to saying it out loud in a face-to-face group, makes it necessary for participants to be more aware of their wording, the length of their writing, their response time and the need to refer and direct comments to a relevant participant.

Many of the difficulties presented by synchronized communication are easily resolved through asynchronous communication through a forum. The ability to communicate whenever it suits them allows participants to choose the right time, logistically as well as emotionally, an advantage that makes this kind of group more convenient and provides users with broader operational space. A forum is chronologically reversed, so that the most recent main message is presented first. A main message heads a thread of messages in which participants interact with one another. A participant may post a message freely, at any time and of any length. The delay in asynchronous communication allows messages to be edited before they are submitted. Use of attachments and links is possible, too. Forums are usually open to anyone and their history can usually be browsed freely. In addition to the active members of the group, passive, reading-only participants (called lurkers) may read and stay informed about developments within the group. While lurkers do not actively take part, they frequently experience a commitment to the group and obtain support from it (Nonnecke & Preece, 2002).

Two of the special features that distinguish online from offline support groups are the textual nature of online communication and the variety of technical aids for the use of participants. Early theorizing predicted that computer-mediated communication would be impersonal because of its invisibility and anonymous nature and the fact that it is not able to convey nonverbal cues. However, the huge number of individuals who choose to take part in this type of communication seems to contradict that notion

(Tanis, 2007). People adapt their linguistic and textual behaviors in an attempt to overcome limitations created by written-only communication; in this way, communication becomes more personal and tends to resemble face-to-face communication. Some of the tools available to online writers constitute attempts to substitute nonverbal communication, such as highlighting text by color, size, or boldness; use of emoticons; elevated punctuation marks; links to other online materials, integrating pictures and sounds with text; and the use of personal signatures. These tools help get the message across in a richer way and with greater accuracy. Additionally, written communication facilitates the creative use of written language through the employment and integration of lingual creative applications, such as rhymes, metaphors, poems and original (invented) terms (e.g., Provine et al., 2007).

PSYCHOLOGICAL PROCESSES IN ONLINE SUPPORT GROUPS

Being part of a group enables participants to go through a process in which they can learn about themselves and about how others see them and receive an opportunity to express themselves authentically. Yalom and Leszcz's (2005) conception regarding therapeutic forces that operate in groups and facilitate change is of high relevance here. These forces include instilling hope, inducing a sense of universality, imparting information and knowledge, offering advice and guidance, developing altruistic attitudes, encouraging interpersonal learning and providing a convenient space for catharsis. Qualitative and quantitative research of online support groups shows that these forces operate in virtual groups just as they do offline, in face-to-face groups.

Additional processes characterize online support groups. Since communication takes place in a virtual arena, one can participate while preserving anonymity and invisibility. This unique procedure operates as an accelerator of disinhibition and consequent self-exposure. These processes thus explain why new members feel comfortable soon after joining the group in sharing personal experiences and relatively quickly develop feelings of intimacy in relationships with other group members. Disinhibition, furthermore, induces dynamic progress in the group by encouraging sharing, self-expression and introspection. It should be noted, at the same time, though, that disinhibition might introduce damage by promoting flaming, acting out and judgmental attitudes (Suler, 2004; Tanis, 2007).

Communicating through writing, in contrast to speech, leads to significant cognitive and emotional self-processes. For example, writing has been found to contribute to the process of thought arrangement and subsequent emotional relief (Pennebaker & Seagal, 1999). Writing is a way for a person to express and share thoughts, emotions and experiences that may not be otherwise expressed. In addition to mere ventilation, the writer is focused on herself or himself while writing, allowing for an examination and re-examination of thoughts, for clarification, explanation and eventually–unlike in face-to-face interactions–the choice of whether to transmit the text to the group. This reflective process contributes to self-awareness, awareness of others and a developing sense of control (Hoybye et al., 2005), all in a safer place than the participants' offline environment (Tichon & Shapiro, 2003).

The evidence that has accumulated shows that involvement in an online support group empowers participants, in addition to providing emotional relief (as opposed to healing users). Several specific processes have been identified as responsible for creating a sense of personal empowerment: the exchange of relevant information and knowledge, undergoing the psychological impact of writing, providing and receiving emotional support, accepting social recognition, sharing personal experiences, developing interpersonal relationships, helping others in need, being assisted in making decisions and taking consequent action and experiencing amusement and fun. These processes produce specific outcomes: clients become better informed, more confident, more accepting of their condition, more optimistic, more active and have generally improved well-being (Barak et al., 2008; van Uden-Kraan et al., 2008).

FACILITATION OF ONLINE SUPPORT GROUPS

There is no consensus or standard directing the management and supervision of online support groups. Some groups are conducted with no officially designated administrator; in others, the administrator is one of the members, chosen either by the group or by its owner (e.g., the portal's administration, a professional association) to oversee and supervise proceedings so that group procedures are successfully maintained. Despite the call for research (e.g., Eysenbach et al., 2004), the personal impact of the group administrator (also termed moderator, facilitator or navigator) and the types of moderating still await scientific inquiry. Recent research

on cancer support groups by Lieberman (2008), however, clearly points to the advantage of professional facilitation as superior to peer facilitation when judged by several criteria.

Facilitators' responsibility has multiple aspects. First and foremost, they should promote cohesiveness, as this is one of the most important and influential factors at work in a group (Yalom & Leszcz, 2005). It is a mission, however, that is particularly complex to achieve in an online group, which is characterized by physical distance, anonymity and invisibility. A second important role played by facilitators is to maintain the rules and practices of the group procedure in regard to ethics, such as preventing unwanted exposure or outing, harsh language and flaming; deleting problematic and misleading messages; negotiating with and solving problems of frustrated or embittered members; making attempts to avoid impersonation and phishing and so on. Facilitators may take such actions openly or secretly in back communication channels. A third function is to make sure that published information is well founded and based on credible sources and to prevent it from misleading and misguiding people in need and distress. Obviously, group facilitators cannot check every piece of information and advice provided, but they should take steps to guide participants and so minimize the effect of any problematic and harmful information that is published. An additional role of the group facilitator entails stimulating discussions related to the group's common topic, raising intriguing questions and posting materials of interest. Another function is to ensure that the group atmosphere is as positive, supportive and constructive as possible. This may be done by both modeling appropriate messages and responses and by providing feedback to members (usually through private communication). As the multiple and responsible role of a group facilitator is highly time- and work-consuming, the different tasks involved could be divided among several people who share the mission (Till, 2003).

RESEARCH ON ONLINE SUPPORT GROUPS

Process Research

Much research has been conducted on processes, behaviors, communication characteristics, personal expressions, emotional experiences and other process-related variables that occur in the dynamics of online support groups. Some process research has focused on psychological factors that take place in the group process (e.g., universality) and found that indeed the act of identifying and comparing oneself with similarly distressed people contributes to emotional relief (e.g., Bane et al., 2005) and empowerment (Bakardjieva, 2003; van Uden-Kraan et al., 2008). Generally, this research shows that online support groups are as dynamic, lively and engaging as offline support (and therapy) groups. Writing, as mentioned earlier, has been found to act as a central therapeutic agent, enhancing emotional relief and promoting well being (e.g., Hoybye et al., 2005). Participants find an online support group to constitute a safer situation than an offline environment in which to share their difficulties (Tichon & Shapiro, 2003). More generally, the expression of feelings, especially more negative ones, was shown to be related to emotional relief (e.g., Buchanan & Coulson, 2007; Lieberman & Goldstein, 2006). Although lurking is typical, participants normally take advantage of their anonymity and actively and in great detail, share with others in the group (actually, with anyone who observes the group's interactions) their individual concerns. This includes feelings, memories, desires, fears and so on. Research also shows that participants are very active in providing help to others, be it ideas and suggestions, referrals to online and offline information resources, or the communication of reassurance, encouragement and acceptance. Providing, as well as receiving, relevant information was found to empower participants in a wide variety of support groups (e.g., Bunde et al., 2007; Coulson & Knibb, 2007; Weis et al., 2003). Research, though, has also found evidence of negative behaviors, such as flaming, outing and impersonating, that do undermine group coherence, diminish a positive atmosphere and generally hinder normal proceedings (e.g., Aiken and Waller, 2000).

Outcome Research

Outcome research attempts to examine the impact of interventions; that is, the effects and changes that intervention procedures have caused in participants. However, whereas the goal of therapy in therapeutic interventions is generally known and clear the objective of support groups is much less clear, as their purpose seems to be more general than specific therapeutic change. Moreover, as indicated by Barak et al. (2008), in contrast to psychotherapy, which is usually aimed at well-defined, pre-planned changes relating to an area of distress, support groups strive to improve general feelings relating to well-being and empowerment and they can be successful in doing so (van Uden-Kraan et al., 2008).

Therefore, studies and literature reviews that refer to therapeutic changes caused by participation in online support groups usually have showed little evidence of actual, distress-specific improvement. However, publications report much empirical evidence from interviews and questionnaires, but also from observations of actual support group writings, in support of the notion that participants gain generally positive feelings directly related to their experiences in the group (e.g., Barak & Dolev-Cohen, 2006; Beaudoin & Tao, 2007; Buchanan & Coulson, 2007). These elevated feelings pertain to increased self-confidence and a sense of independence and decreased anxiety, loneliness and depression—all of which indeed relate to the concept of well-being. The result, as reported, was a better ability to make decisions related to one's distress condition, a better knowledge of, or at least acquaintance with, relevant information resources and the promotion of self-assurance in regard to difficulties—in other words, experiences related to the concept of empowerment.

It seems that these results imply that, for many people, the combination of specific professional therapeutic intervention, on the one hand, and participation in a relevant online support group, on the other, could provide optimal help for their problems. For instance, while evidence-based psychological treatment of PTSD for a woman who was raped could effectively help her overcome anxiety and depression related to her condition, parallel participation in a successful online support group—preferably in coordination with her clinician—could accelerate improvement of her condition by complementing her well-being. Therapists should be aware of this option and encourage clients to take advantage of it.

CONCLUSION

The advent of online support groups approximately a decade ago has dramatically changed the mental condition of many people suffering from various types of personal distress. People who experience emotional hardship—caused by disease, failure, social circumstances and other stressful and painful situations—can now easily find others whom to share their miseries and to consult with, to be helped by and to offer help to. By participating in such virtual groups, not only have many people improved their condition, but they have also gained a sense of personal empowerment that directly contributes to their general well being. Thus, online support groups may serve as an important social agent in enhancing quality of life for disadvantaged, marginal, weak and unhealthy populations. Moreover, online support groups may serve as a significant aid to a therapist in complementing therapeutic services. Obviously, not all support groups are equally valuable and successful; it takes the leadership of a good moderator, advanced and suitable online technology and design, involved group partners and appropriate participants to yield a constructive online support group (McKenna, 2008). With a thoughtful and well-planned approach, however, these groups may make a great contribution to the well-being of many members of society (Barak et al., 2008; Tanis, 2007).

REFERENCES

Aiken, M., & Waller, B. (2000). Flaming among first-time group support system users. *Information and Management, 37*(2), 95–100.

Bakardjieva, M. (2003). Virtual togetherness: An everyday-life perspective. *Media, Culture and Society, 25*(3), 291–313.

Bane, C. M. H., Haymaker, C. M. B., & Zinchuk, J. (2005). Social support as a moderator of the big-fish-in-a-little-pond effect in online self-help support groups. *Journal of Applied Biobehavioral Research, 10*(4), 239–261.

Barak, A., Boniel-Nissim, M., & Suler, J. (2008). Fostering empowerment in online support groups. *Computers in Human Behavior, 24*(5), 1867–1883.

Barak, A., & Dolev-Cohen, M. (2006). Does activity level in online support groups for distressed adolescents determine emotional relief? *Counselling and Psychotherapy Research, 6*(3), 186–190.

Beaudoin, C. E., & Tao, C. (2007). Benefiting from social capital in online support groups: An empirical study of cancer patients. *CyberPsychology and Behavior, 10*(4), 587–590.

Buchanan, H., & Coulson, N. S. (2007). Accessing dental anxiety online support groups: An exploratory qualitative study of motives and experiences. *Patient Education and Counseling, 66*(3), 263–369.

Bunde, M., Suls, J., Martin, R., & Barnett, K. (2007). Online hysterectomy support: Characteristics of website experiences. *CyberPsychology and Behavior, 10*(1), 80–85.

Coulson, N. S., & Knibb, R. C. (2007). Coping with food allergy: Exploring the role of the online support group. *CyberPsychology and Behavior, 10*(1), 145–148.

Eysenbach, G., Powell, J., Englesakis, M., Rizo, C., & Stern, A. (2004). Health related virtual communities and electronic support groups: Systematic review of the effects of online peer to peer interactions. *British Medical Journal, 328*(7449), 1166–1171.

Hoybye, M. T., Johansen, C., & Tjornhoj-Thomsen, T. (2005). Online interaction: Effects of storytelling in an Internet breast cancer support group. *Psycho-Oncology, 14*(3), 211–220.

Hsiung, R. C. (2000). The best of both worlds: An online self-help group hosted by a mental health professional. *CyberPsychology and Behavior, 3*(6), 935–950.

Hsiung, R. C. (2007). A suicide in an online mental health support group: Reactions of the group members, administrative responses and recommendations. *Cyber-Psychology and Behavior, 10*(4), 495–500.

Lieberman, M. A. (2008). Effects of disease and leader type on moderators in online support groups. *Computers in Human Behavior, 24*(5), 2446–2455.

Lieberman, M. A., & Goldstein, B. A. (2006). Not all negative emotions are equal: The role of emotional expression in online support groups for women with breast cancer. *Psycho-Oncology, 15*(2), 160–168.

McKenna, K. Y. M. (2008). Influences on the nature and functioning of online groups. In A. Barak (Ed.), *Psychological aspects of cyberspace: Theory, research, applications.* Cambridge, UK: Cambridge University Press.

Nonnecke, B., & Preece, J. (2002). Silent participants: Getting to know lurkers better. In C. Lueg & D. Fisher (Eds.), *From Usenet to CoWebs: Interacting with social information spaces.* London: Springer.

Pennebaker, J. W., & Seagal, J. D. (1999). Forming a story: The health benefits of narrative. *Journal of Clinical Psychology, 55*(10), 1243–154.

Provine, R. R., Spencer, R. J., & Mandell, D. L. (2007). Emotional expression online: Emoticons punctuate website text messages. *Journal of Language and Social Psychology, 26*(3), 299–307.

Suler, J. R. (2004). The online disinhibition effect. *CyberPsychology and Behavior, 7*(3), 321–326.

Tanis, M. (2007). Online social support groups. In A. Joinson, K. McKenna, T. Postmes, & U. Reips (Eds.), *The Oxford handbook of internet psychology.* Oxford, UK: Oxford University Press.

Tichon, J. G., & Shapiro, M. (2003). The process of sharing social support in cyberspace. *CyberPsychology and Behavior, 6*(2), 161–170.

Till, J. E. (2003). Evaluation of support groups for women with breast cancer: Importance of the navigator role [online]. *Health and Quality of Life Outcomes.* 1(16). [Accessed May 6, 2009]. Available from: http://www.hqlo.com/content/1/1/16.

van Uden-Kraan, C. F., Drossaert, C. H. C., Taal, E., Shaw, B. R., Seydel, E. R., & van de Laar, M. A. F. J. (2008). Empowering processes and outcomes of participation in online support groups for patients with breast cancer, arthritis, or fibromyalgia. *Qualitative Health Research, 18*(3), 405–417.

Weis, R., Stamm, K., Smith, C., Nilan, M., Clark, F., Weis, J., & Kennedy, K. (2003). Communities of care and caring: The case of MSWatch.com®. *Journal of Health Psychology, 8*(1), 135–148.

Yalom, I., & Leszcz, M. (2005). *The theory and practice of group psychotherapy* (5th ed.). New York: Basic Books.

Chapter 6

USING CELL/MOBILE PHONE SMS TO ENHANCE CLIENT CRISIS AND PEER SUPPORT

STEPHEN GOSS AND JOE FERNS

INTRODUCTION

This chapter explores the development and use of SMS (short message service) text messaging systems in counselling and support services with particular attention to the way in which this technology has been applied by Samaritans in the UK. In particular, it will look at the way in which the service was developed, give a brief outline of how the service operates, explore the experience to date and give examples of case material. Samaritans offers 24-hour emotional support services aimed at those in distress including people at risk of suicide. It is perhaps best known for its telephone service, one of the oldest in the world having been founded in 1953. More recently, Samaritans developed email (in 1994) and SMS (in 2007) as additional channels through which their services can be accessed.

Messages restricted to just 160 characters, as is commonly the case with SMS, would appear at first sight to place a major block in the way of creating a freely flowing, in-depth, supportive relationship. Certainly, both participants need to be highly focussed, making the most efficient possible use of the space available. However, as with a number of the other technologies described in this book, the very restriction of communication breadth has been found not only to have less effect on the help that can be offered than might be thought at first glance, but also to have some distinct advantages. Not least is the perception of anonymity, privacy and ease of contact in both practical and emotional terms for the user but there are also advantages in the level of focus and precision required.

SMS systems to provide emotional or psychological help, whether for those in crisis or for longer term difficulties began to be introduced some years ago. Increasing numbers of services now use them, such as What Now?, a youth-oriented service in the North of England and numerous others are planned, such as that for the Campaign Against Living Miserably (CALM), who focus on suicide prevention and facilitating ease of access to mental health support for young men, a population who are generally under represented in mental health support services while disproportionately vulnerable to suicide.

SMS text messaging is also particularly relevant to the needs of services in countries with emerging economies (Chipchase, 2007) where the infrastructure of mental health support may be less well developed. Mobile phones are rapidly becoming ubiquitous, or nearly so, in many such countries (e.g., ITU, 2009; Textually.org, 2009) the fastest growing mobile phone market in the world being Africa (Arnquist, 2009). A number of projects have demonstrated the feasibility of reaching populations hitherto very poorly served by mental health professionals (e.g., Gadebe, 2006).

In the case of Samaritans, 201 branches are staffed by around 15,500 volunteers in the UK. Samaritans has a federal structure, with each branch operating with a fair degree of independence and autonomy. Between them they handle over 2.8 million contacts each year that involve meaningful dialogue. Many more contacts are very brief (e.g., a caller

hanging up as soon as the call is answered) or comprise testing or "prank" calls as people "dip their toe into the water" and use such initial contacts as a way of finding out what the service is like. This is of particular relevance to contact methods like SMS or email, as Samaritans service users have indicated that they have used them as a means of discovering the kind of response they will get, before building up courage to speak to a practitioner directly, live and on a one-to-one basis. Thus, it could be argued that at least some text based services can operate as a gateway to accessing other forms of helping and may be particularly important for those who would not otherwise turn to helping services at all.

It is interesting to note that many of the same comments that the organisation has received regarding its SMS and e-mail services were similar to those received when Samaritans was first established well over half a century ago, when the concept of offering support services by telephone was reacted to with scepticism and, in some quarters, outright resistance.

ADVANTAGES OF SMS

"Distraction"

Sometimes, especially when people are in crisis, it is helpful to have something to do not least as a way of calming immediate emotional turmoil but also to allow increased opportunity for reflection and considered expression. In comparison with making a telephone call, text messaging is a more physically and mentally involving activity that has greater capacity to take the person out of their current state, temporarily, by pro-

viding a task that must itself be concentrated upon through the need carefully to key in the correct characters and so on. Manipulating the technology thus becomes a kind of distraction technique in itself, often helpful for those at risk.

Confidentiality

It is arguable that text messaging is a more confidential means of contacting support services than most other means. Consider the example of children or young people who may not be able to use a phone with privacy and may also be unable to access their own computer for email use without parental supervision. It is very difficult to see what text message someone else is sending, unless looking directly over their shoulder and if deleted after sending, communications can remain completely undetectable unless a third party directly intercepts the message or is paying the bill and obtains access to the numbers contacted. Even then, the content of messages is usually unavailable.

HOW SAMARITANS' SMS SERVICE WAS DEVELOPED

The Samaritans SMS service was developed in a detailed, carefully planned way on the principle that any emotional support, especially for those who may be in crisis, should be done well or not undertaken at all. The care with which this process was undertaken stands as an exemplar of the approach to introducing technologically mediated mental health support services and is one that could be readily and helpfully emulated by practitioners seeking to introduce any of the technologies discussed in this volume. Its thoroughness serves users far better in the long run than rushing to introduce technologies. A service once offered that then has to be withdrawn may have potentially disastrous results for those who could then find themselves suddenly cut off.

Table 6.1 outlines the process undertaken by Samaritans to introduce their SMS service in a safe, carefully planned way.

Table 6.1
Development Process of Samaritans' SMS Service in the UK

Phase 1	Desk research: Consultation with focus groups (aged 13–25 years). Consultation with other service providers.
Phase 2	Internal role plays and consultation with volunteers. Development of basic training systems. Basic software development.
Phase 3	Live trials at music festivals to provide contained, time limited community to test take up rates, utility, systems and training needs.
Phase 4	Limited live 3 month trial by 10 branches.
Phase 5	6 month pilot to test ability to offer 24/7 emotional support by SMS and to test systems and demand levels.
Phase 6	Final troubleshooting phase to address problems of providing an integrated 24/7 SMS service.
Phase 7	Development of an accreditation system whereby branches are accredited to run the SMS service. Gradual roll out of service across Samaritans branches.

Phase One: Desk Research

It is important not to duplicate the work of others in mental health service provision, so that services do not overlap and to ensure that the learning afforded through their development and implementation is not lost. A great deal of effort was put into an initial "desk research" phase, ensuring that the systems and service design were based on a full understanding and awareness of the potential of this method of working, its pitfalls, the current state of the best technological solutions available and the experiences, both published and unpublished, of those who already used SMS communication as part of any kind of support mechanisms. This phase also involved detailed consultation with service users themselves through a series of focus groups, especially with 13–25 year olds, the primary anticipated target audience.

Phase Two: It's a Lot Easier Than We Thought It Was"

The second phase involved development of response protocols, methods and training in collaboration with a sample of the practitioners who would be providing the service. Initial concern regarding the ability to provide adequate support within 160 characters was steadily replaced by recognition that it was indeed possible to create meaningful, empathic and helpful responses through text messaging. Examples of training activities included deliberate circumvention of the technology itself to enable clearer focus on the detail of the process of responding in such short communications by using role play simulations of contacts in which volunteers playing both client and practitioner roles used paper with 160 boxes

in which to write each character by hand. By removing the technology itself, replacing it with the most familiar means of written communication, it was possible to obtain very direct feedback on the ability to express the necessary content in the space available. Participants reported that it was much more possible to do so and to do it well, than they had expected prior to such exercises, a typical response being "it's a lot easier than we thought it was going to be."

Another example of the learning gathered through Samaritans' experience of introducing their SMS service has been that while practitioners were keen to be given guidance on how to use "text speak" (abbreviations, emoticons and so on), service users themselves indicated that they strongly preferred a "plain English" approach as it appeared to show more respect and, perhaps, represented the genuine voice of the practitioner more accurately. While some contractions or simple abbreviations (e.g., "2" for "too" or "4" for "for") were fine, it was found to be important to avoid these when expressing feelings and especially strong feelings.

Phase Three: Limited Initial Trials in Contained, Temporary Community Setting

The next phase of development was to offer the SMS service at a small number of events with the service being carefully promoted to ensure that it was understood to be only for that time and place. Music festivals were deemed to be ideal for this purpose not only because they attracted a relatively young section of society, anticipated to be the main users of SMS support services, but also because they created a community of sufficient size to create a significant level of demand while being small enough to prevent the new service being overwhelmed. The service would also not be expected to continue after the end of the event providing containment of the public trial, so potential service users would not be left without a means of support on which they might have expected to rely.

Phase Four: Limited Three-month Trial at Selection Locations

Ten branches of Samaritans were then selected to offer the SMS service on a trial basis for a period of three months. This meant that the service could be tested in a more typical public setting than that of music festivals but on a scale on which take up rates would not be overwhelming and whereby any difficulties or harm caused, should there be any, would be limited. It also provided a further opportunity for analysis of the experience and for another iterative stage of development for the service. A number of community groups who provided support to young people in crisis, including those who self-harm, were asked to disseminate publicity material about the SMS service. Data was collected and the experience reviewed before progressing to the next phase.

Phase Five: Full Six-month Pilot Phase

At this stage, Samaritans was approaching the "point of no return" with the service and made the decision to commit to adding SMS to it's suite of services. Phase five involved a further trial on a national basis for an initial period of six months. Usage levels were monitored and data was collected regarding the nature of the service with special attention being paid to difficulties that were encountered. Formal systems of training, supervision and caller care were developed in order to facilitate the eventual roll out.

Phase Six: Final Troubleshooting

Some systems were changed and then tested to ensure that any issues were identified before bringing additional branches into the service.

Phase Seven: Roll Out of the New SMS Service

The SMS service formally moved out of development and into implementation. An accreditation system was put in place to ensure that branches who wished to begin delivering the SMS service were sufficiently robust and received the support they needed.

OUTLINE OF THE SMS SYSTEM USED

The Samaritans' SMS system can be outlined very simply (see Figure 6.1).

A caller sends a text. This goes to a SIM Host–a computer that acts as a "hub" to pass on the message. This is then translated into an email that is sent to the organization's central server in encrypted form. At that point the telephone number is stripped out as a further protection of privacy.

When volunteers at Samaritans' branches are ready to answer the next contact, they "pull" the next SMS message from the server. This reliance on

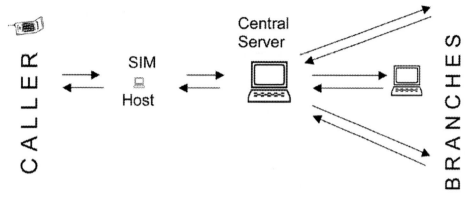

Figure 6.1. Samaritans' SMS system.

"pull," rather than "push," technology is based on the same system Samaritans uses to deal with emails. It has the advantage of managing the rate at which volunteers deal with contacts; ensuring that they are not overwhelmed and that each message receives proper consideration. However, one operational disadvantage is that it results in "pull" services feeling less urgent than the telephone (a "push" service). During the early stages of the SMS development project, when SMS accredited branches were scarce, there were some issues in persuading volunteers in these branches to prioritize SMS contacts above phone contacts (since phone contacts would ultimately trip on to another branch and be answered).

Individual service users can be "assigned" to a branch, ensuring that they receive consistent responses from within the same group. Each branch of the organisation thus has a list of existing service users to whom on-going support is provided and new contacts to add to that list. A very similar system is used for dealing with emails received by the organization. First developed in 1994, it has required very few changes since its inception.

Initial incoming SMS messages are responded to within 60 minutes with subsequent messages being responded to much faster. This is facilitated in part by the system automatically identifying where an on-going conversation is taking place and putting responses from service users to volunteers' texts at the front of the queue. Thus, a service user demonstrating a desire to have continuing contact is able to receive it. For comparison, emails received by the organization are responded to within 24 hours as a maximum, with a typical response time usually being around 12 to 13 hours. Smaller scale services with lower level demand often manage to respond even faster than this.

Since the initial trialling of the SMS service began in April 2006 (going fully operational around a year later), 51 branches now offer the SMS service and they have responded to over 413,000 messages from around 7,600 unique mobile numbers in the 36-month period to April, 2009. Volume of demand is also reported to be continuing to rise with a further 25 percent increase in volume predicted in the rest of 2009.

This level of demand is all the more telling given that it has been achieved without the SMS service ever having been advertised nationally since the initial pilot, other than being noted on Samaritan's website. The influence of Web 2.0 style viral transmission of the number to use and knowledge of the existence of the service itself, is clearly evident in the information sharing among peer groups, forums, discussion lists and so on. As branches are accredited, some limited local publicity is undertaken with schools and colleges, but this is carefully controlled so as not to overwhelm capacity.

The greatest levels of demand have been consistently found to be highest at around lunchtime, when schools finish, and then peaking dramatically at around 9 pm to 10 pm, an important factor when planning service responsiveness. This is in contrast to usage of the telephone service which peaks between 10 pm and 2 am.

It has been a noticeable trend in this service that the average number of text messages per user has been steadily increasing over time. This suggests that the service is developing enduring contacts with the number of exchanges between caller and practitioner averaging around 60 messages. These figures underline that despite the restricted number of characters per message, seen as a whole series they can and do develop into something much deeper than a simple request for information. This is evidence contrary to the impression that text messaging is an inadequate environment in which to support relational helping.

CASE EXAMPLES

The following are examples of the opening sequence of incoming and outgoing SMS messages from Samaritans' service. All have been thoroughly anonymised and are reproduced here with permission. Note that incoming messages can exceed the 160 character limit because some mobile phones allow this functionality; however, outgoing messages remain within the standard limit.

Example 1: A young woman sends a text, early one Thursday evening

Caller   *My friend is suicidal*

Jo   Im sorry to hear that How are you feeling about it? Has she or he spoken to Samaritans?

Caller   *no she doesn't really want to talk to any one its only me and another friend that no she has*

been cutting herself and thinking about pills

Jo   How are you feeling about that?

Caller   *Pretty shit I don't know wat to do. She was meant to be going to uni but dropped out cos she missed home. She didn't say anything about why she is like this*

Jo   That's a lot for you to cope with—has she tried to kill herself?

Caller   *She cuts herself and has thought about over Dosing but didn't . . . does my number get stored*

Jo   No don't worry—I cant see your number and this is completely confidential to Samaritans. This is a safe space for you to talk about it if you want to

Caller *wats your name? sorry I like to know who I am talking to. Do you know If she can go on medication?*

Jo You can call me Jo. I don't know whether she can go on medication—that's not something we can help with—has she spoken to you about medical help?

Caller *Okay . . . can you see my texts from the past?*

Jo Yes, we can read your previous messages. How are you feeling tonight?

Caller *I suppose im okay . . . I don't mean to sound selfish but all of this has made my relationship with my boyfriend complicated*

Jo Would you like to tell us more about how things are with your boyfriend?

Caller *Well my mate is suicidal and I have been trying to help which means spending most my time with her and not him*

This case continued the exchange and included the service user obtaining help with her relationship with her boyfriend as well as with her suicidal friend.

Case 2: A school age caller sends a text at 4.20 pm on Monday afternoon

Caller *I cannot find anuf tme 4 homwrk*

Jo Hi . . . Not enough time for homework . . . Is thisa problem for you? How are you feeling today?

Caller *Im not 2good. Frends ignorin me. Teachr setin way 2 much hmewrk I don't have a lot of*

tme 2 do it

Jo That cant be easy for you—I wonder how long has it been like that—do you feel able to tell me a little more about how you are feeling right now?

Caller *It hz ben goin on sinc I startd high skol. It mkes me feel rejected*

Jo You seem to have had a tough time since you started at this school. Do you know the reason why?

Caller *I went 2 a different skol then the rest of my close frends. They cant even hllp with hmwrk*

Jo I understand you miss your friends and this makes you feel bad. Have you ever felt suicidal?

Caller *yes I have felt suicidal*

Jo are you feeling suicidal now?

Caller *not really. It only happens wen im alone in the house*

Jo Are you alone in the house often? If so, is there a reason you are alone often?

Caller *My mum and dad work a lot so I go home alone 'cause I am an only child*

Jo Do your mum and dad know how you feel? Is it easy to talk to them about the things that matter to you?

Caller *It is not easy 2 talk 2 them 'cause they'll ignore me wen somthin beter comes up*

Jo Who can you talk to when you feel lonely?

Caller *No one*

Jo No? Then I hope you will find this a safe and confidential space where you can share your most difficult feeling. Does it help to text?

This case continued into a much longer conversation. Note the more intense use of "texting language" with this younger person.

SERVICE USER PROFILE

It is a generality that most mental health services find that their clientele is disproportionately composed of women. Atypically, however, just over half of the callers to Samaritans' telephone service are male. While it is quite wrong to think that SMS text messaging is particularly suitable for men (a common but sexist assumption given that women actually make greater use of SMS messaging e.g., Balakrishnan, 2009; Geser, 2006; Proitz, 2004) men and women do seem to make *different* use of text messaging (e.g., Potts, 2004; Rafi, 2009) and it does have the clear benefit of being able to present a means of access to young people which is attractive and accessible (e.g., Ling, 1999; Kaseniemi & Rautiainen, 2002).

In practice, Samaritans' SMS service has found that, as expected, the largest group have indeed been aged under 24 (67%). Eight percent were aged 25–34 with the same proportion aged 35–44 and only 9 percent over 45 (the remaining 8% representing missing data). This represents a much younger age group than use the telephone support service.

In general, the main reasons for contacting the SMS service are similar to those across other Samaritans services. Among the SMS service users the main variation has been a greater proportion of issues that would be expected to arise among this younger audience with more emphasis on peer group pressures, bullying and so on.

However, Samaritans has noted that contacts via any text-based means appear to come from a higher risk group than those who access the service by telephone, with a higher proportion being actively suicidal rather than simply distressed. This may be because it is easier to be open by email (the disinhibition effect, cf Suler, 2004) or that the population is actually different or, to some extent, that those who make "testing" or abusive calls to the helpline have not yet begun to do so by email or text message. In the SMS service, the severity of contacts and proportion of service users in crisis (e.g., the likelihood of the service user being actively suicidal) is *even* greater than with email. This is possibly due to the SMS number having been passed on through crisis services rather than being to do with the nature of SMS use in itself, but neither possibility can be ruled out at the time of writing (December, 2009). Certainly, this evidence is also contrary to the opinion that SMS is not appropriate for those with severe or acute needs.

IMPACT

Of those who contacted the service, 75 percent felt that doing so helped make a decision not to self-harm. 66 percent felt that Samaritans had helped them make a decision not to end their life, at least on that occasion. Feedback from service users has also included comments such as:

- "the text service is great, it helped me build up the confidence inside of me to phone up and speak to someone"
- "its made me delay self harming as I know a response is on its way"
- "the text service has been my saviour Sometimes a feel that if I hadn't contacted the Samaritans I may have seriously harmed/killed myself"
- "I think the text service is really good because I have phoned Samaritans before and ended up hanging up because I didn't have the courage to speak aloud"
- "I think it is a great idea to be able to text and not necessarily having to speak to someone"

While this is not the "hard," randomised controlled trial evidence that would accurately demonstrate the full impact of this kind of service, comments that demonstrate that it has saved or extended a person's life by averting or delaying serious harm testify to its value in ways that are rarely achieved by composite statistics or changes in psychometric scores. Clearly, SMS support services will need to undertake further research to establish outcomes among their own user group. However, even these fairly straightforward findings establish a helpful indicator of how service users reply when asked how helpful an intervention has been, in this case providing a ringing endorsement of the service.

CONCLUSIONS

High quality services are essential for all mental health interventions and the same is true of SMS and other technologically mediated means of access. In short, it is better not to run a service at all than to run it badly.

An inherent risk in developing such services is that the technology becomes the primary focus. Over and above the technical system needs, there is also a need to make sure that people are adequately trained and prepared. Furthermore, resources must be sufficient to ensure that response times are adequate and systems are sufficiently robust. The experience of Samaritans has underlined that while there are many "off the shelf" packages which can help handle incoming SMS messages in volume, most, if not all, are unlikely to be sufficient for the needs of mental health and crisis care

where any difficulties or limitations in functionality can have a serious impact for service users. Specific services will have specific requirements and it is vital for people seeking help that their needs are fully taken into account in system design and implementation. Delivery times of messages, for example, can extend to more than an hour at peak times. High volumes of messages can also create problems (Samaritans' service received over 800 messages in its first hour) unless the resources are made available to ensure that the system is sufficiently robust to handle demand.

It is also important that where a variety of means of contact are possible; they must be integrated with clear policies for how the different channels of communication may be combined. For example, if a person makes contact by SMS clearly indicating that they are in crisis but then ceases to respond to the messages they are sent, is it appropriate for the service to make contact by telephone? How is that handled if a user indicates a preference *not* to use the telephone? Services should also consider whether the introduction SMS services in particular are to be seen as gateways to other kinds of provision or as a service delivery method in themselves. Despite initial expectations to the contrary, the latter proved to be the case for Samaritans. Different services will have different answers to these questions but careful consideration and policy development leading to effective combination of technologies is likely to be a key factor for all.

That meaningful emotional support and mental health interventions are possible through SMS has undoubtedly been demonstrated by Samaritans' service. It appears that, as in the case of many other technologies, the initial doubts of many are being steadily dispelled. Demand from service users is vast and likely to continue to grow.

Developing new means of contact is a challenging and time consuming process. It must be done because there is a clear need rather than simply because the technology is "there" and it must be done in a way which is "safe" and thoughtful. We must be guided in this by the people who use our services, their needs and their preferences in how to make contact.

To use any form of emotional support service requires a huge amount of courage from an individual. It is an act of trust which places on the service provider a duty to continue to improve and to strive to develop more and better ways to enable contact. Therefore, while it may be a time-consuming and difficult process, it is not one which we can afford to neglect.

ACKNLOWLEDGMENT

NB This chapter is based on a presentation by Joe Ferns, *The Work of The Samaritans Online,* at the OCTIA 2009 Conference, Leicester, 25th April 2009.

REFERENCES

Arnquist, S. (2009). In rural Africa, a fertile market for mobile phones. *New York Times* [online]. [Accessed December 21, 2009]. Available from: http://www.nytimes.com/2009/10/06/science/06uganda.html?_r=3&ref=science.

Balakrishnan, V. (2009). A look into SMS usage patterns among Malaysian youths. *Human IT, 10*(2), 55–80.

Chipchase, T. (2007). Jan Chipchase on mobile phones. *Ted.com* [online]. [Accessed December 21, 2009]. Available from: http://www.ted.com/talks/jan_chipchase_on_our_mobile_phones.html.

Gadebe, T. (2006). SMS help for teens in distress. *SouthAfrica.info* [online]. [Accessed December 21, 2009]. Available from: http://www.southafrica.info/services/health/teensindistress.htm.

Geser, H. (2006). Are girls (even) more addicted? Some gender patterns of cell phone usage. *Sociology in Switzerland: Sociology of the Mobile Phone* [online]. [Accessed December 21, 2009]. Available from: http://socio.ch/mobile/t_geser3. htm.

ITU. (2009). *The world in 2009: ICT facts and figures* [online]. [Accessed December 21, 2009]. Available from: http://www.itu.int/ITU-D/ict/material/Telecom09_flyer.pdf.

Kaseniemi, E., & Rautiainen, P. (2002). Mobile culture of children and teenagers in Finland. In J. E. Katz & M. Aakhus (Eds.), *Perpetual contact*. Cambridge, UK: Cambridge University Press.

Ling, R. (1999). 'We release them little by little': Maturation and gender identity as seen in the use of mobile telephone. In *International Symposium on Technology and Society (ISTAS 99) Women and Technology: Historical, Societal and Professional Perspectives. July 29–31,* Rutgers University, New Brunswick [online]. [Accessed December 21, 2009]. Available from: http://www.telenor.no/fou/program/nomadiske/articles/11.pdf.

Proitz, L. (2009). The mobile gender: A study of young Norwegian people's gender performances in text messages. In *Mobile Communication and Social Change, International Conference*. Seol, Korea.

Potts, G. (2004). *College Students and Cell Phone Use: Gender Variation* [online]. [Accessed December 21, 2009]. Available from: http://personalwebs.oakland.edu/$gapotts/rht160.pdf.

Rafi, M. (2009). SMS text analysis: Language, gender and current practices. *Tesol France Online Journal* [online]. [Accessed December 21, 2009]. Available from: http://www.tesol-france.org/OnlineJournal.php.

Suler, J. R. (2004). The online disinhibition effect. *Cyberpsychology and Behavior, 7*(3), 321–326.

Textually.org. (2009). Mobile phone use soars in Africa, unevenly. In *Textually.org* [online]. [Accessed December 21, 2009]. Available from: http://www.textually.org/textually/archives/2009/10/024783.htm.

Chapter 7

USING WEBSITES, BLOGS AND WIKIS WITHIN MENTAL HEALTH

JOHN M. GROHOL

INTRODUCTION

The Internet is the world's leading resource that people turn to for researching information on topics they'd like to learn more about. As such, most people at one time or another have investigated a health topic online (Fox, 2006; iCrossing, 2008). More people turn to the Internet than their own doctor or a friend to get information related to a health concern (iCrossing, 2008).

The vast majority of the Internet is made up of traditional, information-focused websites. A website is simply a collection of information that can sport many features, including a blog, static pages of information arranged by topic, or a wiki. Websites may also be community-enabled, meaning that they allow for social networking to take place. Websites may just be a single page of information (for instance, advertising one's practice), or can be a huge information store containing tens of thousands of articles and features (such as WebMD.com or PsychCentral.com). A website's mainstay–the static article or content page–is usually authored by a single individual, edited and published without comment or further editing by visitors.

Mental health websites today generally contain information about a condition's symptoms, commonly accepted treatments, news and research information on conditions (including clinical trials), links to other online resources of interest to that condition, related book reviews and symptom checkers (sometimes in the form of online screening quizzes). There are many to choose from and most generally offer similar types of resources to users. Two examples of mental health websites are Psych-Central.com and Internet Mental Health (www.mentalhealth.com).

A blog is a shortened form of the term "web log," which is an online journal consisting of individual entries that are arranged chronologically (most recent entries appearing at the top of the page, for example). Blogs may be characterized by their links to other information or opinions online, usually with commentary and perspective by one of the blog's owners. Blogs also usually, but not always, allow for reader commentary, which makes a blog a two-way conversation between the author and his or her readers. A specific and popular type of blog is an online journal, which many people use to diary their daily life. Two examples of mental health blogs are World of Psychology (www.psychcentral.com/blog) and Furious Seasons (www.furiousseasons.com). Blogs and blogging are examined further in Chapter 8.

Blogs can be public or private; private blogs require a password to access and are not indexed by search engines, such as Google. Whether out of ignorance or a desire for attention and popularity, most blogs are kept public, even when people are discussing the most intimate details of their lives. This can lead to some unintended consequences if the blog's author doesn't take into account that what they may write on the blog could someday be linked back to their real name (even if they use a pseudonym to create the blog).

A wiki is a type of web page that allows anyone to add or edit content on the page. The most famous example of a wiki is the free online encyclopedia, Wikipedia, which anyone can edit or add to. Wikis can be stand-alone websites on their own, or a part of a larger website. Because anyone can edit a wiki page, wikis keep copies of every edit ever made. If a malicious edit is made to a wiki page, it can quickly and easily be reverted to a previous untainted version of the page by an editor overseeing the wiki. Wikis are primarily used as a publishing tool when the publisher wants the community of users to help edit or add content on a specific topic. For instance, in companies, wikis are often used as an online space to manage all of the details that go into a project. They can be used anywhere online collaboration is needed amongst a set of people (who don't even need to be on the same continent).

Wikis and blogs are considered prime examples of empowering Web 2.0 tools. Web 2.0 tools allow for the easy editing or adding of content to the Internet with little or no technical knowledge or skill. For instance, free services like Blogger. com allow any individual to setup a blog in less than 5 minutes and start blogging immediately. And the world's largest free encyclopedia, Wikipedia (en.wikipedia. org), allows anyone to edit virtually any article on the site (such edits, however, may quickly be undone by a volunteer Wikipedia editor who disagrees with your edits). Web 2.0 tools such as these also encourage a two-way dialogue between content creator (whether it be a blog or wiki) and visitors who read the content. Blogs and wikis allow for discussion of each entry, which encourages a dialogue that was previously absent on static websites (such as in any corporate or government websites like nimh.nih. gov).

APPLICATION

Websites, blogs and wikis are all primarily used in mental health to help educate people about relevant mental health issues in their lives. Psychoeducation can form a cornerstone of psychotherapy and in helping an individual understand their own or a loved one's mental health concern and the types of treatments most often used. By learning about their mental health concern, the individual becomes an informed and educated patient, one that can play a more active and engaged role in the transformative process. Valuable therapy time can be used to focus on the client's individual needs and issues, rather than in explaining basic components of mental illness or its treatment.

Using such educational tools in therapy is best done as a collaborative process. Clients may be encouraged to research their mental health issues online and also print out pages that speak to them or seemed to offer them valuable insights into their own change process. These pages could then be brought into a future session with the therapist and discussed. Alternatively, clients can e-mail links to websites or individual pages they found interesting.

While everyone may already know this, not all websites are created equally. Since anyone can publish anything online, it can be challenging to determine whether the information found online is relevant, accurate and reliable. Keys to the validity and usefulness of a given website or information found online can be had from:

- helping the client identify the publisher,
- the author of the article,
- whether the article cites any scientific articles or not,
- generally whether the site is a mainstream publisher, or a personal site and just somebody's opinion.

While all different types of sites and information found online may hold potential, clients may need help understanding the difference between well-accepted treatment strategies found online versus scientifically suspect strategies (such as magnet therapy or vitamin therapy). The only difference between a website and a wiki is that usually anyone can edit a wiki. But since creating and publishing a website is only slightly harder, there really is very little difference between these two forms of online publishing when it comes to psychoeducation.

People can vet information found on a website or wiki by looking for confirmation of that information on other websites. So, for instance, if one site says that depression is often treated by antidepressants and psychotherapy, other sites should be in general agreement. Clients can also be counseled to look for some telltale signs of legitimate website publishers—a privacy policy, terms of use, information (including contact information and an address) about who runs the site, authorship and dates on all articles and ideally, a seal such as the HONcode that denotes the site is aware of the unique issues regarding publishing health and mental health information. These are minimal requirements for a mental health site and they don't guarantee any type of quality. But they do immediately help a person distinguish a potentially beneficial site from a potentially unbeneficial or even dangerous site.

Personal sites and blogs can also hold a lot of value. But they may not be the best place for a person to conduct their primary, personal research on a disorder or condition and its treatments.

Beyond simple psychoeducation, blogs offer an additional therapeutic benefit—they provide people with an online "space" in which to diary or chronicle their grappling with a specific mental health concern. A survey conducted by

America Online in 2005 reported that nearly 50 percent of those people who blogged used blogging as a form of self-therapy (Tan, 2008). Online journaling has been conducted for well over a decade at the time of writing (May, 2009) and while there have been no studies specifically chronicling the benefits, they would likely be similar to those detailed for writing in general (e.g., significant physical and mental health improvements, see Pennebaker, 1997) and journal writing in particular (Thompson, 2004). People intending to blog may view blogging as a potential way to alleviate distress, especially when they lack typical social support in their environment (Baker & Moore, 2008). Blogs allow their authors to convey a significant range and depth of emotional experiences. Because blogs also allow an author to receive feedback from others on what they write, it can setup a self-reinforcing mechanism to continue blogging, especially if the feedback is positive (Miura & Yamashita, 2007).

Beyond simple writing in a journal, however, blogging may have additional therapeutic benefits. Increased disinhibition online (Joinson, 2007) suggests that blogging can possibly provide an author with a platform on which to write where their writing is even more honest and open than if writing to only oneself in a traditional paper journal. Additionally, since most blogs allow others to comment on each entry, readers can provide beneficial (or harmful) feedback to the author about what they've written (Nagel & Anthony, 2009). This continuous feedback loop provides another level of potentially therapeutic work outside of the therapy session.

Even if a person has no interest in writing on their own blog, simply reading about other people's experiences can also be beneficial to a client (Richards, 2008). While this sort of psychological benefit is usually gained in reading done in online support group communities, it can also be gained by reading people's blogs who are writing about coping with depression, anxiety or some other concern.

ETHICAL CONSIDERATIONS

Because the Internet is the world's largest information resource today, it is also potentially the world's largest misinformation resource as well. This means that well-meaning people can stumble upon inaccurate or even potentially harmful information online (although there yet remains to be a documented case in the research literature of someone doing so that resulted in serious harm). There are, however, groups on the Internet that help provide a great deal of information and support for committing suicide, anorexic food intake control, self-harm methods and similar.

So while the potential for helping someone is far greater than hurting them, it is still a legitimate concern that should be addressed.

Any website, blog or wiki can be a potential instrument of misinformation and harm. Websites that appear legitimate can simply be advertising portals trying to get the reader to purchase a bottle of placebos or become a patient at an expensive inpatient facility. Blogs can provide people with all sorts of potentially harmful (or at the very least, useless) personal opinions that carry some legitimacy if the blog is popular (regardless of whether the information is good or not). In fact, there is a burgeoning industry of blogs created to purportedly help people "enhance" their minds, but with little scientific data supporting their suggestions and techniques.

Wikis are likely seen as potentially the most harmful form of information online, because anyone can edit one. Yet because they are still fairly rare (a person is far more likely to come across an ordinary website or blog), their potential for harm is probably the least. The most popular wiki, Wikipedia, seems to have enough interested people acting as article editors to keep most articles relatively accurate and relatively unbiased at any given moment. So while an article may contain misinformation for small amounts of time, most articles offer mostly valid information on most mental health conditions. People are often encouraged to use a wiki such as Wikipedia as a jumping off point to understand the basics of a condition, but to research the condition further on specific mental health websites.

People should be made aware of privacy issues related to their sharing of information in a blog or on a website. Even while using a pseudonym or alias, such information could eventually be traced back to one's real identity if used on other, unrelated non-mental health sites, or as a part of one's email address or general online identity. Professionals should discuss such concerns with their clients and make them aware of the limits of such privacy protections, so that if they do choose to share, they do so in a way that limits potential future harm.

CLIENT SCENARIO

Jane is a 42-year-old housewife, married with two children. Lately she's been feeling more run down than usual and sometimes looks at her life and wonders, "What if?" She complains of having little to no energy or motivation to do the daily tasks around the house to keep the household running in the manner in which she usually likes it. When asked by her husband "what's wrong?" or what can he do to help, she has no real answer and instead just brushes off his suggestions or offers of help. While she used to enjoy meeting with her friends every week for coffee and sometimes a movie or shopping, she hasn't seen most of her friends now for over two months. When they call, she avoids picking up the phone to talk, because she doesn't feel like it and has no answers to why she's avoiding them. She feels sad, lonely and distracted. Jane has trouble concentrating and feels her memory is slipping.

After feeling this way for two months, Jane decided to see if there was anything online that could help her understand what her problem was. Like most people, she began her search at Google, a popular Internet search engine, and just typed in many of her symptoms: sad, lonely, concentration, memory. Within the search results, she found many articles about these symptoms, some indicating that perhaps her concern was something called "depression." She clicked on a few of the articles to learn more and came across a website called PsychCentral.com. While there, she read an in-depth guide to depression that explained the common symptoms, possible causes and treatments available to help her. She was still unsure, however, and a little scared about talking to her husband or doctor about her feelings.

So Jane went back to the search results and looked for a blog on depression (now that she knew what term she was looking for). She found a blog called depression introspection online (deepintro.typepad.com/depression_introspection/), which detailed one person's experiences with depression and bipolar disorder. She enjoyed reading it and found she could relate a lot to what the author wrote. It also gave her some perspective and confidence that this was a condition that could be helped through getting the right treatment.

Jane picked up the phone and called her family physician to schedule a checkup. There, she talked to her doctor about her feelings and inability to just "snap out of it." She also mentioned that she had done some research online and thought that maybe she was depressed. Did he know of any professional he could give her a referral to? The doctor listened, asked a few follow-up questions related to Jane's symptoms and gave her a standard physical to rule-out any physical issues that might be the cause of her symptoms. After being satisfied that Jane was suffering from a mental health concern, he gave her the names and numbers of some mental health professionals to call.

When Jane met with her therapist for the first time, she explained that she found the information online helped her not only figure out what might be the problem, but also gave her the strength and courage to ask for help. The therapist encouraged her to continue researching and learning from her online experiences and that if she ever had any questions about something she read online, she could print out a copy and bring it to the next session to review.

Jane returned home later that night and accessed the Internet again, looking for more resources and information about depression. She found a self-help book online entitled *Psychological Self-Help* (www.psychologicalselfhelp.org), written by a psychologist. In the book, she read the chapter about depression and happiness and then a few pages about things she could do to help change her behavior. She thought that while her therapy and medication would help her depression, it wouldn't hurt to continue working on her problems outside of therapy too. She found the exercises challenging and resolved to talk to her therapist in the next session about the point of the cognitive-behavioral techniques she was practicing.

Jane's experience is typical of most Internet health users—they first search for a health or mental health concern online, starting with a regular search engine such as Google. They often don't know the exact name of the condition they are searching for, instead typing in symptoms they know they (or a loved one) have. While such a strategy often provides hit-or-miss results, it is usually sufficient to lead a person to a reputable resource that has scored highly within the search results. It is then the user's journey of learning and discovery begins.

CONCLUSION

The Internet continues to grow at a rapid pace, with thousands of new blogs and websites created each day. People will continue to use these resources primarily as the Internet was intended, as an educational tool meant to inform and reduce the stigma traditionally attached to mental health concerns. Websites, wikis and blogs help inform people who otherwise may not recognize a mental health problem or concern and provide them with specific steps and resources to find help.

However, websites, wikis and blogs can also be platforms for misinformation in rare circumstances. Most people know to be skeptical about information they find online if they can't verify it through other websites, or through some other means (such as reviewing it with a professional). It helps to review signs of legitimate websites and information versus those that may be suspect and it helps to encourage clients to review primary information on well-known and respected mental health websites first before exploring the entire Internet for addi-tional resources.

As video and data sharing become more commonplace, it is likely we will see even more people sharing their mental health experiences through video and their personal health data. Privacy concerns notwithstanding, people seem more inclined to share even the most sensitive information about themselves first and ask questions later. A therapist can help their client understand the potential problems with such sharing and ensure they understand that pseudonyms are not a foolproof anonymity mechanism.

Websites are increasingly becoming not only an information tool, but also an important part of one's social connectedness. People are turning to the Internet not just for information, but also for community and support from others with similar concerns. The Internet is making people feel less isolated and stigmatized because of their mental health issues and the reach and connectivity the Internet fosters will only expand in the years to come.

REFERENCES

Baker, J. R., & Moore, S. M. (2008). Distress, coping and blogging: Comparing new Myspace users by their intention to blog. *CyberPsychology and Behavior, 11*(1), 81–85.

Fox, S. (2006). Online health search 2006. *Pew internet and American life project* [online]. [Accessed May 6, 2009]. Available from: http://www.pewinternet.org/PPF/r/190/report_display.asp.

iCrossing (2008). *How America Searches: Health and Wellness* [online]. [Accessed May 6, 2009]. Available from: http://www.icrossing.com/research/how-america-searches-health-and-wellness.php.

Joinson, A. N. (2007). Disinhibition and the Internet. In J. Gackenbach (Ed.), *Psychology and the Internet: Intrapersonal, interpersonal and transpersonal implications* (2nd ed.). San Diego, CA: Academic Press.

Miura, A., & Yamashita, K. (2007). Psychological and social influences on blog writing: An online survey of blog authors in Japan. *Journal of Computer-Mediated Communication, 12*(4), 1452–1471.

Nagel, D. M., & Anthony, K. (2009). Writing therapies using new technologies–the art of blogging. *Journal of Poetry Therapy, 22*(1), 41–45.

Pennebaker, J. W. (1997). Writing about emotional experiences as a therapeutic process. *Psychological Science, 8*(3), 162–166.

Richards, D. (2008). Towards an informal online learning community for student mental health. *British Journal of Guidance and Counselling, 36*(1), 81–97.

Tan, L. (2008). Psychotherapy 2.0: MySpace® blogging as self-therapy. *American Journal of Psychotherapy, 62*(2), 143–163.

Thompson, K. (2004). Journal writing as a therapeutic tool. In G. Bolton, S. Howlett, C. Lago, & J. Wright (Eds.), *Writing cures.* Hove and New York: Brunner-Routledge.

Chapter 8

THE ROLE OF BLOGGING
IN MENTAL HEALTH

DeeAnna Merz Nagel and Gregory Palumbo

INTRODUCTION

Since the introduction of the Internet, there has been an evolution in human communications. One of the corollaries to this reinvention is that there is a resurgence in the use of the written word. The Internet has inspired collaboration on a scale never before imagined and messaging between people has evolved to take advantage of the unique characteristics of this new medium.

The common theme supporting online communications is sharing and interactivity. Prior to the Internet, the written word was static. Books, magazines and newspapers provided unidirectional communication. Information could be disseminated but interactivity was not supported by these media, other than the occasional letter to the editor. The Internet brought change not only to how people could distribute their writings, but also to how those writings could remain dynamic and alive. Text stored online can not only be accessed by anyone, anywhere, but there exists the potential for that text to be edited by those who view it. There are various forms of technology that support such interactivity and one of the most popular forms is called the "blog."

DEFINITION

The term "blog" is short for "weblog" but can be used as a noun or a verb. As example, noun: "Kate is examining Action Research processes on her blog" or verb: "Kate has just blogged about the woes of getting the Victoria Line to Hanger Lane" (Anthony, 2004). A blog is a form of website that is customarily maintained by an individual who regularly posts commentary, event descriptions or other materials such as graphics or videos. Blogs can provide commentary or news on a subject or they may function as personal online diaries. Typically, blogs will combine text, images and links to other blogs, web pages and other related media. Many blogs provide an opportunity for readers to submit their personal comments, inspiring an interactive and evolving dialogue.

Blogging is a standardized form of online communication and as such, its various elements—which include title, description, keywords, author, date and content—are usually coded with a programming language called "xml" so that the content can be accurately categorized and searched in a standardized format. This standardization gave birth to a new way for the information to be delivered to interested readers—RSS feeds. RSS stands for Really Simple Syndica-

tion. RSS is a web "feed" or "channel" to which readers may subscribe. Thus, as blog content is updated, the "feed" is instantly delivered to all subscribers, eliminating the need for the reader to continually check the blog for new updates.

RSS benefits publishers by providing a way for them to syndicate their content automatically. It benefits readers who want to be updated by their favorite websites and aggregates all of their updates into one place—their RSS reader.

By definition, blogs are regularly updated websites that inspire interactivity. Because they are regularly updated, their content tends to be current. Additionally, the interactivity lends itself to readers providing additional insight and information on the subject, enhancing the relevancy of the content.

BUSINESS APPLICATIONS OF BLOGGING

This combination of current information and interactivity naturally gave way to search engines favorably ranking blogs. In fact, often blogs rank on the first page of search results, alongside major websites. So although blogging began with individuals discussing favored topics, businesses took note of their popularity with readers and favorability with search engines and began to implement blogs as part of their marketing strategy.

The popularity of blogging for business purposes revolves not only around search engine popularity but also around the unique way that blogs allow publishers to maintain a close relationship with their subscribers. Businesses depend upon long-term customer retention. Companies dedicate large portions of their advertising budgets to marketing to pre-

vious customers. Blogs allow companies to provide their previous customers with useful information. Their customers appreciate the on-going support and develop strong bonds with these companies. The businesses are able to inform their customers of additional products, services and promotions to entice customers to make new purchases. As opposed to traditional mailers or telemarketing campaigns, the company incurs virtually no cost to disseminate their offers. This allows companies to focus more on providing useful content that helps cement the bonds with their customers and less on the "hard sell" that is typical of print and telemarketing campaigns.

Businesses that implement blogs find that their cost of acquiring a new customer is mitigated by the increase in long-term business that results from the enhanced relationship afforded by the blog. Instead of focusing on new customer acquisition, companies focus on retention and implementing new products and services that complement the customers' original purchase. Since each subscriber is predisposed to having interest in the company's content, products, services and promotions, they are interested in hearing about additional solutions to challenges that they may be having. In television advertising, it is generally accepted that it takes approximately thirteen exposures to a commercial before a new customer is inspired to make a purchase. Blogging provides a very similar kind of repeated exposure to a company's marketing message, with the distinct advantage of not costing the company to distribute it.

Marketing by using a blog also provides other advantages to businesses. Although the "hard sell" is still a viable approach, recent trends suggest that people are more willing to purchase products and services from companies that provide helpful information and resources. This is a "soft sell" and is very effective in that companies that create compelling content are able to convert people looking for free information into paying customers. Therefore, potential new customers are able to gain useful data from a company which creates an affinity with the company. They may even recommend the company to others without having purchased products or services themselves. Well thought out blogging campaigns can create excitement amongst subscribers and can even result in great PR–even coverage by traditional media outlets (Palumbo, 2008).

Blogs can be used by businesses to help their customers connect with one another. By enabling and encouraging communities around their products and services, companies create a "social network" that allows customers to support one another. This is not meant to replace traditional customer service, but is an adjunct to it that provides an additional outlet for customers to find the answers for which they are looking. This "social network" can also be a source for customers to connect with like-minded people. By providing value to the customer beyond that which is derived directly from a company's products and services, the company creates a "home" for the customer which fosters customer loyalty and brand allegiance.

MENTAL HEALTH APPLICATIONS OF BLOGGING

Mental health providers are typically latecomers to adopting new technologies. A therapist's work is a unique service predicated upon confidentiality and discretion. At first glance it may seem difficult, even ill advised, for a therapist to create a blog for their business. However, it is imperative to look at the big picture. Within a few short years blogs have gone from novelty to necessity for any business looking to maximize its reach and relationship with their customers. Therapy is not an exception. The prerequisite is that the goal and parameters of the blog are clearly defined before setting out, but that should be the case for any business. Therapists know their business; they are clear on what is appropriate, ethical and legal. Within those bounds, therapists will find that there are a few very effective uses of blogging.

One effective use of blogging is to share knowledge that will benefit readers. Self-help articles and articles related to the therapist's niche area are two viable uses of blogs. The therapist has the opportunity to utilize his or her expertise while educating the lay and/or professional audience. See the following blog post as an example of sharing relevant self-help information:

Is Your Spouse or Partner a Sex Addict?

Oct 17th, 2008
by DeeAnna.

Have you recently discovered that your partner or spouse has been involved in sexual activity on the Internet? Perhaps your partner has been having an affair or you are wondering if you may be in a relationship with someone who has a sex addiction. You are not alone. Often, finding out is the toughest part. You may have felt that something was wrong and may have even confronted your partner. Maybe you were lied to or told you were crazy. The initial discovery is sometimes the most difficult time—the shock and overwhelm, wondering if the entire relationship was a lie- these are all normal feelings.

Here's the good news.

It is not your fault.

Your partner's addiction is not about you.

Your partner's recovery is not your responsibility.

Still, living with an addict is not easy. If your partner is in recovery through a12-step program and/or psychotherapy, this is a good first step. Let your partner heal while you seek help and support for yourself. Take the focus off your partner and focus on you. You may feel the need to know details or police your partner's activities. This is not usually helpful and may actually retraumatize both of you.

Be good to you; decide whether you want to give your partner another chance and if so, let that chance take root. Focus on the positive. Commit to your healing while supporting your partner's recovery!

(Nagel, 2008).

While blogging is not the proper method of delivery for therapeutic exchanges (Nagel & Anthony, 2009a) a therapist's effective use of blogging potentially increases client caseload, drawing potential clients to a therapist's particular specialty or location. A blog also serves as an altruistic offering of information to people in an easily accessible, easy to use format. Therapists can not only use a blog as a website, a blog can be used to create community. Therapists can create a blog post and ask participants of a workshop to connect with each other via comments on the blog. Counselor educators can post homework assignments or handouts on a blog (Truffo, 2007). Blogging can be a personal notebook, providing the life and times of, say, a psychology graduate student; blogging can be used as a teaching tool, suggesting that psychology and counseling students find a particular blog topic and comment; blogging can be used as a public service reaching many people about a single topic. Finally, blogging can be used to create a virtual community whereby like-minded people come together around a particular interest (Clay, 2009a). In the blog post example below, the Online Therapy Institute rallies like-minded professionals around pertinent issues related to the promotion of online therapy:

How Professionals Can Promote Online Therapy

by DeeAnna.

Yesterday I completed facilitation of a two-day Distance Credentialed Counselor training in Springfield, IL. Every time I do a training I meet great people and I learn. In this training there was much concern expressed about therapists being able to cross state lines; how to know what each state's law says and whether there is a "clearinghouse" for such information.

Well, OTI has an Ethics and Law wiki and we do our best to keep it updated as we receive information about the legal and ethical aspects of practicing online counseling across the globe. But still, this method relies on all of us to make sure the updates are received in a timely manner and that Kate and I can upload the information that is sent to us if a person does not enter the information to the wiki him/herself . . .

And so on my drive back the hotel it occurred to me that one way we can effect change as professionals in our various states and countries is to become active in our professional organizations. If you are in the states and you are member of APA, ACA, NASW, get involved. Join taskforce committees. To have influence in your state, join a state chapter. Volunteer to be on the board. Be part of a government relations or ethics committee. Become the ethics chair of your state chapter. That is how we can begin to educate our colleagues about the value of online counseling. I do not think we should be legislating WHERE online counseling can occur. I think we should be legislating competency.

It is obvious to me that state licensing boards are way behind the curve when it comes to understanding the global community—and global e-commerce. Placing practice restrictions on licensed professionals does not allow consumers choice in treatment and seems to be a rather paternalistic stance. And clearly, state licensing boards have no clue about the online culture. Most states require practitioners to have taken a class on multiculturalism to obtain a license to practice, yes? Yet the boards do not understand that we have an entirely new culture of people who live within a mixed reality, choosing to receive professional services online through their global community. So if we look at the online community as a culture, then we could make the claim that in this instance, our state boards are not being very culturally sensitive, could we not?

While this issue of "crossing state lines" is rather U.S.-centric, my point in this post is to encourage professionals to become involved in their local professional organizations no matter what country, so that we can all make a difference. We want online therapy to be a viable option within the global community!!

(Nagel, 2009a).

Blogs may be used by organizations to provide their members with timely, relevant and thought-provoking commentary while exposing the organization's mission and work to nonmembers as well. In this way, the organization provides education in the form of a public service to nonmembers and information to members. Nonmembers may in turn decide to join the organization after reading information provided on the blog. One such organization that is utilizing a blog in this manner is the American Counseling Association Weblog found at http://my.counseling.org. At the ACA blog's inception, four individuals regularly blog for the ACA Weblog. Two of the individuals represented the membership and two were employees of the organization. Occasionally, a guest blogger would be hosted as well. Now ACA's blog has several regular bloggers who represent ACA's membership and the counseling profession at large.

Therapists may also offer their own or other blogs to existing clients as additional reading regarding various topics. Therapists should educate clients about the boundaries and perimeters of the use of blogs. For instance, clients should understand that the therapist would not accept a blog comment from an existing or former client. To that end, therapists should monitor blog comments prior to official posting. Therapists can explain that a client's post on a therapist's blog may potentially threaten confidentiality of the therapeutic relationship and explain reversely, that the therapist will not comment on a client's blog for the same reasons.

Additionally, therapists are in a unique position to educate clients about the use of blogs and as well as other Web 2.0 applications. The following blog post is an example of how a therapist can inform the general public and yet specifically target clients who may or may not be the therapist's own client:

Are You in Counseling? Would You "Friend" Your Therapist?

Jun 28th, 2009
by DeeAnna.
I have spent time lately training therapists and writing about a therapist's boundaries online. And so now I am curious from the other perspective, what people think about connecting with their therapist online via social media sites like Facebook, MySpace or other similar social networks?

I guess it might help for those of you who are not in the counseling profession to talk first about our code of ethics—what we as therapists, counselors, psychologists, social workers and psychotherapists must carry out to remain ethical. Regardless of the discipline, we all have a code of ethics that we are expected to follow and with a few differences in intent and wording, there are some ethical tenets that remain universal. Two of these tenets are with regard to confidentiality and dual relationships.

While most ethical codes have not yet addressed social media in their codes, some of us in the field have interpreted the existing codes as applied to social networking as follows:

Friending a client on Facebook or MySpace could potentially breach confidentiality. While the client may agree or even initiate the connection, others who are friends of the therapist and/or the client may "connect the dots" and assume or confirm that the person is indeed a client of the therapist.

Friending a client on Facebook or MySpace could be interpreted as a dual relationship. As a therapist I do not socialize with my clients. I don't meet my clients for coffee and I don't go to their home for dinner. Inviting a client to my Facebook page is like inviting a client into my living room.

Feedback anyone? What do you think?

Have a beautiful summer day!
(Nagel, 2009b)

Blogging may also be used as a form of journal writing or self-help intervention therefore teaching the client about the effects of posting information into cyberspace can be critical (Nagel & Anthony, 2009b). For instance, clients that post personal information to the Internet may not immediately think through the potential hazards of doing so. Many people who use journal writing as a form of self-help may imagine a perceived audience as they write. This works well, but with blogging as a form of journaling the perceived audience becomes the World Wide Web audience, bringing a person's personal information into the psyche of the general public. Therapists can help clients understand the permanence of information posted to the Internet and discuss the impact of posting particularly personal information for everyone to access. Some people now use blogs as a way to conduct self-therapy (Tan, 2008) and not merely as a form of self-help. Take for instance, the case example given in a recent news article in which Stacey Kim blogged about her husband's death to cancer. The day after she blogged about the experience of holding him in her arms as he died. She said she received so many supportive responses from people around the world and she said several people asked her if she was in therapy following such a traumatic loss. Kim replied, "No, but I have a blog" (Grossman, 2008).

It is also advantageous for therapists to discuss record ownership with the client. Informing the client that the therapist owns verbatim transcripts of the actual sessions offsets the risk that a client may decide to post the contents of a therapy session in a blog post. While this scenario may be far-reaching, practicing due diligence ultimately keeps the client's personal information confidential and away from the public eye. Likewise, blogs are not the proper venue to discuss case information even in the most generic of terms. Current or previous clients might read the therapist's blog and realize the seemingly innocuous post is about them (Clay, 2009b).

MICROBLOGGING

Complimenting yet contrasting the blog is what is commonly referred to as a microblog. Microblogging is a networking service that allows mobile users of cell phones and other Internet connected devices to stay abreast of activities within a group by receiving frequent published updates, typically of 140 characters or less. Text messages are uploaded to a microblogging service such as Twitter, Jaiku and others and then distributed to group members. All persons subscribed within a specific group are instantly notified of the microblog, enabling groups to keep tabs on one another's activities in real time (Kayne, 2008).

Many of the same reasons exist for microblogging as blogging, from personal to professional, and many therapists use microblogging to build a professional network and as a public service. Twitter is the most popular microblog site. PsychCentral, a website known for providing information about mental health and psychology recently posted "Top Ten Psych Tweeps" (Kiume, 2009) featuring people who offer useful information about mental health and psychology and many on the list are therapists. Many people who tweet are sending out information in short 140 character messages that may reflect an interesting article, a thought provoking question or a link to the latest blog post of their personal blog or an organizational blog. For instance, the American Counseling Association has a profile on Twitter displayed as CounselingViews and the American Counseling Association Weblog posts are tweeted at CounselingViews. Anyone viewing the CounselingViews profile will have access to blog post links and other relevant ACA information.

Other profiles may represent an individual yet have a username that reflects the majority of the profile content.

DeeAnna Nagel's username is Therapy Online because she tweets mostly about issues related to technology and mental health. Since she blogs at various sites all of her posts can be reached through her profile. Her profile content offers a variety; she offers retweets (reposting a someone else's tweet) of interest, she asks questions, offers links to various news items and tweets self-help content as well. In addition, she announces news related to the Online Therapy Institute, the organization she co-founded.

CONCLUSION

Clearly, the meshing and intertwining of blogs and microblogs along with other Web 2.0 applications such as social and professional networks like Linkedin and Facebook offers the opportunity for a sense of community to grow and learn from one another. These applications add to our ability to rely on the collective intelligence and wisdom across the globe. Whether for professional or personal pursuits, when used responsibly, blogging can make a substantial and positive impact on the counseling profession and the world at large.

REFERENCES

Anthony, K. (2004). The art of blogging. *BACP Counselling and Psychotherapy Journal, 15*(9), 38.

Clay, R. (2009a). Meet psychology's bloggers. *Monitor on Psychology, 39*(11), 34.

Clay, R. (2009b). Think before you post. *Monitor on Psychology, 39*(11), 37.

Grossman, A. J. (2008). *Your blog can be group therapy* [online]. [Accessed August 11, 2009]. Available from: http://www.cnn.com/2008/LIVING/personal/05/07/blog.therapy/index.html.

Kayne, R. (2008). *What is microblogging?* [online]. [Accessed August 10, 2009]. Available from: http://www.wisegeek.com/what-is-microblogging.htm.

Kiume, S. (2009). *Top ten psych tweeps* [online]. [Accessed June 29, 2009]. Available from: http://psychcentral.com/blog/archives/2009/06/29/top-ten-psych-tweeps/.

Nagel, D., & Anthony, K. (2009a). *Ethical Framework for the Use of Technology in Mental Health* [online]. [Accessed August 10, 2009]. Available from: http://www.onlinetherapyinstitute.com/id43.html.

Nagel, D., & Anthony, K. (2009b). Writing therapy using new technologies–the art of blogging. *Journal of Poetry Therapy, 22*(1), 41–45.

Nagel, D (2008). Is your spouse or partner a sex addict? *Mental Health on the Web* [online]. [Accessed November 20, 2009]. Available from: http://www.mentalhealthonthewebblog.com/?p=15.

Nagel, D. (2009a). How professionals can promote online therapy. *Online Therapy*

Institute Blog [online]. [Accessed November 20, 2009]. Available from: http://www.onlinetherapyinstituteblog.com/?p=459.

Nagel, D. (2009b). Are you in counseling? Would you 'friend' your therapist? *Mental Health on the Web* [online]. [Accessed November 20, 2009]. Available from: http://www.mentalhealthonthewebblog.com/?p=48.

Palumbo, G. (2008). *Webinar—Blogs and newsletters to drive traffic to your site* [online]. [Accessed August 10, 2009]. Available from: http://www.securetherapy.com/GregsTest/webinararchives.asp?EUID=.

Tan, L. (2008). Psychotherapy 2.0: MySpace blogging as self-therapy. *American Journal of Psychotherapy, 62*(2), 143–163.

Truffo, C. (2007). *Be a wealthy therapist: Finally you can make living while making a difference.* Saint Peters, MO: MP Press.

Chapter 9

USING THE TELEPHONE FOR CONDUCTING A THERAPEUTIC RELATIONSHIP

DENISE E. SAUNDERS

INTRODUCTION

The telephone has been used for the delivery of counseling services for many decades. Perhaps most widely known and recognized were the crisis hotlines of the late 60s and 70s (Lester, 2002). Samaritans, developed in the United Kingdom, continues to receive 96% of their contacts by telephone (Samaritans, 2009). Using the telephone in the therapeutic relationship grew in acceptance among counselors and clients with the advent of these hotlines and has expanded to the use of contracted counseling delivered exclusively over the phone for individuals, couples and groups. Telephone counseling has grown in recent years to assist clients with varying needs in a variety of settings. One need only Google "telephone counseling" or "telephone counselling" to find multiple pages listing solo practice counselors and therapists, clinics and other mental health service providers offering counseling assistance and support to clients in need. Historically, practitioners utilized this technology primarily for initial contact with clients, follow-up and in-between session contact. Technological advances and client desire for counseling services delivered via telephone have contributed to the increase in the use of this modality for direct service delivery.

DEFINING TELEPHONE COUNSELING

A variety of terms have been used to refer to the use of the telephone in counseling and therapy services. Among those in the literature are telehealth, telemedicine, telephone based counseling, telephonic counseling, telephone counseling and telecounseling. The terms telehealth and telemedicine are used more frequently in referring to medical environments where physicians and other health service providers utilize the telephone for patient care and management and health information dissemination delivered through telecommunication technology, including videoconferencing. Telehealth and telemedicine are umbrella terms encompassing physical and mental health services delivered via electronic transmission of communication. Telephonic refers directly to the technologies used for service delivery, i.e., the telephone (Hughes, 2000; Maheu et al., 2005).

The use of multiple terms and references to similar yet different aspects of telephone technology can be confusing and overwhelming to readers. For this reason a brief definition of telephone counseling may be helpful. For purposes of the discussion in this chapter the term "telephone counseling" will be used and refers to the use of the telephone for contracted counseling and therapy services between a counselor or mental health practitioner and a client (or clients in the case of couples or groups).

THE STATE OF TELEPHONE COUNSELING IN PRACTICE

Evidence-Based Findings

Having been in existence for multiple decades, telephone counseling has seen the benefits of research studies examining both process and outcome variables. Due to the use of telephones in everyday work and play, counselors and clients have developed a comfort level in using the phone for communication. This may help explain researchers' interest in expanding our understanding of the unique therapeutic qualities using this modality as well as clients' willingness to be a part of these research endeavors. It seems only natural then that, with increasing frequency, counseling and psychotherapy would involve the use of the telephone as a means to communicate with clients. Although the research is still limited in scope, it does provide support for the effectiveness and use of this modality for work with clients.

In a study comparing psychotherapy conducted face-to-face, through two-way audio (analogous to telephone) and videoconferencing technologies, Day and Schneider (2002) found that clients participated more in the counseling

process when working in a distance environment. Reese et al. (2002) reported that clients viewed telephone counseling as an effective and satisfactory experience and believed that telephone counseling helped them improve their lives. Clients perceived the counselor's influence and relationship to be strong throughout the therapeutic process. In a more recent study investigating client's perceptions regarding attractiveness of telephone counseling, clients reported satisfaction with telephone counseling indicating that convenience, accessibility, control and inhibition reduction were important features of telephone counseling (Reese et al., 2006).

These studies provide support for the effective use of telephone counseling and suggest overall satisfaction and comfort using the telephone for counseling services. Clients report that they would use telephone counseling again even when initially questioning the benefit of telephone counseling. More than half of those who had received face-to-face counseling prior to their participation in the study indicated a preference for telephone counseling following the counseling intervention (Reese et al., 2006).

ReadyMinds, a provider of "distance career telecounseling," reported similar outcome findings; research on the effectiveness of their counseling program suggests that client areas of satisfaction include:

> . . . convenience, efficiency, strong working alliance with the counselor, helpful and personally useful resources, increased motivation to complete the work of the counseling and a better understanding of the career counseling process. (Djadali and Malone, 2003, p. 16)

ReadyMinds counselors often find that clients are more willing to share with counselors about themselves, their career aspirations and challenges in making career decisions while engaging in telecounseling (Malone et al., 2004). Similarly, the telephone has been found to provide clients with the perception of distance and safety in the counseling or therapy process which allows them to more quickly share and discuss their concerns (Day & Schneider, 2000; Rosenfield, 1997).

Benefits of Use

Accessibility is a significant benefit in the provision of telephone counseling services. Many individuals in the United States and around the world have access to a telephone. Increasing use and availability of cellular phones has contributed to affordable and globally accessible phone access. Clients and counselors report that convenience and ease of use are appealing aspects of telephone counseling (Reese et al., 2006; Djadali & Malone, 2003). With the increasing globalization of our society, many people travel extensively for work. The availability and convenience of counseling sessions via telephone is therefore desirable given the hectic lives many clients lead.

A major advantage of telephone counseling is client control and anonymity. The perceived anonymity of the relationship provides clients with a feeling of greater control in the therapeutic relationship. One could easily choose to end the counseling communication by simply hanging up the phone. This sense of control in the therapeutic process leads to feelings of comfort using the modality and client disclosure of difficult material more quickly in the counseling process. This serves to "jump start" the process and further motivate clients in doing the work of the counseling.

Although at a distance, being able to hear a client's voice over the phone can serve as an important counseling tool. Awareness of voice tone, pace, inflection and silence are all cues to aid the counselor. In the absence of visual cues counselors may find that they rely more heavily on these characteristics. Counselors are afforded the flexibility to use the telephone as the sole means of counseling communication or as an adjunct to face-to-face counseling. Clients receiving counseling in a more traditional face-to-face environment may perceive this additional support as an added benefit to their counseling work, further enhancing the counseling relationship.

Limitations of Use

Critics argue that without visual cues counselors will be unable to develop a strong therapeutic relationship or that important clinical data will be overlooked. Although it is true that some material may be missing when one cannot see the client visually, those same cues may easily be "heard" over the phone as the counselor further develops skill and comfort in listening in a different counseling environment. Telephone counselors may find it useful to engage in more directive counseling work with clients, following up with questions, summarizing more frequently and using inquiry to further clarify client's communication. Rosenfeld (2003) writes "after working by telephone for a few months, practitioners will probably notice that their listening skills become increasingly finely tuned" (p. 99).

Telephone counseling may not be suitable for everyone. Those who are not comfortable using the phone or do not articulate well verbally may feel more comfortable engaging in counseling via a different method of delivery. Clients and counselors with strong accents may not be well suited to telephone counseling and may find communication challenging. Clients need to be able to find a quiet, comfortable space where they will not be disturbed during telephone counseling sessions. Due to the informal na-ture of phone communication, occasionally clients do not recognize the potential for interruption from dogs barking, children in the room or other distractions during the counseling. It is important to discuss such issues prior to beginning telephone counseling so that clients and counselors are aware of the potential for disruptions during phone sessions and work together to minimize them.

Other limitations include the consideration of potential cultural and or socioeconomic issues and concerns when using telephone counseling. Use of the telephone for communication may differ across groups and cultures. Language issues may present potential challenges for engaging in telephone counseling. Despite increased accessibility to phone services, not everyone has the technology to engage in telephone counseling. Perhaps awareness of these issues could serve to inspire counseling professionals in the United States and other countries to advocate for increased accessibility of telephone and other technologies to accommodate those requesting services for distance counseling services.

ETHICAL CONSIDERATIONS

Professional organizations are responding to client and practitioner interest in providing counseling through distance modalities by developing appropriate guidelines and standards for the provision of these services. The American Counseling Association's most recent revision of their Code of Ethics includes guidelines for the use of technology in counseling including telephone contact (American Counseling Association, 2005). The National Board for Certified Counselors (NBCC) created *The Practice of Internet Counseling* to provide a standard of practice using all distance modalities (National Board for Certified Counselors, 2007). The United Kingdom has often been at the forefront of distance services such as telephone counseling. The British Association of Counselling and Psychotherapy's *Guidelines for Telephone Counselling and Psychotherapy* is an example of that (Payne et al., 2006). These guidelines focus entirely on the use of the telephone in a counseling or therapeutic relationship and include case illustrations and suggested reading for further information on this counseling topic.

SECURITY AND CONFIDENTIALITY

Just as counselors work to maintain a high degree of security and confidentiality in face-to-face work with clients, so too must practitioners work toward a similar environment when engaging in telephone counseling. There are numerous phone technologies in existence today. Many households have eliminated home phones, opting for the use of cellular phones for all telephone communication. Despite their convenience, we must be cautious regarding their use and fully inform our clients regarding potential threats to the security of the communication.

Until recently, landline phones were thought to provide the highest degree of security for telephone communication. Cordless phones in the home or office did not provide the same degree of privacy as they could be intercepted. A baby monitor next door or a scanner could easily pick up conversations on these phones. Cellular phones were not considered secure when operating on analog signals. Newer phones, both cordless and cellular, operate predominantly on digital signals for transmission of communication, reducing the opportunity for hackers to break into and access the communication. As technology has advanced in the area of telecommunication, a digital signal, being sent more rapidly, provides a higher degree of security. Despite these advances, one cannot guarantee complete security using these technologies. It is the counselor's responsibility to thoroughly explain potential breeches to confidentiality and work to minimize the risk of these prior to beginning telephone counseling with clients. Information regarding confidentiality, security and privacy issues may be included in the informed consent document of the counseling practice or setting.

Encryption affords the highest level of security. This technology is a form of secure transmission that scrambles the communication making it more difficult for hackers to decipher what is being sent. At present, there are several vendors who provide software for the encryption of telephone communication, although it may be cost prohibitive. Voice over Internet Protocol (VoIP) technologies have led to an increase in telephone communication via the Internet. VoIP allows for the transmission of verbal communication through the Internet (Maheu et al., 2005). Encryption software is available using this technology and should be implemented. Although in existence for a few years now, it remains an evolving technology, with ongoing advancements in sound quality, security and transmission. Caution should still be maintained when utilizing these technologies to engage in telephone counseling.

PRACTICAL APPLICATIONS

Effective telephone counseling utilizes structure as a tool in the counseling process. Brief therapy models work well in this modality. Establishing a contract with clients for telephone counseling services helps to eliminate confusion and uncertainty about how services will be delivered and what clients can expect. The contract would include specifics about number of sessions, length of sessions, understanding of how telephone counseling will occur and fees involved. This information could be discussed when initial contact is made via a website or phone consultation and included in the client terms of agreement or informed consent. Telephone counseling may not be appropriate for all clients or counselors. Some clients may prefer to work with counselors in a different modality or present with high-risk, dangerous behaviors or other issues that may be better addressed through an alternative counseling modality. It is ethically appropriate for counselors to provide clients with referrals when issues presented fall outside of their scope of practice or boundaries of competence. This helps ensure that clients and counselors make informed choices about services being offered.

Logistics of telephone counseling are often dependent on the individual setting or practice providing the service. Many counselors will choose to initiate calls at the scheduled appointment time while others may feel comfortable having clients call in on a toll free number set up for this purpose. Counselors are advised to give careful consideration to the selection of phone used to initiate or receive calls from clients. This is a particularly salient issue for independent practitioners using landlines that are also personal home phone lines.

CASE STUDIES

May

May lost her husband 6 years ago to cancer. She has been living by herself in their home since his death. Her health has declined, limiting her physical mobility. She was told she would need a hip replacement—however, at 81, May doesn't feel the costs and recuperation are worth it. She no longer drives and is dependent on friends or a shuttle service for transportation. Her two children live out of state and visit infrequently.

Lately, she has felt depressed, spends the day looking out of her front window and has limited social contact outside the growing number of visits to healthcare providers. May decided to schedule a telephone counseling session after being encouraged by her primary care physician to work with a counselor on their staff for telephone counseling.

Initial Session

May and the counselor discussed her feelings of loss, not only for loved ones but also the impact of losses she experienced due to physical ailments. May was pleased that the counselor understood her and found it helpful to talk with someone outside her circle of friends and family. After asking questions about telephone counseling and determining that she felt at ease communicating with the counselor over the phone, May expressed interest in continuing work with the counselor and agreed to schedule sessions weekly for the next month.

The Fourth Session

Over the course of the previous month, May found herself appreciating her days more. She and the counselor further explored her feelings of loss. By the third contact, May had felt comfortable sharing with the counselor her disappointment that her children were not more involved in her life. This was difficult for her, as she felt selfish acknowledging this. The counselor assisted her in getting involved with a local organization that knitted baby blankets for the local hospital neonatal unit. She now expressed a willingness to consider medication and surgery options to improve her physical mobility as her doctor felt she was a good candidate for surgery. May felt the telephone counseling experience had been beneficial in many ways and she was appreciative of her physician's initial referral. She requested on-going contact with the counselor and they agreed to continue with weekly sessions.

Jonathan

Jonathan was a thirty-two year old male in a committed relationship of 2 years. He recently asked his fiancé to marry him and she accepted. Since the engagement, he has been physically ill, unable to eat and tense and anxious much of the time. Jonathan had called in sick to work 4 days out of the past two weeks. He had a brief period of tension and worry while in college and could recognize the signs again. Since he was currently unable to work effectively he felt it would be helpful to talk with a counselor. Jonathan's job took him out of town almost every week. In-office visits were not an option. Hoping to find assistance, he searched the Internet and found a therapist online who could provide telephone counseling and who would be available in the evenings when he was free.

Initial Session

Jonathan contacted the counselor as instructed for the scheduled appointment. He felt uncertain about what to expect and how this relationship would develop. His counselor sensed his worry and quickly put him at ease by sharing more about telephone counseling and how the two might work together. As they talked, Jonathan became less anxious. He shared openly his frustration of not having better managed his feelings. The counselor again could hear what Jonathan was communicating and encouraged him to share about his relationship and his fiancé. As they did, Jonathan began to see connections between concerns about the relationship, feelings of responsibility and confusion about marriage with his current physical problems. Jonathan felt comfortable with this modality of counseling and enjoyed the convenience of it. He requested additional calls, which the counselor was able to provide working around his travel and work schedule.

Three Months Later

Jonathan and his counselor worked together for three months varying session frequency dependent on Jonathan's work schedule. To his surprise, he was comfortable engaging in telephone counseling and enjoyed the ability to communicate with the counselor while on the road. During his counseling sessions, Jonathan recognized that he truly loved his fiancé and looked forward to a life with her but had felt a sense of responsibility for her happiness and the security of their life together. With the help of his counselor he was able to share some of what he was feeling with his fiancé, freeing him from the burden he had been bearing alone. They also worked together to further develop stress management techniques from which Jonathan was already benefiting.

CONCLUSION

With the impact of the global workplace, advancements in technology and lifestyle changes, telephone counselors will continue to be a growing part of the provision of mental health counseling and therapy services. As telephone counseling and other distance modalities are given greater favor in the provision of counseling services there will be a need to further explore the process of telephone counseling and its unique contributions to the counseling/therapeutic relationship. Counselor education and postgraduate programs will be called upon to include discussion of these is-

sues, raising student awareness of the options available for counseling, ethical and legal concerns, and research findings supporting the use of telephone and other technologies in counseling. With increased use of telephone counseling it will be equally important for practitioners to enhance understanding of client suitability for this modality through research and professional practice. Perhaps one day it will be commonplace for counselors to provide distance services to clients exclusively. Without a doubt, the telephone will have a prominent role in this movement.

REFERENCES

American Counseling Association. (2005). *ACA code of ethics.* Alexandria, VA: Author.

Day, S.X. and Schneider, P. (2002). Psychotherapy using distance technology: A comparison of face-to-face, video and audio treatment. *Journal of Counseling Psychology, 49*(4), 499–503.

Djadali, Y., & Malone, J. (2003). Distance career counseling: A technology-assisted model for delivering career counseling services. In G. Walz & C. Kirkman (Eds.), *CyberBytes: Highlighting compelling issues of technology in counseling.* Greensboro, NC: CAPS Publications.

Hughes, R. S. (2000). Cybercounseling and regulations: Quagmire or quest? In J. W. Bloom & G. Walz (Eds.), *Cybercounseling and cyberlearning: strategies and resources for the millennium.* Greensboro, NC: CAPS Publishing.

Lester, D. (2002). *Crisis intervention and counseling by telephone* (2nd ed.). Springfield, IL: Charles C Thomas.

Maheu, M. M., Pulier, M. L., Wilhelm, F. H., McMenamin, J. P., & Brown-Connolly, N. E. (2005). *The mental health professional and the new technologies: A Handbook for practice*

today. Mahwah, NJ: Lawrence Erlbaum Associates, Inc.

Malone, J. F., Miller, K. S., & Miller, R. M. (2004). The evolution of the ReadyMinds model of distance career counseling: Implications for training, practice and supervision of cybercounselors. In J. Bloom & G. R. Walz (Eds.), *Cybercounseling and cyberlearning: An encore.* Alexandria, VA: American Counseling Association.

National Board for Certified Counselors (2007). *The practice of internet counseling* [online]. [Accessed May 9, 2009]. Available from: http://www.nbcc.org/AssetManager Files/ethics/internetCounseling.pdf.

Payne, L., Casemore, R., Neat, P., & Chambers, M. (2006). *Guidelines for telephone counselling and psychotherapy.* Lutterworth, UK: BACP.

Reese, R. J., Conoley, C. W., & Brossart, D. F. (2002). Effectiveness of telephone counseling: A field-based investigation. *Journal of Counseling Psychology, 49*(2), 233–242.

Reese, R. J., Conoley, C. W., & Brossart, D. F. (2006). The attractiveness of telephone counseling: An empirical investigation of client perceptions. *Journal of Counseling and*

Development, 84(1), 54–60.

Rosenfield, M. (1997). *Counseling by telephone.* Thousand Oaks, CA: Sage.

Rosenfield, M. (2003). Telephone counselling and psychotherapy in practice. In Goss, S. & Anthony, K. (Eds). *Technology in counselling and psychotherapy: A practitioner's guide.* New York, NY: Palgrave Macmillan.

Samaritans. (2009). *Introduction to Samaritans* [online]. [Accessed January 10, 2009]. Available from: http://www.samaritans.org/about_to_samaritans.aspx.

Chapter 10

USING VIDEOCONFERENCING FOR CONDUCTING A THERAPEUTIC RELATIONSHIP

Susan Simpson and Emma Morrow

INTRODUCTION

Video teleconferencing (VTC) is broadly defined as a live, interactive two-way video-audio electronic meeting between at least two remote sites using video cameras, monitors and communications technology. The potential of videoconferencing as a mode of delivering psychotherapy has become increasingly recognised for those who would not otherwise have access to local therapeutic services. It has been shown to be of enormous benefit to a range of populations, from those living in the far-flung islands of Scotland (Simpson et al., 2001) and rural parts of the U.S. (Glueckauf et al., 2002) to aboriginal settlements in outback Australia (Young, 1995; Forbes, 1996) among many others. In addition to those living in remote and rural areas, early evidence suggests that video therapy may also benefit other marginalized groups such as those in prison, the elderly, military staff or those with mobility difficulties. Those who avoid in-person therapy due to per- ceived stigmatisation or elevated anxiety (e.g., agoraphobia or social phobia) also stand to take advantage of this form of treatment delivery.

Although we know that VTC is a practical means of providing therapy to those who do not have access to traditional in-person treatment, there remains a clear scepticism amongst clinicians as to how suitable VTC is in this setting (Rees & Haythornthwaite, 2004). It is well established that the quality of the therapeutic relationship is central to the process, effectiveness and acceptability of psychotherapy. Several studies have identified therapeutic alliance, widely defined as "the collaborative bond between therapist and client," as a key factor in determining outcome across a wide range of psychotherapeutic models (e.g., Krupnick et al., 1996; Agnew-Davies et al., 1998). Given the importance of the quality of rapport, it remains to be established whether it is possible to develop a positive therapeutic relationship through this mode of treatment delivery and in fact whether there are certain client groups for whom VTC may actually facilitate or hinder therapeutic alliance.

VIDEO THERAPY AND THE THERAPEUTIC ALLIANCE

There seems a general reluctance amongst psychotherapists to use videoconferencing for therapeutic purposes. A study in the U.S. found that only 1% of those psychologists surveyed had used VTC for therapy, whereas 69 percent had provided telephone-based therapy (VandenBos and Williams, 2000). A survey of health professionals working in the UK national health service found that those who had not had any experience in the use of videoconferencing for therapeutic purposes were in general more reluctant to use it. This was due to their expectation that they would be unable to work collaboratively with patients and that nonverbal communication would be impaired, thereby preventing the establishment of a therapeutic rapport. In contrast, the views of those who were experienced users suggested that these concerns had not been borne out by the reality of their video therapy sessions and that a strong positive alliance was possible (Mitchell et al., 2003). This finding was corroborated by a recent study of 30 clinical psychologists who were randomly assigned to watch an identical therapy session, conducted either in-person or via VTC. Psychologists in the VTC condition rated the therapeutic alliance as significantly lower than those in the in-person condition and were concerned that VTC impacted negatively on the therapist's ability to convey warmth, empathy, sensitivity and understanding to clients. Most of these psychologists had no experience of offering video therapy. As sessions contained identical content (verbal and non-verbal), it seems likely that ratings may have been influenced by negative expectations (Rees & Stone, 2005).

So are these negative expectations borne out in reality? In fact, the majority of studies that have compared treatment modalities have found very little difference in ratings of therapeutic alliance by both clinicians and clients. Perhaps the most methodologically sound study to date was conducted by Day and Schneider (2002) who evaluated the delivery of brief CBT via videoconferencing. A sample of eighty clients (treatment completers) with difficulties ranging from weight concerns to personality disorders were randomly assigned to one of three treatment groups (in-person, two-way audio, or two-way video) or a waiting list control group. A closed circuit television system was used with two 20-inch television sets used to simulate a high quality two-way video delivery. The same system was used without a picture to simulate a two-way audio system. No differences in therapeutic alliance were found between the three groups and it was concluded that both therapists and clients were able to adapt according to the peculiarities of each mode of treatment delivery. In fact, in this study client participation was noticeably higher in technology-facilitated sessions. It may be that just as a sight impaired person may become more adept at using other sensory modalities (e.g., Gougoux et al., 2005), so a video therapy participant may utilise the information available to them (e.g., verbal content, tone of voice, gestures) to a greater degree than might have been the case in an in-person setting.

So how exactly does VTC interact with the therapeutic alliance? What are the factors that lead some to prefer video therapy and others to prefer in-person or other treatment modes? The main components of alliance as described by researchers in this area include:

- bond (acceptance, understanding, trust and support);

- partnership/goals and tasks (working collaboratively on therapeutic tasks, cognitions an behaviours within sessions that make up the substance of therapy);
- openness (ability to discuss personal information without feeling anxious or embarrassed) and
- initiative (the level of responsibility taken by clients in determining the direction of therapy) (Agnew-Davies et al., 1998; Alexander & Luborsky, 1984).

BOND, PARTNERSHIP, OPENNESS, INITIATIVE

An important component of video therapy is the availability of visual cues that can be used to gauge emotionality and expression, as well as to express concern or empathy. The development of a therapeutic "connection" or "bond" is likely to be influenced by such factors as nonverbal cues including eye gaze and gestures in facilitating conversational rhythms, conveying meaning and verbal fluency (Fussell & Benimoff, 1995). Several studies suggest that clients rate high levels of therapist empathy in video therapy. Alternative ways of conveying empathy and warmth are often used to supplement nonverbal cues, such as through voice tone and being more explicit verbally. Therapists also describe relying more on verbal cues to detect clients' emotions and on verbal forms of social reinforcement, but this does not appear to interfere with rapport (Himle et al., 2006; Simpson et al., 2002). It might be expected that a low quality videolink might compromise these factors through introducing sound delays, lack of lip-voice synchronisation and image pixilation and there is some evidence that this can delay initial rapport building (Kirk-wood, 1998). However, even at relatively low quality (ISDN 2), it appears to be possible to develop a positive rapport, despite the loss of some nonverbal cues and body language and lip-sound synchronisation (Simpson, 2001).

Although some authors have expressed concerns that "social presence" (developing awareness of and a sense of connection to another through nonverbal cues) (e.g., Allen & Hayes, 1994) may be diminished through video therapy, evidence suggests most patients are satisfied with this, sometimes even after just one session (Capner, 2000; Simpson et al., 2001). A recent case study of 3 clients with OCD who were offered video-CBT described high ratings of therapeutic alliance throughout treatment. Therapists were able to carry out modelling over the video link for exposure and response prevention with some extra preparation required for setting up the required stimuli at the remote site. Participants described high levels of "telepresence" and described feeling as though they were in the room with the therapist. However, having the parallel experience of being in a room on their own helped to reduce their anxiety in the initial stages of treatment. Importantly, clients' confidence and self-efficacy were boosted due to carrying out the exercises in the room on their own. This also increased their belief that they would be able to continue this work independently (Himle et al., 2006).

There is some evidence that many clients feel that the partnership aspect of therapy is in fact enhanced by the presence of the technology due to feeling "less intimidated" and more "in control" of their sessions (e.g., Simpson et al., 2002). This may be partly associated with the fact that they have their own space and room with their own video-conferencing remote-control handset (Allen et al., 1996). Clients can change the image and sound using the remote control to find a level of distance or intimacy that feels comfortable to them. This can give them a greater sense of control over their own therapy process, but for those who are unfamiliar with technology, it may lead to increased anxiety and confusion (Omodei & McLennan, 1998). For some, the extra personal space offered by video therapy may facilitate a more equalising function by addressing the imbalance of power associated with in-person sessions that take place on the therapist's "territory."

Many studies have noted that video therapy does not appear to limit the range or depth of emotions expressed or topics discussed (Ghosh et al., 1997). For some clients the experience of "personal space" within video therapy may offer a sense of safety to talk about difficult issues, but for others, it may hinder openness and trust. Holton (2005) described video therapy as a "safe space" for discussing difficult or painful issues, which can in fact facilitate rapport, alongside other issues such as the ability

to establish relational depth and connection with patients. Similarly, Simpson et al. (2001) found that video-therapy was often experienced as a safe environment that was less embarrassing and confrontational than in-person contact, thus facilitating the expression of difficult feelings. A case series by Bakke et al. (2001) echoed these findings, suggesting that patients value the privacy and anonymity of video therapy.

Preferences may to a large degree reflect idiosyncratic differences between individuals associated with personality traits, need for personal space or control and the nature of presenting problems. For example, clients with dependency issues may be more comfortable with in-person treatment due to their desire for proximity to the therapist, but they may in fact benefit more from the space and independence generated by a video link. Similarly, clients with avoidant coping styles who find intimacy and "connection" uncomfortable may be more suited to video therapy. Videoconferencing may provide enough distance initially to give patients the safety to engage in therapy and to experience some intimacy without feeling invaded or overwhelmed. Video therapy may therefore facilitate the development of a sense of connectedness with another in a setting that enhances their sense of personal control. In particular, those who feel that they lack control in their lives and relationships in general might prefer the extra control offered by videoconferencing. Similarly, those who feel apprehensive or self-conscious by talking about themselves or their difficulties may also prefer the distance and control offered by videoconferencing (Simpson, 2003).

It seems likely that the environment at the remote site will also play a part in determining how relaxed and "safe" patients can feel when discussing difficult and personal issues. For example, an open office in a busy hospital department may be more likely to raise anxieties associated with confidentiality and being overheard than a sound-proofed room in a designated videoconferencing clinic with tissues, telephone, comfortable chair and so on to hand. The availability of other technological aids (e.g., document camera, email (especially for diaries, homework, and fax) may also facilitate collaboration/communication.

The following case study illustrates the way in which VTC can be used even in the context of treating clients with complex and chronic difficulties. The schema therapy model involves a significant amount of experiential work and the emotional connection between therapist and client is of central importance.

CASE STUDY

The following case study provides an illustration of a complex case, which was amenable to schema focused therapy (Young et al., 2003) using videoconferencing technology. This therapeutic approach is an advanced form of CBT that encompasses a variety of cognitive and experiential techniques to allow the client the opportunity to explore and challenge the maladaptive core beliefs underlying their difficulties. The therapeutic relationship is also paramount in providing a secure base for clients to explore their difficulties, to challenge schemas and to experiment with new behaviours. Schema therapists use "limited reparenting" as a way of providing some of the nurturance, guidance and encouragement that may have been missing from their clients' early lives and as a way of modelling healthy adult behaviour. The following case illustration provides evidence of the utility of videoconferencing technology in enabling such a relationship to be formed and furthermore for a schema focused approach to be undertaken with a client residing in a remote setting.

Presenting Difficulties

Angela presented for therapy with Bulimia Nervosa, depressed mood and chronic low self-esteem. At the time of referral, Angela resided on a remote island in the West of Scotland. She described a ten-year history of eating difficulties that included Anorexia Nervosa. Her problems had fluctuated in severity over the years, but she was becoming increasingly concerned that her son would begin to notice her abnormal behaviours. Three months following her referral, Angela learned that she was pregnant.

Angela described long-standing relationship problems, with both her extended family and her partner. She identified her own tendencies to prioritise others and neglect her own emotional and physical needs.

Assessment and the forging of the therapeutic relationship

Assessment and treatment were undertaken by a chartered clinical psychologist (E.M.). Angela attended the sessions at her local mental health department. The clinical psychologist used a videoconferencing unit based in a private clinic room within a psychiatric hospital in Aberdeen. Client and therapist could see each other from midtorso upwards.

Angela's difficulties were assessed using a detailed clinical interview and the Young Schema Questionnaire-3 (YSQ-3; Young & Brown, 2003, www.schematherapy.com). Other measures examining specific eating pathology and general psychological pathology were also used pre and post therapy. Due to the complexity of the presenting difficulties and Angela's long history of problems, the assessment was conducted over six sessions. This allowed the therapist to gently explore the issues most difficult for Angela to discuss.

Angela was invited to contact the therapist using other modes of communication in between sessions, e.g., telephone, letter or email, but she did not take up this offer. The sessions alone were sufficient to allow Angela the necessary "space" to discuss and begin to deal with her difficulties. A high level of therapeutic engagement was facilitated by the videolink, as indicated by Angela's commitment to attending sessions and her openness in discussing her difficulties.

Formulation

It is likely that Angela was predisposed to developing eating difficulties due to her extremely low self-esteem, which had been present since childhood. She has a longstanding perception of herself as overweight, resulting in her feeling different from peers and family members. Throughout her childhood, she regarded herself as being inferior and not good enough and it is likely that her eating disorder emerged through a quest to feel more acceptable. It seems that her periods of food restriction as well as bingeing and vomiting developed as a means of coping with distress as well as an attempt to boost her self esteem.

Angela's predominant schemas, as identified in the YSQ-3, were defectiveness, emotional deprivation, social isolation, failure, self-sacrifice and punitiveness. As a consequence of her schemas she avoided close relationships and social situations and found it difficult to trust others. She also found it hard to express her own opinion or make others aware of her own emotional needs. She prioritised others and experienced extreme guilt if she failed to do so. Her eating disorder allowed her to avoid negative feelings elicited by her schemas being activated.

Treatment

Angela attended 6 initial sessions on a weekly basis via videolink prior to her baby being born. She then had a three-month break from therapy. Following this, she attended 22 weekly sessions and then attended a review appointment two months later, when she was discharged.

The cognitive elements of the treatment involved the use of postal services in order to provide Angela with the materials she required, e.g., schema diaries, flashcards. Entries were discussed during sessions, with Angela reading out the written details.

Experiential techniques were introduced in the latter part of the therapeutic contact. Although Angela had made significant cognitive shifts prior to this, she continued to struggle with the emotions elicited by her schemas. Therefore, it was agreed that guided imagery (Arntz & Weertman, 1999) would be used to allow her to cope more effectively with her difficult early childhood experiences which were fundamental to the development of her maladaptive schemas. Several different imagery exercises were conducted and Angela then practiced imagery at home in between sessions. The imagery commenced with Angela visualising a "safe place." She described the image as being vivid and she experienced a sense of safety and calm when she entered this image. This was a powerful coping tool for Angela, which she was encouraged to utilise in between sessions at times when she felt overwhelmed. Imagery was also conducted around difficult childhood memories. Powerful emotional responses were elicited over the videolink and Angela was eventually able to allow her to access the nurturance and comfort that she required within her images. This technique was extremely significant in encouraging emotional shifts and eventual schema modification.

Outcome

Angela made substantial progress throughout her course of therapy via videoconferencing. By her final review session, she no longer met criteria for an eating disorder, having ceased bingeing and purging entirely. She stated that she now valued herself too much to abuse her body through eating disordered behaviours. She also described vast improvements in confidence, social activity and her close relationships. She reported feeling able to assert herself and also to prioritise her own needs. Angela's schema questionnaires demonstrated clinically important changes to her schema profile. Following therapy, she no longer exhibited three out of her six maladaptive schemas and had developed healthy beliefs in relation to herself and her appearance.

Summary

The use of videoconferencing technology to deliver schema focused therapy did not appear to be a barrier to the formation of a positive therapeutic rela-

tionship. The experiential techniques used in schema therapy are highly specialised but were amenable for use via videolink and were evidently instrumental in helping Angela make significant emotional shifts. Angela commented in her final session that she had been most struck by the way she felt "different" about the difficult memories accessed throughout therapy. She described finding it easy to visualise the situations, in particular her safe place and reported strong affect arising when she accessed these memories. It seems that, even via videolink, it is possible to help a patient use experiential techniques effectively. It may be that the added privacy provided by being effectively alone in the room facilitated this process, possibly by reducing self-consciousness.

As Angela's formulation demonstrated, she exhibited failure, defectiveness and social isolation schemas. Such beliefs can be influential in the therapeutic setting, whereby the patient may experience activation of their schemas within therapy sessions. A significant component of SFT is dealing with schemas when they are triggered or played out within therapy sessions. An example of this was Angela's tendency to seek reassurance in relation to her homework exercises due to anxiety that her efforts would not be "good enough." This issue was easily identified and subsequently addressed within the therapeutic setting via videolink.

The therapist was able to provide "limited reparenting" specifically according to her clients' schemas. Nurturance, attunement and empathy were provided through active listening and validation (both verbal feedback and through facial expression), The client was actively encouraged and positively reinforced for efforts to change (through both verbal praise and nonverbal positive expressions). She was helped to challenge and confront her tendency to blame herself through experiential work, which seemed to be facilitated by the videolink due to reduced self-consciousness.

LEGAL AND ETHICAL ISSUES

Early evidence suggests that video therapy is a promising and effective means of offering psychotherapy to a range of client groups. Although large randomised controlled trials are lacking, it will be important to take note of the small scale research in this area. It may be that to withhold video therapy may be considered unethical in the future, especially from those who live in remote areas and cannot access treatment through other means. Individual professions within the field of psychotherapy should be actively involved in the development of guidelines and protocols that direct the expansion of mental health services through the use of videoconferencing. This will allow us to work more flexibly across a range of settings, whilst putting procedures in place will ensure that patients are aware of their rights and are protected within this technological arrangement. Therapists should also take reasonable steps to ensure effective outcome by measuring client progress in video therapy (Koocher, 2007; Reed et al., 2000).

One of the strengths of VTC is its ability to cross geographical barriers. However, as regulations and registration bodies for psychotherapists vary between states and countries, it will be essential to establish the legal and ethical implications of crossing these boundaries.

Capner (2000) suggests that therapists make explicit to patients that all services are considered to take place at the psychologist's place of work regardless of the location of the remote site in order to provide some protection against litigation, which may confuse this issue. In addition, she cautions that if therapists collaborate with other health professionals at remote sites, it is essential that the boundaries are clarified as to who is responsible and qualified to carry out which tasks, in order to avoid the risk of professional litigation. It is imperative that clinicians adhere to the particular standards governing their health profession and be conscious of upholding their duty of care to clients and most importantly ensuring that they are protected from harm.

Confidentiality of client visits and records must be ensured. Clients should be informed of risks (including the limits of confidentiality) and benefits associated with video therapy and their own responsibilities should be clarified in treatment. Importantly, clients should give their informed consent to take part, which may involve written contracts. This will also necessitate that reasonable security and encryption precautions are taken in providing services (Koocher, 2007).

CONCLUSION

Current evidence clearly supports the view that VTC can provide a milieu which is highly suited to the provision of psychological therapies. Larger randomised controlled trials are required to verify this and to identify the factors that may be crucial in establishing rapport with different client groups. In particular, this holds promise for communities living in remote and rural areas and others who are currently unable to access psychotherapy. The studies that have been conducted in this area point to the particular advantages of video therapy over other modes of delivery. Whilst retaining visual communication cues and "telepresence," video therapy can offer clients more personal space and control over their therapeutic experience. This can lead clients to feel less scrutinised and self conscious, thus making it more appealing to certain client groups such as those with avoidant coping styles and those with shame-based and body-image disorders.

REFERENCES

Agnew-Davies, R, Stiles, W. B., Hardy, G. E., Barkham, M., & Shapiro, D. A. (1998). Alliance structure assessed by the Agnew Relationship Measure (ARM). *British Journal of Clinical Psychology, 37*(2), 155–72.

Allen, A., & Hayes, J. (1994). Client satisfaction with telemedicine in a rural clinic. *American Journal of Public Health, 84*(10), 1693.

Allen, A., Roman, L., Cox, R., & Cardwell, B. (1996). Home health visits using a cable television network: User satisfaction. *Journal of Telemedicine and Telecare, 2*(Suppl. 1), 92–94.

Alexander L. B., & Luborsky L. (1984). The Penn helping alliance scales. In L. S. Greenberg and W. M. Pinsof (Eds.), *The psychotherapeutic process: A research handbook.* New York, NY: Guilford Press.

Arntz, A., & Weertman, A. (1999). Treatment of childhood memories: Theory and practice. *Behaviour Research and Therapy, 37*(8), 715–740.

Bakke, B., Mitchell, J., Wonderlich, S., & Erickson, R. (2001). Administering cognitive-behavioral therapy for BN via telemedicine in rural settings. *International Journal of Eating Disorders, 30*(4), 454–457.

Capner, M. (2000). Videoconferencing in the provision of psychological services at a distance. *Journal of Telemedicine and Telecare, 6*(6), 311–319.

Day, S. X., & Schneider. P. L. (2002). Psychotherapy using distance technology: A comparison of face-to-face, video and audio treatment. *Journal of Counseling Psychology, 49*(4), 499–503.

Forbes, M. (1996). Online in the outback: The use of videoconferencing by Australian aborigines. *Technology Review, 99*(3), 17–19.

Fussell, S. R., & Benimoff, I. (1995). Social and cognitive processes in interpersonal communication: Implications for advanced telecommunications technologies. *Human Factors, 37*(2), 228–250.

Ghosh, G. J., McLaren, P. M., & Watson, J. P. (1997). Evaluating the alliance in video-link teletherapy. *Journal of Telemedicine and Telecare, 3*(Suppl. 1), 33–35.

Glueckauf, R. L., Fritz, S. P., Ecklund-Johnson, E. P., Liss, H., Dages, P., & Carney, P. (2002). Videoconferencing-based family counselling for rural teenagers with epilepsy: Phase 1 findings. *Rehabilitation Psychology, 47*(1), 49–72.

Gougoux, F., Zatorre, R. J., Lassonde, M., Voss, P., & Lepore, F. (2005). A functional neuroimaging study of sound localization: Visual cortex activity predicts performance in early blind individuals. *PLoS Biology, 3*(2), e27. [Accessed May 21, 2009]. Available from: http://www.plosbiology. org/article/info%3Adoi%2F10.1371%2Fjo urnal.pbio.0030027.

Himle, J. A., Fischer, D. J., Muroff, J. R., Van Etten, L., Lokers, L. M., Abelson, J. L., & Hanna, G. L. (2006). Videoconferencing-based cognitive-behavioral therapy for obsessive-compulsive disorder. *Behaviour Research and Therapy, 44*(12), 1821–1829.

Holton, C. (2005). *Telecounselling to Arran: A qualitative analysis exploring client experience.* Unpublished MSc dissertation, University of Abertay and CCPS, NHS Ayrshire and Arran.

Kirkwood, K. (1998). *The validity of cognitive assessments via telecommunications links.* Unpublished PhD Thesis, University of Edinburgh.

Koocher, G. (2007). Twenty-first century ethical challenges for psychology. *American Psychologist, 62*(5). 375–384.

Krupnick, J. L., Sotsky, S. M., Elkin, I., Watkins, J., & Pilkonis, P. A. (1996). The role of the therapeutic alliance in psychotherapy and pharmacotherapy outcome: Findings in the National Institute of Mental Health Treatment of Depression Collaborative Research Program. *Journal of Consulting and Clinical Psychology, 64*(3), 532–539.

Mitchell, D., Simpson, S., Ferguson, J., & Smith, F. (2003). NHS staff attitudes to the use of videoconferencing to deliver clinical services. Poster presentation in: *TeleMed '03.* London: Royal Society of Medicine.

Omodei, M., & McClennan, J. (1998). 'The more I see you?' Face-to-face, video and telephone counselling compared. A programme of research investigating the emerging technology of videophone for counselling. *Australian Journal of Psychology, 50*(suppl.), 109.

Reed, G. M., McLaughlin, C. J., & Milholland, K. (2000). Ten interdiscipli-nary principles for professional practice in telehealth: Implications for psychology. *Professional Psychology: Research and Practice, 31*(2), 170–178.

Rees, C. S., & Haythornthwaite, S. (2004). Telepsychology and videoconferencing: Issues, opportunities and guidelines for psychologists. *Australian Psychologist, 39*(3), 212–219.

Rees, C. S., & Stone, S. (2005). Therapeutic alliance in face-to-face versus videoconferenced psychotherapy. *Professional Psychology: Research and Practice, 36*(6), 649–653.

Simpson, S. (2001). The provision of a psychology service to Shetland via teleconferencing: Patient/therapist satisfaction and ability to develop a therapeutic alliance. *Journal of Telemedicine and Telecare, 7*(suppl. 1), 34–36.

Simpson, S. (2003). Video counselling and psychotherapy in practice. In S. Goss & K. Anthony (Eds.), *Technology in counselling and psychotherapy: A practitioners' guide.* Basingstoke, UK: Palgrave/Macmillan.

Simpson, S., Deans, G., & Brebner, E. (2001). The delivery of a tele-psychology service to Shetland. *Clinical Psychology and Psychotherapy, 8*(Suppl. 2), 130–135.

Simpson, S., Morrow, E., Jones, M., Ferguson, J., & Brebner, E. (2002). Tele-hypnosis–The provision of specialised therapeutic treatments via teleconferencing. *Journal of Telemedicine and Telecare, 8*(suppl. 2), 78–79.

VandenBos, G. R., & Williams, S. (2000). The Internet versus the telephone: What is telehealth, anyway? *Professional Psychology: Research and Practice, 31*(5), 490–492.

Young, J. (1995). Downlinks in the outback: A videoconference between Yuendumu, Australia and San Francisco, California. *Forbes, 156*(13), 68–70.

Young, J., & Brown, G. (2003). *Young Schema Questionnaire-L3a.* New York: Schema Therapy Institute.

Young J. E., Klosko, J. S., & Weishaar, M. E. (2003). *Schema therapy: A practitioner's guide.* New York: Guilford Press.

Chapter 11

USING VIRTUAL REALITY TO CONDUCT A THERAPEUTIC RELATIONSHIP

John Wilson

INTRODUCTION

Second Life is a 3D online digital world imagined and created by its residents (Linden Lab, 2003).

This statement by Linden Labs, the creators of Second Life (SL), well describes the creativity and flexibility of this world for its residents. Residents are given an avatar (a computer generated persona in the virtual world) which can then do everything from building their own home to running a business, performing live music, making movies and, above all, creating relationships. SL is a Massively Multiplayer Online (MMO) game, an environment that is capable of supporting hundreds of thousands of players simultaneously via the Internet (Wikipedia, 2007).

MMO's now represent a significant part of the technology market–in 2006 there were over 12 million active subscriptions to online worlds with members spending more than a billion US dollars a year in subscriptions (Woodcock, 2006). More recently Steven Prentice of research firm Gartner stated that

in 2008 there were 30 million active users in virtual worlds and expects this rise to 50 million by 2011 (Schwartz, 2008). Another research firm, Strategy Analytics, predicts that by 2018 virtual worlds will be a market approaching one billion registrants and an eight billion dollar services opportunity (Gilbert, 2008). With this amount of people experiencing virtual worlds, even if therapists are not practicing there it is becoming more likely that a client will bring an issue which originated in a virtual world. For this chapter, I will be focusing on the virtual world that I have the most experience with–Second Life.

Although SL is not in the top 5 MMO's in terms of active members, there is a particular characteristic that sets SL apart. Many of the MMOs have specific individual and team goals, but SL does not and so is not in that sense a "game" but rather a space to exist in. This difference can be seen where a new resident might ask, "how long have you been playing SL?" whereas a longer-term resident may ask about where you live and work. This is an important realization for any therapist entering into SL. It is much more like traveling to another world than entering a game. This world is a social environment, with interactions ranging from a simple passing conversation with someone never to be seen again to the beginning of a long-lasting relationship and even an online sexual experience.

There is equality to SL that is not diminished by disability; all avatars can build, fly, run, jump, dance and communicate. An avatar called Wilde Cunningham is controlled by a group of nine adults with cerebral palsy (and their nurse). In SL they have built their own houses, have pets, gardens, even a baseball field. They also have many close friends and a large social network (Deeley 2008; Live2Give, 2005). There is also a degree of financial equality as materials can be formed out of thin air and as long as you have a connection to the Internet and a computer that can handle the graphics you can build and create without any more expense.

The feeling of being in another "place" is reinforced by SL having its own economy, the currency being Linden Dollars (L$). This allows residents to buy and sell everything from clothes, cars, houses, land and even the currency itself. In November, 2006, Business Week reported the first second life millionaire, an avatar named Anshe Chung, the online personality of Ailin Graef, who owned assets within SL valued at more than a million US dollars, after only two years inworld (life within SL) (Hof, 2007). Of course, not everyone who is working in SL is amassing such fortunes but more and more people are finding it possible to make some or even all of their living within SL either by setting up their own business or working for one of the many corporations that are now in SL including luxury brands like L'Oreal Paris and Calvin Klein, high street names such as Nokia, Thomson Holidays, Colgate and Nissan. There are even embassies to promote tourism established in SL by Sweden, The Maldives and Estonia. Consulting firms are promoting SL as a place to hold business meetings, allowing staff and clients to meet in the same place while still at their Real Life (RL) desks, saving traveling time and costs and making significant reductions to carbon footprints (Depoconsulting, 2007). This is of interest to therapists wishing to practice in SL, as there is the potential for clients to pay real money for a real service.

THERAPY IN SL

This raises the question, what does therapy look like in SL? How could a therapist communicate with a client? There are two primary ways to communicate in SL. Just typing on the keyboard allows text to be seen by any avatar close enough, which is fine for friendly social interactions. It is also possible to open an instant messaging (IM) conversation between your avatar and either one or several other avatars. This would look like the kind of conversation conducted in an online chat environment such as Windows Live Messenger. Many parts of SL are now voice enabled so you can have voice conversations, although this is still not as smooth as using text conversations due to the limitations of the technology and the volume of traffic experienced in some parts of SL. It also changes the experience of the interaction as it is now possible to hear what the person behind an avatar sounds like in RL. It remains to be seen whether this will become a primary means of communication in SL. It might be easy to conclude that working in SL is just the same as working with a standard online chat environment, or even telephone counseling as in the case of voice enabled conversations in SL. This would be to miss the richness of the visual content of SL and its impact on individuals and relationships.

The first building I used in SL was located on a sandy, sunny island right by the sea. The room I worked in had a large curved bay window that let in the lovely calming blue of the sea and the sight and sound of rolling waves. This kind of location and building would not be affordable to me in RL yet this idyllic setting is possible in SL. I have visited other therapists premises in SL and perhaps they have chosen a location and a building more suited to them and their work; a beautiful woodland setting with log cabin style buildings for example. The visual aspect of SL opens up the opportunity of not only a text-based relationship but of an environment that can be manipulated to the ideal requirements of both the therapist and the client. In RL many clients will be limited to the counselling options that are within a reasonable travelling distance from their home, limited further by their financial circumstances. In SL a client can choose from counselling services located all over the world offering different kinds of counselling approaches and fee scales. This reflects the greater sense of equality that the Internet can deliver and hopefully translates to a much greater choice

of counselling provision for the client within SL.

It is not only the environment that can be manipulated but the avatars' appearance also. It is possible for an avatar to be molded to any size or shape desired by its owner. Many people choose an avatar shape that most fits their vision of what is most sexually attractive in a human being and clothes to suit. This may present a challenge to the therapist if an avatar comes for counseling dressed in a way that is overtly sexually arousing. The client may have a paid role in SL where they dress in a sexually provocative manner and arrives in the therapist's office without changing their appearance. While not impossible in RL, perhaps it is more likely in SL due to the disinhibition that many individuals experience inworld. For many people in SL, it is an environment to meet online sexual partners and it is their norm to dress in a sexually provocative way. This may be rich material for therapy; as dress changes, it could be a sign of moving boundaries and changing conception of self. These are visual clues which are not available in online chat environments and therefore this sexual tone is prevalent in SL as much of the business and work available for avatars is in places that people would go for sexual experiences: pole dancing and strip clubs, for example. It is also easy for avatars to make sexual contact with others; sexual organs for avatars are easily purchased and attached, enabling almost instant virtual sexual contact with another person. This reflects the speed of connection to another human being in SL both sexually and emotionally. The disinhibition effect is very much present (Suler, 2004). The disinhibition is not only apparent in what people say but also in where they can go, visiting places they might not in

RL as they can preserve absolute anonymity. This creates opportunities for new kinds of behavior and for very intimate relationships to be formed extremely quickly.

This is where much of the emotional and psychological difficulties come from in SL. Perhaps someone makes a depth of connection with another human being they never felt was possible, or thought they would never experience again after the loss of a significant relationship. Many of these relationships end just as quickly as they started and can leave people in a great deal of distress. This is where it is really important for therapists to realize that the experience of their client is not within a game. These are real relationships created within a real environment, albeit a virtual one. So the sudden and often traumatic end to a relationship may have become an all-consuming issue to the client in SL and in RL. The therapist's ability to understand the reality of this distress and how it touches and stirs up RL experiences from the past such as relationship difficulties, bereavement and abuse, can be vital in enabling effective support of their client. Remembering that these experiences are not imagined "play" but an extension of the client's RL is essential (Anthony, 2001).

Because of the reality of these experiences, it is often possible to transpose the therapist's face-to-face skills into SL. I am a person-centered trained practitioner and find the online disinhibition effect very helpful in meeting clients at relational depth (Mearns & Cooper, 2005). Of course, this must come with the caveat that there is a risk to the client if allowed to charge into a relationship without boundaries allowing a sudden dependence on the therapist and possibly repeating the behavior apparent in

other SL and RL relationships. As in a face-to-face relationship, I am open to meeting at depth and keep one eye on what is actually beneficial to the client's mental well-being. This may mean a referral on to another kind of practitioner if I am not the most beneficial resource for the client.

Of course, many counseling approaches have the possibility to be transferred into SL. The text-based environment that includes the facility to pass written material between avatars in the form of "notecards" could be particularly useful for counsellors who use Cognitive Behavioural Therapy (CBT) interventions. This approach to counselling is in part educational so the RL CBT counsellor may use pen and paper, a whiteboard, set homework and recommend further reading in the form of books or websites (Willson & Branch, 2006). This can be easily replicated in SL as the counselor and client can share written material between them during the session by using notecards, which may contain the written aspects of the session, the homework tasks, hyperlinks to further reading sources and affirmations for anxiety provoking circumstances. More experiential approaches to counseling such as Gestalt and Process-Experiential/Emotion-Focused Therapy use empty chair interventions to address client's sub personalities and family relationships (Ivey & Ivey, 1999; Greenberg et al., 1993). It is an easy task in SL to introduce multiple chairs and although a little more complicated, multiple avatars could be created which resemble these subpersonalities or family members.

Because the client and the therapist are inworld together, they could engage in activities together. Outdoor and wilderness therapy are growing fields in the UK and could be recreated in SL.

Anxiety provoking experiences could be recreated inworld and therapist and client could work on strategies together– this is already happening using VR Exposure Therapy (VRE) where virtual reality technology is used to present a person with the subject of their phobia, for example a spider, and as their anxiety reduces the exposure is increased until the phobia is either manageable or even eliminated (EmmelKamp et al., 2001). Experiential Cognitive Therapy (ECT) integrates virtual reality technology with CBT to treat eating disorders (Perpiña et al., 1999). Clients experience a virtual environment in order to increase body awareness through the manipulation of body shape and their experience of plac- ing that body shape into various con- texts, including a kitchen and facing attractive persons. To create these virtual reality experiences, therapists have had to use expensive equipment to help their clients become immersed in these envi- ronments. However, SL now offers the possibility of creating similar experi- ences at a much-reduced cost.

The low cost yet immersive experi- ence of SL has also been utilized by The Center for BrainHealth, University of Texas at Dallas, for people with As- pergers Syndrome (Nagel, 2009). So dra- matic is the potential of the work that Dr Chapman of the Brainhealth Center de- scribes interventions as able to rewire the brain. People with Asperger's syndrome have normal intelligence, but they have cognitive deficits that impact on their social skills. People with Asperger's syn- drome often struggle to notice and respond to social cues such as body lan- guage and facial expressions. In a social situation such as ordering a cup of coffee or maintaining a friendship, the impact of not responding to social cues can be immediate and distressing creating avoid- ance of important and nourishing social contact.

The Brainhealth Center is using the virtual environment of Second Life to recreate these situations without the pres- sure or threat of negative outcome if social cues are missed. This allows time and space to practice and strengthen social skills which can then be trans- ferred to life outside the BrainHealth Center.

There is an ethical question of work- ing in an environment where there has been very little or no research done about the efficacy of counseling in SL. So what research and established ways of working can a SL therapist draw on? Firstly, the research and established prin- ciples of face-to-face therapy are invalu- able to the therapist working in SL and form the bedrock of how the therapist works. There is a growing acceptance in the therapeutic community that instead of any one form of therapy being most effective, it is the relationship formed between therapist and client that is most important in arriving at a good outcome for the client: "It's the relationship that heals, the relationship that heals, the relationship that heals–my professional rosary" (Yalom, 1989, p. 92). In a social world such as SL, where many people are there for the purpose of meeting peo- ple and forming relationships, the envi- ronment is already conducive to this form of healing by relationship. Second, the important research already conduct- ed in online counseling is also appropri- ate for SL therapy. Suler's work, already mentioned here, is particularly impor- tant with regard to the powerful disinhi- bition effect experienced in SL as text based communication is combined with a very vivid visual experience (Suler, 2004).

There have been research projects

conducted in MMO environments where the effects of getting to know someone online before seeing a photograph or meeting them face-to-face have been investigated (Jacobson, 1999). There was some evidence to suggest that characteristics from people we know can be transposed onto the people we meet in MMOs. This is as if the brain wants to have answers to the questions we have about the people we meet, how tall are they, what color of hair do they have, where do they come from—and if this information isn't forthcoming from the person we meet, our brains are quite capable of filling in the blanks with information from people we already know. This is of particular interest to therapists working in SL as we might be working with someone who for some reason triggers a memory of someone we know, perhaps someone we are close to and before we realize we seem to talking to this client as if they are our mother/ brother/friend. So the SL therapist has the same challenge as therapists who use text base interventions with the added challenge of the visual presentation of the client via the chosen avatar, how it is dressed and how it is shaped. Any of these factors provide material for the brain that could be filling in the "blanks" inappropriately.

It is important not to underestimate the importance of the visual presentation of the avatar. As it has been created by the client it would make sense that it contains some expression of the client's psyche. Perhaps the avatar may be something very different from the client, formulated to protect the client from being seen by others within SL as they are in RL. This is not always so different from what happens in RL where we find ourselves presenting a "face" to the outside world that we hope is more desirable or

acceptable. The "face" we present might be nearer a person we would rather be, the person we "wish" to be. The possibilities for this in SL are endless. It is possible to choose what we look like, where we "live" and of course how we act. Add to this the reality of being able to change our avatar completely every time we log into SL and suddenly no one knows who we are, which brings great freedom to speech and actions.

This is all rich material for therapy. As the therapist there is the opportunity to meet the person that our clients wish to be, or who they wish to become. Instead of talking about this we can be right there with them, meeting, talking to and, perhaps, challenging this way of being. The most exciting aspect for me about working with people in a virtual environment is experiencing the visual representation of how clients see themselves. It would be a wrong assumption that everyone in SL seeks an avatar that is, to their mind, a sexually attractive human form. I have met people who have adopted animal shapes such as ears and tails into their human form or whose avatar is completely of animal form. Other avatars are molded to shapes that are not visually attractive at all, such as a troll, for example. Some avatars are even able to take on machine like appearances that more resemble something robotic than organic.

Some people have adopted the form of children and while there are different thoughts inworld about the appropriateness and the safety of doing this in an adult world there is also the possibility of the inner child being expressed in a way perhaps not possible in an adult body either in RL or SL. There is a very interesting research question to ask in what the therapeutic opportunities might be for someone who wishes to take care of their inner self in this way. One subject of interest lies is in the avatar representing a "part" of the person, a "sub-personality" or a "configuration of self" (Mearns & Thorne, 2000). Rowan (1990) states that this kind of thinking has been around since the writings of Freud and Jung and he also discusses the various theories and approaches in therapy to working with "parts" of a client's personality (Rowan & Cooper, 1998). What is particularly exciting about SL is the possibility to create a visual representation of a sub-personality. Keith Slyvester, a psychosynthesis therapist, describes being able to live unlived parts of yourself (Daniel, 2008). He states that often in therapy we are invited to connect to a sub-personality through drawing or guided fantasy but in SL people can experience this connection in a much more open way. A client may have a sub-personality that feels like a little boy, mischievous and always up to something; another part may be much more feminine and seductive and yet another part that is more like a scolding elderly lady. It would be possible to shape an avatar to visually represent any of these three sub-personalities. They could even meet one another. All three of these avatars might look nothing like the person in real life, but they may speak to us visually and verbally in a way that wouldn't be possible in our RL office.

Of course, there is a danger in working online where we start to touch the very deep places in another human and we are not physically present to facilitate and hold this process. The SL therapist must always be aware of the safety of their client.

The security of client interaction has become an increasingly important part of online counselling as seen by the guidelines produced by the British Asso-

ciation for Counselling and Psychotherapy for online counselling (Anthony & Goss, 2009) and the Online Therapy Institute's *Ethical Framework for the Use of Technology in Mental Health* (Nagel & Anthony, 2009), both of which give much weight to the need for encrypting all client communication between clients and therapists, from arranging sessions to the actual therapeutic communication. This presents a challenge for therapists working within SL as communication is not automatically encrypted and anyone experienced in accessing communications in SL can have nearly x-ray vision as any structural boundaries are only digital and not material.

There are steps that can be taken to heighten client confidentiality within SL. A counseling room can be moved to a "Skybox," a structure that is positioned hundreds of metres above SL ground level where avatars are not able to walk or fly. In a ground level consulting room an avatar may happen to walk by and be able to see through the walls of the consulting room and notice the client. This is not possible with a skybox, as an avatar would need to make a deliberate attempt to travel to the skybox, which can be prevented by the installation of a simple security device that only allows the therapist and client to be in or near the skybox.

There still remains the issue of the communication between client and therapist traveling through SL servers without any kind of encryption ruling out use of SL's own current text communication methods (even those noted above) for confidential exchanges of information. This can be overcome by mixing platforms, such as being in the SL consulting room with the client but utilizing an encrypted platform such as Skype to communicate by either text or voice.

The nature of the therapy may mean that any kind of contact between the client's avatar with a known therapeutic entity whether it is an avatar belonging to a known therapist or a structure maintained by a known therapist is not acceptable. And yet for the client to show the therapist their current avatar as a visible expression of themselves in the moment may be vital for the therapeutic connection. In that case, it may be possible for the client to meet an avatar controlled by the therapist but not known as a therapist in a location not known as a therapeutic space. Once the client has become visible to the therapist and this part of the communication is over, the avatars can separate and the therapeutic contact can continue in another platform outside of SL which is encrypted and secure.

During an interview with *Inner World* magazine, Kate Anthony and DeeAnna Merz Nagel of the Online Therapy Institute discussed these issues of confidentiality, the lack of encryption in SL and their decision not to work with clients therapeutically within SL (Valeeva, 2009). While happy to meet clients for an initial general consultation within SL, they have decided that actual therapeutic content is better undertaken in a completely encrypted environment. This clear decision by leading authorities on online counselling is not made with the intention to prevent therapeutic contact of *any* kind in SL but is a signal to all who choose to practice within SL that the issues of client confidentiality must be taken seriously and the choices made must reflect the informed choice of a therapist who has taken time to consider the risks and benefits to both themselves and their clients.

CONCLUSION

Thinking of what is ahead for counseling in SL, it seems likely that it will be an area of growth attracting more professionals and more clients. At the moment there are lots of people who would gladly use a counseling service in SL but who do not have the means to pay the RL equivalent counseling fees. They are in SL because it is a way of accessing a lifestyle that their RL financial circumstances wouldn't allow. There are others who can afford counseling but are not sure what is available and what is safe and questions about who is a qualified and trained counselor are harder, but not impossible, to establish in SL. These questions will also be asked by businesses operating in SL who have a duty of care to their employees which at times will mean counselling. This demand for

counselling creates a responsibility for SL counsellors to work to the highest standards of practice and to publish research that establishes and improves counselling within SL. So there is a need for quality training for counsellors wishing to work in SL, there are already training programs for counsellors wishing to work online using email and instant messaging such as the training provided by the Online Therapy Insitute, which is well placed to offer further training to work in SL. SL would do well to offer a specific secure and encrypted environment in which to do this work so that therapists and others with a need to communicate with an assurance of privacy can offer the best standard of care to clients seeking counselling. SL will also need some kind of accrediting body that clients can trust to check counsellors' qualifications and provide an enforceable code of conduct, helping reduce clients' anxiety around choosing a qualified counsellor and protect their safety during the counselling relationship.

SL is much more than a substitute for a Real Life–it is an extension of RL, another place to meet and work and play and by extension receive therapeutic help. As such a place it will want and need many things including a good and effective standard of counselling delivered by committed professionals.

REFERENCES

Anthony, K. (2001). Online relationships and cyberinfidelity. *Counselling Journal, 12*(9) 38–39 [online]. [Accessed May 26, 2009]. Available from: www.kateanthony.co.uk.

Anthony, K., & Goss, S. (2009). *Guidelines for online counselling and psychotherapy including guidelines for online supervision* (3rd ed.). Lutterworth: BACP.

Daniel, J. (2008). The self set free. *Therapy Today, 19*(9), 4–9.

Deeley, L. (2008). Is this a real life, is this just fantasy? *TimesOnline* [online]. [Accessed May 26, 2009]. Available from: http://women.timesonline.co.uk/tol/life_and_style/women/body_and_soul/article1557980.ece.

Depo-consulting. (2007). Saving money while reducing your carbon footprint. *Depo-consulting.com* [online]. [Accessed January 5, 2008]. Available from: http://www.depoconsulting.com/files/saving-carbon-121207.pdf.

EmmelKamp, P. M., Bruynzeel, M., Drost, L., & van der Mast, C. A. P. G. (2001). Virtual reality treatment in acrophobia: A comparison with exposure in vivo. *Cyber-Psychology and Behavior, 4*(3), 335–340.

Greenberg, L. S., Rice, L. N., & Elliott, R. (1993). *Facilitating emotional change.* New York: Guilford Press.

Gilbert, B. (2008). Virtual worlds projected to mushroom to nearly one billion users. *Strategy analytics* [online]. [Accessed May 26, 2009]. Available from: http://www.strategyanalytics.com/default.aspx?mod=PressReleaseViewer&a0=3983.

Hof, R. (2007). Second life's first millionaire. *The Tech Beat* [online]. [Accessed May 26, 2009]. Available from: http://www.businessweek.com/the_thread/techbeat/archives/2006/11/second_lifes_fi.html.

Ivey, A. E., & Ivey, M. B. (1999). *Intentional interviewing and counseling.* Pacific Grove, CA: Brooks/Cole.

Jacobson, D. (1999). Impression formation in cyberspace: Online expectations and offline experiences in text-based virtual communities. *Journal of Computer-Mediated Communication* [online]. [Accessed January 5, 2008]. Available from: http://jcmc.indiana.edu/vol5/issue1/jacobson.html.

Linden Lab. (2003). *Second life* [online]. [Accessed January 5, 2008]. Available from: http://secondlife.com.

Live2Give. (2005). All about live2give. *Live2Give* [online]. [Accessed January 9, 2005]. Available from: http://braintalk.blogs.com/live2give/2005/01/all_about_live2.html.

Mearns, D., & Thorne, B. (2000). *Person centred therapy today.* London: Sage.

Mearns, D., & Cooper, M. (2005). *Working at relational depth in counselling and psychotherapy.* London: Sage.

Nagel, D. M. (2009). People with asperger's syndrome learn social skills in second life. *Telehealth World, 2*(1), 1-8 [online]. [Accessed May 1, 2009]. Available from: http://www.telehealthworld.com/images/Spring09.pdf.

Nagel, D. M., & Anthony, K. (2009). Ethical framework for the use of technology in mental health [online]. *Online Therapy Institute*. [Accessed May 26, 2009]. Available from: http://www.onlinetherapyinstitute.com/id43.html.

Perpiña, C., Botella, C., Baños, R. M., Marco, H., Alcañiz, M., & Quero S. (1999). Body image and virtual reality in eating disorders: Exposure by virtual reality is more effective than the classical body image treatment? *CyberPsychology and Behavior, 2*(2), 149–155.

Rowan, J. (1990). *Subpersonalities: The people inside us.* London: Routledge.

Rowan, J., & Cooper, M. (1998). *Plural self (Multiplicity in everyday life).* London: Sage.

Schwartz, D. (2008). Noted gartner analyst Steven Prentice updates his predictions on virtual worlds. *Fast company* [online]. [Accessed May 26, 2009]. Available from: http://www.fastcompany.com/blog/donald-schwartz/fc-technology-moderator-blog/noted-gartner-analyst-steven-prentice-updates-his-.

Suler, J. (2004). The online disinhibition effect [online]. *The Psychology of Cyberspace* [online]. [Accessed May 26, 2009]. Available from: http://users.rider.edu/~suler/psycyber/disinhibit.html.

Valeeva, A. (2009). *Online Therapy Institute. Inner-World Magazine,* 2 32-35 [online]. [Accessed May 26, 2009]. Available from: http://issuu.com/inner-world/docs/innerworld2eng/33.

Wikipedia. (2007). Massively multiplayer online game. *Wikipedia, The Free Encyclopedia* [online]. [Accessed May 26, 2009]. Available from: http://en.wikipedia.org/w/index.php?title=Massively_multiplayer_online_game&oldid=181066643.

Willson, R., & Branch, R. (2006). *Cognitive behavioural therapy for dummies.* Chichester: John Wiley and Sons.

Woodcock, B. S. (2007). An analysis of MMOG subscription growth. *mmogchart.com* [online]. [Accessed January 5, 2008]. Available from: http://www.mmogchart.com/analysis-and-conclusions/.

Yalom, I. D. (1989). *Love's executioner.* London: Penguin Books.

Chapter 12

USING VIRTUAL REALITY
IMMERSION THERAPEUTICALLY

Giuseppe Riva

INTRODUCTION

How is it possible to change a client? Even if this question has many different answers according to the specific psychotherapeutic approach, in general change comes through an intense focus on a particular instance or experience (Wolfe, 2002): by exploring it as much as possible, the client can relive all of the significant elements associated with it (i.e., conceptual, emotional, motivational and behavioral) and make them available for a reorganization of his or her perspective.

Within this general model we have, for example, the insight-based approach of psychoanalysis, the schema-reorganization goals of cognitive therapy or the enhancement of experience awareness in experiential therapies. What are the differences between them? According to Safran and Greenberg (1991), behind the specific therapeutic approach, we can find two different model of change: bottom-up and top-down.

These two models of change are focused on two different cognitive systems, one for information transmission (top-down) and one for conscious experience (bottom-up), both of which may process sensory input. The existence of two different cognitive systems is clearly shown by the distinction between verbal knowledge and task performance: people learn to control dynamic systems without being able to specify the nature of the relations within the system and they can sometimes describe the rules by which the system operates without being able to put them into practice.

Even if many therapeutic approaches are based on just one of the two change models, a therapist usually requires both. Some clients seem to operate primarily by means of top-down information processing, which may then prepare the way for corrective emotional experiences. For others the appropriate access point is the intensification of their emotional experience and their awareness of it. Finally, different clients who initially engage the therapeutic work only through top-down processing may be able later in the therapy to make use of bottom-up emotional processing. A possible way to address this issue is through use of advanced technologies. In particular, using a novel technology–Virtual Reality (VR)–it is now possible to create synthetic experiences that allow both bottom-up and top-down interventions.

A VR system is the combination of the hardware and software that enables developers to create synthetic life-like experiences. The hardware components receive input from user-controlled devices and convey multisensory output to create the illusion of a virtual world. The software component of a VR system manages the hardware that makes up the VR system. The virtual world may be a model of a real-world object, such as a house, or an abstract world that does not exist in a real sense but is understood by humans, such as a chemical molecule or a representation of a set of data, or it might be a completely imaginary world.

According to the hardware and software included in a VR system, it is possible to distinguish between:

- *Fully Immersive VR:* the user appears to be fully inserted in the computer generated environment. This illusion is produced by providing immersive output devices (e.g., head mounted display, force feedback robotic arms, etc.) and a system of head/body tracking to guarantee the exact correspondence and co-ordination of users' movements with the feedback of the environment.
- *CAVE:* This is a small room where a computer-generated world is projected on the walls. This solution is particularly suitable for collective VR experiences because it allows different people to share the same experience at the same time.
- *Augmented:* the user's view of the world is supplemented with virtual objects, usually to provide information about the real environment.
- *Desktop VR:* uses subjective immersion on a standard PC screen. The feeling of immersion can be improved through stereoscopic vision.

VR IN CLINICAL PSYCHOLOGY

Several VR applications for the understanding, assessment and treatment of mental health problems have been developed in the last 15 years (Riva, 2005).

Typically, in VR Exposure (VRE) therapy the client learns to manipulate problematic situations related to his/her difficulties by working both on its experiential/emotional and cognitive/behavioral aspects. For this reason, common applications of VR in this area include the treatment of anxiety disorders (Emmelkamp, 2005; Parsons & Rizzo, 2008), simple phobias (Krijn et al., 2007;

Rothbaum et al., 2006), to panic disorders (Botella et al., 2007; Vincelli et al., 2003) and posttraumatic stress disorder (Gerardi et al., 2008; Rothbaum et al., 2001).

Indeed, VRE has been proposed as a new medium for exposure therapy (Gorini & Riva, 2008) that is safer, less embarrassing and less costly than reproducing the real world situations. The rationale is simple: in VR the client is intentionally confronted with the feared stimuli while allowing the anxiety to attenuate. Avoiding a dreaded situation reinforces a phobia and each successive exposure to it reduces the anxiety through the processes of habituation and extinction.

VRE offers a number of advantages over *in vivo* or imaginal exposure. Firstly, VRE can be administered in traditional therapeutic settings. This means VRE may be more convenient, controlled and cost-effective than *in vivo* exposure. Secondly, it can also isolate fear components more efficiently than in vivo exposure. For instance, in treating fear of flying, if landing is the most fearful part of the experience, landing can be repeated as often as necessary without having to wait for the airplane to take-off. Finally, the immersive nature of VRE provides a real-like experience that may be more emotionally engaging than imaginal exposure.

However, it seems likely that VR can be more than a tool to provide exposure and desensitisation (Riva, 2005). As noted by Glantz et al. (1997), "VR technology may create enough capabilities to profoundly influence the shape of therapy" (p. 92). In fact, the key characteristics of virtual environments for most clinical applications are the high level of control of the interaction with the tool and the enriched experience provided to the client (Schultheis & Rizzo, 2001).

On the one hand, it can be described as an advanced form of human-computer interface that allows the user to interact with and become immersed in a computer-generated environment in a naturalistic fashion. On the other hand, VR can also be considered as an advanced imaginal system: a medium that is as effective as reality in inducing emotional responses. This is achieved through its ability to induce a feeling of "presence" in the computer-generated world experienced by the user (Riva et al., 2007).

These features transform VR in an "empowering environment," a special, sheltered setting where clients can start to explore and act without feeling actually threatened (Botella et al., 2007). Nothing the client fears can "really" happen to them in VR. With such assurance, they can more freely explore, experiment, feel, live and experience feelings and/or thoughts. VR thus becomes a very useful intermediate step between the therapist's office and the real world (Botella et al., 2004).

Emerging applications of VR in psychotherapy include sexual disorders (Optale, 2003; Optale et al., 1998), pain management (Hoffman, 2004; Hoffman et al., 2008), addictions (Bordnick et al., 2005; Bordnick et al., 2008; Gatti et al., 2008; Lee et al., 2007), persecutory delusions (Fornells-Ambrojo et al., 2008), stress management (Villani et al., 2007) and eating disorders and obesity (Riva et al., 2003; Riva et al., 2006).

In fact, immersive VR can be considered an "embodied technology" for its effects on body perceptions (Lambrey & Berthoz, 2003; Riva, 2008; Vidal et al., 2003; Vidal et al., 2004). VR users become aware of their bodies during navigation: e.g., their head movements alter what they see. The sensorimotor coordination of the moving head with visual displays produces a much higher level of sensorimotor feedback and first person perspective (egocentric reference frame).

For example, through the use of immersive VR, it is possible to induce a controlled sensory rearrangement that facilitates the update of the biased body image. This allows the differentiation and integration of new information, leading to a new sense of cohesiveness and consistency in how the self represents the body. The results of this approach are very promising. As shown by different experimental research, VR is effective in producing fast changes in body experience (Murray & Gordon, 2001; Riva, 1998) and in body dissatisfaction (Riva et al., 1998; Riva et al., 2000; Riva et al., 2002; Perpiña et al., 2003; Riva et al., 2004; Riva et al., 2006) that may improve long term outcome of the cognitive behavioural approach to eating disorders and obesity.

Apparently, a similar approach may be used in other pathologies. Lambrey and Berthoz (2003) showed that subjects use conflicting visual and nonvisual information differently according to individual "perceptive styles" (bottom-up processes) and that these "perceptive styles" are made more observable by the subjects changing their perceptive strategy, i.e., reweighting (top-down processes).

Viaud-Delmon and colleagues (Viaud-Delmon et al., 2000; Viaud-Delmon et al., 2002) showed that subjects with high trait anxiety, such as subjects with symptoms of panic and agoraphobia, have a strong dependence on a particular reference frame in which the sensory information are interpreted and in which the subject would remain anchored. A VR experience aimed at modifying the sensory reference frame may be useful in speeding up the process of change. Future studies are needed both to identify specific perceptive styles in different pathologies and to define the best protocols for changing them.

Future VR clinical applications will also include online virtual worlds (such as Second Life, There or Active Worlds): computer-based simulated environments characterized by the simultaneous presence of multiple users within the same simulated space, who inhabit and interact via avatars (Gorini et al., 2007). Online virtual worlds can be considered as 3-D social networks, where people can collaboratively create and edit objects, besides meeting each other and interacting with existing objects (Gorini et al., 2008). Over the last few years the number of virtual worlds' users has dramatically increased and today Second Life, the largest 3-D on line digital world, counts about 12 million subscribers.

VR IN CLINICAL PRACTICE: FROM THEORY TO PRACTICE

Although it is undisputable that VR has come of age for clinical and research applications, the majority of them are still in the laboratory or investigation stage. In a review, Riva (2005) identified four major issues that limit the use of VR in psychotherapy:

- the lack of standardisation in VR hardware and software and the limited possibility of tailoring the virtual environments (VEs) to the specific requirements of the clinical or the experimental setting;

- the low availability of standardised protocols that can be shared by the community of researchers;
- the high costs (up to 200,000 US$) required for designing and testing a clinical VR application;
- VEs in use today not being user-friendly, as expensive technical support or continual maintenance are often required.

To address these challenges, we have designed and developed NeuroVR (http://www.neurovr.org), a cost-free virtual reality platform based on open-source software, that allows nonexpert users to easily modify a virtual environment (VE) and to visualise it using either an immersive or nonimmersive system.

The NeuroVR platform is implemented using open-source components that provide advanced features; this includes an interactive rendering system based on OpenGL, which allows for high quality images. The NeuroVR Editor is realised by customising the user interface of Blender, an integrated suite of 3D creation tools available on all major operating systems; this implies that the program can be distributed even with the complete source code. Thanks to these features, clinicians and researchers have the freedom to run, copy, distribute, study, change and improve the Neuro VR Editor software, so that the whole VR community benefits.

THE NEUROVR EDITOR

The majority of existing VEs for psychotherapy are proprietary and have closed source code, meaning they cannot be tailored from the ground up to fit specific needs of different clinical applications (Riva, 2005). NeuroVR addresses these issues by providing the clinical professional with a cost-free VE editor, which allows nonexpert users to easily modify a virtual scene to best suit the needs of the clinical setting.

USING THE NEUROVR EDITOR

The psychological stimuli/stressors appropriate for any given scenario (see Figure 12.1) can be chosen from a rich database of 2D and 3D objects and easily placed into the pre-designed virtual scenario by using an icon-based interface (no programming skills are required). In addition to static objects, the NeuroVR Editor allows the user to combine a video with the 3D background to create the appearance of partial transparency (known as alpha compositing).

The editing of the scene is performed in real time and effects of changes can be checked from different views (frontal, lateral and top). Currently, the NeuroVR library includes different pre-designed virtual scenes, representing typical real-life situations, e.g., the supermarket, the apartment, the park. These VEs have been designed, developed and assessed in the past ten years by a multidisciplinary research team in several clinical trials, which have involved over 400 clients (Riva et al., 2004). On the basis of this experience, only the most effective VEs have been selected for inclusion in the NeuroVR library.

An interesting feature of the Neuro VR Editor is the possibility to add new objects to the database. This feature allows the therapist to enhance the client's feeling of familiarity and intimacy with the virtual scene by using photos of objects/people that are part of the client's daily life, thereby improving the efficacy of the exposure (Riva et al., 2004).

Figure 12.1. A screenshot taken from the NeuroVR Editor.

THE NEUROVR PLAYER

The second main component of NeuroVR is the Player, which allows the user to navigate and interact with the VEs created using the NeuroVR Editor. When running simulations, the system offers a set of standard features that contribute to increase the realism of the simulated scene. These include collision detection to control movements in the environment, realistic walk-style motion, advanced lighting techniques for enhanced image quality and streaming of video textures using alpha channel for transparency.

The NeuroVR player can be config-ured for two basic visualisation modalities: immersive and non-immersive. The immersive modality allows the scene to be visualised using a head-mounted display, either in stereoscopic or in mono-mode; compatibility with head-tracking sensor is also provided. In the nonimmersive modality, the virtual environment can be displayed using a desktop monitor or a wall projector. The user can interact with the virtual environment using either keyboard commands, a mouse or a joypad, depending on the hardware configuration chosen.

CONCLUSION

Clients are not all the same. Some clients seem to operate primarily by means of top-down information processing (from cognition to emotions), which may then prime the way for corrective emotional experiences. For others, the appropriate access point is the intensification of their emotional experience and their awareness of it (from emotions to cognitions). Nevertheless, psychotherapeutic approaches usually do not target both paths for change, even if having a dual approach could improve the long-term efficacy of the treatment. The use of Virtual Reality (VR), an experiential technology that puts the client inside a life-like synthetic world, can be a solution for this issue.

The key characteristics of virtual environments for most clinical applications are the high level of control of the interaction with the tool and the enriched experience provided to the client (Schultheis & Rizzo, 2001). For these features, VR is described as a "simulation technology" with and within which people can interact. In summary, VR provides a new human-computer interaction paradigm in which users are no longer simply external observers of images on a computer screen but are active participants within a computer-generated three-dimensional virtual world (Riva, 1997).

Even if the potential impact of VR in clinical psychology is high—as shown by the many articles discussing VR applications for simple phobias (Krijn et al., 2007; Rothbaum et al., 2006), panic disorders (Botella et al., 2007; Vincelli et al., 2003), posttraumatic stress disorder (Gerardi et al., 2008; Rothbaum et al., 2001), sexual disorders (Optale, 2003; Optale et al., 1998), pain management

(Hoffman, 2004; Hoffman et al., 2008), addictions (Bordnick et al., 2005; Bordnick et al., 2008; Gatti et al., 2008; Lee et al., 2007), persecutory delusions (Fornells-Ambrojo et al., 2008), stress management (Villani et al., 2007) and eating disorders and obesity (Riva et al., 2006; Riva et al., 2003)—the majority of the existing clinical VR applications are still in the laboratory or investigation stage.

To address the challenges outlined in this chapter, we have designed and developed NeuroVR (http://www.neuro vr.org), a cost-free virtual reality platform based on open-source software that allows nonexpert users to test VR use in clinical practice using either an immersive or nonimmersive system. Currently, the NeuroVR library includes different predesigned virtual worlds that can be easily adapted for targeting different clinical applications: from phobias to eating disorders.

However, to exploit the full potential of VR tools the development of future clinical applications will require multidisciplinary teams of engineers, computer programmers and therapists working in concert to treat specific problems. Hopefully, by bringing this community of experts together, further interest from clinicians and granting agencies will be stimulated. In particular, information on VR technology must be made available to the health care community in a format that is easy-to-understand and which invites participation.

Acknowledgment

The present work was supported by the Italian MIUR FIRB programme (Project "IVT2010–Immersive Virtual.

Telepresence (IVT) for Experiential Assessment and Rehabilitation–RBIN 04BC5C) and by the European Union IST Programme (Project "INTREPID– A Virtual Reality Intelligent Multi-sensor Wearable System for Phobias' Treatment"–IST-2002- 507464).

REFERENCES

Bordnick, P. S., Graap, K. M., Copp, H. L., Brooks, J., & Ferrer, M. (2005). Virtual reality cue reactivity assessment in cigarette smokers. *Cyberpsychology and Behavior, 8*(5), 487–492.

Bordnick, P. S., Traylor, A., Copp, H. L., Graap, K. M., Carter, B., Ferrer, M., & Walton, A. P. (2008). Assessing reactivity to virtual reality alcohol based cues. *Addictive Behaviors, 33*(6), 743–756.

Botella, C., Garcìa-Palacios, A., Villa, H., Baños, R. M., Quero, M., Alcañiz, M., & Riva, G. (2007). Virtual reality exposure in the treatment of panic disorder and agoraphobia: A controlled study. *Clinical Psychology and Psychotherapy, 14*(3), 164–175.

Botella, C., Quero, S., Baños, R. M., Perpiña, C., Garcia Palacios, A., & Riva, G. (2004). Virtual reality and psychotherapy. *Studies in Health Technology and Informatics, 99,* 37–54.

Emmelkamp, P. M. (2005). Technological innovations in clinical assessment and psychotherapy. *Psychotherapy and Psychosomatics, 74*(6), 336–343.

Fornells-Ambrojo, M., Barker, C., Swapp, D., Slater, M., Antley, A., & Freeman, D. (2008). Virtual reality and persecutory delusions: Safety and feasibility. *Schizophrenia Research, 104*(1–3), 228–236.

Gatti, E., Massari, R., Sacchelli, C., Lops, T., Gatti, R., & Riva, G. (2008). Why do you drink? Virtual reality as an experiential medium for the assessment of alcohol-dependent individuals. *Studies in Health Technology and Informatics, 132,* 132–137.

Gerardi, M., Rothbaum, B. O., Ressler, K., Heekin, M., & Rizzo, A. (2008). Virtual reality exposure therapy using a virtual Iraq: Case report. *Journal of Traumatic Stress, 21*(2), 209–213.

Glantz, K., Durlach, N. I., Barnett, R. C., & Aviles, W. A. (1997). Virtual reality (VR) and psychotherapy: Opportunities and challenges. *Presence, Teleoperators, and Virtual Environments, 6*(1), 87–105.

Gorini, A., Gaggioli, A., & Riva, G. (2007). Virtual worlds, real healing. *Science, 318*(5856), 1549.

Gorini, A., Gaggioli, A., Vigna, C., & Riva, G. (2008). A second life for eHealth: Prospects for the use of 3-D virtual worlds in clinical psychology. *Journal of Medical Internet Research, 10*(3), e21.

Gorini, A., & Riva, G. (2008). Virtual reality in anxiety disorders: The past and the future. *Expert Review of Neurotherapeutics, 8*(2), 215–233.

Hoffman, H. G. (2004). Virtual-reality therapy: Clients can get relief from pain or overcome their phobias by immersing themselves in computer-generated worlds. *Scientific American, 291*(2), 58–65.

Hoffman, H. G., Patterson, D. R., Seibel, E., Soltani, M., Jewett-Leahy, L., & Sharar, S. R. (2008). Virtual reality pain control during burn wound debridement in the hydrotank. *Clinical Journal of Pain, 24*(4), 299304.

Krijn, M., Emmelkamp, P. M., Olafsson, R. P., Schuemie, M. J., & van der Mast, C. A. (2007). Do self-statements enhance the effectiveness of virtual reality exposure therapy? A comparative evaluation in acrophobia. *Cyberpsychology and Behavior, 10*(3), 362–370.

Lambrey, S., & Berthoz, A. (2003). Combination of conflicting visual and nonvisual information for estimating actively performed body turns in virtual reality. *International Journal of Psychophysiology, 50*(1-2), 101–115.

Lee, J. H., Kwon, H., Choi, J., & Yang, B. H. (2007). Cue-exposure therapy to decrease alcohol craving in virtual environment. *Cyberpsychology and Behavior, 10*(5), 617–623.

Murray, C. D., & Gordon, M. S. (2001). Changes in bodily awareness induced by immersive virtual reality. *CyberPsychology and Behavior, 4*(3), 365–371.

Optale, G. (2003). Male sexual dysfunctions and multimedia immersion therapy. *CyberPsychology and Behavior, 6*(3), 289–294.

Optale, G., Chierichetti, F., Munari, A., Nasta, A., Pianon, C., Viggiano, G., & Ferlin, G. (1998). Brain PET confirms the effectiveness of VR treatment of impotence. *International Journal of Impotence Research, 10*(Suppl 1), 45.

Parsons, T. D., & Rizzo, A. A. (2008). Affective outcomes of virtual reality exposure therapy for anxiety and specific phobias: A meta-analysis. *Journal of Behavior Therapy and Experimental Psychiatry, 39,* 250–261.

Perpiña, C., Botella, C., & Baños, R. M. (2003). Virtual reality in eating disorders. *European Eating Disorders Review, 11*(3), 261–278.

Riva, G. (Ed.) (1997). *Virtual reality in neuro-psycho-physiology: Cognitive, clinical and methodological issues in assessment and rehabilitation.* Amsterdam: IOS Press.

Riva, G. (1998). Modifications of body image induced by virtual reality. *Perceptual and Motor Skills, 86*(1), 163–170.

Riva, G. (2005). Virtual reality in psychotherapy: Review. *CyberPsychology and Behavior, 8*(3), 220–240.

Riva, G. (2008). From virtual to real body: Virtual reality as embodied technology. *Journal of Cybertherapy and Rehabilitation, 1*(1), 7–22.

Riva, G., Bacchetta, M., Baruffi, M., Rinaldi, S., & Molinari, E. (1998). Experiential cognitive therapy in anorexia nervosa. *Eating and Weight Disorders, 3*(3), 141–150.

Riva, G., Bacchetta, M., Baruffi, M., Cirillo, G., & Molinari, E. (2000). Virtual reality environment for body image modifica-

tion: A multidimensional therapy for the treatment of body image in obesity and related pathologies. *CyberPsychology and Behavior, 3*(3), 421–431.

Riva, G., Bacchetta, M., Baruffi, M., & Molinari, E. (2002). Virtual-reality-based multidimensional therapy for the treatment of body image disturbances in binge eating disorders: A preliminary controlled study. *IEEE Transactions on Information Technology in Biomedicine, 6*(3), 224–234.

Riva, G., Bacchetta, M., Cesa, G., Conti, S., Castelnuovo, G., Mantovani, F., & Molinari, E. (2006). Is severe obesity a form of addiction? Rationale, clinical approach and controlled clinical trial. *CyberPsychology and Behavior, 9*(4), 457–479.

Riva, G., Bacchetta, M., Cesa, G., Conti, S., & Molinari, E. (2003). Six-month follow-up of in-client experiential-cognitive therapy for binge eating disorders. *CyberPsychology and Behavior, 6*(3), 251–258.

Riva, G., Bacchetta, M., Cesa, G., Conti, S., & Molinari, E. (2004). The use of VR in the treatment of eating disorders. *Studies in Health Technology and Informatics, 99,* 121–163.

Riva, G., Botella, C., Légeron, P., & Optale, G. (Eds.). (2004). *Cybertherapy: Internet and virtual reality as assessment and rehabilitation tools for clinical psychology and neuroscience.* Amsterdam: IOS Press.

Riva, G., Mantovani, F., Capideville, C. S., Preziosa, A., Morganti, F., Villani, D., Gaggioli, A., Botella, C., & Alcañiz, M. (2007). Affective interactions using virtual reality: The link between presence and emotions. *Cyberpsychology and Behavior, 10*(1), 45–56.

Rothbaum, B. O., Anderson, P., Zimand, E., Hodges, L., Lang, D., & Wilson, J. (2006). Virtual reality exposure therapy and standard (in vivo) exposure therapy in the treatment of fear of flying. *Behavior Therapy, 37*(1), 80–90.

Rothbaum, B. O., Hodges, L. F., Ready, D., Graap, K., & Alarcon, R. D. (2001). Virtual reality exposure therapy for Vietnam veterans with posttraumatic stress disorder. *Journal of Clinical Psychiatry,*

62(8), 617–622.

Safran, J. D., & Greenberg, L. S. (1991). *Emotion, psychotherapy and change.* New York: The Guilford Press.

Schultheis, M. T., & Rizzo, A. A. (2001). The application of virtual reality technology in rehabilitation. *Rehabilitation Psychology, 46*(3), 296–311.

Viaud-Delmon, I., Berthoz, A., & Jouvent, R. (2002). Multisensory integration for spatial orientation in trait anxiety subjects: Absence of visual dependence. *European Psychiatry, 17*(4), 194–199.

Viaud-Delmon, I., Ivanenko, Y. P., Berthoz, A., & Jouvent, R. (2000). Adaptation as a sensorial profile in trait anxiety: A study with virtual reality. *Journal of Anxiety Disorders, 14*(6), 583–601.

Vidal, M., Amorim, M. A., & Berthoz, A. (2004). Navigating in a virtual three-dimensional maze: How do egocentric and allocentric reference frames interact? *Cognitive Brain Research, 19*(3), 244–258.

Vidal, M., Lipshits, M., McIntyre, J., & Berthoz, A. (2003). Gravity and spatial orientation in virtual 3D-mazes. *Journal of Vestibular Research, 13*(4-6), 273–286.

Villani, D., Riva, F., & Riva, G. (2007). New technologies for relaxation: The role of presence. *International Journal of Stress Management, 14*(3), 260–274.

Vincelli, F., Anolli, L., Bouchard, S., Wiederhold, B. K., Zurloni, V., & Riva, G. (2003). Experiential cognitive therapy in the treatment of panic disorders with agoraphobia: A controlled study. *CyberPsychology and Behavior, 6*(3), 312–318.

Wolfe, B. E. (2002). The role of lived experience in self- and relational observation: A commentary on Horowitz. *Journal of Psychotherapy Integration, 12*(2), 147–153.

Chapter 13

THE USE OF COMPUTER-AIDED COGNITIVE BEHAVIOURAL THERAPY (CCBT) IN THERAPEUTIC SETTINGS

KATE CAVANAGH

INTRODUCTION

The use of computer technologies is widespread in the psychological therapies. From practice portals offering screening tools and appointment bookings, to patient record systems, peer support networks and psycho-education hubs the idea of a therapeutic practice without the assistance of some computing technology is becoming alien. However, the role of the computer as the therapist–delivering a portion or the entirety of treatment–remains controversial.

Since the 1960s researchers have attempted to identify the replicable ingredients of effective therapeutic encounters both in terms of specific techniques and nonspecific contextual and interpersonal factors. Attempts to translate these features into computer-delivered behavioural health interventions have met with varying success (see Cavanagh et al., 2003a for a review). Most recently technological advances have permitted the development of relatively sophisticated computer systems designed to replicate ingredients of cognitive behaviour therapy (CBT) for a growing range of mental health problems. In contrast to previous waves of development in computer-aided therapy which have largely remained in the lab, computer-aided cognitive behavioural therapy (CCBT) has made its way from the research clinic to the mainstream of patient care in the UK (National Institute for Clinical Excellence, 2006; 2009) and elsewhere (see Marks & Cavanagh, 2009 for a global perspective).

This chapter defines what CCBT is (and what it is not) and describes, with examples, some of the CCBT packages available. It goes on to explore the evidence base for CCBT and its impact on improving mental health for clients through self-help. The ethical considerations of offering CCBT are outlined. Finally, the future of CCBT, as a method of extending the reach of CBT, and increasing access to evidence based psychological therapies, particularly using

the example of the NHS in the UK, is discussed.

DEFINING COMPUTER-AIDED COGNITIVE BEHAVIOURAL THERAPY

Psychotherapeutic software can reduce client-practitioner contact time, can meaningfully and effectively deliver the training elements of the psychotherapeutic intervention and can transmit positive nonspecific ingredients of therapy such as empathy and motivation in the absence of human interaction (Cavanagh et al., 2003b), moreover computer-aided psychotherapy uses patient input to make some computations and treatment decisions and thus is interactive and responsive (Marks et al., 1998). By extension, computer-aided cognitive behavioural therapy (CCBT) does this attuned to the cognitive behavioural therapy (CBT) method. This definition excludes computer systems that only improve access or bridge distance via communication technologies (e.g., telephone therapy, email therapy). It also excludes nonresponsive technologies such as psychoeducation websites or e-workbooks which are not interactive.

As technological advances have permitted, CCBT software has been developed for a range of platforms. Initially, much CCBT was accessed on non-networked personal computers and transferred by loading software from removable discs such as CD-ROMS and DVDs. More recently, networked software can be accessed on intranets and the Internet. As well as access on standard computers, several research teams have developed software that is accessible via interactive voice response technology over the phone, or on hand-held computing devices including mobile phones. To date, virtual reality systems have been used to save therapeutic resource whilst retaining CBT outcomes for many problems but do not make treatment decisions, hence they are not considered CCBT.

WHAT CCBT PACKAGES ARE AVAILABLE?

A recent review of English language literature on computer-aided psychotherapy identified 97 therapy packages, many of which were cognitive behavioural in therapeutic orientation (Marks et al., 2007). These packages covered mental health problems as diverse as anxiety disorders (phobia, panic, generalised anxiety, posttraumatic stress disorder, obsessive compulsive disorder,

"stress"), eating disorders, depression, pain, insomnia, sexual difficulties and schizophrenia as well as alcohol and drug misuse and childhood anxiety and depression. Their evidence base ranged from uncontrolled proof of concept studies to large randomised controlled trials of therapeutic efficacy and practice based evidence of effectiveness. Some programs have been taken to market, some are "under development," and some remain locked away in the filing cabinet of lost-innovations. It is impossible to say how many CCBT packages are out there.

How many evidence based CCBT packages are available might be easier to quantify, although the number of packages falling into this catchment will obviously vary depending on what criteria for "good-enough" evidence is set (see Chapter 25 in this volume). Health technology assessment bodies typically view the randomised controlled trial (RCT) as the "gold-standard" of research evidence, although not all RCTs are designed to answer important questions and many other types of study design may give powerful information about the value of healthcare technologies.

In the UK, the National Institute for Clinical Excellence's (NICE) 2006 Technology Appraisal recommended two CCBT packages for use in the National Health Service (NHS) as treatment choices for depression (Beating the Blues) and phobia and panic (Fearfighter). In the case of depression, this recommendation has been extended by more recent clinical guidelines, which conclude a "class effect" for CCBT for depression (National Institute for Clinical Excellence, 2009).

The next section describes, in a little more detail, two CCBT programs for common mental health problems that are commercially available to healthcare providers and individuals seeking treatment.

Beating the Blues

Beating the Blues is an interactive, multimedia CCBT package for depression and anxiety accessed on a personal computer (PC) either within a healthcare

setting or elsewhere via the Internet. Following an "Introduction to Therapy" presentation of 15 minutes, Beating the Blues comprises an eight-session program (each session lasting about one hour). Sessions are usually accessed weekly and there are individualised "homework" assignments to complete between sessions.

The first interactive session introduces and socialises to the CBT model focusing on problem definition and pleasurable activities with behavioural activation as the first homework exercise. Session two introduces the role of automatic thoughts in depression and anxiety and guides the user to begin one of two parallel behavioural programs (activity scheduling or problem solving). Session three explores

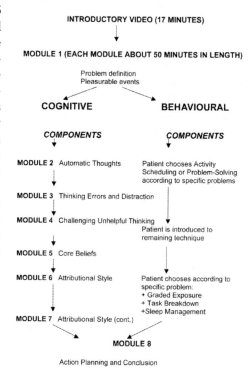

Figure 13.1 Beating the Blues Programme Structure.

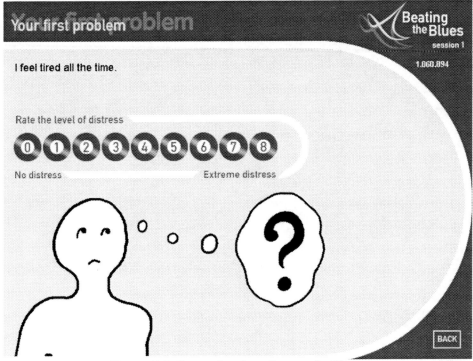

Figure 13.2. Screenshot from Beating the Blues.

thinking errors. Session four guides the user through challenging unhelpful thinking and introduces a second behavioural method. Session five introduces the idea of core beliefs and the downward arrow technique. Session six and seven explore helpful and unhelpful attributional styles and guide the user to work on sleep management, graded exposure or task breakdown in order to manage their own specific problems. Session eight focuses on longer-term goals, action planning and relapse prevention.

Beating the Blues utilises a range of multimedia capabilities. The user is guided through the programme by a narrator (who is a well-known medical doctor) and features a series of filmed case studies of fictional patients who are used to model both the symptoms of anxiety and depression and their treatment by CBT,

as well as animations, voice-overs and interactive modules. Users can work at their own pace and repeat elements of the program if they want to. Session summaries, homework guides and a clinical progress reports are generated during each session. The program is readily usable by patients with no previous computer experience.

The standard delivery model for Beating the Blues is such that clinical supervision and responsibility rest with the primary care doctor or other appropriately qualified professional (such as a nurse or clinical psychologist), to whom reports (including warnings of suicide or other risk) are automatically delivered by the computer program. If accessed in a healthcare setting, a paraprofessional worker typically supports the practical aspects of using the program such as session bookings, logging on and any technical difficulties. If accessed at home, technical support may be given by email or telephone, along with therapeutic support and progress monitoring depending on local implementation, policy and practice.

FearFighter

Fearfighter is a CCBT package for phobia and panic disorder. The program is delivered through the Internet and can be accessed from any computer which is linked to the web. Fearfighter guides patients through nine steps. It explains the exposure therapy rationale with case examples and helps patients to identify their triggers and goals in a step-by-step personalized program, with homework diary, feedback on progress and troubleshooting advice. Patients are also given coping strategies before doing exposure, in order to better learn to cope with the anxiety-provoking situation without escaping from it.

Patients using the programme are supported by a suitably qualified support worker, who has access to the Patient Progress Monitoring System (PPMS) that comes with the programme. On the PPMS, support workers can monitor log-in history, step progression and clinical measures of their patients. Brief support is given by mean of scheduled support calls prearranged with the patients. No more than one hour of telephone support in total is required per patient. Fearfighter has been sold to and is in use by many Primary Care Trusts around the UK.

STEP 1   Welcome to FearFighter

STEP 2   How to bear fear

STEP 3   Problem sorting

STEP 4   How to get a helper

STEP 5   Setting goals

STEP 6   Managing anxiety

STEP 7   Rehearsing goals

STEP8   Carrying on

STEP 9   Troubleshooting

Figure 13.3. Program structure for FearFighter.

EVIDENCE OF OUTCOMES

There is a growing body of evidence reporting on the efficacy, effectiveness, acceptability and cost-effectiveness of CCBT (e.g., Cuipers et al., 2009; Kaltenthaler et al., 2008ab; Marks, Cavanagh & Gega, 2007; McCrone et al, 2004). Large randomised controlled trials in realistic healthcare settings have indicated benefits beyond waitlist control and usual care for a number of CCBT programs including Beating the Blues (Proudfoot et al., 2004) and Fearfighter (e.g., Marks et al., 2004). Subsequent practice-based evidence has supported the generalizability of these findings (Cavanagh et al., 2006; Kenwright et al., 2001; Learmonth et al., 2008) and the acceptability (Cavanagh et al., 2009) of CCBT programs in mainstream practice. Benchmarking and pseudo-experimental studies have indicated similar outcomes between the best evidenced CCBT and equivalent face-to-face therapy (Cavanagh et al., 2006; Kenwright et al., 2001). Evidence for CCBT coupled with that for other self-help CBT methods such as bibliotherapy (e.g., Gellatly et al., 2007) have potentiated enthusiasm for access to "low intensity" CBT, where self-help CBT resources are facilitated or supported by para-professional workers (Department of Health, 2007; National Institute for Clinical Excellence, 2009).

The most recent National Institute for Clinical Excellence guidelines for depression (National Institute for Clinical Excellence, 2009) have advocated a "class effect" for CCBT for depression, echoing sentiments expressed during their consultations, "that any competently created CCBT package will be effective" (http://www.nice.org.uk/media/88D/7A/TA97CommentsTable.pdf).

The NICE guidelines (National Institute for Clinical Excellence, 2009) do not recommend any specific CCBT program as a treatment choice, but indicate some features of CCBT requisite for the treatment of persistent subthreshold and mild to moderate depression, including CBT features (explanation of the CBT model, encourage tasks between sessions, and use thought-challenging and active monitoring of behaviour, thought patterns and outcomes), support features (supported by a trained practitioner who offers limited facilitation and reviews progress and outcome) and service features (treatment program to typically last 9–12 weeks, including follow-up).

However, given the wide range of outcomes for CCBT packages in research trials, claiming a class effect seems premature. We would not champion the pharmaceutical industry if it argued that any "competently created" antidepressant should be recommended to the NHS without a body of high quality supporting evidence for that specific antidepressant. Neither can we do this for CCBT. For the time being, CCBT packages need to demonstrate their value by research rather than judgment, and practice-based evidence for each individual program in context is needed to demonstrate effectiveness. In the future, dismantling studies may help us to learn more about the key elements of CCBT that drive outcome, whether these differ from what works in face-to-face therapies and how we might enhance package outcomes by replicating more of what works and eliminating what is unnecessary or distracting. This will add to a framework for anticipating which CCBT programs will or will not be helpful therapeutically.

ETHICAL CONSIDERATIONS

In addition to the standard ethical considerations needed for any psychotherapeutic encounter, any resource saving technology is bound to carry dilemmas of its own.

Users are typically both screened and assessed for the suitability of CCBT programs and finding a balance between brevity and sufficiency is a clinical challenge. It would be paradoxical for a low intensity service to routinely invest several hours of senior practitioner time in assessing a patient's needs. Equally, it may be unhelpful to triage someone with multiple and complex needs to a CCBT service. A balance must be found.

Risk assessment and risk monitoring need to be part of a program of care, whether this is a feature of the computer program, or a task for human workers managing the program. For example, following initial risk screening by a health professional, the Beating the Blues program assesses risk at each session with the user. The results of this are fed back to a supporting practitioner and if risk is high, the user is advised to stop using the program and seek help.

Subjective distress and problem ratings are also assessed on a session-by-session basis in Beating the Blues. This allows the user and their supporting practitioner to see if any improvement is being made and to note if any deterioration is present. It is up to local protocols to activate alternative help or a treatment review when appropriate.

CCBT programs raise issues of confidentiality and specifically the storage and in the case of web-based products the transfer of digital information. In developing CCBT software, consideration to appropriate levels of data access and data protection must be employed. Entry to the clients' therapeutic sessions should be password protected, the password being generated and held solely by the client. Healthcare professionals holding clinical responsibility for client well-being may wish to have access to progress information regarding mood and problem monitoring, as well as risk information. The parameters of this data access must be made clear to the client. Data entered by the client should be encrypted and retained within the program database for later retrieval by the client but not, without permission, their clinician. The confidential features of psychotherapeutic software may be viewed as an advantage by some clients who wish to work through their problems privately.

Ethical benefits of CCBT include that they may overcome some human foibles and threats to confidentiality. They will never discuss users' difficulties outside of work and will never breach boundaries of therapy by developing an inappropriate relationship with the user. Computers will never forget what your answers to questions are and will never be shocked. The content of CCBT programs can be updated more quickly to reflect the best evidence for therapy than human practitioners can be systematically trained.

CCBT programs raise a number of ethical questions and may solve some others. The mass implementation of a CCBT offer in the NHS will no doubt bring further ethical issues to light.

THE IMPLEMENTATION OF CCBT IN
THE UK NATIONAL HEALTH SERVICE

In the UK, the National Institute for Clinical Excellence (NICE) has recommended CCBT programs as treatment options for common mental health problems (including a range of programs for depression and Fearfighter for panic and phobia) in its guidance to the National Health Service (National Institute for Clinical Excellence, 2006; 2009). In addition, radical new health service initiatives under the Increasing Access to Psychological Therapies (IAPT) umbrella incorporate access to CCBT for depression and anxiety as a routine care option for service-users with mild-moderate difficulties, along with other "low intensity" resources (Department of Health, 2007). The implication of these recommendations is that CCBT will be available to hundreds of thousands of people in the UK suffering from mild-moderate mental health problems as these services roll-out.

In the UK, Primary Care Trusts, the NHS's fund-holding bodies, have been advised to deliver CCBT applications for anxiety and depression (National Institute for Clinical Excellence, 2006). Commissioning guidance advises Trusts to conduct local needs assessment, purchase software licences, ensure any necessary computing hardware is in place, ensure staff are trained to support CCBT and referral pathways are in place. A program of CCBT provision is rolling out across primary care services in the UK.

New services are also directed to facilitate guided CCBT self-help as part of their low-intensity treatment offer (Department of Health, 2007, 2008). It is too early to say how these services will meet population needs for people with depression and anxiety. Training and supervision of low-intensity workers supporting represents a significant workforce demand. CCBT programs will have to evolve to meet the needs of these developing services.

CONCLUSION

CCBT is becoming a hands-on early option for effective self-help in a growing number of mental health problems including anxiety and depression. A number of programs are building a promising evidence base and professionals and healthcare systems are exploring cost-effective ways to employ this new approach to benefit sufferers. While many people will continue to choose and get face-to-face therapy, others may prefer emerging computer-aided options that could reduce overlong waiting lists, increase convenience and confidentiality, and lessen stigma.

REFERENCES

Cavanagh, K., Shapiro, D., Van den Berg, S., Swain, S., Barkham, M., & Proudfoot, J. (2006). Effectiveness of CCBT in routine primary care. *British Journal of Clinical Psychology, 45*(4), 499–514.

Cavanagh, K, Shapiro, D. A., Van Den Berg, S., Swain, S., Barkham, M., & Proudfoot, J. (2009). The acceptability of computer-aided cognitive behavioural therapy: A pragmatic study. *Cognitive Behaviour Therapy, 38*(4), 235–246.

Cavanagh, K., Shapiro, D., & Zack, J. (2003a). Computer plays therapist: the challenges and opportunities of psychotherapeutic software. In S. Goss & K. Anthony (Eds.), *Technology in counselling and psychotherapy: A practitioners' guide.* Basingstoke, UK: Palgrave/Macmillan.

Cavanagh, K., Zack, J. S., Shapiro, D. A., & Wright, J. H. (2003b). Computer programs for psychotherapy. In S. Goss & K. Anthony (Eds.), *Technology in counselling and psychotherapy: A practitioner's guide.* Basingstoke, UK: Palgrave MacMillan.

Cuijpers, P., Marks, I. M., van Straten, A., Cavanagh, K., Gega, L., & Andersson, G. (2009). Computer-aided psychotherapy for anxiety disorders: A meta-analytic review. *Cognitive Behaviour Therapy, 38*(2), 66–82.

Department of Health. (2007). *Improving access to psychological therapies (IAPT) programme: Computerised cognitive behavioural therapy (cCBT) implementation guidance.* London: Department of Health.

Department of Health. (2008). *Improving access to psychological therapies (IAPT) implementation plan: National guidelines for regional delivery.* London: Department of Health.

Gellatly, J., Bower, P., Hennessy, S., Richards, D., Gilbody, S., & Lovell, K. (2007). What makes self-help interventions effective in the management of depressive symptoms? Meta analysis and meta regression. *Psychological Medicine, 37,* 1217–1228.

Kaltenhaler, E., Sutcliffe, P., Parry, G., Beverly, C., & Ferriter, M. (2008a). The acceptability to patients of computerized cognitive behavioural therapy for depression: A systematic review. *Psychological Medicine, 38,* 1521–1530.

Kaltenhaler, E., Parry, G., Beverly, C., & Ferriter, M. (2008b) Computerised cognitive-behavioural therapy for depression: Systematic review. *British Journal of Psychiatry, 193*(3), 181–184.

Kenwright, M., Liness, S., & Marks, I. (2001). Reducing demands on clinicians by offering computer-aided self-help for phobia/panic: Feasibility study. *British Journal of Psychiatry, 179,* 456–459.

Learmonth, D., Trosh, J., Rai, S., Sewell, J., & Cavanagh, K. (2008). The role of computer-aided psychotherapy within an NHS CBT specialist service. *Counselling and Psychotherapy Research, 8*(2), 117–123.

Marks, I. M., & Cavanagh, K. (2009) Computer-aided psychotherapy: State of the art and state of the science. *Annual Review of Clinical Psychology, 5,* 121–141.

Marks, I. M., Cavanagh, K., & Gega, L. (2007). *Hands-on help: Computer-aided psychotherapy.* Hove: Psychology Press.

Marks, I. M., Kenwright, M., McDonough, M., Whittaker, M., & Mataix-Cols, D. (2004). Saving clinicians' time by delegating routine aspects of therapy to a computer: A RCT in phobia/panic disorder. *Psychological Medicine, 34,* 9–18.

Marks, I. M., Shaw, S., & Parkin, R. (1998). Computer-aided treatments of mental health problems. *Clinical Psychology: Science and Practice, 5*(2), 151–170.

McCrone, P., Knapp, M., Proudfoot, J., Ryden, C., Cavanagh, K., Shapiro, D., Ilson, S., Gray, J., Goldberg, D., Mann, A., Marks, I. M., & Everitt, B. (2004). Cost-effectiveness of computerised CBT for anxiety and depression in primary care. *British Journal of Psychiatry, 185*(1), 55–62.

National Institute for Clinical Excellence. (2006). *Guidance on the use of computerised cognitive behavioural therapy for anxiety and depression.* Technology Appraisal no. 97. London: NICE.

National Institute for Clinical Excellence. (2009). *Depression: Management of depression in primary and secondary care–NICE guidance, CG90.* London: Author.

Proudfoot, J., Ryden, C., Everitt, B., Shapiro, D., Goldberg, D., Mann, A., Tylee, A., Marks, I., & Gray, J. (2004). Clinical efficacy of computerised cognitive behavioural therapy for anxiety and depression in primary care. *British Journal of Psychiatry, 185*(1), 46–54.

Chapter 14

THE ROLE OF GAMING IN MENTAL HEALTH

Mark Matthews and David Coyle

INTRODUCTION

Many adolescents experience diffi-culties in engaging directly with traditional face-to-face therapeutic ap-proaches (BMA, 2006). Recent research suggests that computer assisted mental health interventions may provide one potential way of working more success-fully with adolescent clients (Matthews et al., 2008). Research also suggests that the choice of technology is a key factor in the success of computer-assisted interven-tions. For example, it is suggested:

> a quality therapeutic process will active-ly engage the client's participation, by involving their interests, strengths and ideas. Similarly, technologies are most likely to prove effective if they are designed to be client-centred. (Coyle et al. 2007a)

Whilst much attention in recent years has focused on the negative effects of computer games, a review of literature and an initial pilot study (Coyle et al., 2005) has provided strong initial indica-tions that appropriately designed games may have potential to assist in adolescent interventions. Therapeutic games offer the opportunity to engage with adoles-cents through a medium with which they are comfortable. A recent UK survey reported that 53 percent of 11- to 14-year-olds play games four times a week or more and that 44 percent play for more than one hour at a time (McFar-lane et al., 2002). Further surveys in the US and the UK indicate that under-16's rank computer gaming as their number one entertainment form (Gentile & Walsh, 2002; Pratchett, 2005).

This chapter first reviews previous research on the use of computer games in therapeutic settings. The potential benefits of games are discussed. Are games just a useful icebreaker, or can then assist in other ways? Can they, for instance, assist in improving client engagement and the client-therapist rela-tionship? By way of example we discuss

Personal Investigator (PI), a game recently developed for use in professional therapeutic practice. The chapter ends by taking a more speculative perspective on future directions for therapeutic gaming.

ETHICAL CONCERNS

Before discussing ongoing research on therapeutic computer games, it is important to note that many Mental Health Care (MHC) researchers and practitioners are sceptical of the benefits, not just of games, but also of technology in general. Caspar (2004) cites fears such as damage to the client-therapist relationship, ethical and security issues and worries that the current skills of therapists may become obsolete. Others fear that technology in and of itself has a damaging impact on the mental health of society, suggesting dangers such as increased isolation due to excessive time spent online (Caspar, 2004).

In the specific case of computer games, much literature in recent years has focused on the negative effects of computer games. Risks such as addiction and increased aggressiveness and violence have been suggested (Gentile et al. 2004). However, while these fears must be considered, there are strong initial indications that the potential of therapeutic games may be substantial and MHC researchers have begun to show an increased interest in the potential of suitably designed games (Griffiths, 1997; Parkin, 2000). It is important to note that technology-based interventions do not generally seek to replace existing methods. Rather they seek to offer new and complementary options. Rather, than detracting from critical therapeutic factors such as the client-therapist relationship, games, when appropriately designed and used in appropriate circumstances, may offer a way of improving such factors.

PREVIOUS USES OF COMPUTER GAMES

Research on computer games in MHC settings has been limited. Some early research was conducted in the 1980s and early 1990s. Several researchers from a psychology/psychotherapy background developed their own games (Clark & Schoech, 1984; Griffiths, 1997; Hyland et al., 1993; Oakley, 1994; Resnick & Sherer, 1994), while others examined the potential of off-the-shelf commercial games (Gardner, 1991; Hyland et al., 1993). Increases in the costs, development time and technical expertise involved in developing modern games were key factors in the decline of this work. Research on the use of biofeedback-based games for the treatment of anxiety disorders and attention problems has received more recent attention (Pope & Paisson, 2001). Some suggested benefits from research into therapeutic computer games are:

- Games can successfully engage clients previously difficult to engage by other means.
- Clients were more cooperative with their therapists, with whom

they developed effective therapeutic relationships.

- Session attendance rates greatly improved and the stigma felt in attending therapy was reduced (Clark and Schoech, 1984; Hyland et al., 1993).
- Games can help adolescents develop "more self-confidence, a sense of mastery, more willingness to accept responsibility" (Hyland et al., 1993).
- Games can help children displace their aggression, develop problem solving skills and deal with negative and positive outcomes in the game (Gardner, 1991).

It is important to note that these findings must be viewed with a large degree of caution. Research in the area has been largely uncoordinated and the difficulties surrounding clinical evaluations mean that trials typically had limited user numbers. Substantially more work has been conducted in educational and other health care areas, with suggested benefits including increased motivation; increased self-esteem; increased health care knowledge and self-efficacy; improved problem-solving and discussion skills; and improved storytelling skills (Bers, 2001; Gee, 2003; HopeLab, 2006). The degree to which such benefits are transferable to MHC settings remains an open one. The next section highlights one study new study in the MHC area.

PERSONAL INVESTIGATOR (PI)

PI is a 3D computer game that incorporates Solution Focused Therapy (SFT), a goal-oriented strengths-based intervention model. It is the first time this intervention approach has been integrated into a 3D game. The game uses a detective metaphor. Players visit a Detective Academy and play the role of a "personal investigator" hunting for the clues that will help them solve a personal problem. Players are given a detective notebook, where they are asked to record their thoughts and ideas. Five solution-focused conversational strategies are mapped into five distinct game areas. The player meets a master detective in each area who talks with the player in an informal way and asks the player to answer questions in their notebook. Three of the dialogues incorporate videos of adolescents describing how they overcame personal problems using the strategies described.

To complete the game and "graduate" the academy players must complete the tasks set by each master detective. Upon completing the game, they receive a printout of their notebook (further details of PI can be found in Coyle et al., 2005; Matthews et al., 2006; Matthews et al., 2008).

The first character the player meets is the principal of the Detective Academy, whose job is to guide players through the goal setting stage of therapy. He gives the player their detective notebook, which appears at the bottom of the screen and tells them "this book will be a mirror to your mind, it is where you can write all your ideas and hunches as you go along." The player is asked to identify a problem to work on and asked to describe this problem as a solution they would like to achieve. From this point on, the game attempts to focus the play-

Figure 14.1. Screenshots from Personal Investigator.

er's attention on achieving this solution. Goal-setting can be a difficult step to complete in regular therapeutic sessions. When using PI, the goal-setting process is incorporated within the game. Achieving the client's solution becomes the objective of the game.

Inside the Detective Academy, there are four distinct areas to be explored, with four master detective characters, each corresponding to the four remaining aspects of SFT:

- **Recognizing exceptions:** the player meets Damini, a forensic scientist who specializes in spotting hidden evidence. This section aims to help the player recognize times when their problem is less acute with a view to repeating them more often.
- **Coping:** in this area, the player meets Inspector Clueso. He helps players recognize ways they currently have of dealing with their problem and explores how they might have successfully overcome

problems in the past.

- **Indentifying resources:** the player meets Detective Spade, a New York cop. He helps the player identify "Backup," family and friends whose support they can draw on in future times of need. He also discusses other resources, such as their own strengths, which the player can use.
- **Miracle question:** in this area, the player meets Siobhán, an artist, who helps people visualise their life without their current problems. This dialogue is based on the SFT miracle question. By imagining a future without their problems, clients are motivated to seek a solution.

Having met all the other characters and collected the four keys, the player can then open the final door to graduate from the Detective Academy. The player meets the principal again, who congratulates the player and rewards their effort with a printout of their notebook.

USING PERSONAL INVESTIGATOR IN CLINICAL SESSIONS

In clinical sessions the therapist and adolescent sit together at a computer, but the adolescent has full control of the keyboard and mouse. The adolescent choos-

es a username and logs into the game. The game creates an individual account for each adolescent, automatically saving their progress and allowing them to return to saved games at a later date. The adolescent has full control over the game; they play at their own pace and choose their own path through the world. Throughout the game the therapist is a partner in the exploration of the game world and is no longer an interlocutor. If the adolescent asks for help, the therapist can elaborate on the subjects brought up by the game or answer more specific questions from the adolescent in relation to their situation.

A multisite evaluation has been conducted in which 8 therapists used PI with a total of 22 adolescent clients. Approximately equal numbers of male and female clients, experiencing a broad range of difficulties and ranging in age from 10 to 16, used the game. Each therapist agreed that PI had a positive impact in the majority of sessions in which it was used. They also agreed that PI complemented their traditional ways of working and all but one stated that they would like to continue using PI with further clients. All eight therapists agreed that while PI is useful as an icebreaker, it is also more than this. It helped therapists engage constructively with their clients. It helped with the development of the client-therapist relationship and it also helped in structuring sessions.

A key finding to emerge was the importance of the therapist's role in using the game effectively. The real benefit of games such as PI is that they can help to raise issues in a client-centred way and create a context for more detailed discussions between the therapist and client. Games can serve as a therapeutic tool, but the work jointly undertaken by the therapist and client remains critical. This factor is highlighted in the rules one therapist established for using PI with clients. The therapist described the initial discussion she had with clients prior to using PI as follows:

> Prior to commencing the game we have a discussion about the game—and I gauge the interest level. If they are very interested I outline some important things to remember. I describe it as a thinking game. I talk about needing to take time to think before we write down our answers [in the game notebook]. So rule no 1 is the therapist or child reads out the question—and we have a talk about it before we write anything down. Once we have decided we type it and only then press next. Rule 2—if we are going too fast and not taking our time we may need to stop the game completely and work from a page instead. (This is a good strategy for assisting in patience in the game).

Alongside acknowledging therapists' largely positive opinions of PI, it is important to note several concerns raised by the group. These concerns focused on three main issues: difficulties some clients experienced reading and writing in the game notebook, some adolescents engage with the game but not with the therapeutic issues raised and some adolescents engage with the game but not with the therapist, using the game as another way of avoiding discussion with the therapist.

CASE MATERIAL

This case study describes the opinions of the therapist who has used PI most often. He states:

The notable benefit has to be removing the impact of face to face grilling, which for young people who want to oppose adults has to be a plus.

In all, this therapist used PI with seven clients and stated that the game was "helpful" in two cases and "very helpful" in five. The therapist strongly agreed that PI provides benefits as an icebreaker, as an aid to the therapeutic relationship and client engagement. He expressed the opinion that PI had the ability to help clients take ownership of the therapeutic process:

The cognitive goal of PI is to enable and encourage the client towards ownership of the problem. Talking therapy alone can take up to 3 or 4 times longer to reach the same small part of understanding that PI can bring out in 1 session.

One of the issues also addressed in feedback is the importance of the therapist's role in using PI effectively. For example he states:

Skilful use of the introduction of PI into a session just makes for better and better interventions that students/clients can handle at their own pace. Any tool in a therapists "toolkit" that can open a dialogue of any sort can only be of benefit if used with skill.

The therapist describes the way in which he used PI to complement some of his other day-to-day techniques. For example, if he felt that a client had a moment of significant understanding while playing PI, he moves away from the computer and addresses this issue in more detail:

Playing PI created some nice 'Aha moments' . . . Moving away from the PC at these points, using reflection flowcharts, mind maps etc helped to solidify the new learning and turn what was once a block or problem into a manageable challenge that can be dealt with one piece at a time.

What is significant here is that this therapist had integrated the game with his traditional working methods and had begun to use PI as a context for, and complement to, other forms of therapeutic work. As such PI became part of this therapist's overall therapeutic toolkit, rather than a standalone game used in isolation.

THE FUTURE

While more detailed studies are now required to confirm PI's early findings, there are strong initial grounds to suggest that games such as PI offer therapeutic benefits. Alongside use in clinical sessions, there is the potential for games to impact adolescent mental health in many new ways. Between sessions games may help to encourage clients to complete homework activities and reflect on issues raised in sessions. For example, the authors of this chapter recently completed an initial version of an action-based game called Positive Thoughts, which clients will use on their mobile phones between sessions. It is designed to help clients to remember and reinforce positive motivational statements, previously agreed with a therapist in session. To win the game the player collects the letters to complete their motivational statement.

Games may also provide a way to reduce the stigma often associated with accessing mental health information and services. Reach Out Central (ROC) is an example of one such game. Recently launched, it is an online game incorporating a CBT approach, designed for young people aged 16 to 25. It allows players to play through life situations and is designed to help develop a range of skills from general life management skills to dealing with negative feelings or depression.

In the near future, alongside using existing games, it is likely that greater opportunities will exist for MHC professionals to become more directly involved in designing their own therapeutic games. For example PlayWrite is a tool, developed by the authors of this chapter, which allows therapists to easily create character-based games similar to PI. Using PlayWrite it is possible to tailor games to suit particular therapeutic approaches, particular mental health difficulties, or the needs of specific groups or individual clients. To date, 10 games have been designed by MHC professionals to treat a range of issues (Coyle et al., 2007b).

In the long term, research in this area should explore the potential of new and diverse forms of computer games, the merits of which have begun to be seen in other areas. The Nintendo Wii console allows for new forms of physical interaction with games. For example, Wii Fit Yoga, which appeals to a wider audience than traditional games, takes the player calmly through a tailored yoga routine. In West Virginia, 103 high schools incorporated computer games with a physical element to them (Exergames) into physical education classes, to help tackle obesity by offering students an alternative to traditional physical education activities. In the future, Exergames could assist in the treatment of depression. A new generation of daily training games (often called "brain games"), designed to help increase a wide variety of mental skills, have also become popular. The most successful of these games is the Brain Age series (Brain Training in Europe) based on the research of Dr. Ryuta Kawashima. Mind Habits is an online "brain game" based on social intelligence research at McGill University. It is designed to give you a rating on how stressed or focused you are and to help you improve this rating.

CONCLUSION

While there have been few such games targeted specifically at improving mental health, it is not difficult to imagine how similar games might have impact in mental health, by, for example, teaching coping strategies or cognitive skills. As computer games allow for more subtle interactions and appeal to a wider, more diverse, audience, the potential for positive impact on mental health will increase. Games that encourage greater physical activity or socialization are just the beginning. There is the potential for computer games to have a positive impact and offer individuals support in various ways: (1) by encouraging positive mental health and socialization in a general audience, (2) by providing a means in clinical situations through which therapists can engage clients, (3) by acting as a prescribed self-help programme that keeps clients motivated and engaged throughout a tailored programme. What is now needed is a greater concerted exploration of the potential of various computer games, in order to identify how they can best applied to support positive mental health.

REFERENCES

Bers, M. (2001). Identity construction environments: Developing personal and moral values through the design of a virtual city. *The Journal of the Learning Sciences, 10*(4), 365–415.

BMA. (2006). *Child and adolescent mental health–A guide for healthcare professionals.* London: Board of Science of the British Medical Association.

Caspar, F. (2004). Technological developments and applications in clinical psychology: Introduction. *Journal of Clinical Psychiatry, 60*(3), 221–238.

Clark, B., & Schoech, D. (1984). A computer-assisted therapeutic game for adolescents: Initial development and comments. In M. D. Schwartz (Ed.), *Using computers in clinical practice: Psychotherapy and mental health applications.* New York: Haworth Press.

Coyle, D., Matthews, M., Sharry, J., Nisbet, A., & Doherty, G. (2005). Personal Investigator: A therapeutic 3D game for adolescent psychotherapy. *International Journal of Interactive Technology and Smart Education, 2*(2), 73–88.

Coyle, D., Doherty, G., Sharry, J., & Matthews, M. (2007a). Computers in talk-based mental health care. *Interacting with Computers, 19*(4), 545–562 [online]. [Accessed August 14, 2009]. Available at http://dx.doi.org/510.1016/j.intcom.2007.1002.1001.

Coyle, D., Sharry, J., & Doherty, G. (2007b). PlayWrite–publishing and playing 3D computer games in adolescent mental health interventions. XXIV World Congress–*International Association for Suicide Prevention, Killarney, Ireland, 28 August–1 September.*

Gardner, J. E. (1991). Can the Mario Bros. help? Nintendo games as an adjunct in psychotherapy with children. *Psychotherapy, 28*(4), 667–670.

Gee, J. P. (2003). *What video games have to teach us about learning and literacy.* Basingstoke: Palgrave Macmillan.

Gentile, D. A., Lynch, P. J., Linder, J. R., & Walsh, D. A. (2004). The effects of violent video game habits on adolescent hostility, aggressive behaviors and school performance. *Journal of Adolescence, 27*(1), 5–22.

Gentile, D. A. , & Walsh, D. A. (2002). A normative study of family media habits. *Journal of Applied Developmental Psychology, 23*(2), 157–178.

Griffiths, M. (1997). Video games and clinical practice: Issues, uses and treatments. *British Journal of Clinical Psychology, 36*(4), 639–641.

HopeLab. (2006). *Re-Mission™ Outcomes study: A research trial of a video game shows improvement in health-related outcomes for young people with cancer* [online]. [Accessed August 14, 2009] Available at http://www.hopelab.org/docs/Outcomes%20Study.pdf.

Hyland, M., Kenyon, C. A., Allen, R., & Howarth, P. (1993). Diary keeping in asthma: Comparison of written and electronic methods. *British Medical Journal, 306* (6876), 487–489.

Matthews, M., Coyle, D., & Anthony, K. (2006). Personal investigator. *Therapy Today: The Magazine for Counselling and Psychotherapy Professionals, 17*(7), 30–33.

Matthews, M., Doherty, G., Sharry, J., & Fitzpatrick, C. (2008). Mobile phone mood charting for adolescents. *British Journal of Guidance and Counselling, 36*(2), 113–129.

McFarlane, A., Sparrowhawk, A., & Heald, Y. (2002). *Report on educational use of games:*

Teachers evaluating educational multimedia report: St Ives, Cambridgeshire: TEEM.

Oakley, C. (1994). SMACK: A computer driven game for at-risk teens. *Computers in Human Services, 11*(1), 97–99.

Parkin, A. (2000). Computers in clinical practice: Applying experience from child psychiatry. *British Medical Journal, 321*(7261), 615–618.

Pope, A. T., & Paisson, O. S. (2001). Helping video games 'rewire our minds'. Playing by the Rules Conference, Chicago, IL, Oct 26–27.

Pratchett, R. (2005). *Gamers in the UK: Digital play, digital lifestyles* (White Paper). London: BBC.

Resnick, H., & Sherer, M. (1994). Computer games in the human services—A review. *Computers in Human Services, 11*(1), 17–29.

Chapter 15

WEB-BASED CLINICAL ASSESSMENT

REID E. KLION

INTRODUCTION

In an oft-told story, access to the Internet has grown exponentially through the 1990s and into the twenty-first century. Originally developed as a means of communication amongst academics, the Internet has come to have a very broad influence in revolutionizing virtually every aspect of our lives ranging from banking and commerce to travel and dating.

In similar fashion, easy access to the Internet is also reshaping how we are able to provide mental health services and, more specifically, deliver clinical assessments. However, as is often the case when something new and potentially revolutionary emerges in our lives, the growth of web-based clinical assessment has been met with a mixture of both idealization and fear.

The overall theme of this chapter is that while web-based assessment brings with it significant benefits as well as some specific increased risks, the fact that an assessment is being delivered over the Internet does not alter many of the basic clinical and ethical considerations that apply when any form of clinical assessment is used. That is, web-based assessment is simply a means to an end—not an end in and of itself—and must be rooted within the principles of sound clinical work.

HISTORICAL CONSIDERATIONS

Using computer-based applications to assist in the delivery, scoring and interpretation of assessments goes back well over 40 years (Butcher et al., 2004). These early computer applications were largely employed for test scoring and report generation and Meehl's (1954) classic work on the benefits of actuarial (or statistical) scale profile interpretation was predicated upon the use of automated test scoring systems. Through the ensuing decades, computers were often used to deliver and score clinical assessments, typically the MMPI, in large institutional settings such as United States Veterans Administration hospitals. In parallel fashion, the United States armed forces started using computer-based testing system to assign recruits into military jobs in the 1960s (Wiskoff, 1997).

However, the application of computerized assessment methods was of limited interest to most mental health practitioners other than for those who used it for automated MMPI report generation. The situation started to change, though, in the middle 1990s with the advent of widespread access to the Internet. Assessments that only could have been delivered in paper-pencil format (or in rarer situations with a mainframe computer or a diskette-based system running on a personal computer) were now widely accessible and often on demand. Furthermore, not only could a vast array of mental health assessments readily be found online (by both clinicians as well as clients), a web-based assessment could now be created by virtually anyone with

a modicum of familiarity with web-based development tools.

The benefits of web-based assessment delivery are substantial because it allows a test to be administered on virtually any computer with Internet access anywhere in the world with the scored results available almost instantaneously. This way, a client can complete the assessment at a convenient time and place while sparing clinicians the burden of managing, distributing and hand-scoring paper and pencil assessments. Additionally, since certain populations (especially younger and higher socio-economic status groups) often prefer Internet-based to paper-pencil assessments, some clients may be inclined to view clinicians negatively who do not use web-based technology in their practices (Berger, 2006). From the perspective of a test developer, updates and the correction of inadvertent errors can be easily managed. In a similar vein, since the assessment is scored centrally, ongoing data collection is facilitated. Centralized scoring also helps to control the unauthorized use of copyrighted printed testing materials by limiting the need to distribute scoring keys.

APPLICATION OF THE TECHNOLOGY IN RELATION TO THE THERAPEUTIC INTERVENTION

Web-based assessment can readily become part of effective clinical practice and it is easy to envision a broad range of application for these tools. For example, it might be appropriate for clients to be offered the opportunity to complete their initial intake forms and screening checklists prior to their first appointment as opposed to arriving a hour early to do so. (Since it is recognized that clients may have a variety of reactions to completing

this process online–especially in the very early stages of treatment–it would seem reasonable that clients be given the choice and not required to do so). Additionally, if an assessment is required during the course of treatment, the client can be asked to complete it in a web-based format if this is seen as appropriate by the clinician.

Web-based assessments are also particularly well-suited for use in situations where the input of multiple persons would be helpful in developing a fuller understanding of a client but when the informants may not be able to participate in person due logistical or other factors. This especially may be the case when treating children (where obtaining information from teachers can be crucial, for example) or clients who have chronic and severe mental illnesses (whose family members or group home workers can provide much insight into daily functioning and other issues that the client may not be able to provide him or herself during the session). Similarly, web-based assessment strategies can be particularly useful when repeated measures are required to gauge response to treatment. If done appropriately, this may provide a way for clinicians to have frequent updates about a client's condition without the need and cost of an office visit. Even when compared to a phone call, web-based updates may be preferable for clients, their informants, as well as clinicians because they can be completed and accessed when it is convenient for the parties involved.

ETHICAL CONSIDERATIONS

There has been considerable discussion in the literature about the specific ethical considerations which may arise when web-based assessments are used (e.g., Association of Test Publishers, 2000; International Test Commission, 2005; Naglieri et al., 2004). However, the most important concept for clinicians to bear in mind when using web-based assessments is that the same ethical practice standards pertain as they do when carrying out more traditional clinical work. That being said, there are some specific issues that come to the fore when web-based assessments are used that may require special consideration.

APPROPRIATE PROFESSIONAL USE

Given the flexibility of web-based technologies, virtually anyone with a moderate degree of technical knowledge can create and post self-created "assessments" on the Internet. To this end, much concern has been raised about the proliferation of unvalidated, online "pop" psychological test (e.g., Naglieri et al., 2004), which can mislead the public as well as unwitting clinicians. As a first principle, if a clinician implements an assessment, he or she has an ethical obligation to fully understand both its benefits and limitations. Similarly, clinicians should only use assessments in the manner for which they are intended and supported by research. For example, an assessment of depressive symptomatology that is normed on adults will likely not be particularly valid for use in assessing preteens. To this end, unless an assessment is accompanied by validation data, its utility as a clinical instrument cannot be realistically judged. Clinicians may also need to engage in educative efforts if they believe a client has been provided inaccurate or damaging information though a poorly validated assessment that he or she found independently online.

Also, while web-based assessments are often accompanied by a report based upon scoring algorithms created by the test author, it remains the clinician's responsibility to interpret the results and share them with the client within the context of a professional relationship (see Michaels, 2006 for a general discussion). Assessment, be it web-based or not, is a professional activity just as is any other exchange with a client. As a result, assessment must take place within context of a defined professional relationship (American Psychological Association, 1992; 1985). As a result, the use of a computer-generated report does not remove the need for professional judgment and integration of the results. Matarazzo (1990) makes a useful distinction between "testing" and "assessment." While a test may be administered in any number of ways, it remains the clinician's responsibility to carry out assessment by integrating all available clinical data about a client to address the underlying referral question or reason for testing. Berger (2006) touches upon a similar theme in arguing that the critical issue in

> computer-based testing is not so much the technology, empowering as it may be, but more the uses to which such developments are put to meet the needs of clients. . . . Further, whatever the powers of computers and the software that controls what they do, it assumed that the clinician remains central and necessary to the process of understanding what test data mean and how they are relevant to the needs of individuals . . . (p. 66)

PSYCHOMETRIC EQUIVALENCY

Concerns have been expressed in the literature about reports of instances where differences have been found in the results generated by legacy paper and pencil and web-based versions of the same assessment. While clinicians should have an awareness of this (e.g., Barak & English, 2002: Buchanan, 2003), it is becoming less of an issue as test norms are increasingly being derived directly from the web-based version of an assessment and not based upon pre-existing paper and pencil norms. Additionally, there is a large body of literature indicating that this is not a concern for many instruments such as the MMPI (e.g., Finger and Ones, 1999) nor is it typically considered to be an issue when tests are used for pre-employment selection (other than for highly speeded up tests that are heavily dependent upon screen design ergonomics; see Bartram, 2006).

SUPERVISED TEST ADMINISTRATION

While there exist a large number of assessments that can be delivered in a web-based form for clients to complete at their convenience, this may not always be clinically advisable because there are times where a test should be administered in a supervised setting. (The critical factor here is whether the assessment is supervised, not how it is delivered.) One factor is that the content of some assessments must be protected from disclosure. Additionally, there may be clinical situations (e.g., involving the legal system) where it is critical to verify that it was the client him or herself who actually completed the assessment without assistance or coaching. However, if clinically appropriate, a client's completing a web-based assessment in the quiet and privacy of her home may very well be superior to asking her to complete a paper-pencil assessment on a clipboard in the crowded waiting room of a busy community mental health center. As such, it is critical that the clinician be aware of the context and nature of the assessment situation and be fully responsible for managing it.

SECURITY AND INFORMATION PRIVACY

Another factor that often arises is that of security and privacy. Most clinicians cannot be expected to have a deep understanding of the technical issues associated with web-based systems. As a result, they should only work with trusted providers of these services. However, basic considerations include ensuring that clinical and financial data are only transmitted with SSL encryption and that clinicians fully review their provider's privacy policy prior to using it. In the United States, awareness of HIPAA issues is also critical and most countries have equivalent legislation that must be taken into account, such as the Data Protection Act in the UK. An important issue to bear in mind, though, is that most Internet security breaches are due to end-user behavior (e.g., carelessness with passwords, failing to logoff systems), not technical malfeasance due to factors like hacking or interception of Internet transmissions.

RESPECTING INTELLECTUAL PROPERTY

Another important issue to recall is that unless an assessment is in the public domain, it is copyright protected. As a result, a clinician cannot legally create a web-based version of an assessment unless specific permission is granted by the copyright holder. In a similar vein, simply finding an assessment on a website does not mean that the website owner has the right to post the assessment unless copyright notices are prominently placed or the provider is a well-known test publisher. For security reasons as well, it is often best that clinicians rely upon reputably sourced web-based assessments.

CONTEXTUALIZING ETHICAL CONCERNS

While a number of ethical issues may arise when web-based assessment models are considered, they are rarely unique. Rather, the principles of sound clinical assessment practice should always remain at the forefront regardless of the assessment modality to be used. The Internet provides a means of delivering an assessment, nothing more, nothing less. As a result, the same professional considerations apply—regardless of how an assessment happens to be administered.

CLINICAL SCENARIO

Robert is an eight-year-old male referred for concerns about inattention at school, non-compliance at home and borderline failing grades. Robert's family had not sought help for these issues in the past. He was evaluated the previous year by the school psychologist with results indicating average intellectual abilities with no specific strengths or weakness but academic achievement slightly below expectation. Other than seasonal allergies, Robert had no specific health problems.

Robert's parents were divorced when he was three. He lived with his mother (who was not remarried) and visited alternate weekends and during summer vacations with his father who remarried two years ago and lived in a nearby town. His father had a child with his current wife approximately a year ago. Both his mother and step-mother reported a fair degree of distress in managing Robert's behavior with father reporting a lesser degree of concern.

The clinician had a number of initial diagnostic hypotheses after first meeting with Robert and his mother which included Attention-Deficit Hyperactivity Disorder, Oppositional Defiant Disorder and Parent-Child Relational Problem. She was also concerned that Robert's mother might be overwhelmed in her role as a single parent.

The clinician wanted to get a sense of the child's behavior at home, school, community and at his father's home. After explaining this to Robert's mother in person and his father by phone, she asked that Robert's mother, father, stepmother, teacher and afterschool child care provider complete a behavioral disorder inventory that assessed a broad range of child psychopathology and was linked to DSM-IV-R diagnoses. She also asked that all three of Robert's parental caregivers complete a parenting stress inventory. Given her concerns about father's potential lack of involvement with Robert, she requested a face-to-face meeting with him and asked that he complete the assessments in her office during the visit while the other involved adults completed web-based versions of the same assessments at their convenience

Based upon clinical interview, review of assessment data and a brief call to the teacher, the clinician felt that Robert met diagnostic criteria for Attention Deficit Disorder, Predominantly Inattentive Type. Additionally, review of the parenting inventories indicated that both Robert's mother and step-mother (though not his father) showed a moderate degree of stress in fulfilling their parental roles.

The clinician referred Robert to his pediatrician for a medication evaluation and proposed a brief course of behavioral parenting training for his mother, father and stepmother. She also shared with Robert's father the distress experienced by both Robert's mother and his current wife due to child management issues.

The clinician also made Robert's pediatrician aware of the use of web-based assessment tools; the physician subsequently used them to guide her titration of Robert's psychostimulant medication regimen by asking his parents and teacher to complete a behavior rating form on a weekly and then bi-weekly basis until his behavior stabilized.

Robert's caregivers responded favorably to parenting training with father becoming more involved and both his mother and step-mother indicating a lesser degree of stress after completing 8 weeks of parenting training.

CONCLUSION

We are only now beginning to see how web-based assessment can have a revolutionary impact upon the provision of mental health services. To this point, the Internet largely has been used a test delivery mechanism for pre-existing paper-and-pencil assessments. While this does bring value, these web-based testing systems have often been used as little more than electronic "page turners".

Looking to the future, tests will be developed specifically for Internet-based delivery. Not only will this render moot discussions about the method variance due to paper-and-pencil vs. online test delivery, it will take full advantage of Internet technology. For example, we are now starting to see the emergence of web-based adaptive test delivery whereby the sets of questions posed to a client are adapted based upon responses to prior questions. For example, if an earlier set of screening questions have ruled out the presence of psychotic symptoms, the client will no longer be asked about the symptoms related to this. Further, web-based technology can now be used to deliver assessments that could only be delivered by a desktop computer application such as those involving reaction time, intricate branched diagnostic interviews, or complex interactive neuropsychological tests. Finally, the use of web-based assessment also permits the use of audio and video content in assessment, a potentially promising yet largely untapped approach.

In a more mundane yet equally valuable step, web-based assessments can be integrated into electronic medical records. By moving assessments beyond use as stand-alone tools, web-based technologies can facilitate the integration of psychological testing data into the electronic medical record where it can be made differentially available to clinicians based upon their needs. For example, if a web-based tool were used for ongoing monitoring of depressive symptomatology, the mental health clinician could be provided with a detailed report of each client's reported symptoms while providers involved in other aspects of the patient's medical care might only be presented with a high-level overview. Similar, automatic warnings could be generated if specific critical items were endorsed or overall symptomatology reached a predetermined critical level.

In summary, we are at the edge of a revolution when it comes to web-based assessment. The surest path to this goal will involve creating a vision that is based upon a deep understanding of the technological benefits of web-based technology, well-grounded in the principles of sound clinical practice.

REFERENCES

American Psychological Association. (1985). *Standards for educational and psychological testing.* Washington, DC: American Psychological Association.

American Psychological Association. (1992). *Ethical principles of psychologists and code of conduct.* Washington, DC: American Psychological Association.

Association of Test Publishers. (2000). *Guidelines for computer-based testing.* Washington, DC: Association of Test Publishers.

Barak. A., & English, N. (2002). Prospects and limitations of psychological testing on the Internet. *Journal of Technology in Human Services, 19*(2/3), 65–89.

Bartram, D. (2006). Testing on the Internet: Issues, challenges and opportunities in the field of occupational assessment. In D. Bartram & R. Hambleton (Eds.), *Computer-based testing and the internet: Issues and advances.* Chichester: John Wiley and Sons.

Berger, M. (2006). Computer assisted clinical assessment. *Child and Adolescent Mental Health, 11*(2), 64–75.

Buchanan, T. (2003). Internet-based questionnaire assessment: Appropriate use in clinical contexts. *Cognitive Behaviour Therapy, 32*(3), 100–109.

Butcher, J. N., Perry, J., & Hahn, J. (2004). Computers in clinical assessment: Historical developments, present status and future challenges. *Journal of Clinical Psychology, 60*(3), 331–345.

Finger, M. S., & Ones, D. S. (1999). Psychometric equivalence of the computer and booklet forms of the MMPI: A meta-analysis. *Psychological Assessment, 11*(1), 58–66.

International Test Commission. (2005). *International guidelines on computer-based and internet delivered testing* [online]. [Accessed November 27, 2009]. Available from: www.intestcom.org/itc_projects.htm.

Matarazzo, J. D. (1990). Psychological assessment versus psychology testing: Validation from Binet to the school, clinic and courtroom. *American Psychologist, 45*(9), 999–1017.

Meehl, P. E. (1954). *Clinical versus statistical prediction: A theoretical analysis and a review of the evidence.* Minneapolis, MN: University of Minnesota Press.

Michaels, M. H. (2006). Ethical considerations in writing psychological assessment reports. *Journal of Clinical Psychology, 62*(1), 47–58.

Naglieri, J., Drasgow, F., Schmitt, M., Handler, L., Prifitera, A., Margolis, A., & Velasquez, R. (2004). Psychological testing on the Internet: New problems, old issues. *American Psychologist, 59*(3), 150–162.

Wiskoff, M. (1997). R&D laboratory management perspective. In W. A. Sands, B. K. Waters, & J. R. McBride (Eds.), *Computer adaptive testing: From inquiry to operation.* Washington, DC: American Psychological Association.

Chapter 16

THE ROLE OF BEHAVIORAL
TELEHEALTH IN MENTAL HEALTH

Thomas J. Kim

INTRODUCTION

Technology is transforming health-care in extraordinary ways, whether or not providers participate (Fieschi, 2002; Barak, 1999; Bauer, 2002; Swanson, 1999; Tang & Helmeste, 2000). This highlights the prudence of provider engagement to ensure a meaningful transformation. Key to considering technology in healthcare is to first appreciate the challenge and then consider the technology. Too often, the technologically "possible" captivates and risks failing to achieve genuine benefit.

This chapter will examine technology's role in clinical behavioral healthcare (i.e., behavioral telehealth), a challenge of limited resources and rising need. This examination will consider historic efforts, analyze the current landscape, and offer opinions based on clinical and program development experience. The intent is to reframe a frequently stalled discussion towards sustainable progress. To illustrate the value of behavioral telehealth, the following case example is offered as a precursor to this chapter.

This case example is an amalgam of incarcerated Gulf Coast juveniles seen via telehealth both before and after the landfall of Hurricanes Katrina and Rita. Significant postdisaster provider shortages present an opportunity to realize telehealth services impossible by traditional means that in effect drives telehealth maturation. This case material seeks to illustrate the power of telehealth within juvenile correctional care that currently exists as multiple siloed efforts challenged by inter-facility collaboration.

Youth X is a 15-year-old female with a history of mood disturbance, inappropriate behaviors, drug dependence and self-harm (i.e., cutting). Escalating difficulties led to incarceration with a court date six months from detention center arrival.

The youth presented for evaluation to a telepsychiatric detention center clinic. This clinic was built following the loss

151

of an on-site psychiatrist who commuted 45 minutes each way with a history of arrival delays and last minute cancellations. Without an onsite provider, youths are transported with two correctional officers to the nearest clinic one hour away and five weeks from the date of request. With the telepsychiatry clinic, a counselor escorts the youth to a treatment room in five minutes and within one week of detention center arrival. The telepsychiatrist is notable for moving from the Gulf Coast before hurricane landfall while successfully maintaining a clinical telehealth practice despite two moves around the country.

Upon presentation, the youth regarded the teleconferencing equipment with both curiosity and caution. Engaging the youth resulted in her cursing the provider and walking out of the treatment room. As a result of telehealth efficiencies, encounter refusals are rescheduled in one week. For five months, the youth would present weekly only to curse and walk out. Despite this lack of engagement, weekly encounter requests continued based on the observation that the youth would refuse in person. At five months, the youth presented for encounter and sat down without a word. Maintaining eye contact and with the practitioner nonverbally encour-

aging her to say something, the youth finally declared, "Will you please help me?" Treatment then began in earnest.

Following adjudication in court, the youth was sentenced to another correctional facility where the telepsychiatrist also provided clinical services. This resulted in an efficient transfer of service with immediate access to detention center collateral information and treatment recommendations. Service transfer is traditionally a fractured process of incomplete communication and need for redundant effort, activity and cost (e.g., labs and medication plan) now avoided due to telehealth efficiencies.

Youth X was ultimately released to home. Discharge planning included the identification of provider follow up and provision of a 30-day take home medication supply. The Office of Juvenile Justice (OJJ) contacted the telepsychiatrist four weeks after the youth's release. The youth was unable to secure an appointment until two months after release and was about to run out of medications. Given the availability of teleconferencing equipment at OJJ (installed for administrative purposes), the youth was seen at OJJ almost immediately for assessment and renewal of her medication regimen.

BACKGROUND

Terminology

To begin, there is an issue with terminology (Sood et al., 2007). The prefixes tele-, e- and i- precede an already expansive medical lexicon describing telehealth activity. With such a diversity of descriptors, there is little wonder that shared understanding is elusive. Multiple

descriptors also reflect the historically insulated nature of telehealth (Manhal-Baugus, 2001). Given this, consider the following:

Telehealth

The Health Resources and Services Administration (HRSA), Office for the

Advancement of Telehealth defines "telehealth" as:

> The use of electronic information and telecommunications technologies to support long distance **clinical health care**, patient and professional health related **education**, public health and health **administration**. [Emphasis added] (HRSA, 2009, p. 1)

"Telehealth" is favored given its inclusiveness of all potential activities. While an individual may focus on one activity, programs are best served to include all three for reasons to be explored further.

Synchronicity

Synchronicity refers to the nature of telehealth engagements. If participants interact in real time, the engagement is "synchronous." While easiest to imagine in terms of clinical activity (e.g., synchronous behavioral healthcare versus asynchronous radiology services), synchronicity impacts design, operation and support.

TECHNOLOGY

Video Teleconferencing (VTC)

Telecommunications has evolved considerably since the age of the telegraph; perhaps the first applied telehealth technology. Subsequent synchronous innovations include the telephone, cellular/mobile phone, instant messaging and video-teleconferencing (VTC) (via videophone, computer (PC) or dedicated appliance). VTC solutions deliver multi-modal transmissions (audio and video) and offer a distinct value: approximating the face-to-face (FTF) encounter. The focus of this chapter will be limited to VTC solutions. The wide array of VTC solutions prompts further emphasis on dedicated appliances (Polycom, 2009; Tandberg, 2009).

This is not to say that other VTC solutions are unviable (Kaplan, 1997; May et al., 1999; 2000; 2001; Menon et al., 2001). Dedicated VTC appliances, however, invite consideration of acceptance and utilization. Dedicated appliances offer:

- FTF verisimilitude with image fidelity and size
- familiar interface for remote providers
- familiar patient experience with television displays
- higher prices among VTC solutions

Videophones offer a widely deployable, inexpensive VTC alternative though small screens convey a suboptimal viewing experience. This lack of verisimilitude is believed to limit widespread videophone adoption. PC solutions offer a comparable experience to dedicated appliances and are touted as more affordable. Cost savings, however, is a misplaced argument for PC VTC. Those familiar with PC malfunctions can appreciate the expense of PC maintenance and costlier risk of alienating users. User experience and solution stability, then, represents useful benchmarks when considering the appropriate VTC solution to deploy. Appropriateness, in turn, emerges as a helpful construct when engaging those evaluating VTC solutions (Tachakra et al., 1996).

Connectivity

During the 1990s, considerable attention was devoted to "low bandwidth" VTC (Baigent et al., 1997; Zarate et al., 1997; Wheeler, 1998; Haslam and McLaren, 2000; Matsuura et al., 2000; Bishop et al., 2002). This level of service typically required tolerance of suboptimal transmissions. Consequently, attire, lighting and even wall color demanded optimization with varying success. Despite these limitations, low bandwidth solutions supported considerable activity (Allen and Wheeler, 1998). Multiple programs emerged, but few survived beyond initial funding. Several factors contributed to this limited sustainability including the considerable expense of low bandwidth connectivity.

Fortunately, broadband connectivity has since yielded larger, more affordable offerings with a growing footprint of availability (Yoshino et al., 2001). Bandwidth and cost, however, are only two factors impacting connectivity (OECD, 2009a). The US, for example, is lagging behind other industrialized nations in broadband subscriptions (OECD, 2009b). This slowing of broadband penetration reflects the complicated issue of "last mile" connectivity. And while this "last mile" remains to be crossed, the US telecommunications infrastructure is positioned for a new generation of telehealth activity reflecting growth elsewhere in the world.

Acting on this opportunity requires a degree of heroism, as available evidence is scant and includes programs with dated connectivity solutions. Negative anecdotal experiences also persist despite being drawn from low bandwidth initiatives. An appreciation of how environment is outpacing evidence can be found at any Internet Service Provider (ISP). ISP offerings older than one year reveal that additional bandwidth is now available for less money. More bandwidth creates more opportunity and frames a renewed dialogue about the future of telehealth.

The implication of improved connectivity is not to simply endorse high bandwidth solutions, particularly given "last mile" challenges. It is rather to appreciate connectivity as a shared resource. Connectivity should inform telehealth development rather than the reverse (Yellowlees, 1997). The reverse occurs when connectivity is purchased exclusively for telehealth activity despite existing resources or additional needs. As healthcare workflow migrates to the internet (e.g., Internet Protocol (IP) telephony, electronic health record (EHR) solutions, or electronic claims processing), an appropriate connectivity strategy is essential to sustainable growth (Sorensen et al., 2008).

TELEHEALTH MODEL

Model Design

Approach

An appropriately designed telehealth model is vital to success, but there is no readymade template (Dusserre et al., 1995). If a proposed model is flawed or misapplied, success is threatened in even the most receptive environment (e.g., prisons) (Myers et al., 2006). Having established a three-fold purpose, identified core technologies and encouraged a litmus test of appropriateness; the next step involves how materials and personnel come together. Conceptually, telehealth should support rather than replace traditional services (Qureshi & Kvedar, 2003). This speaks to the challenge of developing services and sensitivity required for implementation (Darkins, 2001).

Model design takes into account the challenge of maldistributed personnel and unmet service need. Responding with telehealth reveals some prevalent though unproductive preconceptions. For some, telehealth represents distant engagements to isolated communities. Geography, however, isn't the only service barrier though support is typically reserved for remote areas. Whether six hundred miles or six blocks, "access" rather than "distance" should define an underserved community.

Care fragmentation is another noted concern (Nohr, 2000), but not one specific to telehealth. Consider Australian practitioners who found diagnostic clarity, but limited treatment benefit from a collaborative behavioral telehealth initiative (Clarke, 1997). A potential explanation might be care fragmentation. The lack of perceived benefit might also reflect underutilization of the technology. Model revision could include stakeholders capable of satisfying unmet needs. In this revision, telehealth promotes a more cohesive model rather than an isolated solution separate from traditional resources (Gelber, 2001).

Seeking a finer point with model design highlights a number of publications offering insight. Collectively, they reveal shared elements of model success despite the heterogeneity of constructs. The reader is encouraged to explore the following:

- seven core principles (Yellowlees, 1997)
- readiness model (Jennett et al., 2005)
- appreciating remote site needs (Mitchell et al., 2001)
- identify the inappropriate (Jones, 2001)
- value of shared resources (Brown, 1995)
- whole system thinking (Kalim et al., 2006)
- workforce dilemma approach (Faulkener et al., 1998)
- value of adaptability (Kavanagh & Hawker, 2001)
- four part pilot development (Gelber, 1998)
- integrated global networks (Shannon et al., 2002)
- theory of innovation diffusion (Grigsby et al., 2002; Rogers, 1995)
- human development metaphor (Yellowlees, 2001)

A 1964 RAND memorandum deserves special mention given its continued relevance with distant communications (Baran, 1964). Intended to advise the military on wartime survivability of command and control centers, communication network architecture is classified into three archetypes:

- centralized (single coordinating node)
- decentralized (several coordinating nodes)
- distributed (equally weighted nodes)

These archetypes serve equally well in describing telehealth sustainability. Centralized models adopt the wheel and spoke configuration often found in pilots and suggest a single champion driving activity. This model has limited sustainability when the champion is unavailable. Decentralized models are found in adolescent aged programs with multiple champions and demonstrate higher levels of utilization. Decentralized programs are better able to withstand change given the adaptability of multiple coordinating nodes. Distributed models, therefore, describe mature programs with autonomous encounters across the network. Change within any node has little effect on a distributed program's sustainability.

HUMAN FACTORS

Efforts in Norway determined that non-technical factors (e.g., personality) notably affect telehealth success (Aas, 2001a). Such a conclusion suggests that some factors impacting telehealth may also impact FTF encounters. This is not to say that telehealth is identical to FTF encounters, but that certain factors apply universally. In fact, organizational workflow is affected by telehealth (Aas, 2001b; Aas, 2002a; Ball et al., 1995). Adjustments in expectations, responsibilities and coordination present a host of human factors to overcome prior to widespread acceptance and utilization (Hailey, 2001; Aas, 2002b; Whitten & Rowe-Adjibogoun, 2002; Bulik, 2008).

VTC communication is one such factor requiring support and training (Liu et al., 2007; McLaren & Ball, 1997). It is opined that while VTC communication is a unique skill, it is not unlike FTF communication adjustments (e.g., emergency encounter versus educational presentation). Moreover, as VTC transmission has improved, positive telehealth communication ratings suggest a close approximation to FTF communication (Miller, 2001). Therefore, the cultivation of VTC communicative skill should remain a broader professional competency rather than a technology specific undertaking.

Another notable human factor issue is the cultural defense towards preserving the therapeutic relationship (May et al., 2001; Marcin et al., 2004). While evidence exists that this understandable concern may be unwarranted (Ghosh et al., 1997), some resistance to telehealth is generally assured. An effective response to cultural defenders can be found with full disclosure. Telehealth seeks not to displace existing relationships, but support environments where relationships are wanting or absent. Demonstrating transparency with intent and approach can effectively engage proponent and critic alike.

MODEL IMPLEMENTATION

As circumstances vary, a universal implementation strategy does not exist. There are, however, considerations of which to be mindful.

Integration

The celebration with launching a telehealth program is often fleeting as utilization is likely to progress slowly (Liebhaber & Grossman, 2006). Utilization is a key measure of sustainability and, therefore, requires thoughtful attention (Buist et al., 2000; Yellowlees, 2001). Active promotion and a reliable referral mechanism are two means of encouraging utilization (Cloutier et al., 2008). Whatever the means, it is clear that the "build it and they will come" approach is suboptimal (Doolittle, 2001). A better approach might be "integrate it and they will come." Establish a plan for how a proposed telehealth model supports existing workflow towards enhancing behavioral health care delivery (Greenberg et al., 2006). Revisiting the above mentioned design citations, an integrated telehealth strategy encourages ongoing stakeholder input towards supporting widespread propagation (Yellowlees, 1997; Grigsby et al., 2002).

Model Support

Appropriate telehealth models are not without challenges such as support for encounter completion. This includes an effective electronic health records (EHR) documentation strategy. The number of available EHR solutions continues to grow though many may not survive long term (Makris et al., 1998; Kaufman & Hyler, 2005). The predicted culling is based on the challenge of interoperability (i.e., information transfer between health systems). Solutions fated for demise are often "home grown" and designed for unique workflow needs. Some commercial solutions adopt a similar approach and create limited utility beyond the solution and its subscribers. Though logical for market share, this approach silos information and runs counter to the conceptual benefits of EHR. When evaluating an EHR solu-

tions, inquiry into how data is shared is as important as what data is captured. This would include the capture and sharing of utilization data among telehealth stakeholders (Wootton et al., 2002).

Operational Support

Successful telehealth programs require personnel with the necessary technology skills. This highlights two sources of expertise with Information Systems/Information Technology (IS/IT) and Telehealth. While related, the two camps are seemingly oppositional with the former ensuring network integrity and the latter encouraging network plasticity. Fortunately, the two are not exclusive as balanced inclusion of IS/IT and Telehealth input can prevent avoidable setbacks.

Telehealth operational challenges are still likely to occur. As a general rule, common sense suffices. Miller offers an interesting forensic challenge regarding the inclusion of remote individuals during legal proceedings (Miller et al., 2005). The limits with viewing perspective raises a concern for "witness coaching" off camera. A potential solution might be to place a mirror behind the remote participant thereby providing the local site with a clear view of the remote environment.

Personnel Support

The issue of training and personnel support cannot be emphasized enough (Picot, 2000). Though telehealth is presented as integrating into existing protocols, it helps to prepare for how telehealth will impact personnel. The literature is a good place to gain situational awareness (Health Devices, 1999), but conclusions are often dated or lack generalizability. Professional organizations (Online Therapy Institute, 2010; American Telemedecine Association, 2009; American Association for Technology in Psychiatry, 2009; International Society for Mental Health Online, 2009) offer more timely insight and expertise though specific recommendations (i.e., standards and guidelines) remain a work in progress in some instances (Loane and Wootton, 2002). Formal curricular resources (NARBHA, 2009) also exist

and will likely grow in both quality and number. Ultimately, a brief orientation is sufficient prior to launching a telehealth program (Aas, 2002c). Adaptable and responsive longitudinal support, however, is far more critical (Buist et al., 2000).

If appropriately designed, implemented and supported, telehealth participants will stop thinking about the technology, utilization will rise and the service delivery challenge will abate.

TELEHEALTH CHALLENGES

At present, the principal challenges to widespread telehealth use are neither clinical nor technological. The remaining hurdles are legal, regulatory and financial in nature (Klien & Manning, 1995; Sanders & Bashsur, 1995; Nickelson, 1996; Cohen & Straw, 1996; Stanberry, 1998; Schmitz, 1999; Manhal-Baugus, 2001; Silverman, 2003).

These challenges indicate a still burgeoning field within an environment that pre-dates telehealth innovations. Whether optimistic or apprehensive about telehealth, formal guidance is needed to both encourage appropriate growth and prevent misfortune. Unfortunately, the call for a more hospitable telehealth environment remains unanswered (Wootton, 1998). Prior to exploring these challenges, it bears mentioning that legislation is not itself a barrier to telehealth. Australia appears to have reversed this conventional belief and suggests how lawmakers can be a telehealth propagator rather than an inhibitor (O'Shannessy, 2000). Telehealth propagation is also evident within the US. Moving forward, there remains need for continued engagement between health care, technology and government

stakeholders committed to improving health care service delivery through telehealth (Silverman, 2003; Siwicki, 1997).

Those seeking a deeper understanding of how these challenges impact a particular jurisdiction can find additional information from the American Telemedicine Association, the Telemedicine Information Exchange and the Center for Telehealth and e-Health Law (American Telemedicine Association, 2009; Telemedicine Information Exchange, 2009a; Center for Telehealth and E-Health Law, 2009). Broadly, principal challenges include the following.

Licensure

Licencing or accrediting bodies are essential to maintaining a safe workforce. The challenge lies with regulations negatively impacting workforce adequacy relative to service need. Border regions between Georgia and Florida, for example, reveal patients with high need and available providers on the wrong side. As the challenge of service delivery is blind to borders, the question is whether telehealth should enjoy a comparable lack of discrimination.

Currently, there is progress in the form of special purpose licensure within a few areas (Telemedicine Information Exchange, 2009b). Elsewhere, an unrestricted license is required for both the originating and receiving site. Brief consideration reveals the cost prohibition of securing multiple unrestricted licenses. In the US, the Federation of State Medical Boards is a welcome stakeholder with an interest in exploring national telehealth licensure (Federation of State Medical Boards, 2009). Resolution, however, will be difficult for many reasons including safety concerns highlighted by the 2005 Ryan Haight case (see ryanscause.org, 2009 for details). Though the incident involved e-prescribing, the ensuing legislation underscores the need for a therapeutic relationship prior to treatment. As many areas continue to struggle with provider shortages, telehealth licensure reform holds promise towards ensuring relationships while maintaining citizenry protection.

Licensure reform has also raised concern among providers. Some perceive telehealth as threatening to local practices. As mentioned, telehealth seeks not to replace traditional services, but support areas with unmet need. In locations with adequate provider availability, many patients choose FTF options. One means of assuring local provider interests is requiring partnership with local resources as necessary for telehealth licensure rather than unstipulated direct access to the patient. There is also potential for local provider telehealth service exportation emphasizing the value of an appropriately designed model. Inappropriately restricting telehealth service access at the state level is submitted as counterproductive to resolving service need and supporting provider interests. Licensure reform remains fundamental.

Malpractice

While licensure highlights the challenge of inter-regional telehealth, intra-regional activity is equally challenged. Onerous regulations play some part in discouraging adoption, but another notable barrier is the threat of litigation. At present, there is a lack of legal precedent and uncertainty about how a telehealth malpractice suit would be pursued.

Rather than bog down debating jurisdiction and culpability, it is reassuring to note that providers of professional insurance are now offering coverage for telehealth providers. Another notable exemplar milestone in the US, also encouraging for those elsewhere, is that behavioral telehealth provider enjoyed malpractice coverage under the statutes covering provider liability in their care of vulnerable patient populations. The inclusion of telehealth providers is both appropriate and very encouraging.

Reimbursement

Within the US, securing telehealth reimbursement has met varying levels of success (Center for Telemedicine Law, 2003). Reimbursement remains a substantial barrier to scalable telehealth growth (Smolensky, 2003).

A potentially constructive approach may be to consider why payers are reluctant to reimburse for telehealth (Nesbitt et al., 2000; Whitten and Buis, 2007). As telehealth offers service potential in environments that previously went without, payers are not alone in having concern about additional system costs with a model lacking proof of benefit (Curell et al., 2008). Proving that telehealth merits reimbursement is best served by reframing the anticipated impact beyond the encounter to broader metrics of resource utilization, quality of life effects, relationship to legal proceedings and other downstream costs (Jennett et al., 2003). These societal costs are all too familiar to legislators and others in the public sector, addressing behavioral health care needs. Therefore, the demonstration of telehealth benefit in support of reimbursement aligns perfectly with the behavioral health care legislative agenda.

TELEHEALTH EVALUATION

During the 1990s, telehealth conclusions were far from glowing despite the surge of interest and inquiry (McLaren et al., 1996; Rosen, 1997; Liu Sheng et al., 1998; Werner and Anderson, 1998; Rohland et al., 2000; Mielonen et al., 2003; Webster et al., 2008). These limited findings were possible inevitable given the novelty of VTC, limited functionality and high costs of poorly approximated FTF encounters. Consequently, a cooling of interest and lack of sustainability explains the decline of telehealth publication output (Moser et al., 2004). Fortunately, advances in and acclimation to VTC have resolved many of these limitations. This along with persisting access to care challenges sets the stage for a renewed surge of telehealth activity and evaluation.

A review of the telehealth literature reveals generally positive findings though generalizable conclusions are rare and the necessary support for telehealth has stalled (Hailey, 2001; Neckelson, 1996; Currell et al., 2008; Baer et al., 1997; Hersh et al., 2006; Singh et al., 2002; Whitten et al., 2002; 2007). One approach to increasing rigor has been the standardized comparison of VTC to FTF encounters (Baer et al., 1995; Baigent et al., 1997; Montani et al., 1997; Ruskin et al., 1998; Nelson et al., 2003; Alessi, 2000; Brodley et al., 2000; Elford et al., 2000; Matsuura et al., 2000; Yoshino et al., 2001; Jones et al., 2001; Bishop et al., 2002; McLaren et al., 2002; Simpson et al., 2003; Greenwood et al., 2004; Ruskin et al., 2004; Cuevas et al., 2006; Urness et al., 2006; O'Reilly et al., 2007; Shore et al., 2007a; Singh et al., 2007; Spalding et al., 2008). These assessments employ validated instruments (e.g., structured interviews) and offer notable conclusions. While these findings are of interest, it is opined that this strategy is flawed in two ways.

The first issue relates to the scrutiny that telehealth solutions are subjected to. Undue technology expectations (e.g., frame rates, packet loss, dropped transmissions) are a by-product of low bandwidth VTC solutions inciting worry about missed nuance. Maintaining this concern given current capabilities distracts from more productive lines of inquiry. Put another way, excessive scrutiny of VTC has been compared by colleagues to requiring provider vision and hearing exams prior to FTF encounters. As high bandwidth availability increases, concern about transmission fidelity will subside and attention will refocus on demonstrating the substantive value of telehealth.

A second concern with VTC versus FTF comparisons has to do with context. Considering whether a telehealth solution is viable compared to a FTF alternative presumes that the FTF alternative is available. All things being equal, most people would choose FTF encounters. As FTF options become increasingly scarce, time consuming, or otherwise prohibitive, particularly with vulnerable populations, a more useful approach may be to compare telehealth to available alternatives. Given real world choices, providers and clients alike may favor telehealth (Starling, 2003; Bischoff et al., 2004; Mekhjian et al., 1999). Unless FTF options dramatically improve, the preference for telehealth will continue to grow.

Calling for more rigor in the evaluation of telehealth is far from new (Hailey et al., 1999). One explanation for the pace and quality of published data re-lates to the maturity of reporting programs (Krupinski et al., 2002). Young programs lack the impact to demonstrate clinical efficacy and are left with qualitative inquiries into acceptance and satisfaction. Therefore, a staged evaluation strategy based on model maturity (i.e., maturing towards a distributed model) is both reasonable and recommended (Shaw, 2002). With maturity, agreement on metrics and pooling of interoperable data will yield the necessary rigor supporting the evidence-based practice of telehealth.

FUTURE DIRECTIONS

Utilization is a key to realizing telehealth benefits. Telehealth treatment adherence is one such utilization metric that demonstrates comparable rates to FTF treatments (Ruskin et al., 2004). Attendance is another with rates reported as higher than FTF encounters, suggesting superior efficiency in service delivery (Zaylor, 1999). The influence of telehealth on practice behaviors, however, has revealed conflicting results (Grady & Melcer, 2005; Gruen et al., 2006; Modai et al., 2006). A potential explanation may be the early and unpredictable effects of telehealth within service naive environments. Increases in hospitalization rates attributed to telehealth, for example, results in rising short-term costs, but also potentially improved surveillance, better treatment response and eventual reduction in hospitalization rates. Additional metrics that clarify practice habits in support of telehealth include time to follow up and efficiencies in encounter duration (Zaylor, 1999; Grady & Melcer, 2005). Ultimately, the manner and effect that telehealth has on these and other metrics holds enormous promise that may prove integral to future health care reform.

The economics of telehealth will also remain a fundamental and active area of inquiry adding to the current body of supporting evidence (Trott and Blignaut, 1998; Dossetor et al., 1999; Mielonen et al., 2000; Elford et al., 2001; Simpson et al., 2001a and b; Grady, 2002; Hyler & Gangure, 2003; Young & Ireson, 2003; Ruskin et al., 2004; Harley, 2006; Modai et al., 2006; Shore et al., 2007b). As suggested earlier, a thoughtful economic evaluation strategy is vital. A few notable considerations include maintaining the patient perspective (Simpson et al., 2001b), ensuring real world comparisons (Dossetor et al., 1999) and appreciating a rapidly changing marketplace (Werner and Anderson, 1998).

A final research direction to note is the demonstration of improved clinical outcome (Ruskin et al., 2004; Grady & Melcer, 2005). Though available data remains limited, it is predicted that telehealth's impact on clinical outcome is assured as maturing programs continue to address widespread service needs.

BEHAVIORAL TELEHEALTH CARE

It may be apparent that there has been limited emphasis on behavioral health care in favor of a broader exploration of telehealth. This is intentional and reflects a core recommendation that telehealth initiatives should cast a wide net. Whether in terms of organizational investment or stakeholder recruitment, the underlying technology facilitates encounters regardless of content or purpose. Seeking equitable inclusion of any interested parties ensures appropriateness, encourages adoption and enables long-term sustainability. It should be noted that behavioral health care practitioners enjoy the enviable position of engaging in telehealth without the need for additional remote enhancements (e.g., scope attachments). As such, behavioral telehealth has and will continue to be a sustaining presence within telehealth.

CONCLUSION

It has been presented that the promise of telehealth represents many things to many people. Examining the application of VTC technologies towards synchronous service delivery has revealed a long standing though periodically stalled history of progress. Identified challenges reflect an understandable and possibly inevitable developmental evolution affecting acceptance, deployment, adoption, utilization and sustainability. And while challenges persist, technological advancements and persisting service need primes the next generation of telehealth.

It is clear that a universal telehealth solution is nonexistent given the heterogeneity of needs, interests, capabilities and environments. As such, it is opined that the right strategic approach is far more essential to success. Persons interested in developing or maturing telehealth initiatives would do well to routinely consider appropriateness and context. This approach lends clarity to recruiting partners, aligning expectations and responding to anticipated critics.

Behavioral health care stakeholders occupy a unique position in assuming leadership and advocacy roles towards demonstrating the virtue of telehealth across disciplines and purposes. Such a demonstration will be complicated, but the rising burden of mental illness and ensuing call for meaningful health care reform may offer sufficient leverage towards mitigating service delivery challenges through telehealth.

REFERENCES

Aas, I. H. (2001a). Telemedical work and cooperation. *Journal of Telemedicine and Telecare, 7*(4), 212–218.

Aas, I. H. (2001b). A qualitative study of the organizational consequences of telemedicine. *Journal of Telemedicine and Telecare, 7*(1), 18–26.

Aas, I. H. (2002a). Changes in the job situation due to telemedicine. *Journal of Telemedicine and Telecare, 8*(1), 41–47.

Aas, I. H. (2002b). Telemedicine and changes in the distribution of tasks between levels of care. *Journal of Telemedicine and Telecare, 8*(Suppl 2), 1–2.

Aas, I. H. (2002c). Learning in organizations working with telemedicine. *Journal of Telemedicine and Telecare, 8*(2), 107–111.

Alessi, N. (2000). Child and adolescent telepsychiatry: Reliability studies needed. *CyberPsychology and Behavior, 3*(6), 1009–1015.

Allen, A., & Wheeler, T. (1998). Telepsychiatry background and activity survey. The development of telepsychiatry. *Telemedicine Today, 6*(2), 34–37.

American Association for Technology in Psychiatry. (2009). *Homepage* [online]. [Accessed November 25, 2009]. Available from: http://www.techpsych.net.

American Telemedicine Association. (2009). *Homepage* [online]. [Accessed November 25, 2009]. Available from: http://www.atmeda.org.

Baer, L., Cukor, P., Jenike, M. A., Leahy, L., O'Laughlen, J., & Coyle, J. T. (1995). Pilot studies of telemedicine for patients with obsessive-compulsive disorder. *American Journal of Psychiatry, 152*(9), 1383–1385.

Baer, L., Elford, D. R., & Cukor, P. (1997). Telepsychiatry at forty: What have we learned? *Harvard Review of Psychiatry, 5*(1), 7–17.

Baigent, M. F., Lloyd, C. J., Kavanagh, S. J., Ben-Tovim, D. I., Yellowlees, P. M., Kalucy, R. S., & Bond, M. J. (1997). Telepsychiatry: 'Tele' yes, but what about the 'psychiatry'? *Journal of Telemedicine and Telecare, 3*(Suppl 1), 3–5.

Ball, C. J., McLaren, P. M., Summerfield, A. B., Lipsedge, M. S., & Watson, J. P. (1995). A comparison of communication modes in adult psychiatry. *Journal of Telemedicine and Telecare, 1*(1), 22–26.

Barak, A. (1999). Psychological applications on the Internet: A discipline on the threshold of a new millenium. *Applied and Preventive Psychology, 8*(4), 231–46.

Baran, P. (1964). *On distributed communications: I. Introduction to distributed communication networks.* Santa Monica, CA: The-Rand-Corporation.

Bauer, K. A. (2002). Using the Internet to empower patients and to develop partnerships with clinicians. *World Hospital Health Services, 38*(2), 2–10.

Bischoff, R. J., Hollist, C. S., Smith, C. W., & Flack, P. (2004). Addressing the mental health needs of the rural underserved: Findings from a multiple case study of a behavioral telehealth project. *Contemporary Family Therapy, 26*(2), 179–198.

Bishop, J. E., O'Reilly, R. L. Maddox, K., & Hutchinson, L. (2002). Client satisfaction in a feasibility study comparing face-to-face interviews with telepsychiatry. *Journal of Telemedicine and Telecare, 8*(4), 217–21.

Brodey, B. B., Claypoole, K. H., Motto, J., Arias, R. G., & Goss, R. (2000). Satisfaction of forensic psychiatric patients with remote telepsychiatric evaluation. *Psychiatric Services, 51*(10), 1305–1307.

Brown, F. W. (1995). A survey of telepsychiatry in the USA. *Journal of Telemedicine and Telecare, 1*(1), 19–21.

Buist, A., Coman, G., Silvas A., & Burrows, G. (2000). An evaluation of the telepsychiatry programme in Victoria, Australia. *Journal of Telemedicine and Telecare, 6*(4), 216–221.

Bulik, R. J. (2008). Human factors in primary care telemedicine encounters. *Journal of Telemedicine and Telecare, 14*(4), 169–172.

Center for Telehealth and E-Health Law. (2009). *Homepage* [online]. [Accessed November 25, 2009]. Available from: http://www.ctel.org.

Center for Telemedicine Law. (2003). *Telemedicine reimbursement report.* Center for Telemedicine Law: Washington, D.C.

Clarke, P. H. (1997). A referrer and patient evaluation of a telepsychiatry consultation-liaison service in South Australia. *Journal of Telemedicine and Telecare, 3*(Suppl 1), 12–14.

Cloutier, P., Cappelli, M., Glennie, J. E., & Keresztes C. (2008). Mental health services for children and youth: A survey of physicians' knowledge, attitudes and use of telehealth services. *Journal of Telemedicine and Telecare, 14*(2), 98–101.

Cohen, J. L., & Strawn, E. L. (1996). Tele-medicine in the '90s. *Journal of the Florida Medical Association, 83*(9), 631–633.

Cuevas, C. D., Arredondo, M. T., Cabrera, M. F., Sulzenbacher, H., & Meise, U. (2006). Randomized clinical trial of telepsychiatry through videoconference versus face-to-face conventional psychi-atric treatment. *Telemedicine Journal and E-Health, 12*(3), 341–350.

Currell, R., Urquhart, C., Wainwright, P., & Lewis, R. (2008). Telemedicine versus face to face patient care: Effects on profession-al practice and health outcomes. *The Cochrane database of systemic reviews. Issue 2.* Chichester: Wiley. Updated quarterly.

Darkins, A. (2001). Program management of telemental health care services. *Journal of Geriatric Psychiatry and Neurology, 14*(2), 80–87.

Doolittle, G. C. (2001). Telemedicine in Kansas: The successes and the challenges. *Journal of Telemedicine and Telecare, 7*(Suppl 2), 43–46.

Dossetor, D. R., Nunn, K. P., Fairley, M., & Eggleton D. (1999). A child and adoles-cent psychiatric outreach service for rural New South Wales: A telemedicine pilot study. *Journal of Paediatrics and Child Health, 35*(6), 525–529.

Dusserre, P., Allaert, F. A., & Dusserre, L. (1995). The emergence of international telemedicine: No ready-made solutions exist. *Medinfo, 8*(Pt 2), 1475–1478.

Elford, R., White, H., Bowering, R., Ghandi, A., Maddiggan, B., St John, K., House, M., Harnett, J., West, R., & Battcock, A (2000). A randomized, controlled trial of child psychiatric assessments conducted using videoconferencing. *Journal of Telemedicine and Telecare, 6*(2), 73–82.

Elford, D. R., White, H., St John, K., Maddigan, B., Ghandi, M., & Bowering, R. (2001). A prospective satisfaction study and cost analysis of a pilot child telepsy-chiatry service in Newfoundland. *Journal of Telemedicine and Telecare, 7*(2), 73–81.

Faulkner, L. R., Scully, J. H., & Shore, J. H. (1998). A strategic approach to the psychi-atric workforce dilemma. *Psychiatric Serv-ices, 49*(4), 493–497.

Federation of State Medical Boards. (2009). *Advocacy, key issues and goals* [online]. [Accessed November 25, 2009]. Available from: http://www.fsmb.org/grpol_key issues.html

Fieschi, M. (2002). Information technology is changing the way society sees health care delivery. *International Journal of Medical Informatics, 66*(3), 85–93.

Gelber, H. (1998). The experience of the Royal Children's Hospital Mental Health Service videoconferencing project. *Journal of Telemedicine and Telecare, 4*(Suppl 1), 71–73.

Gelber, H. (2001). The experience in Victoria with telepsychiatry for the child and ado-lescent mental health service. *Journal of Telemedicine and Telecare, 7*(Suppl 2), 32–34.

Ghosh, G. J., McLaren, P. M. , & Watson, J. P. (1997). Evaluating the alliance in videolink teletherapy. *Journal of Telemedicine and Telecare, 3*(Suppl 1), 33–35.

Grady, B. J. (2002). A comparative cost analysis of an integrated military telemen-tal health-care service. *Telemedicine Journal and E-Health, 8*(3), 293–300.

Grady, B. J., & Melcer, T. (2005). A retro-spective evaluation of telemental health-care services for remote military popula-tions. *Telemedicine Journal and E-Health, 11*(5), 551–558.

Greenberg, N., Boydell, K. M., & Volpe, T. (2006). Pediatric telepsychiatry in ontario: Caregiver and service provider perspec-tives. *The Journal of Behavioral Health Services and Research, 33*(1), 105–111.

Greenwood, J., Chamberlain, C., & Parker, G. (2004). Evaluation of a rural telepsychi-atry service. *Australasian Psychiatry, 12*(3), 268–272.

Grigsby, J., Rigby, M., Hiemstra, A., House, M., Olsson, S., & Whitten P. (2002). Tele-medicine/telehealth: An international per-spective. The diffusion of telemedicine. *Telemedicine Journal and e-Health, 8*(1), 79–94.

Gruen, R. L., Bailie, R., Wang, Z., Heard, S., & O'Rourke, I. (2006). Specialist outreach to isolated and disadvantaged communities: A population-based study. *Lancet, 368*(9530), 130–138.

Hailey, D. (2001). Some successes and limitations with telehealth in Canada. *Journal of Telemedicine and Telecare, 7*(Suppl 2), 73–75.

Hailey, D., Jacobs, P., Simpson, J., & Doze, S. (1999). An assessment framework for telemedicine applications. *Journal of Telemedicine and Telecare, 5*(3), 162–170.

Harley, J. (2006). Economic evaluation of a tertiary telepsychiatry service to an island. *Journal of Telemedicine and Telecare, 12*(7), 354–357.

Haslam, R., & McLaren, P. (2000). Interactive television for an urban adult mental health service: The Guy's Psychiatric Intensive Care Unit Telepsychiatry Project. *Journal of Telemedicine and Telecare, 6*(Suppl 1), S50–2.

Health Devices. (1999). Telemedicine: An overview. *Health Devices, 28*(3), 88–103.

Hersh, W. R., Hickam, D. H., Severance, S. M., Dana T. L., Pyle Krages K., & Helfand, M. (2006). Diagnosis, access and outcomes: Update of a systematic review of telemedicine services. *Journal of Telemedicine and Telecare, 12*(Suppl 2), S3–31.

HRSA. (2009) *Telehealth* [online]. [Accessed January 11, 2010]. Available from: http://www.hrsa.gov/telehealth/.

Hyler, S. E., & Gangure, D. P. (2003). A review of the costs of telepsychiatry. *Psychiatric Services, 54*(7), 976–980.

International Society for Mental Health Online. (2009). *Homepage* [online]. Available from: http://www.ismho.org.

Jennett, P. A., Affleck, H. L., Hailey, D., Ohinmaa, A., Anderson, C., Thomas, R., Young, B., Lorenzetti, D., & Scott, R. E. (2003). The socio-economic impact of telehealth: A systematic review. *Journal of Telemedicine and Telecare, 9*(6), 311–320.

Jennett, P. A., Gagnon, M. P., & Brandstadt, H. K. (2005). Preparing for success: Readiness models for rural telehealth. *Journal of Postgraduate Medicine, 51*(4), 279–85.

Jones, B. N. (2001). Telepsychiatry and geriatric care. *Current Psychiatry Reports, 3*(1), 29–36.

Jones, B. N., Johnston, D., Reboussin, B., & McCall, W. V. (2001). Reliability of telepsychiatry assessments: Subjective versus observational ratings. *Journal of Geriatric Psychiatry Neurology, 14*(2), 66–71.

Kalim, K., Carson, E., & Cramp, D. (2006). An illustration of whole systems thinking. *Health Services Management Research, 19*(3), 174–185.

Kaplan, E. H. (1997). Telepsychotherapy. Psychotherapy by telephone, videotelephone and computer videoconferencing. *Journal of Psychotherapy Practice and Research, 6*(3), 227–237.

Kaufman, K. R., & Hyler, S. E. (2005). Problems with the electronic medical record in clinical psychiatry: A hidden cost. *Journal of Psychiatric Practice, 11*(3), 200–204.

Kavanagh, S., & Hawker, F. (2001). The fall and rise of the South Australian telepsychiatry network. *Journal of Telemedicine and Telecare, 7*(Suppl 2), 41–43.

Klein, S. R., & Manning, W. L. (1995). Telemedicine and the law. *Healthcare Information Management, 9*(3), 35–40.

Krupinski, E., Nypaver, M., Poropatich, R., Ellis, D., Safwat, R., & Sapci, H. (2002). Telemedicine/telehealth: An international perspective. Clinical applications in telemedicine/telehealth. *Telemedicine Journal and E-Health, 8*(1), 13–34.

Liebhaber, A. B., & Grossman, J. M. (2006). *Physicians slow to adopt patient e-mail. Data Bulletin No. 32.* Washington DC: Center for Studying Health System Change.

Liu Sheng, O. R., Jen-Hwa Hu, P., Chau, P. Y. K., Hjelm, N. M., Yan Tam, K., Wei, C. P., & Tse, J. (1998). A survey of physicians' acceptance of telemedicine. *Journal of Telemedicine and Telecare, 4*(Suppl 1), 100–102.

Liu, X., Sawada, Y., Takizawa, T., Sato, H., Sato, M., Sakamoto, H., Utsugi, T., Sato, K., Sumino, H., Okamura, S., & Sakamaki, T. (2007). Doctor-patient communication: A comparison between telemedicine consultation and face-to-face consultation. *Internal Medicine, 46*(5), 227–232.

Loane, M., & Wootton, R. (2002). A review of guidelines and standards for telemedicine.

Journal of Telemedicine and Telecare, 8(2), 63–71.

Makris, L., Kopsacheilis, E. V., & Strintzis, M. G. (1998). Hippocrates: An integrated platform for telemedicine applications. *Medical Informatics, 23*(4), 265–276.

Manhal-Baugus, M. (2001). E-therapy: Practical, ethical and legal issues. *Cyberpsychology and Behaviour, 4*(5), 551–63.

Marcin, J. P., Schepps, D. E., Page, K. A., Struve, S. N., Nagrampa, E., & Dimand, R. J. (2004). Using telemedicine to provide pediatric subspecialty care to children with special health care needs in an underserved rural community. *Pediatrics, 113*(1, pt 1), 1–6.

Matsuura, S., Hosaka, T., Yukiyama, T., Ogushi, Y., Okada, Y., Haruki, Y., & Nakamura, M. (2000). Application of telepsychiatry: A preliminary study. *Psychiatry and Clinical Neurosciences, 54*(1), 55–58.

May, C. R., Ellis, N. T., Atkinson, T., Gask, L., Mair, F., & Smith, C. (1999). Psychiatry by videophone: A trial service in north west England. *Studies in Health Technology and Informatics, 68*, 207–210.

May, C., Gask, L., Ellis, N., Atkinson, T., Mair, F., Smith, C., Pidd, S., & Esmail A. (2000). Telepsychiatry evaluation in the north-west of England: Preliminary results of a qualitative study. *Journal of Telemedicine and Telecare, 6*(Suppl 1), s20–22.

May, C. R., Gask, L., Atkinson, T., Ellis, N., Mair, F., & Esmail, A. (2001). Resisting and promoting new technologies in clinical practice: The case of telepsychiatry. *Social Science and Medicine, 52*(12), 1889–1901.

McLaren, P. M., Laws, V. J., Ferreira, A. C., O'Flynn, D., Lipsedge, M., & Watson, J. P. (1996). Telepsychiatry: Outpatient psychiatry by videolink. *Journal of Telemedicine and Telecare, 2*(Suppl 1), 59–62.

McLaren, P., Ahlbom, J., Riley, A., Mohammedali, A., & Denis, M. (2002). The North Lewisham telepsychiatry project: Beyond the pilot phase. *Journal of Telemedicine and Telecare, 8*(Suppl 2), 98–100.

McLaren, P. M., & Ball, C. J. (1997).

Interpersonal communications and telemedicine: Hypotheses and methods. *Journal of Telemedicine and Telecare, 3*(Suppl 1), 5–7.

Mekhjian, H., Warisse Turner, J., Gailiun, M., & McCain, T. A. (1999). Patient satisfaction with telemedicine in a prison environment. *Journal of Telemedicine and Telecare, 5*(1), 55–61.

Menon, A. S., Kondapavalru, P., Krishna, P., Chrismer, J. B., Raskin, A., Hebel, J. R., & Ruskin, P. E. (2001). Evaluation of a portable low cost videophone system in the assessment of depressive symptoms and cognitive function in elderly medically ill veterans. *Journal of Nervous and Mental Disease, 189*(6), 399–401.

Mielonen, M. L., Ohinmaa, A., Moring, J., & Isohanni, M. (2000). Psychiatric inpatient care planning via telemedicine. *Journal of Telemedicine and Telecare, 6*(3), 152–157.

Mielonen, M. L., Väisänen, L., Moring, J., Ohinmaa, A., & Isohanni, M. (2003). Implementation of a telepsychiatric network in northern Finland. *Current Problems in Dermatology, 32*, 132–140.

Miller, E. A. (2001). Telemedicine and doctor-patient communication: An analytical survey of the literature. *Journal of Telemedicine and Telecare, 7*(1), 1–17.

Miller, T. W., Burton, D. C., Hill, K., Luftman, G., Veltkemp, L. J., & Swope, M. (2005). Telepsychiatry: Critical dimensions for forensic services. *Journal of the American Academy of Psychiatry and the Law, 33*(4), 539–546.

Mitchell, J. G., Robinson, P. J., McEvoy M., & Gates, J. (2001). Telemedicine for the delivery of professional development for health, education and welfare professionals in two remote mining towns. *Journal of Telemedicine and Telecare, 7*(3), 174–180.

Modai, I., Jabarin, M., Kurs, R., Barak, P., Hanan, I., & Kitain, L. (2006). Cost effectiveness, safety and satisfaction with video telepsychiatry versus face-to-face care in ambulatory settings. *Telemedicine Journal and E-Health, 12*(5), 515–520.

Montani, C., Billaud, N., Tyrrell, J., Fluchaire, I., Malterre, C., Lauvernay, N., Couturier,

P., & Franco, A. (1997). Psychological impact of a remote psychometric consultation with hospitalized elderly people. *Journal of Telemedicine and Telecare, 3*(3), 140–145.

Moser, P. L., Hauffe, H., Lorenz, I. H., Hager, M., Tiefenthaler, W., Lorenz, H. M., Mikuz, G., Soegner, P., & Kolbitsch, C. (2004). Publication output in telemedicine during the period January 1964 to July 2003. *Journal of Telemedicine and Telecare, 10*(2), 72–77.

Myers, K., Valentine, J., Morganthaler, R., & Melzer, S. (2006). Telepsychiatry with incarcerated youth. *Journal of Adolescent Health, 38*(6), 643–648.

NARBHA. (2009). *Telepsychiatry seminars* [online]. [Accessed November 25, 2009]. Available from: http://www.rbha.net/index_seminar.htm.

Nelson, E. L., Barnard, M., & S. Cain, (2003). Treating childhood depression over videoconferencing. *Telemedicine Journal and E-Health, 9*(1), 49–55.

Nesbitt, T. S., Hilty, D. M., Kuenneth, C. A., & Siefkin A. (2000). Development of a telemedicine program: A review of 1,000 videoconferencing consultations. *Western Journal of Medicine, 173*(3), 169–174.

Nickelson, D. (1996). Behavioral telehealth: Emerging practice, research and policy opportunities. *Behavioral Sciences and the Law, 14*(4), 443–457.

Nohr, L. E. (2000). Telemedicine and patients' rights. *Journal of Telemedicine and Telecare, 6*(Suppl 1), S173–174.

OECD. (2009a). *OECD Broadband portal* [online]. [Accessed November 25, 2009]. Available from: http://www.oecd.org/sti/ict/broadband.

OECD. (2009b). *Broadband subscribers* [online]. [Accessed November 25, 2009]. Available from: http://www.oecd.org/dataoecd/21/35/39574709.xls.

Online Therapy Institute. (2010). *Homepage* [online]. [Accessed January 15, 2010]. Available from: www.onlinetherapyinstitute.com/.

O'Reilly, R., Bishop, J., Maddox, K., Hutchinson, L., Fisman, M., & Takhar, J. (2007). Is telepsychiatry equivalent to face-to-face psychiatry? Results from a randomized controlled equivalence trial. *Psychiatric Services, 58*(6), 836–843.

O'Shannessy, L. (2000). Using the law to enhance provision of telemedicine. *Journal of Telemedicine and Telecare, 6*(Suppl 1), S59–62.

Picot, J. (2000). Meeting the need for educational standards in the practice of telemedicine and telehealth. *Journal of Telemedicine and Telecare, 6*(Suppl 2), s59–62.

Polycom. (2009). *Polycom* [online]. [Accessed November 24, 2009]. Available from: http://www.polycom.com.

Qureshi, A. A., & Kvedar, J. C. (2003). Telemedicine experience in North America. *Current Problems in Dermatology, 32*, 226–232.

Rogers, E. M. (1995). *Diffusion of innovations.* New York: Simon and Schuster.

Rohland, B. M., Saleh, S. S., Rohrer, J. E., & Romitti, P. A. (2000). Acceptability of telepsychiatry to a rural population. *Psychiatric Services, 51*(5), 672–674.

Rosen, E. (1997). Current uses of desktop telemedicine. *Telemedicine Today, 5*(2), 18–19.

Ruskin, P. E., Reed, S., Kumar, R., Kling, M. A., Siegel, E., Rosen, M., & Hauser, P. (1998). Reliability and acceptability of psychiatric diagnosis via telecommunication and audiovisual technology. *Psychiatric Services, 49*(8), 1086–1088.

Ruskin, P. E., Silver-Aylaian, M., Kling, M. A., Reed, S. A., Bradham, D. D., Hebel, J. R., Barrett, D., Knowles, F., & Hauser, P. (2004). Treatment outcomes in depression: Comparison of remote treatment through telepsychiatry to in-person treatment. *American Journal of Psychiatry, 161*(8), 1471–1476.

ryanscause.org. (2009). The Ryan Haight bill (the Internet pharmacy consumer protection act) *ryanscause.org* [online]. [Accessed November 25, 2009]. Available from: http://www.ryanscause.org/ryan-haightbill.html.

Sanders, J. H., & Bashshur, R. L. (1995). Challenges to the implementation of telemedicine. *Telemedicine Journal, 1*(2), 115–123.

Schmitz, H. H. (1999). Telemedicine and the role of the health information manager. *Topics in Health Information Management, 19*(3), 52–58.

Shannon, G., Nesbitt, T., Bakalar, R., Kratochwill, E., Kvedar, J., & Vargas, L. (2002). Telemedicine/telehealth: An international perspective. Organizational models of telemedicine and regional telemedicine networks. *Telemedicine Journal and e-Health, 8*(1), 61–70.

Shaw, N. T. (2002). 'CHEATS': A generic information communication technology (ICT) evaluation framework. *Computers in Biology and Medicine, 32*(3), 209–220.

Shore, J. H., Savin, D., Orton, H., Beals, J., & Manson, S. M. (2007a). Diagnostic reliability of telepsychiatry in American Indian veterans. *American Journal of Psychiatry, 164*(1), 115–118.

Shore, J. H., Brooks, E., Savin, D. M., Manson, S. M., & Libby, A. M. (2007b). An economic evaluation of telehealth data collection with rural populations. *Psychiatric Services, 58*(6), 830–835.

Silverman, R. D. (2003). Current legal and ethical concerns in telemedicine and e-medicine. *Journal of Telemedicine and Telecare, 9*(Suppl 1), s67–69.

Simpson, J., Doze, S., Urness, D., Hailey D., & Jacobs P. (2001a). Evaluation of a routine telepsychiatry service. *Journal of Telemedicine and Telecare, 7*(2), 90–98.

Simpson, J., Doze, S., Urness, D., Hailey, D., & Jacobs, P. (2001b). Telepsychiatry as a routine service–The perspective of the patient. *Journal of Telemedicine and Telecare, 7*(3), 155–160.

Simpson, S., Knox, J., Mitchell, D., Ferguson, J., Brebner, J., & Brebner, E. (2003). A multidisciplinary approach to the treatment of eating disorders via videoconferencing in north-east Scotland. *Journal of Telemedicine and Telecare, 9*(Suppl 1), s37–8.

Singh, G., O'Donoghue, J., & Soon, C. K. (2002). Telemedicine: Issues and implications. *Technology and Health Care, 10*(1), 1–10.

Singh, S. P., Arya, D., & Peters, T. (2007). Accuracy of telepsychiatric assessment of new routine outpatient referrals. *BMC Psychiatry, 7*(1), 55.

Siwicki, B. (1997). Telemedicine. Legal issues could slow growth. *Health Data Management, 5*(4), 107–110.

Smolensky, K. R. (2003). Telemedicine reimbursement: Raising the iron triangle to a new plateau. *Health Matrix: Journal of Law-Medicine, 13*(2), 371–413.

Sood, S., Mbarika, V., Jugoo, S., Dookhy, R., Doarn, C. R., Prakash, N., & Merrell, R.C. (2007). What is telemedicine? A collection of 104 peer-reviewed perspectives and theoretical underpinnings. *Telemedicine and e-Health, 13*(5), 573–90.

Sorensen, T., Rivett, U., & Fortuin, J. (2008). A review of ICT systems for HIV/AIDS and anti-retroviral treatment management in South Africa. *Journal of Telemedicine and Telecare, 14*(1), 37–41.

Spaulding, R. J., Davis, K., & Patterson, J. (2008). A comparison of telehealth and face-to-face presentation for school professionals supporting students with chronic illness. *Journal of Telemedicine and Telecare, 14*(4), 211–214.

Stanberry, B. (1998). The legal and ethical aspects of telemedicine. *Journal of Telemedicine and Telecare, 4*(Suppl 1), 95–97.

Starling, J. (2003). Child and adolescent telepsychiatry in New South Wales: Moving beyond clinical consultation. *Australasian Psychiatry, 11*(Suppl), s117–121.

Swanson, B. (1999). Information technology and under-served communities. *Journal of Telemedicine and Telecare, 5*(Suppl 2), s3–10.

Tachakra, S., Mullett, S. T., Freij, R., & Sivakuma, A. (1996). Confidentiality and ethics in telemedicine. *Journal of Telemedicine and Telecare, 2*(Suppl 1), 68–71.

Tandberg. (2009). *Tandberg* [online]. [Accessed November 24, 2009]. Available from: http://www.tandberg.com.

Tang, S., & Helmeste D. (2000). Digital psychiatry. *Psychiatry and Clinical Neurosciences, 54*(1), 1–10.

Telemedicine Information Exchange. (2009a). *Homepage* [online]. [Accessed November

25, 2009]. Available from: http://tie.tele
med.org.

Telemedicine Information Exchange. (2009b). *Law and policy in telemedicine* [online]. [Accessed November 25, 2009]. Available from:http://tie.telemed.org/legal/state_data.asp?type=licensure.

Trott, P., & Blignault, I. (1998). Cost evaluation of a telepsychiatry service in Northern Queensland. *Journal of Telemedicine and Telecare, 4*(Suppl 1), 66–68.

Urness, D., Wass, M., Gordon, A., Tian E., & Bulger T. (2006). Client acceptability and quality of life–Telepsychiatry compared to in-person consultation. *Journal of Telemedicine and Telecare, 12*(5), 251–254.

Webster, K., Fraser, S., Mair, F., & Ferguson J. (2008). Provision of telehealth to the Scottish Police College. *Journal of Telemedicine and Telecare, 14*(3), 160–162.

Werner, A., & Anderson, L. E. (1998). Rural telepsychiatry is economically unsupportable: The Concorde crashes in a cornfield. *Psychiatric Services, 49*(10), 1287–1290.

Wheeler, T. (1998). Thoughts from tele-mental health practitioners. *Telemedicine Today, 6*(2), 38–40.

Whitten, P., & Buis, L. (2007). Private payer reimbursement for telemedicine services in the United States. *Telemedicine and e-Health, 13*(1), 15–24.

Whitten, P., & Rowe-Adjibogoun, J. (2002). Success and failure in a Michigan telepsychiatry programme. *Journal of Telemedicine and Telecare, 8*(Suppl 3), s75–77.

Whitten, P. S., Mair, F. S., Haycox, A., May, C. R., Williams, T. L., & Hellmich, S. (2002). Systematic review of cost effectiveness studies of telemedicine interventions. *BMJ, 324*(7351), 1434–1437.

Whitten, P., Johannessen, L. K., Soerensen, T., Gammonand, D., & Mackert, M.

(2007). A systematic review of research methodology in telemedicine studies. *Journal of Telemedicine and Telecare, 13*(5), 230–235.

Wootton, R. (1998). Telemedicine in the National Health Service. *Journal of the Royal Society of Medicine, 91*(12), 614–621.

Wootton, R., Smith, A. C., Gormley, S., & Patterson, J. (2002). Logistical aspects of large telemedicine networks. 2: Measurement of network activity. *Journal of Telemedicine and Telecare, 8*(Suppl 3), 81–82.

Yellowlees, P. (1997). Successful development of telemedicine systems–Seven core principles. *Journal of Telemedicine and Telecare, 3*(4), 215–223.

Yellowlees, P. (2001). An analysis of why telehealth systems in Australia have not always succeeded. *Journal of Telemedicine and Telecare, 7*(Suppl 2), 29–31.

Yoshino, A., Shigemura, J., Kobayashi, Y., Nomura, S., Shishikura, K., Den, R., Wakisaka, H., Kamata, S., & Ashida, H. (2001). Telepsychiatry: Assessment of television psychiatric interview reliability with present- and next-generation internet infrastructures. *Acta Psychiatrica Scandinavica, 104*(3), 223–226.

Young, T. L., & Ireson, C. (2003). Effectiveness of school-based telehealth care in urban and rural elementary schools. *Pediatrics, 112*(5), 1088–1094.

Zarate, C. A., Weinstock, L., Cukor, P., Morabito, C., Leahy, L., Burns, C., & Baer, L. (1997). Applicability of telemedicine for assessing patients with schizophrenia: Acceptance and reliability. *Journal of Clinical Psychiatry, 58*(1), 22–5.

Zaylor, C. (1999). Clinical outcomes in telepsychiatry. *Journal of Telemedicine and Telecare, 5*(Suppl 1), S59–60.

Chapter 17

THE USE OF VIRTUAL REALITY
FOR PEER SUPPORT

Leon Tan

INTRODUCTION

Given that a host of developments in Internet technologies and cultures since the turn of the new century have produced numerous widely accessible and highly immersive virtual reality environments or 3D virtual worlds such as Second Life, Entropia Universe and SmallWorlds, it seems useful to consider how such virtual worlds may, like their offline counterparts, function to deliver therapeutic benefits beyond professionally run programs. In-vivo exposure therapy (IVET) is considered a standard treatment of choice for phobias with wide empirical support (Garcia-Palacios et. al., 2007). As the Latin origin of the term suggests (*in-vivo*–within the living), such therapy involves exposure to actual aversive situations in the so-called "real" world. Thus IVET for the fear of flying involves exposure to actual experiences of flying, and IVET for arachnophobia involves exposure to actual spiders. Since at least the 1990s, however, virtual reality (VR) environments have been successfully deployed by mental health professionals in treating a variety of phobias as well as posttraumatic stress disorder. VR Exposure Therapy (VRET) involves exposure to virtual and not actual aversive situations. As Cote and Bouchard (2005) observe, a large number of outcome studies now support the efficacy of VRET, and "most of them converge towards the conclusion that VRE[T] is as effective as in-vivo exposure" (p. 217). In a controlled clinical trial (n=83), Rothbaum et al. (2006) demonstrated VRET and IVET to be equally effective in treating fear of flying, "suggesting that experiences in the virtual world can change experiences in the real world" (p. 80). Furthermore, "the gains observed in treatment were maintained at 6- and 12-months" (p. 87), indicating that transformative virtual experiences carrying over into the "real" world may be sustained over time.

VRET is typically deployed in offline and/or "gated" VR environments, with elaborate technologies (e.g., computer driven head-mounted displays running

3D simulations) under the control of mental health professionals. The offerings of *Virtually Better* (http://www.virtuallybetter.com/), a leading provider of VRET, are thus located within physical clinics and administered by psychotherapists. Yet as Garcia-Palacios et al. (2007) observe, "most people who suffer phobias (around 60–80%) never seek treatment" (p. 722), meaning that the benefits of VRET may be restricted to a minority of sufferers with the fortune or inclination to access professional clinic based services.

The goal of this chapter is to portray the mental health affordances of 3D virtual worlds for populations of individuals engaging socially as peers. This will be accomplished by way of a portrait of an adult woman overcoming agoraphobia through the social use of Second Life (SL), reported recently by Tracy Smith (2008) for CBS News on the *Early Show*. A case is chosen from popular culture in order to emphasize the wide accessibility of online virtual world based therapeutic affordances. In contrast to relatively scarce clinical virtual environments reliant on interventions by trained mental health professionals (such as psychiatrists, psychotherapists and psychologists), the mental health affordances of online virtual worlds derive from interactions in supportive peer-based communities.

Quantifying the spread of mental illness and the associated impacts on individual quality of life and community health is never a simple task. Nevertheless,

> Data developed by the massive Global Burden of Disease study conducted by the World Health Organization, the World Bank and Harvard University, reveal that mental illness, including suicide, accounts for over 15% of the burden of disease in established market economies, such as the United States. This is more than the disease burden caused by all cancers . . . (NIMH (video recording) 2001)

If this portrait of the global severity and cost of mental illness is anything to go by, it would seem that mental illness poses a significant and ongoing problem in contemporary societies. Given the seemingly intractable problem of mental illness worldwide and the large numbers of individuals not seeking out professional treatment for various mental illnesses, widely accessible peer driven opportunities for improving mental health deserve greater attention.

AFFORDANCES OF 3D VIRTUAL WORLDS

For those unfamiliar with the term, "affordances" are sets of opportunities and risks particular environments supply or provide (Gibson, 1977). As a virtual social environment, SL provides individuals with a set of opportunities and risks to express identities and interact socially. The expression of identities and the production of social relations are vital dimensions of human existence and indeed of therapeutic and transformative experiences of self. In actual environments, expressing an identity and forming social relations take place largely through conversations involving both linguistic and nonlinguistic means. In the absence of physical bodies in SL, the expression of identity depends largely on the creation and deployment of a 3D avatar (see www.secondlife.com). A high level of visual customization is possible for an avatar, from facial features through to clothing and accessories. As for the production of social relations in SL, this involves the use of an avatar to participate in conversations. It thus relies on SL as an expressive repertoire and social ecology. That is to say, social relations in SL depend on the communicative means SL affords, as well as on SL as a population of peers with whom individuals may interact.

The SL user interface may be viewed by visiting www.secondlife.com; it will be useful to take a look to understand how an individual deploys a virtual life within an online 3D community. In the SL user interface, an avatar is located in the center of the screen looking outwards. SL's expressive means in the form of communication and navigation toolbars are located at the bottom of the screen. The communication toolbar provides options for engaging in conversations with other SL inhabitants using synchronous text and/or voice chat as well as bodily gestures (users can shrug, laugh, show boredom, bow and point, amongst other things). Text clouds follow users throughout the SL world displaying context-relevant information such as the names of surrounding peers and interactive possibilities of various in-world objects. The navigation toolbar allows for movement of an avatar (typically walking or flying) through the 3D spaces of the SL grid. By and large, content and experiences within SL are user-generated, meaning that the spaces, architectures, avatars and social events one is likely to encounter in-world are limited in variety only by the imagination and

the basic rules for behavior known as "community standards." Users are also able to share various media and to perform specialized actions such as building rooms and houses. Together, all these various components can be considered SL's expressive repertoire through which individual users express identities and develop social relationships through conversations.

Mental health affordances can be considered opportunities and risks provided by a social environment to affect the mental health of individuals. In a recent article (Tan, 2008), I demonstrated how blogging (or writing socially) in the online community MySpace could function as a cathartic vehicle as well as to assist an individual in discovering and developing a "voice" in a social milieu. As an online community, SL also offers users opportunities for cathartic expression (tension reduction through affective expressions involving text, voice and gestures), as well as opportunities to express and transform identities in social interactions. There are in fact a wide range of general and mental health groups and communities within SL offering specialized social contexts not only for cathartic tension reduction but also for social support and psycho-education. The Heron Sanctuary, for example, is a group for disabled people gathering for mutual support and social interaction. Support groups also exist for autism, cancer, AIDS/HIV, agoraphobia and so on. Finding one's way to these groups within SL is also relatively easy on account of portal organizations such as the Health Support Coalition and Health Info Island. SL thus offers users a range of opportunities to improve mental health. In the specific case of phobias, SL as a user-generated community allows for exposure situations through which individuals may confront and learn to cope with problematic associations between particular situations and anxious affects, as we will see in the case illustration.

CASE ILLUSTRATION

CBS News recently covered the case of an individual utilizing SL therapeutically to overcome agoraphobia. According to Tracy Smith (2008), Patricia Quig suffered from agoraphobia from an early age; a condition for which medication and psychotherapy offered limited help in her instance. Agoraphobia is a condition where a sufferer experiences an increase in anxiety in social situations, which, left unchecked, may develop into panic attacks. Another way of putting this is to say that agoraphobia involves the production of associations between social situations and anxiety. Anxiety and panic triggers for Quig included "too much people, too much noise, too much stimulation" leaving her feeling "too exposed" to the point where she became more or less house-bound and incapable of maintaining regular employment. Quig however discovered SL a little before her 40th birthday and became an active SL user through her avatar "Baji." For Quig, there is little doubt that virtual living in SL enabled her to gain traction in her battle with agoraphobia. As she herself says,

> You can go and be with a group of people and discover that it's not the worst thing in the world . . . and that you don't feel strange doing it and enjoy it. And once you've learned that it's an enjoyable experience, you're not scared of it anymore. (Smith (video recording) 2008)

A vital aspect of Quig's recovery can be explained in terms of IVET and VRET. In the application of exposure therapy, sufferers are equipped by a psychotherapist with coping components such as relaxation training and cognitive reappraisal of imagined outcomes and then gradually exposed to (actual or virtual) conditions associated with a phobia and its anxious affects. Through repeated encounters coupled with the practice of coping skills, an individual experiences a new possibility—that of being in a "phobic" situation without being overwhelmed by anxiety. If we conceive of this new possibility as a new identity (differing from that of say an "agoraphobic"), we can say that the rehearsal of this new identity over time produces new associations between social situations and affective states. The portrayal of Quig's recovery by CBS shows precisely such a transformative process. As Smith observes,

> In Second Life, your alter ego, called an "avatar," can be and do anything. Quig's avatar, Baji, started doing things in second life she wouldn't consider doing in real life.
> . . . Facing her fears over and over again in Second Life freed Quig from her real-life phobias. (Smith (video recording), 2008).

Clearly, the therapeutic possibilities of in-vivo and virtual exposure are not confined to offline clinical contexts involving mental health professionals, but may also emerge for individuals interacting socially within a supportive network of peers in virtual worlds such as SL. Quig it seems found a way of expanding and transforming a self-limiting identity as the unemployed agoraphobic "Patty" to experiment with a virtually articulated new identity "Baji."

"Naïve realism" is a term that refers to conventional wisdoms sharply separating virtual experiences on the one hand and "real"-life experiences on the other. In naïve realism, real is conflated with actual. According to this view, social reality is confined to the actuality of material worlds; in the case of social relations, in the paradigmatic face-to-face encounter. The various experiences afforded by the Internet are by contrast, deprived of reality and validity, fantastic (in the psychoanalytic sense of fantasy) and insignificant (because immaterial). To counter any naïve realist skepticism as to the "real life" effects of such virtual identity transformations, it is important to examine the mixed reality dimension of this case. By mixed reality, I mean the mixing of virtual and actual life worlds through the integration of Internet technologies and experiences into the fabric of everyday reality. The virtual must not be naively dismissed as less real or even unreal, but instead be understood as "real without being actual, ideal without being abstract" (Proust, in Deleuze, 1988, p. 96). Mixed reality provides a framework recognizing the reality of virtuality, allowing us to think virtuals and actuals as consequential and real dimensions of contemporary life.

The CBS news video clearly shows Quig walking through the aisles of an actual supermarket, when six months prior to her interview for CBS she was unable to shop in a grocery store. Furthermore, Quig was also able to travel to New York to participate in a face-to-face encounter with the CBS journalist before a massive American viewership. In discussing how the experience of overcoming her fears of social situations in SL has carried over into her actual daily life, Quig is very specific, saying, "I'm not *just* Patty anymore, I'm Baji . . . I just feel like a different person."

The actual effects of Quig's virtual social experiences testify to the therapeutic potential of 3D virtual worlds for individuals to rework habitual associations between affects, ideas and actual life circumstances. By actualizing the virtual identity developed in SL, Quig effectively transforms her real life. Should she continue along this trajectory of expressing "Baji" and not just "Patty" in actual everyday situations, it is likely that Baji will eclipse Patty as a habitual identity.

DISCUSSION

If as the philosopher Deleuze (1991) argues, "We are habits, nothing but habits–the habit of saying 'I'" (p. x), it becomes possible to think of the mental health of an individual in terms of socially adaptive habits of saying "I" and of mental illness in terms of socially maladaptive habits of saying "I." The habitual saying of "I" is of course another way of discussing identity. In the case of Patricia Quig, we can consider "Patty" as a socially maladaptive habit of saying "I" on the one hand and "Baji" as an adaptive one allowing Quig to break out of self-imposed constraints in virtual and actual life on the other. Whilst Quig's case demonstrates the mental health opportunities of virtual worlds for situational phobias, it must be emphasized that SL's mental health affordances are not just limited to those suffering from agoraphobia, but instead may be deployed by any individual whose mental health is compromised by the existence of problematic habits of saying "I" and limiting self-images.

At the crux of the matter is the identity experimentation set into motion by an engagement in a massively social virtual environment such as SL. Where individuals are caught up in socially maladaptive habits of saying "I," transformations are made possible by an exploration of different habits of saying "I" (different identities or selves). In the illustration above, Quig need not stop at the first socially viable identity or self-image. Like other users of social 3D worlds, she is able to experiment with a multiplicity of possibilities for identity, self-image and social relations and to re-integrate these experimentations back into the fabric of actual social reality.

The capacity to experiment with different identities and self-images in social interactions is not unique to 3D virtual worlds. Non-3D online communities such as MySpace and Facebook also provide such opportunities. SL however differs from non-3D virtual environments in the nature or style of identity expression. Unlike the photographs or videos depicting actual faces and bodies in MySpace type communities, 3D avatars tend to bear less visual relation to actual appearances. This difference lends to a heightened sense of anonymity, accentuating and amplifying what Suler (2004) calls the online disinhibition effect—the tendency of individuals to behave in less inhibited ways in virtual spaces. Such disinhibition can be of tremendous therapeutic value if deployed in supportive contexts, leading to increased imagina-

tive play and risk taking and thus the destabilizing of habitual associations and forming of new habits of saying "I". Where disinhibition inspires experimentation, SL as an expressive repertoire provides the means to express different self-images through the construction and evolution of 3D avatars, as well as the means to explore different social situations and dynamics through conversations and activities with other SL inhabitants.

Opportunities for transformative expressions of identity depend, of course, on the massively social dimension of online virtual worlds, not least because such expressions always take place in the context of social interactions, primarily conversations. In social reality, it is never enough for an individual to simply express an identity. As the work of Goffman (1967) demonstrates, participants in conversations must ratify each other in order to enter into a state of talk. That is to say, the expression of identity requires the validation/acceptance of those addressed. Peers are thus important components contributing to the mental health affordances of virtual worlds. In the first place, supportive peers provide contexts for conversations within which individuals may experiment with new expressions of identity and thus form new habits of saying "I". Second, peers may assist in the development of socially adaptive identities through the repetitive validation of identity expressions, thus consolidating an individual's new habits of saying "I." Finally, peers interacting regularly tend to produce communities (such as the many specialized support groups in SL) within which new habits of saying "I" may be reinforced at a community level. Such peer-based communities may afford individuals a sense of belonging as well as a consensually derived social reality, thus supporting an individual's integration of virtual identity transformations back into actual life.

Thus far this chapter has focused on the mental health *opportunities* of peer-based 3D virtual worlds such as SL. Virtual worlds and the experiences they make possible also come with risks, as Turkle (1995) observes,

> People can get lost in virtual worlds. Some are tempted to think of life in cyberspace as insignificant, as escape or meaningless diversion. It is not. Our experiences there are serious play. We belittle them at our risk. We must understand the dynamics of virtual experience both to foresee who might be in danger and to put these experiences to best use. Without a deep understanding of the many selves we express in the virtual we cannot use our experiences there to enrich the real. If we cultivate our awareness of what stands behind our screen personae, we are more likely to succeed in using virtual experience for personal transformation. (p. 268–269).

Turkle points out that it is possible to get lost in the elaboration of multiple identities online. It is also possible to overemphasize virtual living over actual experiences, or valorize actuality over virtuality as real. Whilst principles governing the provision of online mental health services by professionals have already been endorsed (ISMHO & PSI, 2000, Anthony & Goss 2009, Nagel & Anthony, 2009), no such guidelines exist concerning engaging in peer-based social interactions in popular 3D virtual worlds for mental health benefit. Protection from risk in this case is best achieved by taking Internet virtuality and its experiences seriously, as well as by developing and promoting useful understandings of virtual life experiences and their affective relationships with actual life.

CONCLUSION

In conclusion, this chapter has explored how widely accessible virtual social worlds such as SL afford both opportunities and risks for individual mental health within the context of peer-based social interactions and ongoing relationships. Whilst virtual, transformative experiences of identity and self in SL relationships nevertheless have the power to affect actual lives, as the case of Patricia Quig demonstrates. This is because virtual experiences are no less real than in-vivo ones; IVET and VRET both work because they both involve exposure within the living so to speak. The possibilities for peer-based use of virtual worlds for mental health are not limited to the conditions typically treated by VRET (namely phobias), but in fact apply to any situation where the development and social rehearsal of new and more socially adaptive habits of saying "I" may therapeutically displace maladaptive ones. Whilst a great deal of research has already gone into validating the professional use of VRE for the treatment of phobias and PTSD, relatively little has been done on the professional treatment of other conditions such as depression or generalized anxiety in virtual environments and even less on peer-based models of mental health development, within both 3D and non-3D online virtual worlds. Future research might thus investigate these neglected areas. Whilst this chapter proposes mixed reality as a more accurate and sophisticated reality framework, constraints of space have not allowed for a full elaboration, nor for a comprehensive critique of naïve realism (responsible for the kind of perspectives and attitudes belittling virtuality that Turkle cautions against). Future research might thus address the ontological status of virtuality and the relations of virtuals to actuals, as a great deal of confusion still exists both within academic and mass populations concerning the reality and value of online social experiences.

REFERENCES

Anthony, K., & Goss, S. (2009). *Guidelines for online counselling and psychotherapy including guidelines for online supervision* (3rd ed.). Lutterworth: BACP.

Cote, S., & Bouchard, S. (2005). Documenting the efficacy of virtual reality exposure with psychophysiological and information processing measures. *Applied Psychophysiology and Biofeedback, 30*(3), 217–232.

Deleuze, G. (1991). *Empiricism and subjectivity.* New York: Columbia University Press.

Deleuze, G. (1988). *Bergsonism.* New York: Zone Books.

Garcia-Palacios, A., Botella, C., Hoffman, H., & Fabregat, B. A. (2007). Comparing acceptance and refusal rates of virtual reality exposure vs. in vivo exposure by patients with specific phobias. *CyberPsychology and Behavior, 10*(5), 722–724.

Gibson, J. J. (1977). The theory of affordances. In R. Shaw & J. Bransford (Eds.), *Perceiving, acting and knowing: Toward an ecological psychology.* Hillsdale, NJ: Erlbaum.

Goffman, E. (1967). *Interaction ritual: Essays on face-to-face behavior.* New York: Anchor Books.

International Society for Mental Health Online and Psychiatric Society for Informatics. (2000). *The suggested principles for the online provision of mental health services* [online]. [Accessed July 14, 2008]. Available from: http://www.ismho.org/builder//?p=page&id=214.

Nagel, D. M., & Anthony, K. (2009). Ethical framework for the use of technology in mental health. *Online Therapy Institute* [online]. [Accessed December 4, 2009]. Available from: http://www.onlinetherapyinstitute.com/id43.html.

NIMH. (2001). *The impact of mental illness on society: A fact sheet* [online]. [Accessed February 3, 2006]. Available from: http://www.masterdocs.com/fact_sheet_files/pdf/mental_illness.pdf.

Rothbaum, B. O., Anderson, P., Zimand, E., Hodges, L. F., Lang, D., & Wilson, J. (2006). Virtual reality exposure therapy and standard (in vivo) exposure therapy in the treatment of fear of flying. *Behavior Therapy, 37*(1), 80-90.

Smith, T. (2008). Real-life fears faced in an online world: Having alter-egos in 'Second Life' helps people cope. *CBS News The Early Show* [online]. [Accessed July 14, 2008]. Available from: http://www.cbsnews.com/stories/2008/01/29/earlyshow/contributors/tracysmith/main3763968.shtml.

Suler, J. (2004). The online disinhibition effect. *The Psychology of Cyberspace* [online]. [Accessed July 14, 2008]. Available from: http://www-usr.rider.edu~suler/psycyber/disinhibit.html.

Tan, L. (2008). Psychotherapy 2.0: MySpace blogging as self-therapy. *American Journal of Psychotherapy, 62*(2), 143–163.

Turkle, S. (1995). *Life on the screen: Identity in the age of the Internet.* New York: Simon and Schuster.

Chapter 18

THE USE OF PODCASTING IN MENTAL HEALTH

MARCOS A. QUINONES

INTRODUCTION

Podcasting, as it exists today, began to take hold in 2005, when Apple Computers included a directory of podcasts in its iTunes software. They saw big potential in a technology that could broadcast audio and video content over the Internet and be stored on computers and portable digital devices like iPods. The term podcast comes from the merging of iPod + Broadcast (Wikipedia, 2008). It is often thought of as a radio or television program that is reduced to a computer file. A podcast is a file that is created using a digital camcorder, computer and editing software. Creating podcasts is relatively easy and inexpensive and has therefore inspired thousands of professionals, including mental health professionals, to seek out potential in using this technology to move their industry forward. In this chapter, I will discuss the use of podcasts in improving mental and physical health for clients, best practices in creating and keeping a podcast successful, ethical considerations and the role of podcasting in the future of mental health.

APPLICATION

I have been podcasting since 2005, when I first came across a podcast called Yogamazing. Chaz, the author or podcaster, published a 10-minute yoga class each week that focused on a different part of the body. I recognized that this would be good as a psycho-educational addition to my practice. I decided to undertake this project and chose Self-Help as the theme. Similar to Chaz's Yogamazing podcast, I chose to focus on one problem, disorder, behavior or idea in each podcast. Since then, I have created over 80 podcasts, which have been downloaded and viewed over half a million times by clients in countries as far as India, Thailand, Australia, China, Africa, Argentina, Iraq and many others at http://www.thejoveinstitute.org/podcast.html.

The success of this project has been attributed to the ease of use in hearing the message. From the emails that I receive from clients that use my podcast to help themselves, the overwhelming benefit they take from it stems from learning a basic theory that they can then apply for themselves. Many of my podcast clients do not have access to professional mental health resources in their region or do not have the means to acquire the limited psychological resources that exists.

Others, in regions with sufficient professional help available, are hesitant or reluctant to attend therapy. Individuals have indicated that seeing the podcast showed them there might be a way out of their problems and that solutions could exist. Therefore, clients are eager to learn methods of helping themselves overcome depression, anxiety and other disorders and their causal self-defeating behaviors like social isolation, addictions and self-injury.

Podcast technology is global and can easily be misinterpreted. Not only do clients from different races, languages, cultures and religious backgrounds view the podcasts, but also clients with varying degrees of mental and physical functioning. Therefore it is very important to keep with an empirically proven theory when planning the fundamental underpinning of the podcast. I chose to keep with Cognitive Behavioral and Rational Emotive Behavioral Theories, which work exceptionally well as self-help adjuncts to cultural and religious beliefs (Selmi et al., 1990).

Some of the benefits that clients have reported are as follows:

Psycho-Education on the Theory

Clients report ease of use and understanding of the theory, the practicality of theory, the benefits of semantics on their culture, language and religious belief, the benefit of theory to people of different ages and the sheer number of self-help techniques available to them.

Fictional Case Examples to Reinforce Theory and Self-help Techniques

Clients like the use of fictional case examples, as they say that it makes it seem like I'm not speaking about a theory, but about real people and how they use the exercises to help themselves.

Cognitive Exercises

Clients report benefits of changing the way that they think using self-talk exercises, homework assignments, worksheets, journals and lists.

Behavioral Exercises

Clients mention the benefits of relaxation training and breathing exercises, meditation and awareness and behavioral exercises to control addictions.

Emotive Exercises

Clients benefit from visualization exercises, labeling emotions and emotion logs.

Personable Nature of the Podcast

Clients point out the benefits of seeing me and being able to relate and feel the empathy and compassion coming through the visual medium. They consider valuable the fact that someone puts this kind of effort into solving their particular problem. They report the value of hearing the podcasts in their language at their intellectual level and benefits from the interactive technology that allows them to email comments, opinions and questions related to specific podcasts.

Professional Uses

Teachers have commented that they use my podcasts to present to their students. Website owners use my podcasts targeted at their client audiences (geri-atric, children, etc). Job groups and team leaders use my podcasts to help with common labor and environmental issues. An Iraq aid workers' team leader uses podcasts to help with addictions and secondary trauma. Private Practice therapists use my podcasts to orient the client to therapy or the theory itself.

This is just a short list of the therapeutic benefits of this technology that clients, mental health professionals, nonmental health professionals and I have reported over the years. There are many more benefits, uses and stories from clients that I will never hear, as well as around a million users that have used these podcasts and chosen to keep anonymous.

BEST PRACTICES

Podcasting offers a unique opportunity for someone with a message to reach hundreds of thousands of people. The technology allows for the proliferation of the podcast based on its merits and usually not on expensive advertising. Similar to dogmatic religions where it is an all or nothing belief of the theory, a mental health client can agree or disagree with the message and choose to subscribe to the podcast or not. This is what will determine whether the podcast is successful.

If the client subscribes to the podcast, then every time the podcaster uploads a new segment (podcast), the client's computer automatically receives it. Podcasts are usually free and the more people subscribe to the podcast, the more popular it becomes. Hosting companies and websites that draw millions of users advertise podcasts that are doing well by having a steady increase in the number of subscribers. These websites thrive on successful podcasts to draw users to their sites and subsequent advertising revenue. There are many creative ways for a podcaster to increase subscription numbers, but the bottom line is the message. This is important for mental health professionals who want others to benefit from their theories, because the message has to appeal to a wide range of individuals so that it will proliferate throughout the Internet and subsequently be advertised by these portal websites.

In other words, subscribers = proliferation = success.

This success also works in reverse. Individuals can unsubscribe at any time. If the message does not have merit, or the podcaster does not upload new podcasts regularly, then subscription falls and the podcast becomes less desirable to the websites and individuals.

Therefore, it is important that before a podcaster decides to start podcasting, he or she defines a goal and determines how the podcast technology is going to help him or her to reach his or her goal. Each podcaster has his or her individual goal, but podcast technology is universal and in order to be successful using it, the podcaster needs to consider content and technology. It is similar to starting up a radio station that will potentially broadcast to millions of listeners–it will take a lot of work, dedication and money. Assuming the podcaster has a good work ethic, time to dedicate to creating a weekly or bi-weekly podcast and enough money to fund the project, what is going to be needed? The following outlines the basics of identifying content and technological needs for the project.

Content

- Podcast Program Theme
- List of podcast titles for the first 10 podcasts
- Target Audience
- Length
- Frequency
- Medium (audio only or audio/visual)
- Location

Technology

- Computer
- Digital Video Camcorder
- External Microphone
- Lighting
- Editing Software
- Internet Connection
- Hosting Facility
- iPod
- Email Address

CONTENT

The Podcast Program Theme is the fundamental basis of the podcast. It is derived from the podcaster's goal and will be used by websites that promote podcasts to categorize and list it appropriately. The theme could be self-help, psychology lectures, mind-body, research study results, happiness, relationships, etc. A common mistake when setting the theme is not considering the longevity of the project, as for the most part this theme cannot be changed. If a podcaster wishes to change the theme, a new podcast Program will have to be created and previous subscribers will be lost. Along with the theme the podcaster needs to develop a catchy definition of the podcast that listing directories will use to draw subscribers.

Creating a list of the first 10 podcasts and a definition of each is a good exercise. It gives the podcaster an idea of the work needed to come up with ideas for podcasts, a framework for initiating the project and a starting point to practice as the other logistical details come together. More than 10 may not be needed because if the project takes off, the podcaster should receive emails from clients on suggested titles for future podcasts.

Target audience should be determined when setting the goal of the podcast. The content, message, delivery, time, frequency and medium are all factors to consider depending on the targeted client demographics. For example if the target audience is children, then specific technical arrangements will have to be considered to keep their attention.

The longer the length of time of the

podcast, the larger the size of the file, and the larger the size of the file, the longer it's going to take for it to download to a computer. In this age of speed, clients tend to be impatient and will not wait minutes for a file to download. Therefore, it is important to keep podcasts to less than 15 minutes in length. Some websites have file size restrictions, which will help to limit talkative podcasters.

When beginning a new podcast it is important to get the word out as often as possible. New podcasters may need to publish a new podcast every week or bi-monthly in order to draw subscribers. When the frequency drops below one a month, subscribers lose interest and unsubscribe.

Podcasts can be audio only or audio-visual. The podcast file is much smaller when it's audio only, but there are also limitations, such as competition. There are many more audio only podcasts than audio-visual podcasts. Also, in mental health I have found that it makes a difference for the client to see whom they are hearing. I have received requests for audio only and have created them for those users, but continue to do audio-visual podcast for the vast majority of my subscribers.

Location is the least important of the logistical considerations, but nevertheless important. I have received feedback that noise obstructs and distracts clients from hearing the message. The message should be clear and unobstructed so that it can be understood and internalized. Some of the distractions are noise from cars, people talking, air conditioners and other devices, color of room or office, art, size of the podcaster in relation to the room, clothing and grooming.

TECHNOLOGY

Making a decision on which computer to use early on will alleviate headaches in the future. It will be important to choose a computer with enough memory to store the large files that camcorders create before editing. Anything less than 100GB will become obsolete before you get properly started.

Choose a digital camcorder that is compatible with the computer that you chose above and an external microphone that is compatible to the camcorder.

I have found lighting and noise to be the main obstacles to expressing a clear message to my clients. Although sometimes professional lighting is not necessary, if you have the means, investing in professional lighting could be worth-while.

I decided to use IMovie HD for editing my videos because of ease of use. There are many other editing software suites available in the market that are more flexible and can offer more than IMovie, but the "ramp-up" time (the time it will take you to learn the software and start using it) is longer.

A high-speed Internet connection is necessary because of the large size of the file that will be uploaded to the hosting facility.

A hosting facility is the place on the Internet that will host the podcast. Hosting facilities usually provide you with a website and limited storage capabilities. Depending on the frequency of your podcasts, it will be important to choose a hosting facility that will scale with you. Most hosting facilities allow you to purchase more space and bandwidth as your subscribers grow, but make sure of this in the beginning. The reason you need a hosting facility is because the podcast listing website will only list your podcast, it will not store it. When a new subscriber chooses to download your podcast, the website will direct them to a place where your podcast file is stored and the client downloads it from there. The process of downloading a file takes up bandwidth. Think of bandwidth as traffic on a road–the hosting facility owns this road and will allow a limited amount of your traffic and will charge you more as your traffic increases.

Purchasing an iPod for viewing your podcast is very important. An iPod will be used to test how others view your podcast. It will be necessary for you to go through the process of searching, subscribing, downloading and viewing the podcast on an iPod, as your clients will. That way you will be aware of any problems your clients may face.

When your clients come across a problem it will be important for them to reach you. An email address for the podcast is important for feedback, comments, suggestions, recommendations and problem solving. Stay away from offering your phone number in any of the descriptions of the podcast; it will be impossible to return all of the messages you receive.

FILMING, EDITING AND HOSTING

I have found it useful to write down what I will say in the podcast and run through it a couple of times. Then, I put the sheets down and have a conversation with the camera. I have tried several ways to approach this and most of the feedback I have received supports a conversational approach. Film and edit the podcast using the instructions supplied by the camcorder and computer editing software, respectively. When you are done editing the podcast, the software should supply a file with the extension .mp3, .m4a, .mp4, .m4v, or .mov etc. This is the final file that will be uploaded to the hosting facility.

At this point the podcaster is ready for others to start looking at his or her work. The Apple store is the largest directory of podcasts and I recommend this be the first place to list your podcast. Go to http://www.apple.com/itunes/store/pod caststechspecs.html and follow the online directions to submit your podcast. The podcaster needs to create an .rss file (which according to Wikipedia is called a "feed," "web feed," or "channel" and includes full or summarized text, plus metadata such as publishing dates and authorship) and submit it to Apple for approval. The instructions for creating the file are very clear and there is plenty of online support from other podcasters should you have any questions. Once your .rss file is submitted, you will receive an email from Apple that it was approved and clients can start to download it.

TRACKING

You will want to know how many people are subscribing to your podcasts and there are several companies that do this. I chose Feedburner.com which provides an easy interface to track subscribers and hits to your website and podcasts. It is free and the information you get from the tracking software is invaluable.

FEEDBACK AND ADJUSTING

Finally and most importantly, be open to feedback. Ask your friends and family to go through the steps of finding your podcast and downloading and viewing it. If they have problems with it, most likely others will too. Also, be open to feedback from people you don't know. There are people in different cultures that listen to your message and may have constructive criticism. If you don't take it personally, then you may have an easier time to make adjustments in subsequent podcasts. Being able to listen to others criticize your hard work and make sense of it is a skill that will go well beyond podcasting and will help you develop as a seasoned podcaster.

ETHICAL CONSIDERATIONS

When considering ethical and moral questions, the first thing a podcaster needs is common sense. The Internet has grown to be a global highway of information essentially because of the morality and basic common sense of the people who publish information. Of course, there is plenty of misinformation published on the Internet, sometimes with tragic outcomes, but for the vast majority of web users, the Internet is a safe and useful place for publishing and searching for information.

Also, as mentioned above, the podcast technology serves as a gateway in weeding out messages that are not likely to serve others. The key to being a successful podcaster is subscriptions and subscribers are not going to subscribe for information that is not relevant, lacks evidence or is false. The podcasts that are most successful present a clear message for clients to accept or reject.

Being a Licensed Social Worker in New York, I researched ethical and legal regulations that could be relevant within my professional organization and state law. What I found relevant was the importance of competence and of confidentiality (NASW, 2002). It was easy to stay within the boundaries of competence because of my podcast theme. At the beginning I had chosen to use as the underpinnings of my podcasts a published theory that is empirically proven: Cognitive Behavioral and Rational Emotive Behavioral Theories (Chambless et al., 1998). Second, I chose never to discuss real cases online, instead using fictional case examples that were previously imagined and presented the material to the audience by making the disclaimer that the case example is fictional and names are made up.

Again, common sense comes to mind when I consider competence and confidentiality. Researching your professional organization's ethics and region's legal regulations is also important.

Disclaimers are also a good idea to protect the podcaster and the client. I make it clear in my podcasts that this is a self-help tool and is not meant to replace formal individual psychotherapy with a professional. I also mention that this is not meant to help people who are currently suicidal and that if someone is currently suicidal, he or she should immediately seek emergency help.

CONCLUSION

Based on my experience, podcasts are an effective intervention in providing self-help techniques to clients, including individual clients, mental health professionals, nonmental health professionals and others. Any professional who follows best practices in planning, implementing and maintaining a podcasting project, considering at the same time the applicable ethical and legal regulations, will be able to successfully reach and help a great number of people. The mental health profession needs risk takers with common sense and integrity, willing to experiment with new technology to offer help to people and regions with limited mental health services. This podcast technology and others will continue to evolve and provide tools for these risk takers to test the limits of the technology. In the past, technology has been limited by memory space and bandwidth, but as more efficient hardware becomes available, memory and bandwidth will become cheaper. We are already seeing this with the success of YouTube and Apple TV. YouTube has created data centers and technology to host millions of large video files and making the bandwidth available for users to publish and view as many of these videos as they like free of charge and other companies are following suit.

Apple TV is one of the products that is capitalizing on the video boom. Apple developed a box that can receive movies, podcasts and other large files from the Internet and view them on large screen entertainment systems. The success of Apple TV is at its infancy, but very soon, schools, offices and homes will be using this technology to view podcasts on TVs that are already fixtures in the environment.

In the next few years, it will be very likely for a school teacher, a housewife or a hospital patient to turn on a TV and choose from over a million podcasts to bring joy, understanding and alleviate a bit of stress about the world we live in.

REFERENCES

Chambless, D. L., Baker, M. J., Baucom, D. H., Beutler, L. E., Calhoun, K., & Crits-Christoph, P. (1998). Update on empirically validated therapies, II. *The Clinical Psychologist, 51*(1), 3–16.

Wikipedia. (2008). *Podcast* [online]. [Accessed

August 14, 2009]. Available from: http://en.wikipedia.org/w/index.php?title =Podcast&oldid=222708839.

Selmi, P. M., Klein, M. H., Greist, J. H., Sorrell, S. P., & Erdman, H. P. (1990). Computer-administered cognitive-behav- ioral therapy for depression. *American Journal of Psychiatry, 147*(1), 51–56.

National Association of Social Workers. (1999). *Code of ethics.* Washington, DC: NASW Press.

Chapter 19

THE USE OF ONLINE PSYCHOLOGICAL TESTING FOR SELF-HELP

MARK DOMBECK

INTRODUCTION

This chapter concerns online psychological testing as it applies to self-help efforts. The aims of this chapter are to review how online testing in its various forms supports mental health self-help efforts; to discuss problems and concerns associated with online testing and self-help practices; and to offer informed speculation concerning the ways in which online psychological testing and self-help technologies will likely develop in the future.

PSYCHOLOGICAL TESTING CONCEPTS REVIEWED

Psychological tests can be used for many purposes, one of them being to support psychological self-help efforts. Psychological tests provide a way for people to make tangible what are otherwise intangible psychological attributes like mood. The act of self-monitoring raises awareness and tends to suppress the unconscious emission of undesirable behaviors. Repeated measurement over time enables people to track the progress of their change efforts over time, or understand how they compare to peers.

ONLINE PSYCHOLOGICAL TESTING

The Internet and the visual interface to that worldwide computer network known as the World Wide Web are arguably the most important technological and cultural developments of recent times. The web can be thought of as a digital publishing platform which can be used to present content, such as psychological tests, to consumers. The key word here is "digital." Because content published on the web is digital, it can be easily projected across vast (or local) distances, duplicated, stored, retrieved and manipulated via algorithm. These characteristics make it possible to effectively transcend many of the reproduction, scoring and scaling problems inherent to printed tests and offer dramatically new possibilities for psychological testing and for self-help and therapeutic efforts more broadly.

CURRENT AVAILABILITY OF ONLINE TESTS

The low costs associated with publishing content on the web has led to a rapid expansion of available online psychological tests, many of which have potential to be used for self-help purposes. Unfortunately, a good deal of these tests are of dubious quality. Popular testing websites such as tickle.com and queendom.com, are advertiser supported and thus motivated to produce psychological tests for entertainment purposes so as to generate web traffic necessary to attract advertisers. Many of the tests appearing on such sites have little practical utility as capable measurements.

Though there are some quality and organizational problems present with regard to today's available online psychological tests, there is reason to expect that the situation will improve over time. As the web become ever more integrated into society, commercial publishers will create reliable and valid online versions of popular clinical measures and will integrate them into online self-help programs so that consumer choice of tests for self-help use is responsibly guided. Also, we can expect to see novel testing and self-help platforms built to exploit the rapidly evolving possibilities of the networked environment.

CURRENT SELF-HELP ONLINE TESTING EXAMPLES

Several current online self-help programs bear brief mention here as they illustrate how testing can function in the context of an online self-help program.

Qwitter.tobaccofreeflorida.com, an online smoking cessation tool, uses Twitter to help people track their efforts to quit smoking. Participants follow "iquit" and then use Twitter's response functions to record when they smoke and to keep an ongoing journal of their experience.

Psychtracker.com offers a freely available online behavioral recording tool suitable for use by people who are looking to keep track of various behaviors, moods and symptoms as part of a therapy program or self-help effort. Users may create a free individualized account and then log in daily to make simple Likert ratings on relevant subjects such as suicidality, mood and interest in activities. As part of setup, users select only those subjects that are relevant for themselves to track. At any time, system users may view graphical representations of their progress over time and print out copies of their results so as to share with their therapist or self-help partners.

Myselfhelp.com offers a series of targeted online self-help workbooks which one designed based on cognitive behavioral principles. At the time of writing, the service is available by subscription only. Regular measurement of targeted symptoms such as depressed mood is an integral part of each Myselfhelp.com program. In their Defeating Depression program, for instance, participants take and retake an online version of the Zung Depression Rating Scale and may view a graphical representation of their Zung scores over time as they make progress through the program. People using Myselfhelp.com programs can authorize their therapist to view their data.

Fearfighter.com is another self-help implementation of online cognitive behavioral therapy. It is currently only available in the United Kingdom and only by a subscribing doctor's prescription. Fearfighter participants step through a series of steps designed to teach and implement CBT therapy principles (such as exposure therapy) proven to be helpful for treating anxiety problems. The program authors note that the system has been empirically studied and shown to be as efficacious as working with an actual CBT therapist. As regular symptom measurement is integral to all CBT, Fearfighter participants complete periodic online anxiety and adjustment questionnaires and review their progress over time via online graphs of their test scores.

DOWNSIDES OF ONLINE TESTING AND SELF-HELP

Though there are many benefits associated with online testing and self-help programs, there are numerous downsides as well. All of the psychometric caveats that apply to traditional testing practices also apply to online testing. A variety of security and privacy issues related in part to testing platform reliance on rapidly evolving and often bug ridden web technologies create additional causes for concern.

Reliability and Validity Concerns

Reliability and validity are essential components of any useful psychological test. If either of these qualities are questionable for a given test, that test ceases to be useful as a measurement device and may deserve to be downgraded to a mere means of entertainment at best. Because of the advertisement-driven eco-nomics of web publishing, many currently available online psychological tests are there primarily to attract web traffic and advertising dollars. Other tests have been designed to be biased so as to lead consumers to come to particular marketing-driven conclusions (such as that they may have a problem that could benefit from a specific pharmaceutical aid). At least with regard to free-standing tests that have not been preselected for inclusion in a formal self-help program, there is no simple way for lay people to distinguish tests that are valid and reliable from those with alternative agendas. *Clinicians looking to recommend online tests for client's self-help use should take care to make sure that they are recommending properly validated tests.*

Even if obviously dubious online tests are eliminated from consideration, reliability and validity concerns may linger. Establishing the reliability and validity of a test is a time consuming and expensive and thus infrequent process. Many tests which appear online are translations of tests which were developed and validated offline. It is not entirely clear that the reliability and validity of such tests will have survived this translation process intact. Any online version of a psychological test which has only been evaluated in its original print form (which describes most tests available today) should be considered somewhat suspect until a revalidation has taken place. *Interpretations made based on data taken from suspect tests should be qualified, at least, so as to acknowledge the issue if they are made at all.*

Data Interpretation Concerns

A virtue of online tests is that they are self-scoring and can provide automated feedback as to what scores mean. For instance, a depression screening test can be programmed to make suggestions as to what different score ranges indicate with regard to the severity of a depression condition. A low score may suggest that depression is not a particular problem, while a very high score may suggest that immediate treatment would be a good idea.

Potential problems exist with regard to the accuracy and appropriateness of computerized interpretive feedback. Such feedback can only be made on the basis of numerical scores; it is not possible for the online testing system to take context or history into account, or to make adjustments for cultural variations in terms of how people will respond to questions. Consequently, there is an ever-present chance that test takers will receive inappropriate feedback, either minimizing the extent of existing problems, or, alternatively, making more of

them than is warranted. Screening tests are generally designed to cast a wide net and may lead lay test takers to overly pathologize their experience. *Clinicians should take care to educate their clients as to how to best make sense of automated test interpretations and to the proper purpose of recommended tests. Screening tests should be distinguished from tests more appropriate for repetitive symptom tracking, for instance.*

Data Ownership and Privacy Concerns

Consumers utilizing testing and self-help services may assume that they own the data they produce, but this is by no means a safe assumption. Contemporary online testing and self-help services are generally provided by private, for-profit companies who may assert partial or complete ownership over data stored in their system. Further, testing data generated through the use of such services may not qualify for legal privacy protections afforded to medical records. Consequently, *clinicians should take care to carefully review the privacy and terms of use statements issued by testing services they plan to recommend.* These documents should make explicit who owns data generated by the use of the testing or self-help service, under what conditions that ownership may be asserted and what the disposition of the data is in the event of a sale or similar transaction of the testing or self-help company.

Some uses for stored data a testing company may assign itself may be less palatable than others. For instance, a testing service that states it will use consumer generated data in an anonymized fashion for purposes of quality control and benchmarking might be considered an acceptable use by most individuals. A service that plans to use the same data for direct marketing purposes may be something test-takers would rather avoid.

It is similarly important to know who is considered to be the actual client of testing and self-help services. Some testing services such as Fearfighter.com are sold to healthcare institutions who in turn provide them to health care consumers. In such a resale scenario, it can be confusing to know whether the client of the service (and thus the presumed owner of generated data) is the healthcare institution who paid for the service, or the healthcare consumer actually using the service. Exactly who owns generated data and to what degree each party may assert ownership over that data needs to be made clear in a process of informed consent prior to consumer's use of the service. To the extent that third parties are allowed to access testing data, the terms of service document should address this possibility and outline in detail under what circumstances third parties may see the data.

An obvious issue to explore and document concerns efforts testing services take to protect the privacy of testing system users. Psychological test data are personal and sensitive by nature. It could be embarrassing or even damaging to a system user's career or employment prospects should such data inappropriately find its way into a public arena. The potential for such damage to occur is greatly lessened when the testing service has taken care to properly design their service so as to anonymize and secure stored data. Programmatic encryption of passwords as well as actual data are possible, but the most effective method of all is to keep personally identifiable information wholly separated from all recorded test data. This is easy for most free services to accomplish since they never

need to collect identifying information in the first place. Services that require a credit card or other identifiable payment must take additional precautions. The methods by which testing services secure data will hopefully be documented and discoverable so that potential consumers and recommenders of such services can make informed decisions as to whether or not to participate.

A separate issue to consider has to do with data retention policies. It is important for consumers of a testing service (and clinicians recommending such services) to know how long and under what circumstances a given testing service will retain customer data. If a testing service will delete an account after a period of disuse, a consumer of that service ought to know about that policy in advance. The only way to know this information is to carefully read the privacy and terms of service documents published by testing services.

The possibility of data portability is another area to explore carefully. It is possible for testing sites to allow site users to export and download data stored within the service, but testing services may not be motivated to create such a download feature until multiple requests for it have been logged.

Even if the terms of service and privacy documents are all satisfactory, users of online testing services should be aware and comfortable with the fact that nothing on the Internet is ever truly stable and that data may be lost at any time. Catastrophic equipment failures, unfortunate software problems, malicious hackers and simple bankruptcy may force a testing service offline at any time. Testing service users should consider themselves to be on the bleeding edge of a new and emerging technology and should ensure that they are comfortable with the idea that they may lose all of their stored data without notice.

Security and Availability Concerns

It is *extremely* difficult to secure online services from all possibility of compromise. Web software is often created rapidly so as to gain competitive advantage and as such it can contain bugs and poorly written code that leave it vulnerable to attack by malicious hackers. More than just the testing application itself may be insecure; all layers of software from the server operating system on up through the web server, database and scripting language used will generally contain bugs and vulnerabilities. Internet service provider companies (of which online testing providers are a subset) defense against such vulnerabilities is to make sure that server software is updated regularly with applicable security patches, to make sure scheduled security audits are performed, to properly apply firewalls and similar network boundary, encryption and monitoring measures and to expend resources fixing vulnerable code when it is found. While most companies make best efforts to do these things, inevitably, some vulnerability remains.

If the need to fend off attackers was not enough, Internet Service Providers must contend with the vagaries of hardware and network failures and other events that can temporarily disable a service. Companies can partially mitigate such failures by hosting their application with a high end service provider which makes available 24/7 network engineering support and monitoring, server spare parts, redundant high speed connections to the Internet, physical security measures and backup services, but even when this is the case, temporary periods of downtime will probably still occur.

Measures taken by testing companies to identify and correct unwanted software vulnerabilities and mitigate damage from hardware and network failures may be documented somewhere on their respective websites. It is a good idea for concerned clinicians to research this information (or call to obtain it if it is not otherwise posted) so as to take it into account when deciding on which service to recommend or use.

In light of the inevitable security and availability issues that will exist, people using online testing or self-help services should be made aware of, and hopefully become comfortable with, the idea that data may be compromised or become temporarily unavailable. This comes down to an informed consent issue. The potential for compromise or failure is, of course, easier to stomach when little or no personally identifying information is attached to stored data.

FUTURE DIRECTIONS FOR ONLINE TESTING AND SELF-HELP

Online testing and self-help will undoubtedly continue to rapidly evolve both as network technologies evolve and as psychologists become more knowledgeable about how to put these technologies to work. I close this chapter with a few speculations as to the probable shape some of these future developments will take.

The trend towards designing web resources for consumption on mobile devices such as the cell phone and ebook as well as for traditional web browsers will undoubtedly continue. Online testing applications that incorporate behavioral recording (such as counting the number of cigarettes smoked, or types of foods consumed across the day) will benefit most greatly from this trend, as the use of such networked mobile devices will enable practical end-to-end digitization of vital in situ data.

Applications will be built up around online testing technologies so as to harness their potential as technologies of description and change. We are already seeing this in the form of self-help psycho-educational services such as Fearfighter and Myselfhelp and in the form of various personality testing websites which, for a fee, will help you learn about yourself. As these applications mature and as more money becomes available to businesses offering these services, we will hopefully also see continuing efforts to empirically validate these services. The early example set by Fearfighter and Myselfhelp in this direction is encouraging.

It is still the case that relatively few clinicians have actively embraced online therapy at this moment in time, in part because of the strangeness and lack of body-language feedback current implementations of such services offer and also, in part, because professional associations and licensure boards have not always encouraged the practice.

What seems far more likely to happen, in my opinion, is for clinicians to incorporate online testing and self-help technologies into their face-to-face practice. For example, therapists might create homework assignments for their clients and enable them to keep an online journal and daily mood record through an online resource while still seeing clients face-to-face on a weekly basis. One can imagine future empirically validated therapies being shipped in manualized online workbook format, via an online application not unlike Myselfhelp that therapists could offer to their clients as a practical therapeutic resource. This sort of application would, of course, appeal most of all to behaviorally oriented clinicians treating highly specific and targeted disorders, as it would aid them in holding their clients to an organized and empirically validated track towards the resolution of their troubling issues.

FURTHER GENERAL READING ON PSYCHOLOGICAL TESTING

Cohen, J. (1960). A coefficient of agreement for nominal scales. *Educational and Psychological Measurement, 20*(1), pp. 37–46.

Cronbach, L. J. (1951). Coefficient alpha and the internal structure of tests. *Psychometrika, 16*(3), 297–334.

Nunnally, J. C. (1978). *Psychometric theory* (2nd ed.). New York: McGraw-Hill.

WEBSITES

http://fearfighter.com/
http://www.myselfhelp.com/
http://www.psychtracker.com/
http://queendom.com/

http://qwitter.tobaccofreeflorida.com/
http://twitter.com/
http://web.tickle.com/

Chapter 20

USING EMAIL TO ENRICH COUNSELOR TRAINING AND SUPERVISION

JOHN YAPHE AND CEDRIC SPEYER

INTRODUCTION

The growth of online counselling as an effective therapeutic modality has created the need for ongoing supervision of e-counsellors. This chapter will describe one model of online supervision as it applies to asynchronous communication, as well as reviewing practices that have emerged within the framework of one specific e-counselling service. It will present the principles of online supervision used in this service, discuss common challenges faced by counsellors and present some online supervisory interventions using composite case excerpts. It will conclude with reflections on future developments for Internet supervision of distance counselling. Case material is drawn from a variety of different cases.

Online supervision is defined as the provision of supervision to e-counsellors providing online clinical service delivery. It is intended to assure the quality of online counselling and the effectiveness of therapeutic outcomes. It also promotes the knowledge, skills and clinical attributes required by e-counsellors who

are making the transition to text and supports their online professional development. Nagel et al. (2009) include a discussion of recent developments in their review of the influence of new technologies in clinical supervision.

Asynchronous exchanges provide an effective way to supervise e-counsellors. Asyncnhronous communication does not take place in "real time," but rather whenever the participants have a chance to respond to one another (Rochen et al., 2004). Asynchronicity allows reflection, but as with online counselling between client and counsellor, asynchronicity is not immune from misunderstandings. As is the case with online counsellors, online supervisors must be aware of the lack of spontaneous clarification (Speyer & Zack, 2003). Nevertheless, the raw material of case management (transcripts of the correspondence when ethically appropriate) is readily available to the supervisor; therefore quality assurance can be hands-on. Supervision is more directly accessible. It is not necessarily based solely on the therapist's perception and report of the therapeutic interchange. Supervisors can offer guidance by reading the client's text independently of the e-counsellor's response and review the e-counsellor's clinical process before, during or after the asynchronous session.

IN-SERVICE SUPERVISION

Counsellors in the service described here, an e-counselling program of a major Canadian EAP provider, are drawn mainly from the fields of social work, counselling and psychology with a Master's degree and a minimum of five years of in-person counselling experience as minimal requirements. There is also a family physician on staff. Counsellors pass through three stages of screening to assess the level of integration of their writing and therapeutic skills and are subsequently provided with extensive on-the-job training and ongoing supervision.

The pioneer of the service (and coauthor of this chapter) serves as clinical supervisor for case management challenges of all kinds and a consultant specializing in the approach named "Inner View." The training for this approach uses a template known as CARE for e-counselors to follow as a framework for case management. The acronym stands for Connect and Contain ("your challenge is human and manageable"); Assess and Affirm ("you've got what it takes to get through this"); Reorient and Reaffirm ("you are not defined by your life situation"); and Encourage and Empower ("keep going, one step at a time") (Speyer, 2010).

Recently, a second experienced e-counsellor has taken on the role of clinical co-supervisor for "e-team" counsellor management and in-service professional development. The family medicine specialist on the e-team, with experience supervising the clinical work of medical residents and students, has served as a consultant for case conferencing and conducted an in-service training workshop. In principal, supervision follows the general guidelines established for the practice and principles of online clinical supervision by the British Association for Counselling and Psychotherapy (Anthony and Goss, 2009).

E-counsellors benefit from both individual and group supervision. Individual supervision occurs as the need arises at the counsellor's initiative, at regularly scheduled intervals, or at the initiative of the supervisor, using selected cases as teaching vehicles to follow-up feedback from clients.

Continued collaboration, consultation and training occur via an ongoing listserv and in-person at an annual in-service training workshop. ViewPoint (the listserv) is a private professional development forum for E-team networking and sharing. Members are pre-authorized by the Clinical Supervisor. Discussions pertain to the quality, effectiveness and influence of online counselling in an EAP setting. Members offer support, encouragement, and resources to each other in the interests of the growth and evolution of the E-team. Peer support takes place in the context of the development and expansion of E-Counselling. The group also serves as an extension of orientation, training and supervision for the e-counselling program. Counsellors can also receive individual supervisory guidance upon request at any time before, during, or after case exchanges. Supervision is mandatory for high-risk cases needing offline intervention and/or contracting with the client for safety.

CASE MANAGEMENT CHALLENGES

In the following section we present clinical material to illustrate best practices and common challenges encountered in e-counselling. The material has been modified to preserve anonymity of counsellors and clients and uses composite case excerpts to illustrate key principles.

Close Attention to the Client's Text

The client in the following example is a 40-year-old woman who requested help in dealing with sources of stress in her life.

> Client (intake form): This is all absorbing. I'm avoiding social occasions, not in the mood. I stopped going to tango nights, my dance partner senses my stress which just escalates his and that spoils the fun, plus I can't really concentrate and when really into tango you need to.

The e-counsellor replied to the client in the first exchange using the following formula in order to obtain information on the client's interests and activities without addressing one of the client's passions, namely dancing the tango:

> E-Counsellor (1st exchange): I am curious to know what your life outside of work is like at this time. What sort of life-work balance do you have at this time? Who are the significant people in your life? What sort of activities do you participate in outside of work? What do you do to relax/de-stress? Taking care of yourself during an emotionally stressful time like this is very important. What can you do at this time to take care of you?

The counsellor continues with psycho-education and the following homework assignment for the client:

> E-counsellor: During emotionally stressful times there is a tendency for thoughts and feelings to be chaotic. Journaling is a wonderful way of releasing the thoughts and feelings onto paper. You can also type them into your computer, if you feel more comfortable doing that.

In supervision the supervisor reminded the counsellor that the client has registered for counselling and had already told her story online, thereby connecting with a counsellor. A generic response recommending homework for the same client misses the opportunity to reinforce that this is what the client is already doing in her relationship with the counsellor.

PERSON-CENTRED VS. PROBLEM-SATURATED APPROACH

Clients usually present their issues in a problem-saturated manner. E-counsellors in this service are encouraged to "find out what's right with the client" rather than make an in-depth discussion of dysfunction the central theme of the online dialogue (in the name of removing blocks to the client's happiness and well-being). Instead, in this approach, e-counsellors are coached to focus on the "person behind the problem" and draw upon inner resources that will enable the client to choose a response to their life situation rather than continue to feel victimized by it.

In the following example, a 24-year-old woman requested help in dealing with many challenges of her daily life:

> Client: I am really stressed out with many family issues such as my father possibly having MS . . . brother on crystal meth . . . guilt that my parents are barely keeping a roof over their heads . . . me having money problems . . . missing sisters who are in another country . . . weight issues . . . lonely and depressed. I wish I would not want to cry all the time I would be skinny lol I would want to be out there having fun rather than sitting at home.

The counsellor, who was a novice, responded in her first exchange in this way.

> Counsellor: Hi Doreen and welcome to e-counselling which is a place that you can feel free to share your feelings and thoughts without having to worry about what you should or should not say. My name is Christine and I will be your e-counselor. I look forward to having a few back and forth exchanges with you to help you try and figure out what

has you feeling so unhappy.

She continued with the following synopsis:

> Counsellor: From reading your email I see that you are feeling pretty unhappy and seem to be lacking in energy and motivation—kinda' like your get up and go has got up and went?

The supervisor picked up on this problem-centered approach and suggested a more person-centered approach:

> Supervisor: Instead of leading with the negative as a goal and buying into client's line of depressive thinking when you say, "I am here to help you try to figure out what it is that has you feeling so unhappy," you might try relating to the person behind the problem. You could lead with a capsule summary of the life situation in positive terms. For example: "You are coping with many family issues such as your father's illness, your brother, money issues and weight issues. Yet you have a clear idea of your goals when you say: "I would not want to cry all the time, I would be skinny, I would want to be out having fun rather than sitting at home." I wonder what kind of fun that would be Doreen?
>
> You have a good upbeat, conversational tone and offer some excellent guidance. Now you need to instill the feeling that so-called depression doesn't define her and transmit that along with the empathy of the first exchange by connecting with the person who was able to write "lol" in the midst of listing her burdens.

POSITIVE CORE ISSUE: THE GLARE AND THE GAZE

When e-counsellors apply the full scope of their clinical expertise to the etiology of the negative core issue, this is the necessary "glare" of the assessment phase. Yet the tone of the online dialogue is the antidote to client discouragement. E-counselling exchanges are characterized by a positive *gaze* on client strengths. While the "glare" provides valuable insight into self-defeating attitudes and patterns, the "gaze" is focused squarely on the inherent capacity to overcome, transform, or transcend painful life predicaments.

> E-supervisor: I am talking about *listening* to the client in a solution-focused way, by acknowledging that she is a *survivor* of sexual abuse, in response to her disclosures. You can also ask her if it is something she had received help with in the various forms of therapy she has undergone. We are not looking for cause and effects in any clinical way, because we are not using the medical diagnostic model in this short-term EAP service, nor actively revisiting past trauma.

There has been much clinical discussion at all levels, as well as trial and error on the ground among numerous e-counsellors, and this perspective has emerged as perhaps the best way to field revelations of past abuse, in the authors' view. We cannot explore the abuse in the name of "decathecting" the trauma, yet we also need to honour the trust clients place in us when they reveal painful episodes of the past. Therefore, here's a generic take on how we acknowledge and reframe past abuse (as modified to address specific client scenarios):

> The good qualities that came to the surface as a result of childhood abuse, and which still do, enabled you to survive at the time and continue to build a life for yourself in which you can thrive. Those strengths say more about who you are than how the original trauma made you feel, which is powerless and of no value.
>
> As an adult, you have the power to experience yourself with compassion as someone susceptible to feelings which may lead you to believe something is wrong with you. However, those feelings can cue what is most right with you: the ability to take care of yourself in exactly the ways your caretakers were unable to do.

ONLINE GUIDANCE WITHOUT PENPAL DEPENDENCE

Clients are encouraged to view their e-counsellor as a guide at the crossroads who is trained to point them in the right direction (for them), rather than serve as a virtual companion or penpal as the need arises. E-counselors encourage clients to be emotionally self-sufficient, rather than position themselves as helpers who will "be there for them" on an ongoing basis. The general goal, as much as possible, is to cut to the chase of the client's essential qualities, values and strengths.

In this example, the counsellor consulted with the supervisor because of difficulties in terminating counselling with a client.

Client: Gotta go now . . . hope to chat soon . . . thanks for being there in my InBox . . . getting your take on things is the highlight of my day!

The supervisor responded in this manner.

E-supervisor: It is a challenge to set parameters for certain clients, with no perceived loss of compassion. As in all forms of therapy, you need to stay in charge of the process (not the person) by keeping control over the framework. Otherwise, some clients will just keep coming back to the well, as thirsty as ever. What we mean by "issue based" case management is the ability to support clients without propping them up; that means clearly leaving the responsibility for their health and wholeness with them, again with no loss of compassion. The general goal is to leave clients with confidence in their own resources. So be explicit about how you are a guide for a short while on the journey; it's all about which direction to take at the crossroads. You're a guide, not a companion, so every case is about handing the compass to the client so they can find the direction (inner and outer) that's right for them. Keep the clinical goal of closure in mind from the beginning: guiding, advising and concluding in the spirit of "My voice will go with you" (Rosen, 1982).

This counsellor adopted the supervisor's advice during the closure phase:

E-counsellor: "I am often a little sad when I come to the end of a brief journey with people I meet in counselling. It has been a pleasure and a privilege to correspond with you and I admire the way you have faced your difficulties and dealt with them. You are now on your way! Sometimes I see my job like that of a guide who helps people across a swift-flowing river. It's tricky but it helps if someone shows you where the solid stones are so you can get firm footing. Now it's time for me to go back and help someone else across."

FINDING OUT WHAT'S RIGHT WITH THE CLIENT

In the "InnerView" approach, e-counsellors encourage clients to separate their sense and source of identity or self-fulfillment from the circumstances of their unhappiness (at first by simply witnessing their predicament with borrowed functioning coming from the e-counsellor's compassion and loving-kindness). When we see through the self-concept shell of damaged goods that many clients present at intake, we discover essential qualities at the heart and core of client personhood that allow us to reframe the challenging crux of their issues in terms of personal hope and faith already accessible to the client's essential self.

E-supervisor: I hear a tone of bitter resignation in the client's sign-off to you and that goes with the territory of what she's been through lately. You can understand the conclusions she comes to without buying into the spirit of them; just the opposite. You started this case off well, but the problem-saturated story took over with you in the more traditionally therapeutic role of uncovering layers of her distress. You tried to get at her underlying positive values as an entry point for believing in herself, yet she succeeded in steering the dialogue towards her grievances. You need to keep your gaze on the redemptive aspects of her personhood and attune the client to the vision of her strengths, which you steadfastly hold on the client's behalf (which is different than any facile praising or "cheerleading" of good traits).

The clinical microscope revealing the deep-seated roots of her flaws and failings needs to be put aside in favour of the magnifying glass applied to what's right with the client; not what's wrong with her. You're the role model for those perceptions.

E-counsellor (supervisory recommendations): When I first read your letter, a number of thoughts and feelings surfaced in me and I would like to share them with you to see how that can help us get started. The first thought was a question. "Who is Fiona?" I read about diagnoses, medications and doctors, but I don't think that gives me a good picture of you. I don't see you as a patient in need of treatment. I read a little more and learned about a wife, a daughter, a worker with lots of experi-

ence in a responsible position and felt "that's more like it!" Then I heard someone who is looking for a new way to make progress in the personal, family, work and social spheres. This sounds like a person who is ready to work with me and move forward. That is the person I want to get to know better.

E-supervisor (responding to another case consultation): Meanwhile, if your role is not to diagnose any condition or treat any mental illness, then guess what? You can explore what's right with her—by writing a full, compassionate, soul-making 1st exchange inviting her to explore the personhood that is not defined by "severe anxiety/depression/stress issues" but instead highlights the following:

Client (at intake): I still value life and my family really matters to me. I want to do work that gives me a reason to get up in the morning.

I need an emotional boost and could use some advice on how to stop hating my ex. I'd be able to walk into the layer's office to complete the divorce settlement with confidence and have nothing to fear.

LETTING GO OF OUTCOMES
(NOT WORKING HARDER THAN THE CLIENT)

After supervised practice, experienced e-counsellors may become adept at sensing what healing may come for the client at whatever point in their life they may be ready to own it. This is the big picture or the view from the mountaintop. When guiding the client through the valley of their present predicament, e-counsellors can see the forest for the trees and pace themselves accordingly; they can walk their client towards the

nearest clearing without necessarily taking them through all the tangled thickets of the negative core issue.

One e-counsellor was advised as follows:

A, B, C's of "not working harder than the client":

A. Hold the vision of the healing and enjoy the soul-restoring effect of writing accordingly, without disregarding the client's pain (where it hurts).

B. Pace and lead the client one or two steps further than where they are, while encouraging their progress, no matter how minimal.

C. Be vigilant of all feelings that signal taking responsibility for the outcome.

Counsellor impatience, irritation, or anger at lack of client "movement" are all clues.

Increasingly, e-counsellors are facing situations in which on-line clients are at apparent risk of harm to themselves or others. This is a situation that calls for consultation with a supervisor. A counsellor who consulted on a potential high risk case was advised:

E-supervisor: The first exchange serves as a context in which to connect with the whole person. The clients usually initiate a dialogue "organized around the problem." Without minimizing their pain, we do not have to do the same. The empathy and compassion for what clients are going through, no matter how extreme, needs to be accompanied by great interest in the life in which this life situation is taking place. "Where attention goes, energy flows" and that's why you don't want to focus the first exchange exclusively on the pain that leads to "thoughts of hurting yourself." More importantly, the contracting for safety (which needs to be *part* of the first exchange and not set the whole tone) is counterproductive if it displaces connecting with the client on the basis of the positive core issue.

INTUITIVE ASSESSMENT WITHOUT DIAGNOSTIC QUESTIONING

E-supervisor: Every intake comes with a feeling and a core issue behind that feeling. In this case, there is a tone of insecurity and vulnerability. Connecting on a feeling level always comes first, before the psycho-education starts to build on the (positive) core issue. It appears the client could be ready to grow in the direction of self-validation. Strengthening her own emotional "container" could help with the mutual boundary-setting that helps make the marriage a safe container. All this needs to be addressed by connecting with the client on the basis of what she's already shared rather than asking "further assessment" questions about the problems in her marriage.

Prepare your response in a way that signifies to the client that you have carefully read and understood the presenting issues. This can be achieved through validating the client's experience, reflecting what the client is communicating and expressing unconditional positive regard, with a minimum of strategic questions to move the dialogue forward.

Uncover client strengths and refer to these often in the context of the presenting problem, quoting the client's words to illustrate themes.

In the process of the correspondence, read between the lines to ascertain if there are underlying issues that need to be addressed. As long as you are making educated guesses and resonating with the client's agenda, rather than assuming hidden issues, it is an important part of the assessment process to follow hunches, trust gut feelings and lead with an intuitive sense of the person on the other side of the computer screen.

CLIENT-FRIENDLY LANGUAGE AND "VOICE"

A counsellor consulted with the supervisor regarding the tone or "voice" to be used in first exchanges.

E-supervisor: In the process of communicating with the client, keep in mind both the purpose and the overall goal of the exchanges, which is to reinforce what is right with the client rather than diagnose and treat what is wrong with them. To that end, write in the tone of a close friend, without being presumptuous about it, especially at the beginning. Be aware that the most important goal is to create a therapeutic bond with the client, which has the tone of warm, respectful, caring letter writing. Validate the client's experience within the client's frame of reference. Comment often on the progress being made. Express appreciation for the depth of honesty in the person as it emerges through the correspondence. Be transparent about your thoughts and feelings in "real time."

MAINTAINING CONSISTENT ONLINE FRAMEWORK AND PARAMETERS

The e-counsellor sets the parameters for short-term correspondence. This spells out the pace, momentum and rate of replies on both sides and the need for a theme, in order to take charge of the case management. Initial parameter-setting sends the message that clients have a few focused back-and-forth exchanges to work with over a limited period of time. In the short-term model, the window clients have to communicate with a counsellor does not stay open indefinitely. Files are opened when clients register and closed when the correspondence concludes, within a flexible time frame. Short-term asynchronous cases are not designed for periodic contact. Clients need to perceive their e-counsellor as a guide who is trained to point them in the right direction for them and make sure that they are equipped for their own journey, rather than someone who is there for ongoing consultation or an on-call consultant who they can turn to as the need arises.

E-supervisor: The emphasis is always on the perspective or direction that the client needs to move forward and the "remaining exchanges" invoked in the context of the positive core issue. Sometimes you have to explicitly orient the client on how to make the most of the short-term nature of the service.

READING BETWEEN THE LINES FOR FEELING TONE

Writing can be reflecting the thought processes and emotional state of the client, even when the personality or attitude behind the core issue is not directly expressed. Experienced e-counsellors learn to intuitively assess the nature of their correspondent by paying close attention to the text. Consider the difference between these two ways of presenting the same marital issue and what it says about the personality behind the words.

> Client A: I am seeking professional assistance for marital difficulties that have led to temporary separation from my spouse.
>
> Client B: Hope someone there can help me! My husband just walked out on me and I don't know what I'm going to do. I knew there were some problems, doesn't everyone have them? But this feels like a kind of amputation. I feel cut off and torn in half!
>
> E-supervisor: When you read an intake, you really have to sit with it for awhile, so you can enter into the client's world and get a sense of their felt presence through paying close attention to what they're saying as well as feeling, making the connection warm, close, empathic and heartfelt.

MASTERING THE NUANCES OF TELE-PRESENCE

Since the writing process mirrors a person's thought process, it can provide opportunities to explore the client's irrational beliefs and distorted perceptions through text-based input alone. Writing style can be as revealing as body language. It's a way of "composing oneself" in more ways than one, revealed in writing as visible "self-talk." There is also an intangible *attunement,* as Suler (2004) observed: "There is a special type of interpersonal empathy that is unique to text relationships. Some claim that text-only talk carries you past the distracting, superficial aspects of a person's existence and connects you more directly to the other's psyche."

> E-supervisor: There are three ways of writing to a client. The first and least evolved is when we write "at" the person with all the expertise on the issue in mind. The second is when we write "to" the person—however, it is still the person who has the problem, while we have possible solutions. The third and most evolved form of e-counselling is when we are writing "with" the person by entering their world from our side of the computer, where healing takes place as a result of the layered intersection of perspectives that produces new possibilities.
>
> Client feedback: While the traditional therapeutic relationship is ideally a collaborative process, I felt that this medium moved things in that direction much more quickly. It seemed that we were both beginning on the same level with no preconceived notions. By this I mean that there was no room for outside influences—for example, the physical characteristics of either of us, the office, other people, tones of voice etc. . . . These were not present and as such, allowed for the "pureness" of the words to be heard. The true content of our discussions is the focus, not the other stuff that can often impede effective communication. I had no idea it was possible to form a bond and a trust with someone based solely on the written word. Thoughts and feelings just seemed to flow out of me in a way I never could have imagined. My e-counsellor helped me put things in perspective and look at

things going on in my life in a whole different light. I was apprehensive about

trying e-counselling but find it was the best move I ever made.

LEADING THE PROCESS WITHOUT IMPOSING AN AGENDA

E-counsellors are trained to focus on client strengths and resources. From that point of view they are able to reframe significant stresses and traumas. The problem and its consequences are then situated within a more meaningful story, allowing choices to be made in freedom and out of self-love. Yet it all starts with the joining and the client's gut feeling that no matter what else is being discussed, the counsellor is saying *"I'm with you, I sense your pain, I know what's wrong, but I also know it's not bigger than you; so let's walk through this together and find out how what's right with you can point the way forward."* That allows for a "cut to the chase" effect when it comes to the (positive) core issue.

E-supervisor: Your assessment of the core issue still needs some fine-tuning, in that you tend to use a wide-angle lens in the 1st exchange due to good in-person, client-centered training in which there's an open-ended unconditional positive regard. In the InnerView approach we keep the unconditional positive regard, yet it is not as open-ended as in face-to-face counselling. In this case, for example, you can "cut to the chase" of the (positive) core issue. In a few exchanges you can plant the seeds of what she needs to achieve more emotional intimacy in her marriage. I like the way you're prescribing getting to know her preferred state first, i.e., what true intimacy means to her. The first exchange also sets the theme and this is where you need a working hypothesis that contains a vision of her healing, i.e., what would be an antidote to: "I can't really figure out what is wrong lately but I'm not happy."

CONCLUSION

The early days of e-counselling and online supervision have presented many challenges and opportunities for creative solutions. In the next phase of development of this modality we will be looking for more evidence of the benefits of this approach and these methods. Both quantitative and qualitative methods can be applied to study the effects of e-counselling and e-supervision. Many questions arise in this field. What kinds of issues are most effectively dealt with in this format? What kinds of counsellors are most suited to this modality? What techniques of supervision are most effective in training and guiding counsellors? How will these methods be incorporated into the traditional repertoire of skills taught to professionals who use counselling methods in their daily work? We expect that the coming decade will see continued development in these directions.

REFERENCES

Anthony, K., & Goss, S. (2009). *Guidelines for online counselling and psychotherapy including guidelines for online supervision* (3rd ed.). Lutterworth: BACP.

Nagel D. M., Goss, S., & Anthony, K. (2009). The use of technology in supervision. In N. Pelling, J. Barletta, & P. Armstrong (Eds.), *The practice of clinical supervision.* Bowen Hills, Qld.: Australian Academic Press.

Rochlen, A. B., Zack, J. S., & Speyer, C. (2004). Online therapy: Review of relevant definitions, debates, and current empirical support. *Journal of Clinical Psychology, 60*(3):269–83.

Rosen, S. (Ed.). (1982). *My voice will go with you: The teaching tales of Milton H. Erickson.* New York: Norton.

Speyer, C., & Zack, J. (2003). Online counselling: Beyond the pros and cons. *Psychologica, 23*:2.

Speyer, C. (2010). From products to persons: Psychology with a soul. *Psychologica, 32*(1): 20–26.

Suler, J. R. (2004). The psychology of text relationships. In R. Kraus, J. Zack & G. Stricker (Eds.), *Online counseling: A handbook for mental health professionals.* San Diego, CA: Elsevier Academic Press.

Chapter 21

USING CHAT AND INSTANT MESSAGING (IM) TO ENRICH COUNSELOR TRAINING AND SUPERVISION

DeeAnna Merz Nagel and Sara Riley

INTRODUCTION

Using text-based, real-time chat to conduct supervision is quickly becoming an integral part of many educational, organizational and employment settings. This chapter will describe the use of chat and instant messaging in a work setting, offering the reader an opportunity to envision how this particular use of technology may be incorporated into various controls.

We will begin by defining the following four terms:

- online chat
- clinical supervision
- peer supervision
- field supervision

Online chat is a generic term for what is commonly known as instant messaging (IM). This is normally a computer program that enables mutual typing to connected users as an "instant" form of communication.

Online chat can refer to any kind of communication over the Internet, but is primarily meant to refer to direct one-on-one chat or text-based group chat (formally also known as synchronous conferencing), using tools such as instant messaging applications. (Wikipedia, 2009, p. 1).

This is a process whereby users of the Internet engage in real time or synchronous conversations using their computers. Online chat consists of these users exchanging text messages. In order to engage in online chat, a chat client must log-in to a chat channel and contact a chat server. There are a large number of chat channels, ranging from those that support general conversations to those that are devoted to a specific topic. Other terms include Internet Relay Chat (IRC), instant messaging and private chat (Ince, 2001).

Clinical supervision is,

... an intervention provided by a more senior member of a profession to a more junior member or members of that same profession. This relationship is evaluative and hierarchical, extends over time and has the simultaneous purposes of enhancing the professional functioning of the more junior person(s), monitoring the quality of professional services offered to the clients, she, he, or they see ... and serving as a gatekeeper for those who are to enter the particular profession. (Bernard & Goodyear, 2009, p. 7)

Peer supervision, also referred to as peer consultation, has been proposed as a potentially effective approach to increasing the frequency and/or quality of supervision available to a counselor (Benshoff, 1989; Remley et al., 1987). Peer supervision may also be defined as a process that allows counselors to assist one another in becoming more effective and skillful helpers by using their relationships and professional skills with each other. Counselors can develop their own peer consultation relationships to fill a "supervision void" or to augment traditional supervision by providing a means of getting additional feedback from their peers (Wagner & Smith, 1979).

Field supervision is also referred to as field education and the term is often associated with the social work profession. In addition, the term is used in counselor and social work education to refer to the student's placement in the field and resulting supervision of field work. Field supervision may also be referred to as "direction." For instance, direction can be defined as

... the ongoing administrative overseeing by an employer or superior of a Professional Counselor's work by a director. The director shall be responsible for assuring the quality of the services rendered by that practitioner and shall ensure that qualified supervision or intervention occurs in situations which require expertise beyond that of the practitioner. (Georgia Composite Board of Professional Counselors, Social Workers and Marriage and Family Therapists, 2003, p. 8).

The field supervisor may be external or internal from the organization. Depending on the geographic region, internal and external supervisors, whether clinical or field, supervisors may be assigned different roles and expectations (Franséhn, 2007).

Regardless of the particular role a supervisor plays, supervision generally involves consultation about specific client information including background and presenting issues. The supervisor may be an employer, a peer, a professor or a clinician. The role of supervision may be to satisfy the coursework necessary to complete a degree, or to satisfy requirements toward certification or licensure. Supervision may also be considered a professional growth endeavor that is neither required nor expected.

THE ARGUMENT FOR SUPERVISION VIA CHAT

The age of the portable laptop and response on demand has arrived (Reisch and Jarman-Rohde, 2000). It is easier for some to sit in front of their computers and schedule appointments, confirm dates, times, locations and/or discuss cases with peers. Online forums, chat rooms and instant messaging give professionals other options for communication that deviate from the traditional face-to-face and telephone encounters. As with any supervisory relationship, this connectivity via chat warrants several considerations to include informed consent, confidentiality, crisis situations, jurisdiction and technical competence (Fenichel, 2000; Paños et al., 2002; Watson, 2003).

Supervisees and supervisors should be aware of the limitations of online consultation and supervision. Confidentiality is paramount. Depending on the particular setting, actual names and identifying information may be blinded to further protect the client's record. For instance, in the case of peer supervision, it is advised that identifying information such as name, demographics or details of the case be avoided so that the actual client identity is not revealed to peer professionals. This would apply to educational settings or group supervision in which all of the participants are not part of the same organization. If the supervision occurs within a work setting, client information may be revealed, assuming the employer is the owner of the record and employees take on various roles within the organization as is the case in the illustration that follows. To further ensure that all communication is as confidential as possible, chat and IM dialogue online should always be encrypted (Anthony & Goss, 2009). Encryption is no longer cost prohibitive and can be achieved with relative ease. Programs such as HushMail and Skype offer encrypted chat. At the time of writing, chat options through HushMail and Skype are free to the user. Other more formal platforms are available, offering organizational branding, email and file storage options. Supervisors who are interested in incorporating encrypted chat should be sure to use a service, program or platform that is encrypted. Supervisors should take extra steps towards protecting the process and effectiveness of their supervision. Supervisors have a professional, ethical and legal responsibility to monitor the quality of care that is being delivered to their supervisees' clients (Vaccaro & Lambie, 2007).

At many times, professionals feel isolated, struggling with written documentation, direction of treatment, appropriate referral(s) or an ethical or professional dilemma. It is now accepted, respected and expected to seek professional connectedness through the Internet. It is easy to instantly chat with a peer, a supervisor, a supervisee, or a group, to assist with a case that may benefit from a variety of insight and objective input. Supervision is critical in the development of a counselor (Gladding, 2002).

CASE SCENARIO

The authors of this chapter worked together for a period of several years in an agency setting that offered in-home counseling and evaluation services to clients in several rural and remote parts of Georgia, USA. The agency served 20 counties in the southern-most and northern-most areas of the state. While the agency had offices in both northern and southern locations, the office was still a two-hour drive for some employees. It became crucial to create an online environment that allowed communication between manager and supervisors and their employees and supervisees. Field work was conducted by a constellation of people comprising a team of parent educators, mental health professionals and supervisors. Mental health professionals held varying degrees and were either fully licensed or working toward licensure. While it is not considered ideal for a clinical supervisor to fill the role of both supervisor and employer, because of the rural and remote nature of the work, the clinical supervisor was sometimes also the employer. Other supervisors also offered clinical input and direction to workers in the field. The owners of the agency were fully licensed and qualified clinical supervisors and often filled the role of clinical supervisor for employees who would not have otherwise had access to clinical supervision under the rules of the state licensing board.

While the clinical supervisor offered therapeutic and clinical input online via chat in real-time, that time did not meet the requirement for supervision hours needed for licensure. Clinical supervision was, at that time, interpreted as occurring face-to-face. To further meet the requirements of the state and despite the distance and inconvenience, face-to-face clinical supervision was also offered.

In between face-to-face opportunities for further training, professional development and clinical supervision, the day-to-day "operations" were conducted online. The agency utilized a platform that offered email, chat and file storage options. Email worked much like standard email programs such as Eudora or Outlook, but the platform was web-based. All emails sent within the agency were encrypted. All emails sent outside the agency were not encrypted. At any given time, once logged in, an employee could see everyone online at the same time. Anyone online and showing "available" could engage in chat with one or more employees. Since the owners and supervisors of the agency were hundreds of miles apart and employees numbered up to 70 at the agency's peak, the ability to reach out online became the essence of clinical operations.

Formal times were sometimes set aside for chats online but often, "chatting" became the preferred method for communicating about cases when the employee or clinician had a specific question or needed direction. Because many of the employees used cell phones and often did not have a landline phone at home, case consultation was not conducted on the phone. Employees were instructed to use cell phones to communicate with or on behalf of a client only in cases of scheduling or cancelling appointments or in times of client crisis. When the employee returned home or to the office, he or she would often login, check email and chat any necessary information or questions resulting from the day's work.

In addition, the chat platform served as a way for employees to gain a strong sense of community within the agency. Often, employees could rely on each other for support as well as answers to administrative questions. Employees in the field had instant access to administrative employees who worked from the office. Clinicians and paraprofessionals worked from home writing progress notes, reports and other clinical documentation. While using, say, Microsoft Word, an employee could move quickly to the online chat platform and ask a question of his or her supervisor if necessary. The employee was able to avoid a break in concentration avoiding the shift to aural input that a phone call would require. Since chat is in real time, the employee did not have to wait for an email response.

Sometimes a clinician and paraprofessional were both assigned to a case. Chat made it convenient for both to discuss the case and when necessary a supervisor could open a chat with two or more people creating a group discussion. This real-time collaboration allowed for open discussion about possible interventions. Employees were often more responsive online than on the phone or face-to-face because the intervention was immediate and offered a level of anonymity which was not afforded in-person or on the phone. Text-based communication would allow the disinhibition effect to work in favor of the case consultation, leveling out authority of positions within the agency and allowing all parties to participate with equal weight (Suler, 2004).

Employees, whether administrative, paraprofessional or clinical, also benefited from having ready access to supervisors. Despite the lack of face-to-face interaction in this rural agency setting, employees could often seek immediate consultation.

While chat was but one way in which communication was delivered, it allowed for everyone to be able to maintain a constant presence within the agency and offered a connection to clinicians and employees in the field. Supervisors, clinicians and paraprofessionals often reported that communicating through chat was as effective as communicating in-person or on the phone. While this is anecdotal information, it does speak to the power of the written word offered in real time. Supervision offered through chat, whether as stand-alone or as adjunct to in-person and other technological delivery methods is an effective way to process clinical supervision issues (Nagel et al., 2009).

CONCLUSION

It should be noted that scheduled online clinical supervision should be revered in the same way as a scheduled online therapy session. Whether the supervision is within a work setting, or an external and contracted clinical supervision relationship, parameters should be set that suit the particular purpose of the interaction. Clinical supervision often relies on the supervisee's disclosure about his or her interpersonal and psychodynamic experience within the client/therapist relationship. As is the case with an online chat therapy session, when working online in a scheduled clinical supervision session, attention should

be paid to the virtual consultation room, allowing complete focus on the supervisory process and to the supervisee (Nagel, 2009). If the supervisory interaction is impromptu, attention should be paid to the pace of the online conversation and the effect on the supervisee/employee. Particular awareness of emotional content is necessary so that the supervisee feels heard and validated. The supervisor, while not in a scheduled session, should still remain cognizant of the client/therapist relationship even within the context of answering what appear to be administrative or logistical inquiries about the case and intervene as necessary if it appears that the supervisee requires processing of emotional content.

Controversy exists about whether or not online supervision is valid and some professionals state that ideally supervision should be face-to-face with technology only being utilized in an adjunct role (Borders & Brown, 2005). The agency scenario delineated here, because of remote and rural geographical logistics, utilized online supervision as a primary process while face-to-face supervision and interaction remained secondary. The availability of online supervision through chat and instant message allowed the organization to remain vibrant, offering quality services in areas of the state that were not otherwise easily accessible. Many of the reasons for accessing online therapy are valid for accessing online supervision. Another scenario offered for validating the use of distance supervision via technology is offered by Wood et al. (2005). Distance, travel and mountainous roads were but a few of the difficulties supervisors encountered in provid-

ing weekly supervision. The authors believe that more and more rural areas of the world will embrace online supervision. Online supervision should not be viewed as inferior. On the contrary, distance supervision via technology will allow access to skilled experts and clinical supervisors across the globe.

This chapter has summarized how online supervision can work within an agency setting that offers community-based in-home services. These concepts can be applied to other settings including organizations that offer traditional face-to-face therapy and online therapy services. E-clinics offering online therapy exclusively can easily add chat supervision or consultation and other groups of peers can choose to work together online one-to-one and in group chats. Chat supervision can be used as a stand-alone method of delivery or it can be combined with other technology and face-to-face supervision, enriching any supervisory experience.

REFERENCES

Anthony, K., & Goss, S. (2009). *Guidelines for online counselling and psychotherapy including guidelines for online supervision* (3rd ed.). Lutterworth: BACP.

Benshoff, J. M. (1989). *The effects of the structured peer supervision model on overall supervised counseling effectiveness ratings of advanced counselors in training.* PhD Thesis. The American University.

Bernard, J. M., & Goodyear, R. K. (2009). *Fundamentals of clinical supervision.* London: Pearson.

Borders, L. D., & Brown, L. L. (2005). *The new handbook of counseling and supervision.* Mahwah, NJ.: Lawrence Erlbaum.

Fenichel, M. (2000). *Online psychotherapy: Tech-*

nical difficulties, formulations and processes [online]. [Accessed December 19, 2009]. Available from: http://www.fenichel.com/technical.shtml.

Franséhn, M. (2007). The importance of supervision in social work–the example of Sweden. *SP Sociální Práce, 4,* 72–78.

Georgia Composite Board of Professional Counselors, Social Workers and Marriage and Family Therapists. (2003). *Rules of Georgia Composite Board of Professional Counselors, Social Workers and Marriage and Family Therapists* [online]. [Accessed December 19, 2009]. Available from: http://sos.georgia.gov/acrobat/PLB/Rules/chapt135.pdf.

Gladding, S. T. (2002). *Counseling: A comprehensive profession* (4th ed.). Upper Saddle River, NJ: Prentice Hall.

Ince, D. (2001). Online chat. *Encyclopedia.com* [online]. [Accessed December 19, 2009]. Available from: http://www.encyclopedia.com/doc/1O12-onlinechat.html

Nagel, D. M. (2009). Filling the void in the virtual consultation room. *Voices: The Art and Science of Psychotherapy, 44*(1), 98–101.

Nagel, D. M., Goss, S., & Anthony, K. (2009). The use of technology in supervision. In N. Pelling, J. Barletta & P. Armstrong (Eds.), *The practice of supervision.* Bowen Hills, Qld: Australian Academic Press.

Paños, P. T., Paños, A., Cox, S. E., Roby, J. L., & Matheson, K. W. (2002). Ethical issues concerning the use of videoconferencing to supervise international social work field practicum students. *Journal of Social Work Education, 38*(3), 421–437.

Reisch, M., & Jarman-Rohde, L. (2000). The future of social work in the United States: Implications for field education. *Journal of Social Work Education, 36*(2), 201–214.

Remley, T. P., Benshoff, J. M., & Mowbray, C. (1987). A proposed model for peer supervision. *Counselor Education and Super-*

vision, 27(1), 53–60

Suler, J. R. (2004). The online disinhibition effect. *Cyberpsychology and Behavior, 7*(3), 321–326.

Vaccaro, N., & Lambie, G. W. (2007). Computer based counselors in training supervision: ethical and practical implications for counselor educators and supervisors. *Counselor Education and Supervision, 47*(1), 46–57.

Wagner, C. A., & Smith, J. P. (1979). Peer supervision: toward more effective training. *Counselor Education and Supervision, 18*(4), 288–293.

Watson, J. (2003). Implementing computer technology into the delivery of counseling supervision. *Journal of Technology in Counseling, 3*(1) [online]. [Accessed December 19, 2009]. Available from: http://jtc.colstate.edu./Vol3_1/Watson/Watson.htm

Wikipedia. (2009). *Online chat* [online]. [Accessed December 21, 2009]. Available from: http://en.wikipedia.org/wiki/Online_chat.

Wood, J. A. V., Miller, T. W., & Hargrove, D. S. (2005). Clinical supervision in rural settings: a telehealth model. *Professional Psychology: Research and Practice, 36*(2), 173–179.

Chapter 22

USING FORUMS TO ENRICH COUNSELOR TRAINING AND SUPERVISION

Linnea Carlson-Sabelli

INTRODUCTION AND DEFINITIONS

This chapter is designed to introduce you to technical developments over the past 15 years that are being used to enhance clinical supervision for Psychiatric Mental Health–Nurse Practitioner students and professionals and to discuss the impact that asynchronous forums have had on the way we are able to supervise psychotherapy interventions.

Our goals are to provide definitions, applications, ethical considerations, illustrations of supervision techniques and speculation on the future of online text based clinical supervision based on our extensive experience supervising graduate level Psychiatric Mental Health–Nurse Practitioner students at a major medical center university located in the Midwest United States.

Through "Project Aha!" we designed and implemented the Aha Center for Clinical Reasoning, a virtual networking community for advanced practice psychiatric nurses. Project Aha! was initially designed to overcome practical difficul-

ties of delivering online clinical practicum supervision for Psychiatric Mental Health–Nurse Practitioners (PMH-NP) for whom on-campus participation would never be possible. Through this program we develop innovative asynchronous tools useful in delivering online psychotherapy supervision to PMH-NP students at distant clinical practicum sites.

Our clinical supervision program is competency based. It is asynchronous and is conducted within a fully accredited university where registered nurses are earning an advanced practice degree or advanced practice nurses are earning a postmasters certificate in psychiatric mental health nursing. Graduates of our program are eligible to take the American Nurses Credentialing Center (ANCC) national certification exams for PMH-NPs. The techniques we will describe here are text based and are suitable for long-distance supervision that is conducted in online forums used by the faculty and onsite supervisors and student supervisees.

Because the techniques are asynchronous forums they support 24-7 student access, allowing students to work at the times that are most convenient. Responses can be given more thought encouraging reflection. Group supervision is possible as students can post and discuss their assignments with each other. Copies of selected assignments and assessments can be compiled into a student controlled portfolio. Students can share clinical stories with one another, ask and answer questions and role play "what if" scenarios with faculty supervisors. These are some of the ways that we have improved the way we are able to supervise psychotherapy interventions. We can replace tape recorded therapy sessions with process recordings where students not only recreate the dialogue, but also type in what they might have been thinking and feeling and saying or showing. The rationale for interventions can be interspersed within dialogue snippets. Assignments can be selectively released to provide additional competency practice, student by student, based on the quality of previous work. In these ways, text-based online forums provide methods for overcoming challenging aspects of a providing a competency based curriculum for advanced practice nursing students of diverse backgrounds and experience, living in underserved and rural locations.

Within our program we have two types of clinical supervisors–faculty clinical supervisors who are based at the University and onsite clinical preceptors who are based at the clinical site. All faculty clinical supervisors are doctorally prepared and are certified nurse practitioners or clinical specialists. Faculty supervisors have extensive practice experience and are currently in practice roles as well as educator roles. The third year of our part-time program is a clinical practicum. During the clinical year, each student does a 500 hour clinical practicum and residency with an additional 120 hour clinical supervision component. For this experience, each student is assigned to a clinical site near where they live. The site must have an onsite "clinical preceptor," whose role is to facilitate students' learning as mentor, teacher and supervisor. The onsite clinical preceptor must be credentialed as a certified advanced practice nurse in psychiatric mental health, or be a board certified psychiatrist.

CLINICAL SUPERVISION

The onsite preceptor provides mentoring and direct supervision in a number of competencies, including psychotherapy and medication management and may bring in other mental health professionals to model and mentor the student in specific modalities such as group psychotherapy. The preceptor compiles evaluations across multiple experiences when needed and rates the student's progress on a Competency Development System (CDS), described further below. During the first week of the quarter the preceptor and student discuss competencies and corresponding clinical experiences needed to practice them. They also identify competencies that will be difficult to complete within the setting. Later discussion is about congruency of student and preceptor ratings to guide the student toward the development of an action plan, to maximize strengths and overcome weaknesses.

Onsite preceptors evaluate development in psychotherapy competencies through direct supervision, viewing the student's clinical notes on individual patient interactions which are recorded onsite and in specialist "Typhon" software (described in more detail below) and through reviewing student "moment map" assignments (also described further below) and comments from faculty staff. They post numerical scores in the CDS software as the student progresses through the course. Faculty supervisors evaluate students based on the Typhon clinical note entries, assignments and an analogue rating scale based on student postings, clinical stories and participation in online clinical supervision. "Learn More" activities are developed by faculty supervisors for students who are unable to meet a particular competency at their site. One type of activity is the "Branching Story Simulation." We will now introduce you to the application of these technical developments in providing online clinical supervision.

APPLICATION OF THE TECHNOLOGY IN PROVIDING ONLINE CLINICAL SUPERVISION

Discussion Forums / Groups

The majority of supervisory interaction among students takes place in discussion forums. To keep discussions organized and focused, we divide them into a variety of topics such as announcements, ice breaker, questions and answers, folders for each assignment with due date, private discussion topics for each student, private discussion topic for faculty and a topic for socializing. The discussions are used to post up to the minute faculty announcements, ask and answer questions about the course, share and discuss assignments among classmates and faculty, keep social conversations in one place and provide private feedback. We always include an introductory message in each discussion topic in which we detail what the discussion topic is about, directions for posting and sometimes the rationale for the topic. We socializae the students into posting within this scheme by moving postings to the correct place if students post in the wrong topic. We try to engender lively discussions by breaking students into groups of 12 or less to prevent overwhelming a discussion. We give feedback more frequently at the beginning of the course, model what we want the students to do and give specific praise.

We organize the course by weekly assignments. The assignments are then posted by students in a discussion topic and shared with each other. Students are taught to become the discussion facilitators of their own assignments to engender the kind of feedback that is most useful to them from their classmates. In addition to the assignment discussions we use clinical stories as a springboard for weekly here and now discussions.

Clinical Stories

We ask students to share clinical stories with each other throughout the clinical year. We prescribe the type of story that is to be told on a weekly basis. We modify the type of story we request based on the learning that we are supporting in the management courses that accompany clinical practice.

We start out with stories about forming therapeutic relationships and move into stories of "Wow!" experiences. These stories include moments where students learned something new. We also ask students to relay stories of therapy that illustrate how they use various modalities such as cognitive, narrative, motivational interviewing, dialectic behavioral and process therapy. Next we move into evidenced based stories–where students present clinical questions that arose in the course of clinical practice and the process by which the student explored the answer. Classmates invite each other to address their clinical questions with evidenced based responses. The guidelines for clinical stories are that they are to be in story format. Students are encouraged to respond with a another story, whenever possible, rather than give advice. Stories are posted in asynchronous discussion topics and students are required to respond to at least one or two other stories each week. Faculty staff moderate the story discussions as needed. While we use asynchronous discussions for clinical stories, this activity could also take place in a blog.

Here is a short discussion thread illustrating faculty moderated clinical story discussion.

Title: Swap Clinical Stories— "Being with" a patient.

Initial faculty posting with discussion topic instructions:

This is a weekly activity

As you are in your clinical sites, you have many opportunities for "being with" patients. Each week we want you to tell us a story of a meaningful interaction that you have with a patient. In the story, detail the aspects of the interaction.

The main purpose for these stories is to continuously focus your awareness on "being with" a patient and exploring ways of being an active participant in helping the patient create meaning in their continuing life story. This involves cultivating reflection, mindfulness and patience.

It can be helpful to include in your stories some of the thoughts you were thinking about, but not saying.

The expectation is that you will read everyone else's stories and respond to at least 1 other story per week.

Rationale for the assignment

As you progress through the supervision, it is expected that the quality of your contributed stories will increase enabling you to build a repository of narratives that can be adapted for use as formative peer teaching-learning activities.

In this way, you are socialized into the process of clinical reasoning and into the role of a facilitator of reflection. This provides you excellent experience in guiding reflective practice in others which will be useful to you as you later serve to facilitate the clinical growth of other nurses, is a crucial role of the expert psychiatric nurse.

We will organize feedback toward helping you develop increasing skills in three areas:

Reflection on Practice
Clinical Reasoning
Engagement in Supervision.

Posting 1 Title: "Being with" the family member of a patient.

Mary Student's Initial Story Posting

I have repeated this conversation with just minor variations four times in the past three weeks. This is about "being with" the family member of a patient.

LC is a 75-year-old married male admitted to our unit from the nursing home where he has been a resident for one month. He was placed in the nursing home after he became unable to ambulate and was incontinent. He has a history of strokes and had been cared for at home by his wife until his admission to the nursing home. The patient's wife requested the patient be admitted to this unit for a medication evaluation and to assess his behavior. Problematic behaviors include restlessness at night with poor sleep, a.m. somnolence with poor intake at breakfast and inability to feed himself, pushing staff away that attempt to feed him, resistance to taking medication, combativeness with staff with personal care and raising his fist at his wife. The patient had orders for Valium severe agitation, Tylenol and, Lunesta. Psychiatric medications in place included: Seroquel , Zoloft, and Xanax. The patient's wife believes he has been on Zoloft for about one year. All other psychotropic medications were initiated within the past month.

The patient's admission MMSE (Mini-Mental State Examination) was 9/30. His MSE showed him to be restless, alert, but oriented only to self, with poor concentration, poor recall and poor short-term memory and long-term memory.

I visited with the patient's brother while the patient's wife was talking with the social worker. He lives across the street from the patient and is eager for his brother to return home. Later I visited with the patient's wife and asked her about her plans for her husband after he is discharged from the hospital. She said, "I know I can't take care of him at home anymore, but his kids and brother

think I should." I felt empathy for this elderly woman who has been the sole care-provider for this man for many years as his health has declined. She has endured lack of sleep, back breaking work of caring for a man twice her size and emotional strain. I hypothesized that she might feel guilty for being unable to continue homecare and would benefit from support in her decision. I explained to her that we often see family members who are not involved in the day-to-day care of patients insist that they can be cared for at home. I assured her that she had made the right decision. Based on her husband's cognitive functioning and physical limitations, he was no longer a candidate for homecare. I also supported her decision for evaluation of her husband's medication in this setting as I believed we could address his sleep, appetite, daytime somnolence, restlessness and agitation with medication adjustments. She was not surprised to hear that her husband's cognitive function would not improve dramatically and that his physical improvement would most likely be modest in that he should improve in his ability to feed himself and follow directions.

Most importantly, I assured the patient's wife that we supported her decision and would be happy to talk with any family members that needed information as to why nursing home placement was the best decision for her and the patient's wellbeing. I told her that there was no need for guilt in this situation and that she had done an admirable job in caring for her husband and continuing to oversee his care.

This woman seemed relieved after we visited. I believed she benefited from professional support in her decision making and a sense of hope that her husband would make some improvement.

Mary

Posting 2 Title: "I vowed I'd never do this [nursing home placement] to any of my loved ones."

Peter Classmate's Response

Mary,

I like what you're doing! We need to see that often our treatments are not "just for the patient" but include the entire family—therefore you're treating the entire family in this case—this will impact the outcomes for the patient.

Family dynamics are very interesting. There's so much guilt about nursing home placement. I can't tell you the number of times I've had family members tell me, "I vowed I'd never do this [nursing home placement] to any of my loved ones." "Family Rules" about caring for and not abandoning are all so very real and part of the discourse—but this is where psycho education comes in. Often I find myself having to "reframe" their beliefs and have them look at the "big picture" asking, "what's this doing to you [having the loved one at home]?" Directly addressing the "guilt" is important as they won't talk about it often unless it is directly addressed. Then "reframing" the situation to a realistic context saying, "you're needing help . . . the nursing home is one way that you can help him . . . they can be a support . . . you're not giving up so much as you are finding new ways of helping him and taking care of yourself as well . . . you're not giving up on caring . . ."

Regardless, this is a "gut wrenching" decision on the part of families who are entrenched with beliefs/guilt about the thought of abandoning someone—like the nursing home is a "death sentence"—it doesn't have to be—it can be what is needed.

The vast majority of families are relieved after the move. They have to "work through" the emotional issues—but ultimately they begin to see the wisdom with their decision and find they are able to be "better involved" (if they choose to be). Nevertheless, it's rough.

Peter Classmate

Posting 3 Title: Amazing things have happened.

Mary Student's Response to Peter Classmate:

Thanks for your feedback, Peter. . . . And now, for the rest of the story!

Amazing things have happened since we took this patient off all the psychotropic medicines and got his sleep stabilized! It took a combination of Trazodone 100 mg and Ambien 10 mg, given together, to assist his sleep. Now that he is rested and eating well, he is gaining strength and began walking by himself today! When I expressed my surprise at seeing him walking independently, he said, "What's the big deal? I've been doing this all my life." Also, when his family visited him today and started playing the guitar, he really did a great job of singing! What a comeback for this man who was having so many problems on admission!

I celebrated with this patient's wife! I reminded her that this is the benefit of not having to be the constant caregiver. You can enjoy the visit, bring people in with you that your spouse enjoys and then go home and get a good night's sleep!

Mary Student

Posting 4 Title: I'd celebrate too!

Theresa Classmate's Response to
Mary's Second Posting:

Mary,

Wonderful story! I was wondering
about some of the med combo's that
you had described in the previous post.
Elderly folks don't do so well with a lot
of the medications and dosing that you
had described—kind of made him a bit
of a "zombie"—never-the-less I've seen
weaning people off meds—especially
those that exacerbate dementia (or
delirium symptoms) who make remark-
able recoveries. I'd celebrate too!

Theresa Classmate

**Posting 5 Title: A long-range
perspective.**

Clara Faculty's Response:

This is indeed one of the happier
endings of this story set.

It may become difficult for this
woman if her husband keeps improving.
She may be back into the dilemma of
"Can I care for him?" But as you state,
this story is an excellent example of
"being with" a patient.

I'm curious to know what the literature has to say about best practice and
withdrawing patient's from psychotropic
drugs to reassess baseline symptoms
and behaviors.

Cara Faculty

**Posting 6 Title: Lewy body demen-
tia? An evidence-based inquiry.**

Anita Classmate's response
Mary and others,

I typed "Prescribing psychotroic
drugs for the elderly" into a google
search box and found two interesting
articles. The first article is from 1994,
but indicates several key learning points
at that time: One of them is: "patients
with Lewy body dementia are particular

sensitive to neuroleptics."
http://apt.rcpsych.org/cgi/reprint/1/1/23.p
df

Do you know if the patient you were
talking about had Lewy body dementia?

Anita Classmate

Posting 7 Title: Good question.

Mary Student's Reply

Anita, you have a good point. I will
have to check on this.

Mary

**Posting 8 Title: Inappropriate
prescribing of psychotropic
medication in the elderly.**

Sally Classmate's response

I found another interesting research
article (1999) which suggests that inappropriate prescribing of psychotropic
medication in the elderly has become a
public health concern. The study polls
physicians about their practices and attitudes in prescribing psychiatric medications.
http://www.cmaj.ca/cgi/content/full/161/2
/143.

An interesting finding of this study
was that physicians often had patients
who had been taking psychiatric medications for years, medications they did-
n't initially prescribe. They overwhelm-
ingly decided to keep prescribing these,
because they reported having difficulty
dealing with the suffering they witness
without prescribing medication. They
were also afraid the patient's would
change doctors.

Sally Classmate

Posting 9 Title: Wrap-up.

Clara Faculty's second response

What are the some of the learning
points to consider as we wrap up this
particular story discussion thread?

"Being with" a patient means "being

with the family," as well.

Psychotropic medication can cause side effects that impair cognition and behavior

As patients grow older and their metabolism changes, their psychotropic medications and dosages may need to change too.

Things change and it may be that this woman will want to bring her husband home and it is ok to support this decision as well.

There is a rich literature available to guide clinical practice, which we encourage you to share with us as the clinical year progresses.

Clara Faculty

Posting 10 Title: Thanks for the lead.

Mary Student's final posting

Anita and classmates. I mentioned Lewy Body Dementia to my preceptor. She thinks it is a distinct possibility. We will follow-up on this. Perhaps it was removing the Seroquel that was most effective? Wow! I am really learned a lot from this experience.

This example from a discussion forum is a single thread of a student's posting of a weekly clinical story and corresponding classmate and faculty comments. Since each student posts and facilitates their own thread the discussion topic is rich, interactive and allows issues that are relevant to the students to emerge. Students learn what their classmates are doing, serve as mentors for each other and have experience facilitating discussions. A major goal of our online clinical supervision program is to guide our students to learn how to think, to problem solve and to base their responses on evidence beyond personal experience. Faculty monitor the discussions and

attempt to focus or deepen a discussion, while allowing most of the material to emerge from the students.

While the purpose of this chapter is primarily focused on discussion forums, the Aha! platform offers additional applications to enhance the supervision process.

Competency Development System (CDS) Evaluation

The Competency Development System described here is a work in progress. It is designed to personalize competency development to fit each particular student's individual needs. It serves both as an evaluation system for students to self evaluate and for preceptors to evaluate students. It is administered online and can be accessed by enrolled students, assigned preceptors and university faculty anywhere there is internet access. The current version records and tracks an initial student self-assessment and from this data, prioritizes competencies according to importance for the role and the student's level of experience with the competency in the past. Students are required to discuss the self-assessment report with their preceptors at the beginning of each clinical quarter as a tool to facilitate planning of clinical experiences. The tool also provides a method for continuous self and preceptor assessment. It contains a feature where students who are not progressing on specific competencies are prompted to create action plans for demonstrating the competency. It also contains "Learn More" simulations, such as branching stories, that can be used to fill gaps. It is only available for students enrolled in our university. Plans are being made to make it more widely available for use in other competency-based nursing programs.

The CDS is divided into domains. Delineated domains, are based on nationally recognized core and specialty guidelines National Organization of Nurse Practitioner Faculties (NONPF). Each domain is divided into related competencies and cues integrated from the professional psychiatric nursing associations that guide nursing practice and education in the USA. In addition, competencies within domains are weighted according to the 2003 ANCC Role Delineation Report.

Psychotherapy competencies are integrated within all of the domains.

Students can easily access the CDS through any learning management system by an imbedded link to the internet. Access to individual rating entry and reports is password protected. Clinical preceptors can access only the information for their assigned student.

When a self- or preceptor rating is requested, the rater can access a series of drop down cues for each competency to be rated.

Drop down cues are available for every competency.

Self and preceptor ratings are requested on a 5 point scale, which assess the degree to which the student is meeting a competency. These ratings are:

1=Does not meet objective,
2=Routinely needs continual guidance to meet objective,
3=Demonstrates progress toward meeting the objective,
4=Meets specific objective frequently,
5=Meets specific objective consistently
NA=Not applicable. Student action

was not evaluated.

Faculty staff can print reports of all student and preceptor ratings for the permanent student file. Students and preceptors can print all reports to which they contribute.

The CDS tracks skill development toward meeting clinical competencies, identifies substandard areas of performance, highlights gaps in clinical site experiences and promotes reflection by students on the core competencies, weekly.

The responsibility is with the student to negotiate competency experiences through the initial discussion with the preceptor and student generated-action plans. The student-generated action report is another feature of the CDS.

Student-Generated Action Plan

The CDS also provides "Learn More" activities through which the student can gain competency experience.

If a student receives a rating less than three from the preceptor, or receives an NA rating indicating that competency practice was not available at the clinical site, a call for an action plan is generated by the software. The student is notified, fills out the form indicating how they have met or will meet the competency and submits the plan. The preceptor is prompted to review and sign off on the plan. One way a student can meet a competency is by completing a "Learn More" activity.

"Learn More" Activities

Based on Shulman's (2002) table of learning, integrated with Sabelli's bios theory (Sabelli, 1989; Sabelli & Carlson-Sabelli, 2006), the conceptual model for development of online clinical supervision components focuses on three sets of interacting opposites. We strive to move students from engagement in our learning program to commitment to an advanced practice role. We help students translate knowledge into clinical judgment. Finally we emphasize a continuous cycling between reflection and action. Reflection on practice is necessary for skills to develop. The CDS started off as a reflection tool but has expanded to incorporate judgment building "Learn More" activities as well.

Branching Story Simulations

Branching story simulations provides a student with an imaginary role that allows the student to try out new behaviors in a "mistakes allowed atmosphere" where consequences are experienced, but no-one gets hurt. In this way we connect reflection on action with clinical reasoning, building judgment.

The branching story is an "as if" simulated clinical practice reasoning experience that requires the student to make judgments, take actions, experience consequences and report progress. Branching stories are asynchronous text-based activities that allow students to practice and demonstrate core competencies that might otherwise not be accessible in their particular clinical area. They are ideal for helping students to grapple with common misconceptions related to psychotherapy and avoid some of the problems that are likely to encounter in actual practice. One of our branching stories lures students into making mistakes during a therapy session with a potentially suicidal patient. Those students that act on a misconception, experience consequences of the mistakes and are guided to find additional information to change their course of action. They are able to

revisit the point where the mistake was made and try another path. A sample of a branching story can be found at the URL http://demo.knowledgeanywhere .com/Rush/by using the username: student and password: test.

Moment Maps

The moment map is another asynchronous text-based tool that we have pioneered for psychotherapy supervision. The moment map is an advanced level process recording that the student prepares in PowerPoint. The task is to present various elements of a clinical therapy session in a formalized way using a template. The purpose of the moment map is to promote development of self as a therapeutic instrument, provide the student with a format with which to present, analyze and discuss a meaningful psychotherapeutic intervention and to organize thinking in the context of the patient's life story. The moment map is similar to a process recording, but with additional elements. It was designed to replace taped recordings of a session—which most of our clinical sites no longer allow. Before constructing the first moment map, students are provided with a PowerPoint template, the grading rubric and samples of mediocre, good and excellent examples of moment maps prepared by previous students. It is a required activity several times during the clinical year. The moment map is shared among all students in a clinical cohort for feedback and discussion. Discussion is monitored by the university supervisor. For the initial moment map, we assign a case study of a standardized patient scenario. Students read the case material and then create the moment map. For this assignment they create the dialogue for a therapy session, including the patient responses. This exercise illuminates similarities and differences in therapy knowledge and the skills of students as they enter their clinical year.

"Typhon" Student Tracking Software

Students provide a record of the clinical sessions of the patients they see in "Typhon," an outsourced nurse practitioner student tracking system. Typhon is used by many nurse practitioner students in the US. The software provides a method for each student to enter a clinical chart for each patient they see and to update the chart each time they see the patient for follow-up. We require students to write an intake record and then write an integrated psychotherapy/medication management clinical note for each patient visit. Students with a very large clinical load enter all patients, but only need to write seven follow-up notes each week. Clinical preceptors are given access to this data for the students they supervise. University faculty supervisors can compile custom reports by student or by student group. These reports allow faculty to review clinical notes and give feedback to the student within the learning management system. The feedback is provided privately in a discussion topic that can only be accessed by the faculty supervisor and the assigned student.

Clinical Evaluation Analog Scale

This scale is used by faculty supervisors to evaluate clinical reasoning skills, self awareness skills and student participation in online clinical supervision. Data that is analyzed to support ratings are discussion forums, moment map reflections and branching story reflections.

Faculty supervisors rate students at the middle and end of each clinical quarter and include the scale and a short summary of clinical progress as part of the mid-term and final clinical evaluations.

Mid-term and Final Clinical Evaluations

The student clinical performance evaluations include the CDS report of competency development, a summary of reporting from the Typhon system, the clinical analog scale and a separate summary of clinical psychotherapy skills as reflected in the moment map and clinical story assignments.

ETHICAL CONSIDERATIONS

We provide both formal faculty supervision and supply avenues for peer to peer supervision. Formal supervision requires contractual agreements. We require two contractual agreements. The first contract is an agreement between the university and the clinical site. This contract outlines requirements of both the university and the clinical site related to student professional liability insurance, confidentiality issues and site requirements. The second contractual agreement is the course syllabus. This lays out the responsibilities of the university course to the student and what the student has to do to pass the course.

Confidentiality of patient and student information is regulated, in this instance, by the Family Educational Rights and Privacy Act of 1974 (FERPA) and the

Health Insurance Portability and Accountability Act (HIPAA). FERPA is federal legislation in the US that provides protection of a student's right to privacy by specifying rules about public disclosure of student academic records and guidelines for the handling, storage and release of student data. HIPAA is federal legislation that requires health care providers to protect the privacy of patient information and to ensure the security of patient/client health data. Faculty supervisors are required to take FERPA and HIPAA training on a yearly basis and to socialize students into understanding and following the guidelines.

Because of HIPAA and FERPA guidelines, all students are required to remove any information that might identify a specific patient before submitting clinical notes, stories or moment maps. Students may use pseudonyms as long as they also state in the document that they are not using real patient names. The CDS does not collect patient information. The Typhon clinical tracking software is in compliance with HIPAA and FERPA. Patients are identified only by a number. Students assign pseudonyms for their patients and refer to them in clinical notes by the pseudonym initials.

Additional ethical considerations beyond maintaining patient confidentiality when doing psychotherapy include adequate performance evaluation and the ability to work with alternative perspectives. We have presented our extensive performance competency based evaluation system which addresses many roles of a psychotherapist beyond psychotherapy. We also encourage our students to explore and provide evidence to support alternative perspectives. A competency that students need to demonstrate is the ability to find, evaluate and present evidence to support treatment approaches. We believe that teaching students how to apply evidence to practice and how to evaluate the quality of their practice promotes lifelong learning as progress is made in the assessments and treatments available for promoting mental health of individuals and communities.

CONCLUSION–A LOOK TO THE FUTURE IMPACT OF THE INTERVENTION

We are continuing to create partnerships with online educational development companies to build additional "Learn More" activities as vehicles to translate knowledge into action related to mental health nursing competencies. As these are created they will be added to the CDS.

Todays online learning management systems have improved vastly over those introduced in the 1990s. Many of these programs already have features where learning activities can be mapped to competencies and an e-portfolio system where items demonstrating competency development can be stored and displayed by students. Our plan is to create a CDS which gathers student and preceptor ratings, identifies gaps in clinical psychotherapy education, provides simulations to fill these gaps, and links seamlessly with other learning management systems that map learning activities to competencies. Such a product could be useful for the clinical supervision of mental health professionals beyond nursing because the competencies and cues can be fully customized by the clinical supervision team.

We also have plans to expand psychotherapy education into the virtual world Second Life, which is being used more and more for educational purposes by universities and companies across the world. Second Life lends itself very well to role-playing with simulated patients. It is a synchronous online activity, so we will not go into much detail. We will briefly say that we see it as a venue where faculty supervisors can model group and individual psychotherapy for students, supervise student therapy practice in a safe setting with simulated patients and provide student practice with principles for setting up groups and methods for evaluating the efficacy of psychotherapy.

REFERENCES

Sabelli, H. (1989). *Union of opposites: A comprehensive theory of natural and human processes.* Lawrencefille, VA: Brunswick Publishing.

Sabelli, H., & Carlson-Sabelli, L. (2006). Bios, a process approach to living system theory: In honor of James and Jessie Miller. *Systems Research and Behavioral Science, 23*(3), 323–336.

Shulman, L. S. (2002). Making differences. A table of learning. *Change, 34*(6), 37–44.

Note

The technology described here was developed in part by funds from the Division of Nursing (DN), Bureau of Health Professions (BHPr), Health Resources and Services Administration (HRSA), Department of Health and Human Services (DHHS) under Project Aha! grant number 1D09HP02987 Advanced Education Nursing Grants for $478,739. It is continuing under a second BHPr DHHS grant, Filling in Competency Gaps, number D09HP09354 for $585,220. The information here, is supplied by the author and should not be construed as the official position or policy of, nor should be endorsements be inferred by the Division of Nursing, BHPr, DHHS or the U.S. Government.

Chapter 23

TEXT-BASED CREDENTIALING IN MENTAL HEALTH

DANIEL M. PAREDES

INTRODUCTION

Continuing Education (CE credits) or Continuing Professional Development (CPD) is frequently included among the requirements for membership in professions. Continuing education requirements imposed by credentialing bodies often are met through text-based methods. The inclusion of such requirements, in addition to specialized training, assures that members of a particular profession are continuously offering high quality services (Daniels & Walter, 2002; Lundgren & Houseman, 2002). Requirements imposed upon working professionals are intended to assure that practitioners remain up-to-date on the latest trends in their respective field. In the case of mental health/educational professions such as counseling, this could include, for example, new epidemiologic data; new trends in theory and skills; and alerts to professional issues, such as updates to ethical codes, government policies, or third-party pay-

ment considerations (National Board for Certified Counselors, 2008). Taking into consideration the fact that, due to time constraints, many training programs prepare students in a generalist model, continuing education also plays an important role in facilitating the specialization of working professionals (Latham & Toye, 2006). Despite its ubiquity, there are some concerns with the relevance of compulsory continuing education, including that provided by text-based methods. In this chapter, the author will briefly provide an introduction to text-based continuing education, present a model other authors have developed for the classification of continuing education activities, discuss the ethical implications of the use of text-based continuing education and present recommendations for entities requiring participation in continuing education that can promote the appropriate use of text-based methods.

WHAT IS TEXT-BASED CONTINUING EDUCATION?

One could argue that continuing education activities have been a part of professional practice for millennia. Depending on one's view of continuing education, the guild model where master craftsmen trained and supervised apprentices could be seen as a continuing education process. Text-based continuing education methods and the implementation of systems for documenting continuing education are much more recent and have been associated with professionalization (Daniels & Walter, 2002). Defining text-based continuing education requires that continuing education as a whole first be defined.

Continuing education has been described as postgraduate participation in learning activities that are intended to provide up-to-date knowledge and skills pertinent to professional practice (Cividin & Ottoson, 1997; Daniels & Walter, 2002; Davis et al., 1999; Jameson et al., 2007; Lundgren & Houseman, 2002; Smith et al., 2006). Activities are generally didactic, experiential, or a combination of both. Defining which specific activities generally constitute continuing education is challenging as acceptable activities are defined by the bodies requiring continuing education for the maintenance of professional status and there is often little consistency with professions, across jurisdictions (Daniels & Walter, 2002; Latham & Toye, 2006). In the case of counseling in the United States, for example, it is not uncommon for policies to include continuing education credit for assuming a leadership position in a professional association (National Board for Certified Counselors, 2008; North Carolina Board of Licensed Professional Counselors, 2007). Other organizations may choose

not to accept association leadership as a continuing education activity.

Text-based continuing education consists of professionals completing a reading selection, either in paper or electronic format and then demonstrating proficiency by obtaining a passing score on an assessment of learning (Davis et al., 1992). Recent attention has been directed to the use of computers and other technology as a means to delivering continuing education (Ellery et al., 2007; Krupinski et al., 2004; Smith et al., 2006). However, the fundamental process of text-based continuing education has been in place for decades. Correspondence courses and dedicated continuing education providers have been sending readings, sometimes accompanied by media such audio- and videotapes since well before the Internet was invented. Didactic, text-based continuing education may be especially helpful for providing information about practice issues rather than training in how to implement new information into practice (Aylward et al., 2003; Cividin & Ottoson, 1997; Davis et al., 1999; Vaughn et al., 2006). The selection of which topics to approach is largely at the discretion of the individual practitioner. In some cases, continuing education topics are prescribed by management at a professional's employer (Daniels & Walter, 2002; Latham & Toye, 2006). Ideally, however, the decision to participate in continuing education of any kind is preceded by a critical self-evaluation of what areas of professional knowledge and practice could be strengthened rather than a determination of what means is most expedient to meet recredentialing or agency requirements (Brown, 2002; Xiao, 2006).

Mental health/education professionals who have determined what topic they need to address and which continuing education method would be appropriate should consider that continuing education is known by several terms. Some terms (e.g., continuing medical education (CME), continuing nursing education (CNE)) are designed with certain professionals in mind. Nonetheless, they may be of value of professionals from other disciplines. For example, a text-based update on medications frequently used to treat attention-deficit/hyperactivity disorder would be helpful to many counselors as well as physicians or nurses. Other terms that are frequently used by scholars and continuing educational providers alike include professional development, continuing professional development, in-service training and lifelong learning, among others. Professionals seeking to engage in text-based continuing education also would be well served by choosing the source of their education provider carefully. In an industry worth more than nine billion dollars, it is imperative that credible sources be identified (Vaughn et al., 2006). Some professional bodies, incidentally, have chosen to accredit certain continuing education providers. One example of how professional bodies have interceded to assure the quality of continuing education is the American Psychological Association's (2007) *Standards and Criteria for Approval of Sponsors of Continuing Education for Psychologists.*

ISSUES IN THE USE OF TEXT-BASED CONTINUING EDUCATION

A major criticism of continuing education activities is the apparent lack of a relationship to either practitioner behaviors or client outcomes (Aylward et al., 2003; Davis et al., 1999; Lundgren & Houseman, 2002; Smith et al., 2006). This criticism, however, warrants further study as there is some evidence that continuing education is helpful (Chakraborty et al., 2006; Davis et al., 1992; Smith et al., 2006; Xiao, 2006). Another criticism of continuing education activities is that they are susceptible to falsification. Continuing education credit at conferences and workshops, the most common type of continuing education, is given simply for attendance and not necessarily a demonstration of learning (Vaughn et al., 2006). As part of the general field of continuing education, text-based methods are not immune to such criticisms. Many text-based methods use post course tests to provide evidence of learning. It is unclear, however, what steps are taken to assure unethical participants are not simply choosing to participate in activities in which they already hold mastery. In other words, it is unclear what measures are in place to assure that an expert in a particular area is not fulfilling his or her continuing education requirements by participating in the easiest activity rather than one that promotes the development of new knowledge and skills.

Another criticism of didactic text-based learning methods, not solely those that are used in continuing education, is that they are an ineffective means of teaching skills (Davis et al., 1999; Livneh and Livneh, 1999; Jameson et al., 2007). In the counseling field, practica and internships are an integral part of training. The Unites States' Council for Accreditation of Counseling and Related Educational Programs' *2009 Standards* require training programs to provide supervised practica and internships with the expressed purpose of facilitating the translation of specialized knowledge into practice.

ETHICAL CONCERNS

The limitations and strengths of text-based continuing education mean that it can be used ethically–especially when included among other learning strategies. Ethical concerns arise in situations where the practitioner, intentionally or unintentionally, does not engage in a breadth of activities ensuring their professional development. As noted earlier in the chapter, text-based continuing education is helpful for providing new and updated knowledge to practitioners (Davis et al., 1999; Smith et al., 2006). Undoubtedly, it is helpful for practitioners to be informed of new developments in theory and policy. In this respect, text-based continuing education should be a part of every practitioners' professional development plans. An optimal design of continuing education would include requirements based upon a system of classifying activities more precisely and understanding how practitioners planned to implement new knowledge and skills into practice. In the remainder of the chapter, a way that credentialing bodies could increase the relevance of continuing education is presented.

CLASSIFYING CONTINUING EDUCATION ACTIVITIES

Frameworks explaining continuing education and the continuing education process have been developed that are helpful in discussing text-based methods. One of these, the Application Process Framework (APF), explains the process by which continuing education activities are implemented in practice (Cividin & Ottoson, 1997; Ottoson, 1995, 1997). The APF is useful because it helps address one of the principal criticisms of continuing education–that participation has limited bearing on changes in practitioner behavior or patient/client/student outcomes. The other classification system discussed in the chapter, developed by Daiches, Verduyn and Mercer (2006), provides a structure for classifying continuing education activities may be classified. The classification of content will be critical to discussion how text-based continuing education methods can be included in credentialing/membership organizations' requirements.

APPLICATION PROCESS FRAMEWORK (APF)

The APF is designed from the standpoint of what practitioners need to implement knowledge and skills developed through continuing education

(Cividin & Ottoson, 1997). As such, the framework addresses barriers to implementation and may or may not address all of the limitations identified by researchers exploring the relationship between practitioner participation in continuing education and client outcomes. The framework is based on the premise that application considerations and training programs are in a continuous feedback loop. The influence of training on application is understood to be mediated by predisposing, enabling and reinforcing factors (Aylward et al., 2003; Cividin and Ottoson, 1997; Davis et al.,1992). A characteristic that distinguishes predisposing factors is that they pertain to the individual practitioner rather than their work setting. Predisposing factors such as intrinsic interest in a particular continuing education topic have been identified as the most influential in predicting application of learning. Enabling and reinforcing factors refer to steps a practitioner's employer provides in support of the application of knowledge and skills gleaned from continuing education activities.

An example of the feedback loop between application and training programs in the context of text-based continuing education is practitioners' identification of a spike in the incidence of self-injurious behaviors among teenagers in the United States. An increased amount of research was focused on the topic and materials for those who self-injure, as well as those providing support were developed (National Center for Trauma-Informed Care, 2008; Trepal and Wester, 2007). A predisposing factor might be the selection of the activity by a counselor working in a secondary school who constantly seeks to understand trends he or she sees in the student population. An example of an enabling factor would be the school administration's support for a comprehensive school counseling program. Reinforcing factors–those that support the individual practitioner–could be exemplified by other school staff with which the counselor can debrief periodically.

Requiring practitioner reflection upon how a text-based continuing education activity is being applied could encourage greater intentionality in identifying follow-up strategies. Practitioner use of the APF could also close the gap between the intended goals of continuing education and improved client outcomes. In addition to examining how text-based education is being applied upon completion, greater specificity in classifying content can facilitate the ethical use of this type of continuing education.

DACHIES, VERDUYN AND MERCER FRAMEWORK

Dachies and colleagues (2006) suggest classifying continuing education activities according to general content area. This strategy allows for more precise selection by professionals creating their professional growth plans (a plan indicating what knowledge and skills could be improved). The plan development process could be based on a list of profession-related job behaviors, such as that created by Brown (2002) or those routinely used to underpin accreditation and credentialing schemes, such as those developed by the Council for Accreditation of Counseling and Related Educational Programs (2009) and the National

Board for Certified Counselors (2008). Dachies et al. identified five general categories into which continuing education activities could be clustered: *practice-centered activities, issue-centered activities, population-centered activities, specialism-centered activities and service-centered activities.*

Practice-centered activities focus on refining one's training within a particular kind of therapy modality. Such activities may be especially salient for early-career professionals who were trained from either a generalist model or an overly specific model and who have found an interest in another theoretical framework. Issue-centered activities might include those related to programmatic issues such as improving a school environment or community advocacy. Population-centered activities focus on specific subgroups, such as at-risk youth, immigrants, or methamphetamine users. Specialism-centered activities focus on what Dachies et al. refer to as interest network issues. Activities in this arena might

include those related to the practice of counseling internationally–such as the American Counseling Association's International Interest Network. Service-centered activities focus on administrative and professional association aspects of the profession. Counseling examples of service-centered activities might include updates on third-party payer reimbursement processes or political advocacy issues.

Revisiting how text-based continuing education is classified and the process by which it is reviewed could improve the relationship between this particular kind of professional development and the services provided to clients. Increased intentionality in selecting continuing education activities that are related to practice and are a different content area than one typically attended to could prevent professionals from simply choosing the most convenient activities or those that merely confirm what the professional is already doing.

ASSURING TEXT-BASED CONTINUING EDUCATION IS USED ETHICALLY

Given the limitations of text-based continuing education, its widespread availability and the pressures placed upon practitioners to meet requirements, the onus falls on credentialing bodies to encourage breadth in continuing education participation. Fortunately, existing frameworks for the classification of education methods and content allow for the ready categorization of activities in a way that facilitates the development of comprehensive professional development plans. Credentialing bodies, which have already established parameters for mandatory continuing education, also have

the power to establish parameters regarding the proportion of requirements that are met by text-based or experiential methods as well as parameters regarding content (Davis et al., 1999; Vaughn et al., 2006; Xiao, 2006). Given the lack of research supporting the identification of an optimal proportion of text-based versus experiential methods, each credentialing body should make its own determination. Issues such as time commitment, for both the practitioner and the reviewing agency, costs, and accessibility should be considered when establishing proportional requirements.

CONCLUSION

Continuing education is widely regarded as an important means to assure the public that practitioners are maintaining their knowledge and skills. Prior research suggests that, as it is currently used, continuing education may not be helpful as a strategy to assure competence. One particular kind of continuing education, text-based, may be helpful as a means to provide up-to-date knowledge. It may, however, be an ineffective means to assure that new skills are learned or that existing skills are refined. Therefore, text-based methods should be used in moderation as a strategy to assure professional competence through continuing education. Additional research is necessary to determine the ideal cost/benefit ratio with respect to requirements for continuing education modality and content. Nonetheless, given the doubtful utility of current strategies, revision of current schemes is warranted.

REFERENCES

American Psychological Association. (2007). *Standards and criteria for approval of sponsors of continuing education for psychologists.* Washington, DC: American Psychological Association.

Aylward, S., Stolee, P., Keat, N., & Johncox, V. (2003). Effectiveness of continuing education in long-term care: A literature review. *Gerontologist, 43*(2), 259–271.

Brown, M. (2002). Best practices in professional development. In A. Thomas & J. Grimes (Eds.), *Best practices in school psychology* (4th ed.). Washington, DC: National Association of School Psychologists.

Chakraborty, N., Prasad Sinha, B. N., Nizamie, S. H., Sinha, V. K., Akhtar, S., Beck, J., & Binha, B. (2006). Effectiveness of continuing nursing education program in child psychiatry. *Journal of Child and Adolescent Psychiatric Nursing, 19*(1), 21–28.

Cividin, T. M., & Ottoson, J. M. (1997). Linking reasons for continuing professional education participation with postprogram application. *The Journal of Continuing Education in the Health Professions, 17*(1), 46–55.

Council for Accreditation of Counseling and Related Educational Programs. (2009). *2009 Standards.* Alexandria, VA: Council for Accreditation of Counseling and Related Educational Programs.

Daiches, A., Verduyn, C., & Mercer, A. (2006). Continuing professional development mid career. In L. Golding & I. Gray (Eds.), *Continuing professional development for clinical psychologists: A practical handbook.* Oxford: British Psychological Society/ Blackwell.

Daniels, A. S., & Walter, D. A. (2002). Current issues in continuing education for contemporary behavioral health practice. *Administration and Policy in Mental Health, 29*(4), 359–376.

Davis. D., O'Brien, M. A., Freemantle, N., Wolf, F. M., Maxmanian, P., & Taylor-Vaisey, A. (1999). Impact of formal continuing medical education. Do conferences, workshops, rounds and other traditional continuing education activities change physician behavior or health care outcomes? *Journal of the American Medical Association, 282*(9), 867–874.

Davis, D. A., Thomson, M. A., Oxman, A. D., & Haynes, R. B. (1992). Evidence for the effectiveness of CME: A review of 50 randomized controlled trials. *Journal of the American Medical Association, 268*(9), 1111–1117.

Ellery, J., McDermott, R. J., & Ellery, P. J. (2007). Computers as formal continuing education tool: Moving beyond intention. *American Journal of Health Behavior, 31*(3), 312–322.

Jameson, P., Stadter, M., & Poulton, J. (2007). Sustained and sustaining continuing education for therapists. *Psychotherapy: Theory, Research, Practice, Training, 44*(1), 110–114.

Krupinski, E. A., Lopez, M., Lyman, T., Barker, G., & Weinstein, R. S. (2004). Continuing education via telemedicine: Analysis of reasons for attending or not attending. *Telemedicine Journal and E-Health, 10*(3), 403–409.

Latham, A., & Toye, K. (2006). CPD and newly qualified clinical psychologists. In L. Golding & I. Brown (Eds.), *Continuing professional development for clinical psychologists: A practical handbook.* Oxford: British Psychological Society/Blackwell.

Livneh, C., & Livneh, H. (1999). Continuing professional education among educators: Predictors of participation in learning activities. *Adult Education Quarterly, 49*(2), 91–106.

Lundgren, B. S., & Houseman, C. A. (2002). Continuing competence in selected health care professions. *Journal of Allied Health Professions, 31*(4), 232–240.

National Board for Certified Counselors. (2008). *NBCC continuing education file.* Greensboro, NC: National Board for Certified Counselors.

National Center for Trauma-Informed Care. (2008). Self-inflicted violence: Understanding and treatment. *Trauma Matters* [online]. [Accessed November 27, 2009]. Available from: http://mentalhealth.sam hsa.gov/nctic/newsletter_02-2008.asp.

North Carolina Board of Licensed Professional Counselors. (2007). *License renewal guidelines.* Garner, NC: North Carolina Board of Licensed Professional Counselors.

Ottoson, J. M. (1995). Use of a conceptual framework to explore multiple influences on the application of learning following a continuing education program. *Canadian Journal for the Study of Adult Education, 9*(2), 1–18.

Ottoson, J. M. (1997). After the applause: Exploring multiple influences on application following an adult education program. *Adult Education Quarterly, 47*(2), 92–107.

Smith, C. A., Gant, A., Cohen-Callow, A., Cornelius, L. J., Dia, D. A., Harrington, D., & Bliss, D. L. (2006). Staying current in a changing profession: Evaluating perceived change resulting from continuing professional education. *Journal of Social Work Education, 42*(3), 465–482.

Trepal, H. C., & Wester, K. L. (2007). Self-injurious behaviors, diagnoses and treatment methods: What mental health professionals are reporting. *Journal of Mental Health Counseling, 29*(4), 363–375.

Vaughn, H. T., Rogers, J. L., & Freeman, J. K. (2006). Does requiring continuing education units for professional licensing renewal assure quality patient care? *The Health Care Manager, 25*(1), 78–84.

Xiao, L. D. (2006). Nurse educators' perceived challenges in mandatory continuing nursing education. *International Nursing Review, 53*(3), 217–223.

Chapter 24

ONLINE RESEARCH METHODS
FOR MENTAL HEALTH

Tristram Hooley, Jane Wellens, Clare Madge and Stephen Goss

INTRODUCTION

This book reveals the ways Internet technologies are transforming the professional, social and psychological world available for counsellors and psychotherapists. The penetration of Internet technologies into everyday life has reached such an extent that it is difficult to draw clear lines between people's online and offline lives. For those working in the area of mental health this has profound implications, creating the challenges and opportunities examined throughout this volume.

"Cyberspace" used to be discussed as if it was another country that people visited for their holidays. However, increasingly technologies like Facebook, MySpace and You Tube draw people's social, professional and psychological lives online. The Internet is no longer an exotic destination but is overlaid on our ordinary lives facilitating things as mundane as doctors appointments, train ticket booking, the sharing of holiday snaps and, now, the provision of therapy.

Much of this book has focused on the way in which technology can support or contribute to the counselling experience. However, another area of application for Internet technologies is the investigation of social, cultural and psychological life. This may be about investigating interrelationships between society, psychology and technology in general and therapeutic relationships in particular or about providing tools that speed up or improve research processes, whether that be clinical audit, outcomes or process research or the socio-psychological effects of online clinical relating. This chapter will examine how online research methods can address the kinds of research questions that are likely to interest counsellors and psychotherapists.

WHAT ARE ONLINE RESEARCH METHODS?

Online research methods are methodological techniques used to collect data via the Internet. They cover a wide and growing number of online techniques such as ethnographies, experiments, network analysis, web analytics and a range of engagements with Web 2.0 technologies. This chapter tries to maintain a distinction between the methodology (the approach used to investigate a particular subject) and the technology (the tool used to do this).

For example, in online ethnography, sometimes known as netnography (Kozinets, 1998, 2006; Langer & Beckman, 2005), the methodology draws on conventional face-to-face (often called "onsite" as opposed to "online") ethnography and reapplies it to a new environment (see Hine, 2000; Miller & Slater, 2001). The term ethnography defines the methodology and philosophy that underpins the work of the researcher (qualitative, researcher as participant, holistic and so on) and the type of data likely to be generated. Within the context of the Internet, ethnographies can take a wide range of forms determined by the environment being researched and the technology used. Researchers could, for example, participate in email lists, observe discussions in specialist forums or professional/social networking sites (e.g., www.onlinetherapysocialnetwork.com), engage in video exchanges via You Tube (for example, Wesch, 2008), examine the written record afforded by chat or email therapy exchanges with counselling clients, observe user behavior in online gaming environments or sites intended to address problem gambling (e.g., http://www.GamblingTherapy.org, cf. Anthony, 2005). Despite the variety of technologies used all of these projects could be online ethnographies.

This chapter will concentrate primarily on two methodological approaches, looking at online questionnaires and then at online interviews and focus groups. It is likely that researchers in counselling and psychotherapy might also want to utilise other methodologies such as ethnographies and experiments. However, gaining an understanding of how to collect data online using questionnaires or focus group interviews will provide a good grounding for other types of online research methods.

Online research methods are particularly useful and appropriate when investigating online counselling and psychotherapy (e.g., Kraus et al., 2004; Rochlen et al., 2004; Skinner & Latchford, 2006). The factors that influence a participant's willingness to undertake online counselling, such as IT and web literacy, the desire for anonymity or distance from conventional counselling opportunities, are also likely to mean that such people are suited to participating in studies conducted online.

However, online research is not necessarily confined to investigating online activity. Madge et al. (2006) identified advantages offered by online research methods on the Exploring Online Research Methods website (http://www.geog.le.ac.uk/ORM/) which can be summarised as:

- enabling the researcher to contact geographically dispersed populations (useful in internationalising research);
- facilitating contact with difficult to reach groups, such as the less physically mobile (disabled/in prison/in hospital), the socially isolated (drug

dealers/terminally ill) or those living in dangerous places (e.g., war zones);

- providing savings in costs (travel, venue, data entry);
- enabling a quick supply of data (in comparison to postal, face-to-face and telephone surveys).
- supplying ready transcribed interview data;
- reducing issues of interviewer effect as participants cannot "see" each other.

All these advantages apply regardless of whether the experience being investigated originally took place online or not. So, for example, researchers could investigate a particular therapeutic approach using a survey to investigate levels of satisfaction. This survey could be sent out by post with prepaid envelopes or undertaken as a series of face-to-face meetings using a clipboard and paper questionnaire. Despite the development of online research methods these onsite research approaches still have their place, but both would be slower, potentially more expensive and more complex to administer than an online survey. So, even where the experience under investigation is something that takes place offline, online research methods may offer significant methodological advantages.

Online research methods can contribute to the understanding of both online and offline phenomena. However, while online research methods can be powerful, they are not always the most appropriate methodological tools. There are disadvantages with online research methods just as there are advantages. Both Illingworth (2001) and O'Connor and Madge (2001) found that new technologies can present technical challenges to be negotiated by both researcher and participants. Furthermore, even with increasing levels of penetration of the Internet into the general population, a digital divide still exists between those who have Internet access and those who do not. For example, undertaking research on older age groups, the socially excluded or those outside a western context using an online research method may impact on the validity of the sample. Furthermore online research methods (at least when text based) mean that subjects are responding in circumstances beyond the researcher's control, without visual and auditory cues and where, as Hewson et al. (2003) note, the researcher cannot ultimately be sure of the participant's real identity. However, it is also worth noting that many of these disadvantages can also be the case in other methods. For example, identity can also be difficult to verify in postal questionnaires.

A BRIEF HISTORY OF ONLINE RESEARCH METHODS

Emails and website pop-ups requesting participation in surveys, questionnaires or other online research projects are now extremely common. However, as with many phenomena on the Internet, this is a relatively recent development. While the Internet remained the province of a small minority of the highly IT literate, it did not attract much interest from most social scientists. Nonetheless, researchers such as Bosnjak et al. (2001) were beginning to experiment with the potential of the medium relatively early in its development.

As use of the Internet expanded further into the general population, researchers became increasingly interested in how it could support both quantitative and qualitative social science research. The middle of the 1990s saw further development of online survey research with O'Lear (1996), *Using electronic mail (e-mail) surveys for geographic research;* Coomber (1997), *Using the Internet for survey research* and Harris (1997), *Developing online market research methods and tools.* At the same time, qualitative researchers and ethnographers were also starting to explore the opportunities that the Internet offered to their research with Gaiser (1997), *Conducting online focus groups* and Clodius (1994), *Ethnographic fieldwork on the internet* both serving as examples that still offer useful advice today. Around the same time, online research into counselling and mental health began to develop using a broader range of methodologies (e.g., Walther & Burgoon, 1992; King, 1994; Cohen & Kerr, 1998) and continues to offer an increasingly detailed range of evidence to inform practitioners, their clientele and the profession as a whole (c.f. Barak, 2008).

The level of interest in online research methods continued to grow with the publication of large numbers of articles utilising these methods. Whilst the increasing penetration of the Internet into the wider population made it ever more interesting to researchers, it was the gradual improvement in the usability of online technologies that enabled researchers to experiment more regularly and on a much larger scale. The rapid growth in the use and uptake of online research methods has been accompanied by continual technological developments. This has resulted in a situation where methodological questions have had to be solved rapidly and where best practice in the conduct and analysis of online research is still in flux. So, for example, Wakeford (2000) has argued that

> The quantity of information that may be generated and the speed at which responses can be collected, can result in pleasing piles of data—but we should be wary of being seduced by sheer quantity; data is only useful if it is representative of the larger population. (p. 33)

Just because an online survey is fast and cheap does not necessarily mean that it is good. However, concerns, such as this one about sampling, are likely to be changing as the Internet is used by an ever-wider audience. Riva et al. (2003) report no significant differences in responses gained from the same questionnaire from online participants compared to those completing a paper survey, even when the online sample is not controlled. Furthermore, Reynolds and Stiles (2007) reported equivalence between results from paper and pencil and online testing with comparable distributions of participant responses. It must be remembered that online research methods operate in a changing social and technological environment which means that making absolute statements can be difficult.

DEALING WITH ETHICAL ISSUES

Undertaking research in the area of counselling and psychotherapy requires researchers to be aware of the ethical implications of their work. The potential to unwittingly do harm becomes even greater when working with a research subject who cannot be seen and who the interviewer has never met. The Internet does not present an ethical challenge in and of itself, but rather adds new complexities to already existing ethical dilemmas.

Despite the fact that research ethics has been becoming a much bigger issue for social researchers (see for example the ESRC's (2005) *Research Ethics Framework*) there is a general wariness about how these ethical issues play out in the online environment. Online research ethics is a relatively new area which is subject to rapid changes in methodological practice and technological capability. Nonetheless, it is possible to draw out some general thoughts about online research ethics in this chapter that may be helpful to the researcher without offering a "one size fits all" ethical prescription.

One of the main issues for the researcher to consider is whether there is anything special about the online environment that requires new ethical guidelines. Are online communications necessarily different from those that happen offline? Hine (2005) argues that online research is "a special category in which the institutionalised understandings of the ethics of research must be re-examined" (p. 5). However, the problem is not necessarily that the online space is a "special category" but rather that it masks a wide range of spaces and categories. The researcher needs to analyse these spaces when considering the ethical implications of conducting research in that space. For example, writing that appears in an online journal or newspaper clearly has a different status from that which appears on a person's Facebook profile.

The balance between private/public

and identified/anonymous can be very difficult to tease out online. It is difficult to make clear statements about the status of a particular forum or technology. Consider a BBC forum that deals with the latest government budget. It might be concluded that postings within it were public, available to quote and likely to be personally (if not politically) uncontentious. On the other hand, we might feel much less clear about how far the contributors felt their postings to be public and available for general use and republishing on a forum that dealt with the experience of psychotherapy. Yet, in this example the technology and the rules governing the forums would be identical. The law also gives researchers little guidance in this area and is, in many countries, generally highly permissive. Therefore it is difficult to produce absolute guidelines and thus the decision about how to proceed ethically sits with the researcher (and an appropriate research ethics committee). The Association of Internet Researchers (AoIR) Ethics Working Committee (Ess, 2002) supports this ethical pluralism and concluded that there is likely to be more than one ethically defensible response to an ethical dilemma and that ambiguity, uncertainty and disagreement are inevitable.

There are a number of considerations that researchers might want to make when making ethical judgments about research using online methods:

- Is the space being researched public (like a town hall meeting) or private (like a bedroom) or is it somewhere in between (like a café or bar)?
- Is the author of the words consciously publishing (as in a book)

or engaging in private communication (as in a phone call) or somewhere in between (perhaps like a local newsletter)? Shirky (2008) makes the point that most conversations on the Internet are available to all but are consciously written for a small group of like-minded people. Researchers need to consider the ethical implications of moving the conversations of these "small worlds" into a new and possibly larger, context.

- Does the author perceive that they are publishing anonymously (as if to a priest or counsellor) or are they keen on publishing to advance their reputation and gain greater renown (as in a professional journal)? Or, as will often be the case, are they happy to be known within their community without necessarily seeking wider fame or publicity for their opinions.

Many of the ethical considerations discussed above are not particular to online research. The boundaries between categories are more blurred than in traditional research, but the same questions need to be asked of any research project, online or onsite. There is an extensive literature on undertaking ethical research in counselling and psychotherapy (see for example West, 2002; Bond, 2004 and British Association for Counselling and Psychotherapy, 2002) but the following questions are a useful starting point.

- is there potential to do harm?
- how can informed consent be sought and agreed with the participants?
- can the participant withdraw from the research if they feel uncomfortable?
- is deception a defensible research strategy? For example, can "lurking" as socialisation into the online culture of a group be an important prerequisite for research?
- what will happen to the data and how will the participants be informed/involved in this feedback process?

Researchers are likely to have to gain ethical approval for any research they undertake. To show an awareness of the ethical issues and the potential difficulties raised by the research and the methodology is a much more powerful way to negotiate ethics approval than trying to mask or diminish any ethical difficulties.

COLLECTING DATA USING ONLINE SURVEYS AND QUESTIONNAIRES

Online questionnaires and surveys offer some powerful advantages, which have been discussed above. However, despite obvious attractions, their use must be appropriate and justified for each particular study. Even when the decision has been made that an online questionnaire is an appropriate research tool, it is necessary to design an appropriate methodology considering the balance of qualitative and quantitative questions, deciding on questionnaire type, establishing a justified sampling strategy and ensuring an appropriate response rate.

Many decisions facing online survey researchers are similar to those that face the onsite researcher. If you are new to research, obtaining specialist supervision and accessing the literature (e.g., Rea & Parker, 2005; Leong & Austin, 2005; Timulak, 2008) should help guide you through the basic issues around survey design and analysis in counselling and psychotherapy, whereas this chapter concentrates on issues relating specifically to the online environment.

As has already been noted, use of online surveys and questionnaires has proliferated in recent years. The bombardment of potential participants with invitations to take part in online surveys, many of which are poorly designed, has resulted in a situation where response rates to online surveys are often very low, with less than 10 percent not being uncommon. As a result, online researchers need to think carefully about their sample frame and the usability and design of their questionnaire in order to maximise their response rates and generate useful data.

In comparison with onsite research, the lack of detailed information about online populations in general and difficulty in gaining access to accurate online databases, such as directories of email addresses, means that it is very difficult to undertake probability-based sampling in online surveys. Consequently, many online surveys rely on nonprobability-based samples where participants are not selected at random, but instead positively elect to participate in the survey, for example by following a link or invitation to participate from a website. However, where the population to be surveyed is closed and known, such as all the clients of a particular counsellor

or the members of a particular professional group, researchers may have sufficient information to enable use of a random or stratified sampling frame. Where respondents are self-selecting, a crucial issue is whether this introduces nonresponse bias into the survey—where the characteristics of those responding to the survey are different from those who have chosen not to respond.

Another sampling issue to be considered, particularly where more traditional psychotherapy research techniques are being converted into an online format, is the issue of measurement error, which occurs when survey responses differ from the "true" response. For example, an individual respondent may produce a different answer online than they would when faced with the same question in a paper-based or face-to-face survey, although as noted above this certainly does not always occur (Reynolds & Stiles, 2007). When it does, it may be due to respondents feeling able to answer different types of survey formats more honestly than others, or it could be that there is something about the way in which the survey is presented online that produces the difference. In some cases, respondents have been found to prefer the online environment for the sense of anonymity it provides them. Such anonymity may, of course, be illusory and researchers should inform respondents of the limits that may exist, such as an employer or Internet Service Provider examining the content of emails for perfectly legitimate reasons.

A further key issue in encouraging respondents to complete online surveys and questionnaires is the ease with which respondents can complete them. Careful consideration needs to be given to the length of the survey and the number and type of questions. In general, response rates are likely to be higher if the survey is short and participants are given an honest indication of the amount of time required to complete the survey (Crawford et al., 2001). In addition, whilst online surveys offer researchers a vast array of possible question formats and types (such as inclusion of multimedia stimuli), it is best to stick with formats common to most online surveys (such as option buttons, drop down lists and tick boxes) unless there is a very good reason for using more complex question types. Online surveys must also be thoroughly tested to ensure they operate as expected across different types of computers and operating systems. Thought also needs to be given to how accessible the survey is to those using assisted technologies such as screen readers.

ONLINE FOCUS GROUPS AND INTERVIEWS

Focus groups and interviews can be powerful tools in exploring people's experiences, attitudes and psychologies. These techniques are therefore applied regularly in counselling and psychotherapy research (see for example Grafanaki, 1996; Read, 2001). However, they require easy access to research subjects which is not always possible. Online research may enable researchers to overcome barriers of distance and access and to contact research participants that would otherwise be out of reach. However, they also pose some significant challenges which this section will discuss.

Undertaking face-to-face interviews or focus groups requires strong inter-personal skills and draws on the researcher's ability to build rapport and relationships with people. Madge et al. (2006) note that traditional guidance on interviewing and focus groups "rely heavily on the use of visual and physical clues and pointers in order to build rapport and gain the trust of the interviewee." So Robson (1993) recommends smiling and dressing ". . . in a similar way to those you will be interviewing" (p. 236) whilst Glesne and Peshkin (1992) advise that "your appearance, speech and behaviour must be acceptable to your research participants"

(p. 95). In the online environment these key research skills, basic or perhaps fundamental though they may be for most mental health practitioners, have to be reimagined. More sophisticated interpersonal processes such as empathy or appropriate handling of transference, perhaps augmented by disinhibition, are also likely to be of importance in much online research relating to counselling and psychotherapy.

In the online environment, many of the interpersonal tools used face-to-face to develop rapport are absent. Furthermore, as Paccagnella notes "a stranger wanting to do academic research into online communities is often viewed as an unwelcome arbitrary intrusion" (1997, p. 3). So online researchers need to overcome these barriers and find new ways of establishing trust and rapport before beginning to gather data. In the online environment this process relies on a host of other signals and skills from the onsite researcher's armoury of clothes, smiles and exchanges of cups of tea or coffee. It is useful to gain insights into the culture and communication style of the environment being researched. Mastering, or at least understanding, jargon, slang and paralinguistic expressions like "lol" and emoticons such as ";-)" are just as important as they are for online therapists. There are a number of other techniques that researchers may consider when thinking about building rapport with their research subjects. For example:

- establishing web pages with photographs and brief biographical information so that potential interviewees can gain some knowledge about the interviewer;
- establishing some relationships before the start of the interview or focus group by meeting, telephone or email exchanges;
- using any similarities or insider status that you have to encourage identification;
- sharing your own profile data and encouraging others to do so.

However, it is important not to paint the experience of online qualitative research as second rate. There are good reasons to believe that it enables researchers to gather different kinds of data more effectively than onsite interviewing. As Poster (1995) notes:

> without visual clues about gender, age, ethnicity and social status conversations open up in directions which might otherwise be avoided. Participants in these communities often express themselves with little inhibition and dialogues flourish and develop quickly. (p. 90)

Online focus groups can be synchronous, when all participants are online simultaneously, or asynchronous when participants respond at their own convenience. The researcher also needs to make decisions about whether to use a one-to-one interview or a focus group. Each of these methods has its own advantages and disadvantages and also associated technological challenges. Synchronous interviews and focus groups are most similar to onsite methods and generally use some kind of Internet chat software. Key considerations are to ensure that the technology is easy to use, that the online conversation will be private to participants (e.g., encryption) and that discussions can be downloaded for later use by the researcher. Conversely asynchronous methods offer powerful tools for longitudinal work and can encourage reflective and thoughtful responses.

Managing an online focus group can be a challenging experience. It is more difficult to impose order than in a face-to-face focus group. In onsite focus groups much of the management is done implicitly via body language and tone of voice. However, in the online environment it may be more important to formally set grounds and to be prepared to challenge people openly if they repeatedly move off topic etc. The change in dynamics from the onsite focus group also has benefits in allowing different people to contribute (for example, the fastest typist, not just the most dominant personality), encouraging reflection and ensuring that the researcher does not miss any contributions.

CONCLUSION

Online research offers powerful tools for undertaking research in counselling and psychotherapy. They are particularly effective when investigating online experiences but their use does not need to be confined to the online world. They offer advantages of geography, cost and efficiency and may encourage respondents to engage with research in interesting and reflective ways. However, as Dodd (1998) argues, we must ensure that "cheap entry costs and glowing attractiveness of Internet fieldwork do not result in shoddy 'cowboy research'" (p.

60). Online research should not be seen as a replacement for traditional onsite methods or as a quick fix to the methodological problems of researchers. However, if they are used in a considered way where ethical and methodological concerns drive the use of appropriate technologies, they will continue to be an essential part of the researchers' toolkit.

REFERENCES

Anthony, K. (2005). Counselling problem gamblers online. *BACP Counselling and Psychotherapy Journal, 16*(6), 9–10.

Barak, A. (2008). *References related to the Internet and psychology* [online]. [Accessed December 12, 2008]. Available from: http://construct.haifa.ac.il/~azy/refindx. htm.

Bond, T. (2004). *Ethical guidelines for researching counselling and psychotherapy* [online]. [Accessed January 27, 2009]. Available from: http://www.bacp.co.uk/admin/stru cture/files/pdf/e_g.pdf.

Bosnjak, M., Tuten, T. L., & Bandilla, W. (2001). Participation in web surveys: A typology. *ZUMA Nachrichten, 48,* 7–17.

British Association for Counselling and Psychotherapy. (2002). *Ethical framework for good practice in counselling and psychotherapy* [online]. [Accessed January 27, 2009]. Available from: www.bacp.co.uk/ethical_ framework.

Clodius, J. (1994). Ethnographic fieldwork on the Internet. *Anthropology Newsletter, 35*(9), 12.

Cohen, G. E., & Kerr, A. B. (1998). Computer-mediated counselling: An empirical study of a new mental health treatment. *Computers in Human Services, 15*(4), 13–27.

Coomber, R. (1997). *Using the Internet for survey research. Sociological Research Online, 2*(2) [online]. [Accessed January 27, 2009]. Available from: http://www.socreson

line.org.uk/2/2/2.html.

Crawford, S. D., Couper, M. P., & Lamias, M. J. (2001). Web-surveys: Perceptions of burdens. *Social Science Computer Review, 19*(2), 146–162.

Dodd, J. (1998). Market research on the Internet—threat or opportunity? *Marketing and Research Today, 26*(1), 60–66.

ESRC. (2005). *Research ethics framework* [online]. [Accessed February 21, 2009]. Available from: http://www.esrcsocietyto-day.ac.uk/ESRCInfoCentre/Images/ESR C_Re_Ethics_Frame_tcm6-11291.pdf.

Ess, C. (2002). *Ethical decision-making and Internet research: Recommendations from the AoIR Ethics Working Committee* [online]. [Accessed February 21, 2009]. Available from: http://www.aoir.org/reports/ethics. pdf.

Glesne, C., & Peshkin, A. (1992). *Becoming qualitative researchers: An introduction.* White Plains: Longman.

Grafanaki, S (1996). How research can change the researcher: The need for sensitivity, flexibility and ethical boundaries in conducting qualitative research in counselling/psychotherapy. *British Journal of Guidance and Counselling, 24*(3), 329–338.

Gaiser, T. (1997). Conducting online focus groups: A methodological discussion. *Social Science Computer Review, 15*(2), 135–144.

Harris, C. (1997). Developing online market research methods and tools. In *ESOMAR*

Worldwide Internet Seminar. July. Lisbon.

Hewson, C., Yule, P., Laurent, D., & Vogel, C. (2003). *Internet research methods.* London: Sage.

Hine, C. (2000). *Virtual ethnography.* London: Sage.

Hine, C. (Ed.) (2005). *Virtual methods: Issues in social research on the Internet.* Oxford: Berg.

Illingworth, N. (2001). The Internet matters: Exploring the use of the internet as a research tool. *Sociological Research Online, 6*(2) [online]. [Accessed January 27, 2008]. Available from: http://www.socresonline.org.uk/6/2/illingworth.html.

King, S. A. (1994). Analysis of electronic support groups for recovering addicts. *Interpersonal Computing and Technology, 2*(3), 47–56.

Kozinets, R. V. (1998). On netnography. Initial reflections on consumer investigations of cyberculture. In J. Alba & W. Hutchinson (Eds.), *Advances in consumer research.* Provo, UT: Association for Consumer Research.

Kozinets, R. V. (2006). Netnography 2.0. In R. W. Belk (Ed.), *Handbook of qualitative research methods in marketing.* Cheltenham: Edward Elgar.

Kraus, R., Zack, J., & Stricker, G. (Eds) (2004). *Online counseling: A handbook for mental health professionals.* San Diego, CA: Elsevier.

Langer, R., & Beckman, S. (2005). Sensitive research topics: Netnography revisited. *Qualitative Market Research: An International Journal, 8*(2), 189–203.

Leong, F., & Austin, J. (2005). *The psychology research handbook: A guide for graduate students and research assistants* (2nd ed.). London: Sage.

Madge, C., O'Connor, H., Wellens, J., Hooley, T., & Shaw R. (2006). *Exploring online research methods in a virtual training environment* [online]. [Accessed November 24, 2008]. Available from: http://www.geog.le.ac.uk/orm.

Miller, D., & Slater, D. (2001). *The Internet: An ethnographic approach.* New York: Berg.

O'Connor, H., & Madge, C. (2001). Cyber-mothers: Online synchronous interviewing using conferencing software. *Sociological Research Online, 5*(4) [online]. [Accessed January 27, 2009]. Available from: http://www.socresonline.org.uk/5/4/o'connor.html.

O'Lear, R. M. (1996). Using electronic mail (e-mail) surveys for geographic research: Lessons from a survey of Russian environmentalists. *Professional Geographer, 48*(2), 209–217.

Paccagnella, L. (1997). Getting the seat of your pants dirty: Strategies for ethnographic research on virtual communities. *Journal of Computer Mediated Communication, 3*(1), 267–288.

Poster, M. (1995). Postmodern virtualities. In M. Fetherstone & R. Burrows (Eds.), *Cyberspace/cyberbodies/cyberpunk: Cultures of technological embodiment.* London: Sage.

Rea, L., & Parker, R. (2005). *Designing and conducting survey research: A comprehensive guide.* San Francisco: Jossey-Bass.

Read, S. (2001). A year in the life of a bereavement counselling and support service for people with learning disabilities. *Journal of Intellectual Disabilities, 5*(1), 19–33.

Reynolds, D., & Stiles, W. (2007). Online data collection for psychotherapy process research. *Cyberpsychology and Behavior, 10*(1), 92–99.

Riva, G., Teruzzi, T., & Anolli, L. (2003). The use of the Internet in psychological research: Comparison of online and offline questionnaires. *CyberPsychology and Behavior, 6*(1), 73–80.

Robson, C. (1993). *Real world research: A resource for social scientists and practitioner researchers.* Oxford: Blackwell.

Rochlen, A., Zack, J., & Spayer, C. (2004). Online therapy: Review of relevant definitions, debates and current empirical support. *Journal of Clinical Psychology, 60*(3), 269–283.

Skinner, A., & Latchford, G. (2006). Attitudes to counselling via the Internet: A comparison between in-person counselling clients and Internet support group users. *Coun-*

selling and Psychotherapy Research, 6(3), 158–164.

Shirky, C. (2008). *Here comes everybody: The power of organizing without organizations.* Penguin: London.

Timulak, L. (2008). *Research in psychotherapy and counselling.* London: Sage.

Wakeford, N. (2000). New media, new methodologies: Studying the web. In D. Gauntlett (Ed.), *Web.studies: Rewiring media studies for the digital age.* London: Arnold.

Walther, J. B., & Burgoon, J. K. (1992). Relational communication in computer-mediated interaction. *Human Communication Research, 19*(1), 50–88.

Wesch, M. (2008). An anthropological introduction to YouTube. *You Tube* [online]. [Accessed January 28, 2009]. Available from: http://uk.youtube.com/watch?v=TPAO-lZ4_hU.

West, W. (2002). Some ethical dilemmas in counselling and counselling research. *British Journal of Guidance and Counselling, 30*(3), 261–268.

Chapter 25

EVALUATING THE ROLE OF
CCBT IN MENTAL HEALTH

EVA KALTENTHALER, KATE CAVANAGH AND PAUL McCRONE

INTRODUCTION

As new computer programmes are introduced, it is important to use appropriate methods for appraising their quality and suitability. This chapter explores issues to consider when evaluating computer-based psychological therapies. Emphasis is placed on computer software programmes for depression and anxiety as this area is most developed. The chapter explores key issues to consider when evaluating trial reports of interventions and discusses aspects around software programmes as well as client and logistical issues. One of the primary reasons for the development of computerised packages to treat mental health disorders is to increase access to effective interventions. A second is to reduce the costs associated with therapist treatment and therefore cost effectiveness issues are also considered.

ISSUES RELATED TO TRIAL DESIGN

Issues to consider in the evaluation of CCBT packages include those related specifically to trial design. These are illustrated in Table 25.1 below. Randomised controlled trials (RCTs) are considered the best possible study design to answer questions of comparative efficacy. They are used routinely in trials of pharmacological treatments. In the established hierarchy of study design RCTs with concealed (blinded) allocation are considered to be of highest quality as variables that may influence outcome independently of the intervention are distributed between groups.

Power calculations are undertaken to calculate how large the trial needs to be in order to detect an effective intervention condition. Intention to treat is the preferred form of analysis as all clients initially randomised to take part in the trial are taken into account. Including only those who complete the trial may give a false impression of how effective a treatment was as everyone who dropped out could have deteriorated.

RCTs are expensive to conduct and RCT data is often unavailable in regards to specific research questions. It therefore becomes necessary to draw conclusions about evidence from studies using less vigorous research designs. RCTs were initially developed for investigating pharmacological treatments and are not entirely applicable to psychological treatments. For example, the use of double blinding, where both the client and clinician are unaware if treatment or a control is being administered, is rarely possible in trials of psychological therapies. Both clinician and client will have at least an idea of what type of therapy they are giving or receiving. However, there are still ways to reduce bias, such as blinded assessment, where the clinician interpreting the results is unaware of what treatment the client has had. Different types of evidence are obtained from different study designs. For example, an RCT would not be the best place to find information on treatment acceptability. For this type of information, it may be best to seek out observational studies or qualitative studies based on interviews or questionnaires.

Effectiveness and Efficacy

Effectiveness refers to the extent to which an intervention produces beneficial outcomes under ordinary day-to-day circumstances. This reflects "real-life" conditions. *Efficacy* refers to the extent to which an intervention can produce a beneficial outcome under ideal circumstances (Khan et al., 2003). For example

a randomised controlled trial where a strict protocol is adhered to and only certain types of clients are suitable for inclusion is an efficacy trial. An intervention may appear to work in an efficacy trial but be found to be ineffective in ordinary day to day situations. In efficacy trials, there is often careful monitoring throughout the trial, clients may be carefully selected and have frequent contact with study personnel. These conditions are not necessarily met in effectiveness trials. Trials of effectiveness often include a much broader spectrum of clients more accurately reflecting the type of client who may come forward for treatment in a routine care situation.

Client Group

It it important to consider the features of the client group participating in research trials and evaluation studies, as this may have implications for the generalisation of findings. Most research on software packages of psychological therapies has been done on client groups that consist mainly of women between the ages of 30–45, mostly Caucasian and from higher education level and higher socio-economic groups (Kaltenthaler et al., 2006). There is less evidence for the suitability or acceptability of such programmes for other groups.

Follow-up

Follow-up is a particularly important issue in trials of psychological therapies which traditionally have high drop-out rates (Kaltenthaler et al., 2008). The length of follow-up in the trial needs to be recorded as well as the percentage of participants who completed the program. For those that did not complete, information should be collected as to why. Was it because they felt worse, improved or just didn't like the treatment?

Comparators

It is important to consider whether or not the comparators used in the trial reflect current and local practice. Some studies include no comparator group. Caution is needed when interpreting these trial results. Clients often get better on their own without treatment (although more slowly) and improvement may be a result of the natural course of the condition rather than as a result of the treatment. Trials that do include comparators may use a whole spectrum, but not all may be appropriate comparators reflecting current treatment. Appropriate comparators may include treatment as usual or therapist led CBT, while other options include bibliotherapy, other self-help interventions, group CBT, short course CBT or primary care counselling.

Table 25.1
Trial Considerations

Effectiveness vs. Efficacy	What type of trials:
Study design	RCT is the "gold standard" but others provide useful data on some outcomes.
Client group	Was the client group in the trial representative of clients who will receive the intervention?
Allocation concealment	Was this undertaken by the research team during randomisation to ensure that there are no differences between the study groups in terms of prognosis or response to treatment?
Blinding	Was this undertaken, where appropriate, to ensure that there are no differences in treatment or care (apart from the intervention) and no differences in the interpretation of study outcomes?
Power calculation	Was the trial large enough to identify anticipated effects?
Intention to treat analysis	Were all randomised clients included in the final analysis?
Follow-up	Were numbers lost to follow up reported?
Description of non-completers	Were reasons for clients not completing treatment reported?
Comparators	Were these appropriate and do they reflect current practice?
Outcome measures	Were these clinically relevant outcome measures and were they well validated?

Outcome Measures

Outcome measures used should be clinically relevant and well validated. This makes it easier to compare results with other trials and/or software programmes. A whole spectrum of outcome measures has been used in trials of software packages, making comparisons between programmes difficult. (Kaltenthaler et al., 2006). The most commonly used outcome measures for CCBT of depression are the Beck Depression Inventory (Proudfoot et al. , 2004), Core Outcomes in Routine Evaluation (CORE)

(Cavanagh et al., 2009) and Center for Epidemiological Studies Depression Scale (Clarke et al., 2002, 2005; Christensen et al., 2004). In order to determine whether or not there has been an improvement, baseline scores of outcome measures are compared with post treatment scores and ideally follow-up scores. Statistical tests are used to compare scores between groups. Indices of reliable and clinically significant change may be reported. Care must be taken to ensure appropriate methods are used and to determine changes that are clinically relevant.

SOFTWARE PROGRAMMES CONSIDERATIONS

Components of CCBT Packages

Translation of the intervention, in this case cognitive behaviour therapy (CBT), into a software package is an essential first step for a successful CCBT programme. The components of CBT that are recognised as integral to effective treatment must be included. In order to determine whether or not this is the case, there should be a description of what aspects of CBT are included in the package. Programmes must meet recognised standards of proof for psychotherapeutic interventions (Department of Health (DoH), 2001), but to date there has been little research as to what essential components of CCBT might be. The National Institute for Clinical Excellence (NICE) has offered some guidance as to important features of CCBT programmes for depression (NICE, 2009, see Chapter 13). Packages aimed at different client groups will have emphasis on different techniques to meet the needs of the clients for which they were developed.

Specific approaches to client engagement and motivation, change techniques (such as identification, monitoring and evaluation of negative automatic thoughts and strategies such as sleep management, problem-solving, graded exposure, task breakdown and behavioural experiments) and methods of monitoring and feedback vary between programmes. Beating the Blues, for example, uses different types of media to present interactive CBT which includes work with negative automatic thoughts, core beliefs, unhelpful attributions and a variety of behavioural methods. FearFighter uses computerised graded exposure. Some programmes may use video clips of clients or clinicians. They may use touch screens or have boxes for typing in free text. It is important to have a clear understanding of what CBT components are included in a computerised programme and how they are delivered.

Keeping diaries or experience in between sessions, recording of other data and completing behavioural experiments are integral to the CBT approach and the generation of such "homework" exercises is equally incorporated in many software programmes. Homework may be an integral part of the process or an extra if required.

Delivery of Software Programs

When considering a CCBT software programme it is important to take the mode of delivery into account. Some programmes may require a stand alone computer, some telephone access and some Internet access. They also vary in terms of the extent and complexity of interaction with the programme itself, from a single brief interaction to a lengthy relationship. Moreover, the programme of treatment including a computer-assisted psychotherapy system might range from one where the client for themselves finds a single episode to interact with anonymously, to one where a client is referred to a complex programme offered over several weeks including a mixture of multiple attendance at a computerised-therapy clinic, sched-

uled or on-demand phone calls and ongoing monitoring by primary care staff.

Therapist Input

CCBT programmes may be designed as pure self-help (with no support), guided self-help (with some support from either a paraprofessional or practitioner), or to complement or augment more traditional therapeutic work. It is important to consider the type of worker needed to administer or support a software package as well as how much support time is needed. As with therapist-led psychological therapies, it may be that therapist training and experience will have an effect on client outcomes (Horvath & Luborsky, 1993). Another consideration is how support is provided: by telephone (scheduled or on-demand), by e-mail or other online methods or in person (each session or on request). It may also be important to consider the researched health care provider's attitude towards the treatment programme. Provider acceptability may be important for the successful implementation of a programme. If provid-

Table 25.2
Programme Considerations

CCBT components	What components are included for client engagement, motivation, change techniques, monitoring and feedback?
Mode of delivery	Is a standalone computer, laptop, Internet or telephone needed?
Sessions	What is the number and frequency of sessions?
Homework	Is this integral or extra? Who reviews the homework and is it private or for the health care provider to see?
Therapist input	What type of therapist is needed and for what amount of time?
Provider acceptability	Is the health care provider willing to use this programme and convinced of its effectiveness? What training is required?

ers do not believe that the treatment package is appropriate, useful and value for money this may impact on program uptake, retention and outcomes. Provid- ers also need support and education and resources to incorporate the new pro- grammes so that they are not over bur- dened.

CLIENT CONSIDERATIONS

In order to determine the boundaries of generalisability for a study (how many clients and what type of clients may use the programme), care must be given to how clients are recruited and screened and to how depression and/or anxiety are diagnosed. Self-referral routes may capture a different group of clients to health-care professional referral. Screen- ing criteria may determine who is eligi- ble for the study and who is suitable for use of the programme. Which, if any diagnostic criteria are applied and how any diagnostic instruments are adminis- tered and by whom, may also influence uptake and outcomes. Methods of screening reported in trials include the Programmable Questionnaire System

(PROQSY) to diagnose depression used by Proudfoot et al. (2004) and the Kessler Psychological Distress Scale used by Christensen et al. (2004). Clarke et al. (2002, 2005) identified participants who had received medical services in the pre- vious 30 days with a recorded diagnosis of depression. It is important to ask whether or not the method used to diag- nose the disorder is appropriate and who is meant to administer the instrument.

Some software programmes include monitoring of symptoms, problem se- verity and risk. If suicide risk is identi- fied, mechanisms must be in place to manage this. Monitoring may be at each session or regular intervals and may be via computer or through brief discus-

Table 25.3
Client Considerations

Method of diagnosis	Is the method for diagnosis appropriate? Who is responsi- ble for this?
Screening	How is suitability and risk assessed?
Monitoring	When does this occur and is it via computer or brief discus- sions? What options are there if the client wants to drop out if his/her condition deteriorates?
Safety	How are suicide risk and adverse events identified? What happens to noncompleters?
Acceptability	How is acceptability to clients measured and when?
Satisfaction	How is treatment satisfaction measured and when?
Referral	Are program users self-referred or referred by a health care professional?

sions with the therapist or other person. If clients try CCBT and do not like it, other options must be made available to them. Likewise, the clients whose condition deteriorates must have other options made available to them.

Client Acceptability

Consideration needs to be given to how client acceptability and treatment satisfaction will be measured and when. Acceptability may vary with different groups of people depending on age, sex, education, socioeconomic group, type of illness, experience with computers and preconceived ideas about effectiveness. Self-report measures, treatment uptake, continuation and dropout can be used as measures of treatment acceptability and satisfaction (Cavanagh et al., 2003; Waller & Gilbody, 2009).

ETHICAL CONSIDERATIONS

Many CCBT software packages include some safety mechanisms. In evaluating any programme it is important to note what mechanisms are included to monitor safety throughout the use of the programme. For example, Beating the Blues monitors suicide risk at the beginning of each session and generates a note to the person's doctor, informing him/her of the client's suicide risk. Very little information is reported on side effects or adverse events associated with CCBT packages. These may include a worsening of symptoms or generation of additional symptoms. Clients who drop out of treatment are often not followed up and reasons for dropping out not identified. This may not be different from conventional treatment regimens and poses an ethical dilemma in research where participants reserve the right to withdraw from treatment without giving any reason and pursuing this could invade this basic right.

Some consideration needs to be given to how client data will be stored in order to protect client privacy, including the question of who will have access to this data and how will it remain confidential? There are considerable privacy issues associated with programmes provided via the Internet.

LOGISTICAL CONSIDERATIONS

Clinical support may be provided in brief face-to-face sessions, or by phone, email or other media. The content and style of such support may significantly affect outcomes in ways that are as yet unclear from research evidence, although brief, regular, scheduled support from a trained worker offered face-to-face or by phone has the strongest evidence base. Administrative support needs to be provided in order to ensure all necessary equipment is functioning, to answer client queries and to alert staff to problems. Office space is often but not always necessary as some programmes may be administered via the Internet at home, or in a library, community resource centre or Internet café. Implementation will require training of staff and identification of sources of support.

Table 25.4
Logistical Considerations

Costs	What costs are there for hardware, software, administrative and technical support and office space? How many clients will be using the service? Relevant services used over a defined period can be recorded.
Hardware and software components	What is required and who sets up and services the components?
Administrative support	Who provides this and who will pay for it?
Office space	Will this be required, if so where? Room for a single user or multiple users? Only at home use?
Implementation	How will this be managed and paid for?
Training and supervision	What training and supervision is required for staff providing client guidance to the programme?

It is crucial to assess the cost-effectiveness of CCBT interventions if they are to be used widely. Costs of CCBT programmes can vary considerably, and evaluation of costs may consider programme development costs and delivery costs, including clinical and technical support, as well as any direct commercial costs to the provider. It is to be expected that costs of therapy itself are reduced by using CCBT rather than (only) face-to-face therapy, but overall service costs may not necessarily be reduced. Clients receiving CCBT may possibly still seek direct contact with healthcare professionals such as doctors, practice nurses and counsellors and therefore any evaluation needs to consider all service costs. To date, few studies have achieved this. McCrone et al. (2004) showed that compared to treatment as usual within a primary care setting, CCBT resulted in slightly higher costs. Here though CCBT was additional to usual care and did not substitute for other forms of psychological therapy. However, these additional costs were justified by the additional benefits achieved (reductions in symptoms of depression and anxiety and improved social functioning). Higher treatment costs may also be considered acceptable if savings are achieved elsewhere, for example in the form of reduced work loads. Therefore, evaluations need both to measure costs comprehensively and to combine costs with outcomes. Future evaluations need to incorporate full economic evaluations including established measures of quality-adjusted life years in order to make comparisons with interventions in other clinical areas.

CONCLUSION

In order to adequately evaluate a CCBT package for depression and anxiety and be able to compare packages, a series of predefined criteria as described above should be considered. This enables informed comparisons between packages to be made and ensures that health care providers are able to offer optimal client care. The criteria can be applied to new programmes to assess suitability. These criteria can be used to ensure that CCBT programmes providing optimal care for appropriately selected clients are chosen. Other relevant issues may become apparent so it is important that these issues are updated regularly.

REFERENCES

Cavanagh K., Shapiro D., & Zack J. (2003). The computer plays therapist: The challenges and opportunities of psychotherapeutic software. In S. Goss & K. Anthony (Eds.), *Technology in counselling and psychotherapy: A practitioner's guide.* Basingstoke: Palgrave/Macmillan.

Cavanagh, K., Shapiro, D., Van den Berg, S., Swain, S., Barkham, M., & Proudfoot, J. (2009). The acceptability of computer-aided behavioural therapy: A pragmatic study. *Cognitive Behavioural Therapy, 38*(4), 1–12.

Christensen, H., Griffiths, K. M., & Jorm, A. F. (2004). Delivering interventions for depression by using the Internet: Randomised controlled trial. *British Medical Journal, 328*(7449), 1200–1201.

Clarke, G., Eubanks, D., Reid, E., Kellerher, C., O'Connor, E., DeBar, L., Lynch, F., Nunley, S., & Gullion, C. (2005). Overcoming depression on the Internet (ODIN) (2): A randomized trial of a self-help depression skills program with reminders. *Journal of Medical Internet Research, 7*(2), e16.

Clarke, G., Reid, E., Eubanks, D., O'Connor, E., DeBar, L., Kellerher, C., Lynch, F., & Nunley, S. (2002). Overcoming depression on the Internet (ODIN): A randomized controlled trial of an Internet depression skills intervention program. *Journal of Medical Internet Research, 4*(3), e14.

DoH. (2001). *Treatment choice in psychological therapies and counselling: Evidence based clinical practice guidelines.* London: Department of Health.

Horvath A. O., & Luborsky, L. (1993). The role of the therapeutic alliance in psychotherapy. *Journal of Consulting and Clinical Psychology, 61*(4), 561–573.

Kaltenthaler, E., Brazier, J. E., de Nigris, E., Tumur, I., Ferriter, M., Beverley, C., Parry, G., Rooney, G., & Sutcliffe, P. (2006). Computerised cognitive behaviour therapy for depression and anxiety update: A systematic review and economic evaluation. *Health Technology Assessment, 10*(33), All.

Kaltenthaler, E., Sutcliffe, P., Parry, G., Beverley, C., Rees, A., & Ferriter, M. (2008). The acceptability to patients of computerized cognitive behaviour therapy for depression: A systematic review. *Psychological Medicine, 38*(11), 1521–1530.

Khan, K. S., Kunz, R., Kleijnen, J., & Antes, G. (2003). *Systematic reviews to support evidence-based medicine: How to review and apply findings of healthcare research.* London: Royal Society of Medicine Press Ltd.

McCrone, P., Knapp, M., Proudfoot, J., Ryden, C., Cavanagh, K., Shapiro, D., Illson, S., Gray, J., Goldberg, D., Mann, A., Marks, I. M., & Everitt, B. (2004). Cost-effectiveness of computerised cognitive behavioural therapy for anxiety and depression in primary care. *British Journal of Psychiatry, 185*(1), 55–62.

National Institute for Clinical Excellence. (2009). *Depression: Management of depression in primary and secondary care, CG90.* London: Author.

Proudfoot, J., Ryden, C., Everitt, B., Shapiro, D., Goldberg, D., Mann, A., Tylee, A., Marks, I., & Gray, J. (2004). Clinical effectiveness of computerized cognitive behavioural therapy for anxiety and depression in primary care. *British Journal of Psychiatry, 185*(1), 46–54.

Waller, R., & Gilbody, S. (2009). Barriers to the uptake of computerized cognitive behavioural therapy: A systematic review of the quantitative and qualitative evidence. *Psychological Medicine, 39,* 705–712.

Chapter 26

TRADITIONAL USES OF TECHNOLOGY IN COUNSELING TRAINEE SUPERVISION

GINGER CLARK

INTRODUCTION

Supervision of trainee practitioners is one of the most highly valued aspects of the preparation for practice required for mental health providers. Close monitoring of clinical work, over a defined period of time, is a mandatory requirement for licensure as a mental health provider in every state in the U.S. and required throughout a counsellor's career in the UK, and several other countries. Supervision, as defined by Bernard and Goodyear (2008), includes the following components. It is a relatively long-term relationship, between an experienced and novice professional, where evaluation, teaching, mentoring and guidance take place. Supervisors are expected to oversee the quality of care received by their supervisees' clients and are responsible for making sure only competent and fit practitioners go on into professional practice.

HISTORY OF SUPERVISION

Traditionally, supervision has been conceptualized as the trainee recounting to the supervisor the critical events that occurred in the counseling session. This approach emerged out of the psychoanalytic movement, where it was expected that supervisors would pick up on areas of countertransference or omission as a result of how the trainee described the events (Salvendy, 1984). Numerous studies on the supervision process have refuted that idea (Goin & Kline, 1976; Muslin et al., 1967; Stein et al., 1975) and have served to stimulate development of different approaches to supervision that provide more accurate data to the supervisor.

TYPES OF SUPERVISION

There has been relatively little research comparing the effectiveness of different types of supervision modalities on developing counselor competencies. Most articles that investigate the approaches to supervision focus more on describing the modalities used and the trainees' level of comfort with those methods. Relatively little data is available on the effects of supervision modalities on improved therapeutic outcomes (Anderson et al., 1995).

There are, in general, two types of supervision that are used in counselor training programs: delayed and live supervision. Delayed supervision takes place after the counseling session has ended. The trainee is expected to either talk about the case or review an audio or video tape of the counseling session and feedback will be given to the trainee by the supervisor and, possibly, other trainees in the supervision group. Live supervision takes place during the counseling session. Until the advent of CCTV, observation of the session was usually done through a one-way mirror or observation room, where some form of communication between the supervisor and trainee is possible using a particular type of technology (e.g., phone, bug-in-the-ear, computer communication).

Studies assessing the types of supervision used in counselor education programs found that most reported some use of delayed supervision formats, such as: case review, audio tapes and video tapes, in addition to some live supervision approaches (Bubenzer et al., 1991; Lee et al., 2004).

Delayed Supervision

Case Review

Definition:

Case review requires the trainee to bring in pertinent information about their client to their supervision meeting, where they will present this information to their supervisor and fellow trainees. Typically, a standard format of presentation about the client is provided by the supervisor for the trainee to follow, such as: demographic information, description of the problem, psycho-social history, diagnosis, theoretical conceptualization, therapeutic relationship, treatment plan, progress made, areas of concern and questions.

Effects on Trainee, Client and Therapy:

Case review gives the trainee the opportunity to think more systemically about the client and how their issues developed. This encourages a more global perspective on the part of the trainee. Biggs (1988) describes three essential elements to case presentation designed to increase conceptualization skills. The first is using clinical observations to support conclusions about the client such as critical incidents in session, diagnosis and formulation of the problem. The second is incorporating the trainee's view of the therapeutic relationship and its effects on treatment. The third is laying out the treatment plan and tying it back to the client's problem, the theory being used to conceptualize the problem, the strategies being used and possible obstacles. It is assumed that the process of compiling this information will engage the trainee in the assessment, conceptualizing, problem solving and anticipatory planning that are crucial in mental health treatment.

The drawback to this approach is that it lacks the objective observation by the supervisor of how a case is progressing and relies solely on the perspective of a novice therapist (Anderson et al., 1995). Because of their inexperience, trainees may lack the knowledge needed to know what the critical incidents in therapy are and how they as counselors may affect their client. Novice trainees do not yet have the schematic structure to organize information from the session into the meaningful categories expected in a case review.

Example Scenario:

A new trainee was asked to review one of her cases in supervision. The client was a 21-year-old Latino female suffering from depressive symptoms. The trainee had chosen Cognitive Therapy as her theoretical framework. She began by explaining the clients' cognitive distortions (e.g., dichotomous thinking, mind reading) and proceeded to list the client's automatic thoughts (e.g., "I am no good because I'm not helping my family while I'm in college" and "My mother resents the time and money I'm spending on school"), reflecting a basic level of understanding of the tenets of the theory and its application. But, when asked how she thought the clients' distortions developed, she had a difficult time tying the theory into the

psychosocial assessment. She didn't categorize the information into the organizational structure of Cognitive Theory and only tried to apply the theory to pieces of what stood out to her *after* the session, so key elements of the theoretical conceptualization were missing from her thought process.

Ethical Considerations:

In order for supervisors to adequately supervise the work their students are doing, multiple methods of assessment should be used. The supervisor should not rely solely on the trainee for information about how they are progressing in their work, but should directly observe the work they are doing to do a more objective evaluation of the trainee's clinical skills and interpersonal appropriateness for the field. Case reviews provide valuable practice in teaching students how to think about their cases and should be utilized in conjunction with other forms of supervision to help students form a more accurate view of their work and the history and progress of the client.

Relevance in Training:

When clear structure is provided early in training as to what is expected in case review, it can be a valuable tool in helping students to learn how to organize the information they learn from their clients. It can give them a cognitive framework for categorizing important elements of a case so that they can learn how to determine what information is missing and how key elements of a case may be contributing to the problem or may be able to contribute to the solution.

Audio and Video Taping

Definition:

The video and audio taping of counseling sessions for supervision began in earnest in the 1960s. Capturing a full counseling session on tape provided supervisors a way to view a trainee's work without distracting from the process by being in the room. Audiotapes provided a record of the conversation, including all of the relevant inflections, silences and side comments that reflect therapeutic process that would not be captured in a case review. Audio recorders were less obtrusive than video cameras and clients were often more willing to be audio recorded than recorded on video. Most supervisors, however, prefer video taped records of sessions because it includes the non-verbal communication between the counselor and client that is so important in assessing the dynamics within a session. For that reason, most supervision research has focused on video taping.

Effects on Trainee, Client and Therapy:

Video and audio taping preserves the data and process of the session for the supervisor to review. Whiffen (1982) describes the benefits of using video taping in self review and supervision. It allows for stop action analysis of particular moments during a session, or patterns of behaviors across sessions. Antecedents and consequences to critical events in the session can be examined. It allows trainees to view themselves objectively, as a part of the therapy session, rather than only recalling clients' behavior. Video permits the supervisor to observe a trainee's facial expressions, attending

behaviors and reactions to resistance. The supervisor has direct access to most of the visible and audible data from the session, rather than relying on the trainee's memory (which includes biases and lack of self awareness).

Binder (1999) argues for the use of in-depth analysis of video to help trainees recognize complicated interpersonal patterns and how their reactions to these patterns affected the outcome of the session. Kagan (1980) describes a similar approach: Interpersonal Process Recall (IPR), where the trainee controls and reviews different segments of the tape during supervision. The trainee is encouraged to discuss how they were feeling at particular times in the session and to comment on their reactions to the client. Kagan reports that IPR is especially useful in helping novice practitioners comment on underlying feelings they observed in their clients, but were afraid to address. It also gives them a chance to see things they didn't notice in the session because they were too distracted with their own performance. Trainees who used IPR as their supervision model made more gains in developing effective counseling skills than those who received traditional types of supervision (Kagan and Krathwohl, 1967).

Example Scenario:

A common scenario in supervision with students is that they are often shocked at how they appear on videotape. One remark that is often heard is: "I look so scared!" Students are often surprised that the emotions they felt in the session with the client were apparent in their facial expressions and body language. It is a powerful tool for showing trainees their impact on their clients.

Ethical Considerations:

Informed consent is necessary in order for clients to feel in control of what is happening to them in therapy. If clients are uncomfortable with the taping process, I encourage my trainees to explore their discomfort and to educate their clients about how the tape will be used and when it will be destroyed. But, ultimately the decision for consent to recording lies with the client (or their parents, if the client is a minor). Confidentiality is paramount when considering the use of audio or video tape. Trainees and supervisors must take all necessary precautions to ensure the security of the tape while it is in use and its proper destruction and disposal after it is no longer needed.

Relevance in Training:

Videotapes, in particular, still hold a very valuable place in the training and supervision of counselors. Technology has come a long way from large, cumbersome, expensive recording equipment. The benefits of being able to observe a trainee's work, of having them critique their own work and breaking the session down into component parts, is a crucial part of clinical training that should be retained as one of many training modalities in counseling programs (Romans et al., 1995). Although, immediate feedback is not possible within the session, there is value in taking time to reflecton, review and analyze one's work.

Live Supervision

Live supervision has most commonly been used in the supervision of marriage and family therapy, where teams of supervisors (and often trainees) would observe a session through a one-way mirror and would consult with the therapist through some form of communication (Frankel & Piercy, 1990). In a 1991 survey, approximately 50 percent of responding counselor training programs across the nation used some form of live supervision in their training curriculum (Bubenzer et al., 1991). Many programs reported using more than one form of live supervision (e.g., 53% used co-therapy, 46% used phone-in and 25% used bug-in-the-ear). After studying student reactions to live supervision, Anderson et al. (1995) suggest that the skill of the supervisor is a strong factor in the effectiveness of live supervision practices. Locke and McCollum (2001) found that clients were comfortable with the interruptions of live supervision as long as they perceived an improvement in treatment as a result.

Knock at the Door

Definition:

The lowest tech type of live supervision is the "knock at the door," where the supervisor will observe the therapy session from an observation room and will physically enter the session to call the therapist out of the room when a change of direction in the therapeutic work is warranted. In some cases, the supervisor will join the therapist as a co-therapist, but this is not seen as desirable as the trainee is likely to lose credibility with his/her client if the client perceives the supervisor joining the session as a "take over."

Effects on Trainee, Client and Therapy:

Smith et al. (1991) found minimal changes in the flow of the therapeutic process occurred when there was knock-at-the-door or phone-in supervision interruptions, supporting the argument that they are not distracting enough to prohibit their use. However, they point out that interruptions should be infrequent and brief. If more interruptions seem necessary, then it might be more appropriate to terminate the session.

Berger and Dammann (1982) argue that knock at the door supervision can quicken the pace of therapy. Because the observers are not required to join in the family dynamics, they are better able to objectively observe patterns within the family and are able to make recommendations without concern for how the family will react to them. A suggestion from the observation group can be seen by the family as an "expert prescription" that may not feel comfortable, but might be worth trying. However, the counselor's intimate knowledge of the family's culture and values and how that might inform intervention strategies should be considered.

Live supervision allows the supervisor to view the session more objectively, to observe nonverbals between the client and counselor and to observe how the counselor implements the feedback they receive from the supervisor (this last not being possible with delayed forms of supervision). Knock at the door techniques can be effective as long as clients and trainees are well prepared for these interruptions and see them as part of the therapeutic process and not an interruption of process or indication of failure.

Example Scenario:

The knock at the door technique can be particularly useful when a trainee is feeling overwhelmed with a client crisis. For example, a trainee was doing her

first intake and in the midst of the interview, the client (an adolescent caucasian girl) disclosed that she often wished she were dead. The trainee commented on the statement and asked the client what she meant. The client reported that she thought about suicide often, but when asked, said she did not have a plan or any means. This is where the trainee got stuck. She wasn't sure whether to move on with the interview since the client was apparently not an imminent threat to herself, or to process the depressive feelings surrounding the statement and inform the parents. After the trainee was asked to join the supervisor in the hall, she was instructed to do further assessment (e.g., drug and alcohol use, support system, history of prior attempts) and then to discuss with the client how her parents might be helpful to her if they knew she was feeling this bad. The parents were later brought in and a safety plan was established. The trainee said later she was very relieved to have a moment to think outside of the presence of the client and to be able to consult with her supervisor about such a critical and potentially dangerous issue.

Relevance in Training:

Knock at the door supervision can be very powerful when used sparingly. It can help trainees take a moment to gather their thoughts and consult with their supervisor, which has particular importance during the initial experience of crisis situations. Both trainee and client can feel cared for and supported when they physically see supervisors actively participating in assuring the proper standard of care and skillfully using such occasions as teachable moments for trainees (Charlés et al., 2005).

Phone-in Supervision

Definition:

Phone-in supervision takes place in an observation room (often in the presence of other trainees) with a telephone connected to a phone in the counseling room. When the supervisor wants the trainee to change his or her path of inquiry or intervention, they phone the suggestion into the counseling room. The counselor, who answers the phone, is the only one who hears the suggestion, but the clients are aware that the counselor is receiving a message from the observers. This approach lessons the time between when something occurs in session that requires feedback and when the counselor gets that feedback from the supervisor, but keeps the physical presence of another person out of the room. It allows the counselor to recognize the critical moment in session, to try a particular intervention and to see the outcome of that feedback live. It also allows other trainees to observe the effects of the change (Wright, 1986).

Effects on Trainee, Client and Therapy:

Frankel and Piercy (1990) reported that both supervisors and trainees found that phone-in supervision, when used appropriately, was effective in helping the counselor produce client change. When supervisors used high quality teaching and supportive statements in their calls to trainees, these counselors tended to improve their own teaching and supportive skills toward the client. The opposite was true as well. When supervisors used poor teaching skills and did not provide support in their calls, trainees' teaching and supportive behavior toward clients diminished. Support

skills in supervisors made the most impact on trainees' supportive behavior toward the clients and this behavior in turn predicted the most change in client resistance. The more support the trainee showed in the session, the more likely the family members were to be cooperative in the plan for change. These researchers point out, however, that phone-in supervision is not meant to be co-therapy, but is meant to help trainees develop their own skills. Therefore, it should be done only when the supervisor believes the trainee will not make the change on their own, when the supervisor believes the trainee *must* change directions altogether (rather than *might* try a different path) and when there is a clear, concise, supportive message that can be given to the trainee (Frankel & Piercey, 1990; Wright, 1986). Too much use of both knock at the door and phone-in supervision may be disruptive for both the trainee and the client (Liddle, 1991; Scherl & Haley, 2000).

Example Scenario:

In observing two marriage and family therapy trainees working with a couple, a supervisor noticed that one of the trainees seemed to be exploring the option of divorce to the exclusion of assessing the strengths of the relationship and possible reasons to stay in the marriage. There appeared to be collusion between this trainee and the wife that fostered a sense of hopelessness in the session and the second trainee and the husband were trying to approach the relationship more constructively. The supervisor made a call to the second trainee and asked her to point out this dynamic to the couple and her co-therapist. The supervisor wanted to draw attention to the covert strategies that were taking place, so that an overt assessment could be made about what everyone wanted for the relationship. The trainee that had been colluding had a chance to think about his part in taking sides and was able to change his approach to be more constructive.

Later, he discussed how his own recent divorce was coloring his optimism about the chance this relationship had to survive.

Relevance in Training:

While a ringing phone, with a phantom observer on the other end, might be more disorienting than a knock at the door from a visible person, it does have its advantages. It has the effect of stopping what is happening immediately in the room, in order for the trainee to pick up the phone and listen to what is being said. This can accomplish a few things. It can first teach the trainee that it is sometimes necessary to interrupt what is happening in a session in order to stop a destructive process or focus on something important that is being missed. It can also serve as an *in vivo* demonstration of the process of interruption and refocus, so that the trainee can see that it can take the session down a more fruitful path.

Bug in the Ear (BITE)

Definition:

Bug-in-the-ear (BITE) supervision consists of observing a session in an observation room with a direct audio connection to the trainee through a discreet earpiece. The trainee's earpiece receives radio transmissions from a microphone used by the supervisor. These messages are only heard by the

trainee and not by the client. The client is unaware of any statements made to the trainee unless the trainee indicates she is hearing something through her body language. The equipment is inexpensive and allows the supervisor to give real-time guidance and encouragement to the trainee during the session with the client. Other trainees can observe this process and learn from the comments being made to the counselor during the session (Boylston & Tuma, 1972; Byng-Hall, 1982; Gallant et al., 1991).

Effects on Trainee, Client and Therapy:

BITE appears to be more advantageous in developing specific clinical skills (such as supportive or facilitative statements to clients) than delayed supervision (Gallant et al., 1991; Tentoni & Robb, 1977). BITE supervision also allows for the shaping of appropriate therapeutic skills through the use of immediate reinforcement, correction of ineffective behaviors, pointing out client non-verbal behavior and guidance when the counselor feels "stuck" (Gallant & Thyer, 1989). This form of supervision allows the supervisor to give the trainee feedback about their work that can be implemented immediately, without interrupting the flow of the session and to the client, appears to be coming from the therapist. This prevents any loss of credibility for the therapist when the supervisor makes a suggestion, since the client is not aware of the interruption and doesn't know the therapist may have been stuck or making an error (Byng-Hall, 1982).

In an empirical study on the effects of BITE technology on trainees, McClure and Vriend (1976) found that clients were not disturbed by the use of the BITE technology. Trainees in their study reported no development of dependence upon their supervisor, other than their reliance on it for guidance in their initial sessions. Counselors actually felt more comfortable knowing that they could utilize their supervisors' expertise to competently work with their client during the session, without having to wait for supervision for feedback.

Example Scenario:

A trainee is working with an African American male client in his thirties whose mother just died of cancer. The client admits having a hard time experiencing his feelings about his mother's death. The trainee, also an African American male in his late twenties, is using language that side steps the enormity of the loss experienced by the client. The trainee seems to be treading lightly around the issue of death and the expression of emotion with this client. The supervisor gives brief, supportive, instructive statements through the microphone, such as, "Use more direct language about the death." And later, "I can see you noticing his nonverbals as he holds back the emotion. Reflect that to him." The trainee then begins to use language like "the death of your mother," rather than "the loss of your mother." He also points point out that the client seems to be holding back his tears.

Relevance in Training:

BITE technology is still an effective option for a nonintrusive approach to live supervision. It is relatively simple, inexpensive technology that allows a direct connection between supervisor and trainee during the session that is not distracting to the client.

Computer Mediated Supervision

Definition:

Computer-mediated supervision is a form of live supervision, where a computer monitor is placed in the counseling room, usually behind the client in clear view of the trainee. The supervisor and other observers are in an observation room and provide written or symbolic feedback about the trainee's performance that is displayed on the computer monitor (Klitzke & Lombardo, 1991; Neukrug, 1991).

Effects on Trainee, Client and Therapy:

Neukrug (1991) suggested that the visual cue of messages on a computer screen may be more easily integrated into the trainee's work than audio cues (BITE) that may interfere with the trainee's thinking process. Scherl and Haley (2000) found this approach to be less intrusive than knock at the door and phone-in supervision and effective in guiding trainee behavior. They reported that shorter messages were more likely to be implemented by the trainee, because the simple messages didn't interfere with their cognitive processing about the client.

"Direct Supervision," described by Smith et al. (1998), used a computer monitor to display symbols communicating the supervisor's perception of the client's behavior, how to respond to the client's behavior and a rating on how well the trainee did in matching those interventions. Follette and Callaghan (1995) also used symbolic communication through a "performance line," where they showed a line on a computer screen representing the trainee's performance during the session. When the trainee was on target the line rose; when the trainee was less effective during the session the line fell. There was no qualitative feedback given to the trainee during the session.

Rosenberg (2006) combined live supervision techniques with delayed supervision strategies in her approach called "real-time training." This method provides real-time written feedback visible on a monitor to trainees *observing* a session (not the counselor), so that observing trainees are able to learn from the work of their colleague and their professor at the same time. The feedback is available to the trainee who conducted the interview after the session is over. This way the feedback does not impede the counselor's higher order clinical thinking or foster dependence on the supervisor's feedback.

Example Scenario:

A trainee is seeing an Asian family of four. The parents are first generation immigrants and seeking counseling because they cannot convince their 16-year-old daughter to stay in school. Seeking counseling was their last resort and brings them shame, since the matter could not be handled within the family. The trainee begins the session by focusing on how the family is feeling, resulting in visible discomfort in the parents. A note is sent over the computer monitor to remember to focus on the parents first, as a sign of respect for them as the head of the family. The therapist shifts focus and a supportive symbol is sent over the computer. The next message is to remind the trainee to be more directive, since the family has communicated that they came to therapy to get an expert opinion on what to do with their child. The family may decide not to return to therapy if the therapist continues to focus on feelings.

Relevance in Training:

Computers can facilitate communication between supervisors and trainees and can be programmed to provide some of the predictable/rote training that previously required a great deal of faculty resources. A distinction should be made, however, about what is best handled by computer-based platforms and what needs to be closely monitored by faculty members. Live supervision, for example, takes a very high level of resources in terms of time, vigilance and clinical evaluation on the part of the supervisor (Rosenberg, 2006) and cannot be done without that human interaction (whether it be in person or online). Computers can facilitate, but not replace, this process.

Ethical Considerations:

Preparing both trainees and clients for the disruption caused by live supervision is paramount to its effectiveness. They should expect to be interrupted as the therapy progresses. This preparation will help trainees to maintain their focus and composure so that they don't compromise their credibility with their clients and will help them integrate the feedback seamlessly into their work. There is an ethical obligation to clients to clearly inform them that they are being observed and that the observers may participate in their therapy. They have a right to know who is treating them, how their information is being used and who has access to it.

Because BITE and computer-mediated supervision is not immediately known to clients when it is given, it is vitally important that they be informed about its use, how it works and how it may affect the progress of their therapy. This empowers the client to make informed decisions about their own treatment. All communication should be kept on professional level and given in the best interest of the client.

CONCLUSION

It is not likely that any of these technologies will disappear in the near future, because they each hold value in providing different forms of information and skill building for trainees. Their implementation is what will change and much has already changed. Computers are already being used to teach basic counseling and interviewing skills to trainees (Kenny et al., 2008). Videos continue to be used for supervision, but video cameras are much smaller, less distracting and in many cases less expensive than used to be the case. Case review is likely to remain for the value it retains in teaching students how to conceptualize their clients, but case reviews can now take place over the Internet with e-portfolios that include elements of one's clinical work (e.g., video, case notes, conceptualization and questions) (Coursol & Lewis, 2000). Live supervision can take place electronically through secure, Internet-based video feeds, where supervisors and other trainees can observe sessions live and send messages through the internet by voice (BITE), text, or symbol (computer monitor or handheld device) (Casey et al., 1994). The delivery may change, but the key concepts being taught by these techniques appear to still be of value to the field.

REFERENCES

Anderson, S. A., Rigazio-DiGilio, S. A., & Kunkler, K. P. (1995). Training and supervision in family therapy: Current issues and future directions. *Family Relations, 44*(4), 489–500.

Berger, M., & Dammann, C. (1982). Live supervision as context, treatment and training. *Family Process, 21*(3), 337–344.

Bernard, J. M., & Goodyear, R. K. (2008). *Fundamentals of clinical supervision* (4th ed.). Needham Heights, MA: Allyn and Bacon.

Biggs, D. A. (1988). The case presentation approach in clinical supervision. *Counselor Education and Supervision, 27*(3), 240–248.

Binder, J. L. (1999). Issues in teaching and learning time-limited psychodynamic psychotherapy. *Clinical Psychology Review, 19*(6), 705–719.

Boylston, W., & Tuma, J. (1972). Training mental health professionals through the use of a "bug in the ear." *American Journal of Psychiatry, 129*(1), 124–127.

Bubenzer, D. L., West, J. D., & Gold J. M. (1991). Use of live supervision in counselor preparation. *Counselor Education and Supervision, 30*(4), 301–308.

Byng-Hall, J. (1982). The use of the earphone in supervision. In R. Whiffen & J. Byng-Hall (Eds.), *Family therapy supervision: Recent developments in practice.* London: Academic Press.

Casey, J. A., Bloom, J. W., & Moan, E. R. (1994). Use of technology in counselor supervision. In L. D. Borders (Ed..), *Counseling supervision.* Greensboro, NC: ERIC Clearinghouse on Counseling and

Student Services, University of North Carolina.

Charlés, L. L., Ticheli-Kallikas, M., Tyner, K., & Barber-Stephens, B. (2005). Crisis management during "live" supervision: Clinical and instructional matters. *Journal of Marital and Family Therapy, 31*(3), 207–219.

Coursol, D. H., & Lewis, J. (2000). *Cybersupervision: Counselor supervision in a technological age.* Alexandria, VA: American Counseling Association.

Follette, W. C., & Callaghan, G. M. (1995). Do as I do, not as I say: A behavior-analytic approach to supervision. *Professional Psychology Research and Practice, 26*(4), 413–421.

Frankel, B. R., & Piercey, F. P. (1990). The relationship among selected supervisor, therapist and client behaviors. *Journal of Marital and Family Therapy, 16*(4), 407–421.

Gallant, J. P., & Thyer, B. A. (1989). The "bug-in-the-ear" in clinical supervision: A review. *The Clinical Supervisor, 7*(2/3), 43–58.

Gallant, J. P., Thyer, B. A., & Bailey, J. S. (1991). Using bug-in-the-ear feedback in clinical supervision: Preliminary evaluations. *Research on Social Work Practice, 1*(2), 175–187.

Goin, M. K., & Kline, F. (1976). Countertransference: A neglected subject in supervision. *The American Journal of Psychiatry, 133*(1), 41–44.

Kagan, N. (1980). Influencing human interaction—eighteen years with IPR. In A. K. Hess (Ed.), *Psychotherapy supervision: Theory, research and practice.* New York: Wiley.

Kagan, N., & Krathwohl, E. R. (1967). *Studies in human interaction: Interpersonal process recall stimulated by videotape.* East Lansing, MI: Michigan State University.

Kenny, P., Parsons, T. D., Gratch, J., & Rizzo, A. A. (2008). Evaluation of Justina: A virtual patient with PTSD. In *Eighth International Conference, Intelligent Virtual Agents.* Tokyo, Japan.

Klitzke, M. J., & Lombardo, T. W. (1991). A "bug-in-the-eye" can be better than a "bug-in-the-ear": A teleprompter technique for on-line therapy skills training.

Behavior Modification, 15(1), 113–117.

Lee, R. E., Nichols, D. P., Nichols, W. C., & Odom, T. (2004). Trends in family therapy supervision: The past 25 years and into the future. *Journal of Marital and Family Therapy, 30*(1), 61–69.

Liddle, H. A. (1991). Training and supervision in family therapy: A comprehensive and critical analysis. In A. S. Gurman & D. P. Kniskern (Eds.), *Handbook of family therapy* (Vol. 2). New York: Brunner/Mazel.

Locke, L. D., & McCollum, E. E. (2001). Clients' views of live supervision and satisfaction with therapy. *Journal of Marital and Family Therapy, 27*(1), 129–133.

McClure, W. J., & Vriend, J. (1976). Training counselors using absentee-cuing system. *Canadian Counselor, 10*(3), 120–126.

Muslin, H. L., Burnstein, A. G., Gredo, J. E., & Sadow, L. (1967). Research on the supervisory process. I. Supervisor's appraisal of the interview data. *Archives of General Psychiatry, 16*(4), 427–431.

Neukrug, E. S. (1991). Computer-assisted live supervision in counseling skills training. *Counselor Education and Supervision, 31*(2), 132–138.

Romans, J. S. C., Boswell, D. L., Carlozzi, A. F., & Ferguson, D. B. (1995). Training and supervision practices in clinical, counseling and school psychology programs. *Professional Psychology: Research and Practice, 26*(4), 407–412.

Rosenberg, J. I. (2006). Real-time training: Transfer of knowledge through computer-mediated, real-time feedback. *Professional Psychology: Research and Practice, 37*(5), 539–546.

Salvendy, J. T. (1984). Improving interviewing techniques through the bug-in-the-ear. *Canadian Journal of Psychiatry, 29*(4), 302–305.

Scherl, C. R., & Haley, J. (2000). Computer monitor supervision: A clinical note. *The American Journal of Family Therapy, 28*(2), 275–282.

Smith, R. C., Mead, D. E., & Kinsella, J. A. (2007). Direct supervision: Adding computer-assisted feedback and data capture to live supervision. *Journal of Marital and Family Therapy, 24*(1), 113–125.

Smith, C. W., Smith, T. A., & Salts, C. J. (1991). The effects of supervisory interruption on therapists and clients. *The American Journal of Family Therapy, 19*(3), 250–256.

Stein, S. P., Karasu, T. B., Charles, E. S., & Buckley, P. J. (1975). Supervision of the initial interview. A study of two methods. *Archives of General Psychiatry, 32*(2), 265–268.

Tentoni, S. C., & Robb, G. P. (1977). Improving the counseling practicum through immediate radio feedback. *College Student Journal, 10*(3), 279–283.

Whiffen, R. (1982). The use of videotape in supervision. In R. Whiffen & J. Byng-Hall (Eds.), *Family therapy supervision: Recent development in practice.* London: Academic Press.

Wright, L. M. (1986). An analysis of live supervision "phone-ins" in family therapy. *Journal of Marital and Family Therapy, 12*(2), 187–190.

Chapter 27

THE USE OF TELEPHONE TO ENRICH COUNSELOR TRAINING AND SUPERVISION

MELISSA GROMAN

INTRODUCTION

For many, although there are a variety of good options for distance communication, there is still no replacement for the sound of a familiar voice. The mental health community has long been using the telephone to conduct business, facilitate distance learning, contact distant personnel and provide services. However, its use remains surprisingly underreported in the clinical supervision literature (Driscoll et al., 2006, pp. 1–4) and while agencies have employed the phone as a matter of course for years, the last decade has seen a swell of telephone usage among private practitioners to both offer and accept services. Teleconferences for ongoing training, continuing education, practice building coaching, and supervision and consultation remains one of the easiest, most convenient ways to access intimate, connective experiences across distance, with colleagues, experts and consultants of choice and to pursue personal and professional development without the constraint of geographic boundaries.

SUPERVISION vs. CONSULTATION

While definitions of supervision vary widely depending on the applicable regulations, licensure requirements, personal needs and preferences one example includes:

the terms supervisor and consultant are often used interchangeably. A central distinction between the two is that a supervisor has the authority to implement sanctions on a worker if there are problems with the management of a case, whereas a consultant can make recommendations but has no power . . . professional credentialing bodies have specific definitions of supervision for their purposes and it is the responsibility of both supervisor and supervisee to know what is expected from them. (NASW, 2009, p. 15)

Additionally, supervisors may, in some circumstances, be held accountable for the cases their supervisee is working with. Consultants are generally not considered responsible, nor are they ever in decision-making roles.

Where professional bodies require practitioners to have supervision with a qualified supervisor (e.g., throughout a practitioner's career in the UK, pre-licenced practice in the USA and so on) phone supervision with a supervisor out of state or country may not meet professional bodies' requirements for standards such as accreditation. Practitioners are well advised to check with their individual licencing board or professional body to learn if they may seek supervision from a distance supervisor.

A GOOD EAR

Reaching into the ethics of good practice for professionals, consultation with a trusted colleague, expert or professional "good ear" can be considered a must for professional self care, quality of service to clients and continued satisfaction and professional growth. While agency professionals are often given the opportunity to present cases and discuss work issues, private practice clinicians often work in isolation, without the routine opportunity to connect with colleagues in real time and share ideas, process feelings and unpack transferences. Schools of psychoanalysis and other training institutes tend to mandate supervision/consultation as part of the learning process; however outside the circle of such learning programs and of agency directives, many professionals go it alone in the US, at least.

DEFINING SUPERVISION AND CONSULTATION

Semel (2004) quotes Spotnitz (1976) who presented three goals of supervision:

. . . to increase the (supervisee's) understanding of the (client's) psychodynamics
. . . to help the (supervisee) tolerate the feelings induced in him by the (client)
. . . and to use those feelings to facilitate the progress of the case, [recognizing that the supervisee often represses those feelings rather than accept them because] feelings appear to be connect-

ed with tendencies in the [supervisee] himself
. . . to help the therapist communicate in an appropriate fashion with the (client). (Semel, 2004, p. 195)

By listening to the stories of treatment with trained and kind analytic attention, supervisors also model good practice, encourage personal, professional and practice growth and provide support. Having a "good ear" listen both analytically and empathically to the nuances of cases, the transferences, the communications and the concerns of both clinician and client is likely to yield insight, new ideas and give the therapist the feeling of being taken care of.

Other uses of supervision and telephone supervision specifically broadly include training, both individual and group, for specific specialist qualifications. In such instances, calls may be more structured, require advanced reading or preparation and verification of time spent.

In general, however, private consultation can really be whatever the clinician wants and needs it to be. The consultation room is the place for reflection, discovery and dialog about cases and therapeutic relationships. And just as in the work of psychotherapy, the relationship between supervisor and supervisee, consultant and consultee, can be a model for a clinician's work with clients, the key to professional resilience and an emotional safety net, especially for independently working therapists. Additional benefits and uses of consultation include having a place to discuss and plan practice building, career advancement, business decisions and practices, ethical compliance and applications of theory and technique. Overall, the value of being able to say whatever is on one's mind to a trusted colleague trained to guide a good supervisory relationship cannot be underestimated.

While it is true that supervision is not therapy or psychoanalysis, many therapists who seek clinical consultation find that they may appropriately use consultation to learn more about themselves. This is a natural outcome of discussing counter transference and benefits not only the therapist, but clients as well. Being understood, heard, supported, accessing new ideas and ways of thinking not just about cases, but about the work of psychotherapy and how the therapist functions has far reaching benefits for everyone.

WHAT'S IN THE WAY?

Because the need for supervision and consultation throughout a practitioner's career is not routinely practiced in all countries or all parts of the mental health care professions, it is worth noting some of the resistances against it. Perhaps the most important function of clinical consultation is to tend to the needs of the therapist. So, with so many good reasons to engage in clinical consultation/supervision, why do some therapists hesitate to weave supervision into the fabric of their work? In an informal survey among consultation group members at the Good Practice Institute (a host of telephone supervision groups), clinicians voiced obstacles to seeking out supervision/consultation that included, but were not limited to, "lack of time or money, feelings of general competency and the idea that supervision was only necessary for new professionals or for very difficult cases" (Groman, 2009, p. 1).

These ideas were further analyzed and understood to be, in part, a defense against fear of appearing incompetent or unknowledgeable; anxiety over professional presentation (how they will be viewed by supervisor or group members); fear of rejection by peers; fear of having to share personal information; fear of conflict with other members (in group supervision), supervisor, or group leader; a wish to be seen as the expert;

attachment to a fantasy that others always know how best to work; or that they as the therapist ought to know how to work without having to reflect on their cases and feelings. Though many therapists do regard consultation as a necessity for good practice and normal for therapists at all levels of experience and skill, the same resistances that sometimes surface with regard to in-person supervision may apply to phone supervision.

Ambivalence over establishing a new relationship, potentially encountering difficult feelings, skepticism about the benefits of and necessity for ongoing process by way of consultation, fear of market competition among colleagues and fear of investing resources into an unknown entity, also help explain why many fully licensed professionals waver about seeking organized opportunities to process their work and deny themselves the often much needed and relieving opportunity to talk and tell their own stories of treatment experiences.

Psychotherapy practice by nature may necessitate rigorous self-care in the form of a dedicated personal space to study and reflect upon our work experiences. Overcoming these resistances well enough to seek out good clinical consultation as a fundamental component of good ethical practice requires a commitment to the belief that we are all humanly in need of supportive ongoing process, self and case study.

Given the extent of resistance among some professionals, as well as objective realities of time, money and accessibility of clinical supervisors, consultants and trained group supervision leaders, phone supervision offers a simple, resource efficient opportunity to benefit from the experience of consultation without having to work through both internal and external obstacles all at once.

A ROOM ON THE PHONE

In considering phone supervision, some clinicians are afraid that they will not feel truly connected to, or understood by, someone that they cannot see. As one participant stated, being on the phone is "like speaking into a black hole . . . talking into a void [or] . . . like sitting in a group with a blindfold on and no spatial awareness" (Driscoll et al., 2003, p. 3).

So can the relationship between consultant and therapist become established and develop over the phone and do the benefits of clinical consultation and supervision apply across the airways? Can the goals of supervision be met without visual cues and sight induced transferences? As with face-to-face consultation, the relationship between the two parties becomes the cornerstone for good clinical work. The development of this relationship mirrors in-person supervision in several key ways. As with in-person supervision, it is recommended to have a committed and regular time to meet and an understanding of what is expected from the work. As a supervisee, possessing the willingness to voice concerns, feelings and ideas freely, not only about cases being presented, but about the supervisee's own experience of the supervision itself, is an often unstated, but essential component of a satisfying supervisory experience.

Informal surveying of phone supervision participants supports the idea that, while some therapists do prefer to actually see their supervisor, the sensation of being "with" their consultant and being listened to attentively so that they may talk openly and freely, can be conveyed over the phone by the supervisor's tone, words, cadence and verbalization of visual cues as necessary. "Rather than resisting telephone supervision . . . [clinicians may find] it a more flexible (and necessary) response to life's contingencies. In some instances, telephone supervision can increase freedom of expression and may even deepen the supervisory process" (Manosevitz, 2006, p.581).

> As part of the good work of supervision, supervisors, help the therapist develop an ability to step back from the reaction to the patient and talk about the experience in an emotionally relevant fashion. It may in fact be this ability to be in the moment—to step back and talk about the experience—that is the essential indication that our students and we (as supervisors and teachers) are more fully understanding the patient. So when Spotznitz described the goal of treatment as helping the patient to "say everything," he might also be describing the process of psychoanalytic education, where teachers and supervisors help students "say everything" about the patient with the goal of helping the patient do the same. (Semel, 2009, pp. 210–211).

It is the job of a good supervisor to try to make it comfortable and possible for supervisees to say everything on their mind and to be open to checking in about the consultation process and the experience of phone supervision.

> In using telehealth technology supervisors must maintain a moderate level of arousal. The supervisor must be cautious to see that the supervisee is stimulated to grow without becoming overly threatened by the use of the telehealth equipment. Therefore, the supervisor, as always, must be alert to multiple levels of experience and the possibilities as well as restrictions telehealth places on both the supervisor and supervisee. (Miller et al., 2003, p. 4).

In most cases where consistent regular appointments are met, the relationship between supervisor and supervisee develops on the phone as it would in person and therapists usually find that after a short period of time, they become accustomed to the feel of the phone room and it is not necessary to process the modality itself very often.

Frequency of meetings can also affect the way therapists experience phone supervision. Some clinicians choose weekly supervision, some biweekly and some meet monthly. Others choose to call to schedule on an "as needed" basis to process a particular case, or discuss issues as they present, instead of scheduling regular meetings where this is allowed by their relevant regulatory body. This kind of arrangement works quite well for many professionals, but does not necessarily promote the same kind of reflection and learning, or relationship development, that regular sessions can. When evaluating the feelings, experience and usefulness of phone supervision, meeting frequency should be taken into account.

CAVEATS AND ADAPTATIONS: WORDS AND SILENCES

When meeting on the phone, additional verbal check-ins can often be useful. Without visual cues, participants in phone supervision often find that they become much more focused on their internal experience and become accustomed to deeply concentrated listening, which many who work on the phone believe to be an added benefit of this modality. It is often customary to verbalize particular actions such as smiling, head nodding, wincing and so forth and to name the feeling behind the cue in order to express it. Participants can tend to express would-be actions, even subconscious ones, with words. Verbalizing a head nod or smile ("I am nodding vigorously right now" or "I am smiling") become more normalised over the phone in order to foster connectedness and a feeling of being present over the wire. Moreover, without the interruption of visual cues, phone participants may become internally focused and more readily aware of feelings and sensations. Voice tone, cadence and pace take on more meaning. Likewise, the ability to express feelings and say everything may become finely tuned in phone work and can benefit case presentation greatly, as well as highlighting parallel process in action. In a discussion on supervision using the telephone during the 2005 Spring meeting of Division 39 (Psychoanalysis) of the American Psychological Association, one participant likened the experience of working without visual cues to:

> Freud's use of the couch to reduce the social influence and to deepen and facilitate his access to unconscious process in both participants. [She suggested] that these factors contributed to a highly enriched experience in supervision by telephone and one that was often more productive than face to face sessions. (Manosevitz, 2006, p. 580)

Phone supervision tends to facilitate mindfulness, due to the lack of social and visual distractions and the need to focus on voice and feeling only. This can often be used effectively to understand more about a case. If, for example, when discussing a particular case, phone participants (either supervisor or supervisee) can identify, in the moment and express or explore a particular feeling or sensation, such as inadequacy, hunger, annoyance or distraction, or excitement (for example), these feelings can very often be traced back to the case being presented and lead to a deeper understanding of the client's experiences. This can then be used to discuss interventions, ideas and to help supervisees build resilience and work more steadily with difficult feelings and difficult cases.

Similarly, when there is silence on the line, supervisors may ask (as they might in face-to-face supervision) if the silences are comfortable, what the function of the silence is and if it should be filled, tolerated or enjoyed. Silences over the phone can produce more anxiety than silences in a face-to-face setting. In the absence of visual cues and especially at the beginning of a phone supervisory experience, a discussion about the use of silences can help supervisor and supervisee learn about how they both prefer to employ and respond to silences and what is most helpful to the process. In phone supervision, silence may induce a more tangible fear of having been disconnected physically, not just emotionally or psychically. For this reason, participants in phone work may interrupt silences earlier than in face-to-face work. Actual phone line disconnections occur most often if one party is on a cell phone and use of cell phones is strongly discouraged for this, as well as for security reasons.

BENEFITS AND APPEAL

Many professionals are choosing phone supervision for its convenience and ease of use. The ability to arrange access to distance learning programs, experts, colleagues or group experiences that are otherwise geographically off limits is compelling for many professionals. Many clinicians have become acquainted with the work of topic experts and specialists, authors, practice building coaches and others who they believe can offer them training, new ideas, understanding and advancement. The phone is then an obvious choice for overcoming the obstacle of distance.

Clinicians also find that consultation over the phone saves time and is efficient use of scheduling. Therapists can factor out travel time and participate from their office. Many clinicians who use the phone from their office find that they are more readily able to focus on cases, problems in cases and ideas that they want to discuss. Though some miss the change of environment and the appeal of being in a different space physically, others believe that they are better able to concentrate and recall cases and dialogue from the familiar setting of their own office.

In rural locations and small towns, or where members of the therapy community know one another, clinicians may choose phone supervision for its anonymity and out of town feeling, in addition to convenience and accessibility of experts.

THE PHONE GROUP EXPERIENCE

The coming together of colleagues from far and wide is an experience like no other. Group supervision/consultation traditionally offers a rich dynamic experience, the opportunity to glean different viewpoints, study group process, get support and contribute to the work of others. As McWilliams writes in *Some Observations about Supervision and Consultation Groups:*

The chief purpose of a supervision group is to increase the therapeutic skills of members. It offers fringe benefits in friendship, networking, comparing notes on professional issues and learning for its own sake. It provides a rare kind of sanctuary, a place where therapists—who suffer self-conscious concern about their impact on others to a greater extent than any other professionals I know—can let their hair down, kvetch, laugh, compare experiences and find consolation. Members report that belonging to a group helps them contain their most problematic feelings when working with difficult patients because they know they can vent later to a sympathetic audience. In a group they can also build on their strengths, increase their facility in giving feedback, try out their own supervisory style and develop a realistic appreciation of their capacity to make helpful contributions. "I found my own voice here," one participant recently reflected. (McWilliams, 2004, p. 2)

Group benefits and dynamics on the phone are similar to in person group dynamics except for the absence of visual cues. Over the course of several group meetings, members tend to become familiar with each other's voices, the use of silences and the general feeling and tone of the call.

In 2002, seeking a way to provide more accessible convenient supervision to nurses in England, Wales and Northern Ireland, the Developing Practice Network, a UK wide network for healthcare practitioners that exists to promote, support and enable developments in practice in health care settings, piloted a project to provide and study phone supervision for ten of its members.

While the overall response was positive, group members concluded that naming one another before speaking and having a round of introductions each time and checking everyone could hear each other, was evaluated positively and gave the opportunity for everyone to participate in the group. Whilst some participants reported early in the life of the group that it was easier to express feelings to others you did not know on the telephone, other self reports of meetings contradicted this, suggesting that the group appeared "cosy" and could have challenged each other more. Towards the end of the project the latter had begun, evidenced by increased levels of reflective questioning, but is suggestive that the telephone group clinical

supervision method takes three to four meetings before participants can gauge others levels of comfort or discomfort and use questioning techniques and silences effectively. (Driscoll, 2006, p. 3)

Groups on the phone function best when a trained group leader runs them. It is the leader's job to make sure each participant gets their share of talking time, that participants understand the rules and guidelines for the group and to facilitate the beginning and ending on time. The leader also takes care of all administrative duties and business issues. It is also the responsibility of the group leader to protect the group and the participants from potential emotional pitfalls of group dynamics and to assure that ethical boundaries are maintained.

The nature of group phone supervision can vary greatly depending on the members, the purpose of the group and the training and theoretical orientation of the leader and the number of participants. Some groups are set up as coaching calls, mentoring sessions, continuing education or lecture-oriented learning experiences. Other groups are designed to encourage a group process, help clinicians build a support network and create an experiential learning opportunity. Certain groups may be strictly case presentation or business oriented, while others are more attuned to countertransference issues. As with in-person groups, phone groups, while supervisory in billing and nature, can take on the feel or experience of a therapy group. This largely depends on the leader and the participant's wishes. When choosing a phone group, professionals should have a clear understanding of the purpose of the group, how it is run, what kind of experience is being offered and what to expect.

Group leaders should be accessible to group members outside of the group for individual supervision or consultation as needed to process any feelings that come up in the group that may be outside the scope of the group. It is a widely accepted practice in many training institutes for group members to meet individually with the group leader as needed to discuss issues that seem too personal to share with the supervision group, however issues that involve the group are usually redirected back to the group for processing.

SAFE AND SECURE

To ensure that supervision on the phone is private, use of a landline is recommended for person-to-person calls. Even with current technological advances, cell phones are not only considered unprotected, but they can suffer static, delay in voice delivery and disruption in service. Similarly many cordless phones are not only static producing, but may be subject to interference and should not be considered private.

Most group calls take place over teleconference lines, through teleconference companies. Most companies provide secure conferencing, but participants should be certain to discuss security with the company they are using or the group leader.

Both in individual and group phone consultation, it is rarely if ever necessary or ethical to use exact names of cases being presented. If clinicians are employing phone supervision for accountability, licensure or directive purposes, and though landlines are to be considered secure, it is advisable to use pseudonyms or first names only.

LOGISTICS

Most phone supervision is done by simple direct dialing at an appointed time, with the supervisee calling the supervisor. Some consultants prefer to use secure conference lines, but most often this is used for training, education, group supervision and consultation and not for individual appointments. Long distance charges may apply, so callers are advised to have a cost effective long distance rate as part of their phone service.

Conference calling is as simple as dialing the teleconference number and putting in the access code, (arranged and given to participants by the group leader) and speaking normally into the phone. When scheduling phone sessions, all parties need to attend to differences in time zones and, if the issue applies, it is good practice to be clear about what time the call is scheduled for in everyone's home zone.

As with face-to-face supervision, fees are agreed upon between clinician and consultant. Many distance consultants have the ability to accept credit cards through online payment services. Others usually accept a check sent by regular mail.

Although not face-to-face, the supervisory call should be treated as if clinician and consultant, leader and colleagues, are in the same room. Engaging in other activities, or the temptation to do so, can be viewed as a resistance to the supervision and can, if the supervisee is willing, be studied as such and used to gain insight into the case being presented (parallel process), the therapist's own feeling state, and/or the phone supervision experience itself.

CONCLUSION

In the midst of our rapidly advancing technologically developed world, there are many proponents of the traditional face-to-face way of conducting business. There may in fact be something intangible and of real value that gets lost over the phone. Visual cues, such as eye contact and facial expressions are a powerful means of conveying connection and providing a reassuring feeling of being tended to and understood and while, "communicating [verbally] effectively is a prerequisite for any clinical supervision meeting . . . [it is] magnified [when participants cannot] see each other or in some cases [do]not know each other (Driscoll, 2006, p. 3).

> But supporters of phone supervision suggest that it is:
> not wise to focus exclusively on what is lost when the telephone is used, [as] . . . there is something to be gained when using the telephone because of the heightened acuity to auditory cues that can result in expanded [intersubjective] supervisory space, . . . and that [phone supervision] might provide greater opportunities for expanding and deepening the supervisory process. (Manosevitz, 2006, p. 580)

Phone supervision's appeal will likely continue to grow as technology continues to dissolve geographic limitations. The growing telehealth community only serves to increase accessibility to and familiarity with colleagues from all over the world. Professional communities are springing up in interesting and innovative forums, offering opportunities for professional, practice and personal growth, connection, peer support and continuing emotional and idea based education. Phone supervision in its focus and simplicity connects us easily and allows us to delve deep or just review some cases. For those who appreciate the benefits, working on the phone can be richly rewarding, satisfying and productive.

REFERENCES

Driscoll, J., Brown, B., & Buckley, A. (2006). Exploring the use of telephone group clinical supervision to support the work of practice development nurses in the Developing Practice Network (DPN). In T. Shaw & K. Sanders (Eds.), *Foundation of nursing studies dissemination series, 3*(6), 1–4.

Groman, M. (2009). Phone supervision: Unpacking resistence. *Good practice, good care for professional psychotherapists* [online].

[Accessed August 13, 2009]. Available from: http://goodpracticeinstitute.blogspot.com/2009/03/phone-supervision-unpacking-resistance.html.

Manosevitz, M. (2006). Supervision by telephone: An innovation in psychoanalytic training: A roundtable discussion. *Psychoanalytic Psychology, 23*(3), 579–582.

Miller, T. W., Miller, J. M., Burton, D., Sprang, R., & Adams, J. (2003). Telehealth: A model for clinical supervision in allied health. *The Internet Journal of Allied Health Sciences and Practices, 1*(2) [online]. [Accessed August 14, 2009]. Available from: http://ijahsp.nova.edu/articles/1vol2/MilleretalTelehealth.html.

McWilliams, N. (2004). *Some observations about clinical supervision and consultation* [online]. [Accessed August 14, 2009]. Available from: http://www.apadiv31.org/Coop/SupervisionConsultationGroups.pdf.

NASW. (2009). *Private practice resource packet.* Edison, NJ: National Association of Social Workers: New Jersey Chapter.

Semel, V. G. (2004). Understanding the fieldwork experience: How do we know when students "get it" about narcissism? *Modern Psychoanalysis, 19*(2), 193–213.

Spotnitz. (1976). Trends in modern psychoanalytic supervision. *Modern Psychoanalysis, 1,* 201–217.

Chapter 28

THE USE OF VIDEOCONFERENCING TO ENRICH COUNSELOR TRAINING AND SUPERVISION

Diane H. Coursol, Jacqueline Lewis and John W. Seymour

INTRODUCTION

Clinical supervision in the helping professions refers to a process in which a supervisor is responsible for promoting supervisees' professional competencies and growth while concurrently monitoring and evaluating their performance to ensure client welfare (Haynes et al., 2003). Clinical supervisors serve as providers of information, challengers of "blind spots" and consultants to supervisees. Regardless of the supervisory model or theory, the relationship between the supervisor and supervisee is paramount to successful outcome for the supervisee and the client (Corey et al., 2007; Haynes et al., 2003). Ideally, the supervision process is based upon mutual respect and technology can enhance the supervisory relationship while serving as a vehicle to review critical data (Wood et al., 2005).

Historically technology has been used to enhance the supervision process through a variety of formats (Borders & Brown, 2005; Trolley & Silliker, 2005; Wood et al., 2005) such as audio and videotape, bug in the ear, bug in the eye, electronic mail, chat rooms, instant messaging, mp3 and mp4 players and videoconferencing. Technology and networked communication is fast becoming the norm and worldwide use of the Internet has increased (Lewis et al., 2004; Lewis & Coursol, 2007; Maples & Han, 2008; Sampson et al., 1997). This suggests that as "digital natives" many students entering counseling programs are likely to have greater levels of comfort and experience with technology.

This chapter will discuss the concept of cybersupervision, describe the process, the requirements for implementing it and provide an example of the process using videoconferencing. It will also discuss ethical implications of cybersupervision for the field of mental health.

CONCEPT OF CYBERSUPERVISION

Cybersupervision is the process of providing supervision over the Internet to clients at physically distant sites (Coursol & Lewis, 2000; Vaccaro & Lambie, 2007). It involves the use of the Internet to provide both individual and group supervision over long distances allowing supervisors and supervisees to communicate with each other from the convenience of their computer (Coursol & Lewis, 2000; Watson, 2003). When originally conceived, cybersupervision was seen as providing supervision across distances using videoconferencing (Coursol & Lewis, 2000); however, it can also include instant messaging and chat with video. Cybersupervision allows supervisors and supervisees at remote sites to interact with each other synchronously at a time that is convenient to them.

Cybersupervision offers several advantages that include convenience, ease of access, cost effectiveness, time efficiency, practicality and increases the number of available supervisors (Chapman, 2005; Sampson et al., 1997). Of all the evolving technologies, videoconferencing offers the advantage of an audiovisual format where supervisors and supervisees can see and hear each other in real time. It also offers the additional benefit of synchronous text chat. Some of the limitations include cost, security, user technology competence and potential technology malfunctions (Barak, 1999; Coursol & Lewis, 2000; Jerome & Zaylor, 2000; Kanz, 2001; Paños et al., 2002; Vaccaro & Lambie, 2007).

IMPLEMENTATION OF CYBERSUPERVISION

This section will describe the implementation of cybersupervision through videoconferencing. In order to maximize the cybersupervision experience, it is important to have the appropriate hardware and software.

The minimum hardware requirements for videoconferencing include a computer, microphone and camera. Many computers today come prepackaged with cameras and software. If the computer does not have a built in camera, it is possible to find a stand-alone camera that is compatible with the user's computer.

Software requirements include appropriate videoconferencing software such as Adobe Acrobat Connect Pro, Apple iChat, Microsoft NetMeeting and Skype. These software programs allow one-to-one communication and also allow for multiple users to communicate simultaneously in real time. Additional software is available that allows the supervisor to record a videoconferencing session and utilize it for supervision of supervision.

Both participants are required to have an Internet connection with an Internet Service Provider (ISP) address that will allow them to connect with each other. In order for videoconferencing to be successful, a high-speed Internet connection is recommended. Finally, it is important to request that the ISP offer the appropriate security assurances for confidentiality such as encryption, authentication and a private, secure connection.

A key element of effective cybersupervision is to ensure privacy and confidentiality of the supervisor and supervisee communication. Therefore, cyber-supervision should be initiated through a private designated server housed and managed locally by a trusted ISP. Complete encryption should be provided utilizing a Virtual Private Network (VPN) connection. Each individual participating in cybersupervision should have a private user account with access managed through authentication protocols at sign on. Additionally, all forms of communication should be encrypted (i.e., video, audio and text [Coursol & Lewis, 2000; Nagel & Anthony, 2009] for example).

CYBERSUPERVISION PROCESS

Initially, both supervisors and supervisees should be trained in the use of videoconferencing technology and the protocols for connectivity (Coursol & Lewis, 2000; Paños et al., 2002; Vaccaro & Lambie, 2007). This training should include set-up of the camera and implementation of the videoconferencing software package. It is also recommended that the supervisor and supervisee practice supervision simulations. This will allow the participants to become comfortable with using videoconferencing, adjust to the nuances of the technology and learn how to troubleshoot potential difficulties that they may encounter.

Once the training is completed, individuals need to identify a private location where they can engage in the cyber-supervision process and establish a pre-set time for the cybersupervision meeting. At the designated time the supervisor initiates the cybersupervision process by signing on to the account with a password to ensure security and then proceeds to contact the supervisee through the videoconferencing software. Once the point-to-point connection has been established the supervision session can proceed much as it does during face-to-face supervision. One recommendation to facilitate the supervisory relationship is for the supervisor and supervisee to meet face-to-face prior to cybersupervision and as needed throughout the supervision process (Coursol & Lewis, 2000; Vaccaro & Lambie, 2007; Wood et al., 2005).

CASE STUDY EXAMPLE A

The authors conducted a cybersupervision project in which five therapists received post-degree supervision toward professional licensure one-hour a week over the course of a year. Prior to beginning the project, both supervisors and supervisees received training with videoconferencing technology and were introduced to the protocols of cybersupervision. The purpose of the training was to ensure that all participants learned how to use the technology so that their technological proficiency did not impact the cybersupervison experience. The training consisted of basic equipment set-up (e.g., procedures for ensuring ethernet cable connection, headphone connection, logging into the computer and logging into the videoconferencing software).

The training taught the participants how to establish a cybersupervision session using the videoconferencing software. This included practicing the protocols for connecting with the private secure server, meeting with the supervisee in a private secure online room and using synchronous chat software as a back-up in the event that audio-video connections were lost. Supervisors and supervisees practiced these skills simulating a distance supervision session until they reported comfort with the technology and demonstrated skill proficiency. Supervisors also learned how to trouble-shoot using the synchronous chat option in the event of a loss of audio video contact.

Early on some supervisors experienced connection challenges particularly in agencies that had firewalls that blocked the private videoconferencing connections. Dealing with firewalls was more commonly encountered with government based agencies. However, with the support of IT personnel these initial challenges were easily remedied when the ISP opened a port for connectivity.

Developmental models of clinical supervision suggest that anxiety is a normal part of a new supervisory relationship, particularly when faced with new challenges (Loganbill et al., 1982; Stoltenberg & Delworth, 1987). The participants of this project encountered the predictable new challenges for beginning clinicians and supervisors in the new medium of videoconferencing. In the early weeks of the project when the supervisors were settling into the cybersupervision experience, they reported some anxiety and frustration with connection challenges. In order to address these challenges, the authors conducted discussions that helped to alleviate the supervisor's frustrations and anxiety which allowed them to focus on the clinical issues usually covered in supervision.

CASE STUDY EXAMPLE B

In the following example, the supervisor and supervisee have been working together for over six months. Each was at their work place, located in secure counseling rooms to ensure confidentiality of the supervisory session. Both chose to use a headset for the best sound quality while a split-screen display allowed them to simultaneously see each other during the 45-minute supervisory session. The cybersupervision session began like most face-to-face sessions, with a greeting and reminder that the session would be recorded consistent with the written supervision contract. The supervisee immediately began discussing impressions of a new family counseling case seen earlier that week. The family included a single parent (age 42) and daughter (age 20) who both have histories of anxiety and depressive symptoms, a number of family and social stressors and a relationship characterized by conflict and closeness. After the overview, the supervisor asked about the immediacy of the family's concerns:

Supervisor: Well they've been living with a lot of this for a very, very long time.

Supervisee: Mm-hmm.

Supervisor: And they each, it sounds like, have a lot of very difficult things that they deal with. A lot of challenges. What happened recently that really got them in the door? I mean, how did they sit down and decide they need to go and talk to somebody about this specifically?

Supervisee: Well, the mom is seeing another clinician in our agency and she had contacted that clinician and said, you know I'd like to come back and do some family work. Mom reported that everybody, I guess the few social connections she has and extended family, is saying you need to let your daughter grow up, you need to have some separation, your daughter needs to start doing things more independently because her daughter, there is also some financial strain and her daughter is living at home and not working and not contributing to the family . . . (continues with details)

With the supervisee having described the more immediate pressures on the family, enmeshment was identified as a major concern within the family dynamics to be addressed in family counseling. When considering the challenges that might be faced in helping the family navigate this chal-lenge, the supervision shifted to a consideration of how to build the therapeutic relationships with both family members. This lead to a discussion about the intervention of whether to segment (split session times) or see the family members together:

Supervisor: Ok, how would you say relationship wise, how are things going in establishing a relationship with the mom and the daughter? How do you think rapport is going for you and for them?

Supervisee: Well I think initially it's going pretty well because they are open to something working and excited on one hand about starting to do something, but there is also some resistance just because this is so ingrained and this will be a huge, any small change is going to be a huge change for their relationship.

Supervisor: Mm-hm

Supervisee: I felt like when I met with them both, I don't know that I can keep working with both of them together all the time. I feel like there is an individual thing with both mom and daughter that needs to be addressed as well as doing some sessions where we are all together.

A long conversation continued on the

pros and cons of how to manage the sessions (split or together) and how this choice had the potential to either reinforce the old patterns or allow new patterns to develop in the family. Several strategies were discussed for helping family members address their ambivalent feelings and try new ways of interacting. At the end of the session, the supervisor and supervisee came back to the original themes of discussing immediacy, considering judicious use of techniques for managing enmeshment and continuing to develop the therapeutic relationship with each family member:

Supervisor: So we are going to need to wrap up in a minute. I'm wondering if there's anything else you'd want to throw out or loose

ends we want to tie up?

Supervisee: No, I think this discussion was helpful. You know finding out the risks and benefits and finding out like you said their internal dialogue. I think that's going to definitely be helpful for me to really understand more about where each of them are coming from and what each of them are wanting and needing in this process too.

In the end, the cybersupervision session was very much like a face-to-face supervision session in dealing with the various aspects of the supervisory process.

ETHICAL IMPLICATIONS

While cybersupervision offers several benefits, it is important to recognize the ethical issues associated with it. Some of the most significant ethical issues are confidentiality, informed consent, the welfare of clients and supervisees, the response to emergency situations (Coursol & Lewis, 2000; Greenwalt, 2001; Kanz, 2001; Paños et al., 2002; Vaccaro & Lambie, 2007; Watson, 2003) and privacy (Baltimore, 2000). Confidentiality has unique implications online and supervisors and supervisees must establish procedures for protecting the confidentiality and the welfare of clients and supervisees before initiating the cybersupervision process. It is critically important to protect the confidentiality of supervisees, who during the supervisory process will share information about their attitudes,

values, beliefs, biases and limitations. Both supervisors and supervisees can protect confidentiality by using a location that ensures privacy and confidentiality, sharing only information relevant to the case, avoiding the use of identifying information, using a secure server, using appropriate authentication protocols and ensuring the encryption of all information. Because cybersupervision is a relatively new modality for many supervisors, supervisees and clients, the informed consent form should provide a clear explanation of the cybersupervision process. Supervisors, supervisees and clients should have an understanding of the length of the process, the durations of the supervisory sessions and the limitations of the cybersupervision process (Coursol & Lewis, 2000).

One way to ensure awareness among supervisees of the ethical issues is to train them in cybersupervision before they engage in the process. The training can address issues such as maintaining confidentiality and privacy, effective informed consent and strategies to ensure the welfare of clients and supervisees. Supervisees are likely to encounter crises, so it is imperative that there is a plan to deal with such situations (Lewis et al., 2004). Proactively, supervisors can discuss the procedures for dealing with these crises as discussed in the case study in this chapter during the training, prior to the initiation of the cybersupervision process.

As there are no current guidelines that specifically address cybersupervision via videoconferencing (Baltimore, 2000; Trolley & Silliker, 2005), the training should require supervisees to read their professional association's code of ethics (e.g., ACA, 2005) with special attention to the application of technology in counseling, the National Board of Certified Counselors (NBCC) Practice of Internet Counseling (2005), the National Career Development Association (NCDA) Guidelines for the Use of the Internet for Provision of Career Information and Planning Services (1997) and the International Society for Mental Health (ISMHO) Suggested Principles for the Online Provision of Mental Health Services (2000) that were developed to guide the online delivery of counseling services. In addition, a requirement to read the British Association for Counselling and Psychotherapy Guidelines (Anthony & Jamieson, 2005; Anthony & Goss, 2009) is appropriate as they include guidelines specifically for online supervision via text and are relevant to work via videoconferencing. It is extremely important that supervisors and supervisees are familiar with such statements because apart from the BACP publications in the UK, the ethical codes of key mental health organizations have generally not addressed the impact of technology with online supervision (Baltimore, 2000; Trolley & Silliker, 2005; Vaccaro & Lambie, 2007). Hopefully, in time, there will be guidelines about the practice of cybersupervision via video similar to the existing guidelines about online counseling.

CONCLUSION

There is an increasing perception that cybersupervision is a viable modality (Chapman, 2005; Coker et al., 2002; Coursol & Lewis, 2000; Court & Winwood, 2005; Trolley and Silliker, 2005) and this attitude is likely to continue as technology becomes more sophisticated and integrated into society. However, as a newer protocol, it is important to support research that provides insight into the cybersupervision process and to identify ways to make it more effective. With the accessibility that many supervisors and supervisees have to e-mail, text and videoconferencing, the counseling profession needs to find ways to enhance the process so that it is practiced in a manner that ensures the good of the client.

REFERENCES

ACA. (2005). *ACA Code of Ethics and Standards of Practice* [online]. [Accessed December 13, 2008]. Available from: http://www.counseling.org/Resources/CodeOfEthics/TP/Home/CT2.aspx.

Anthony, K., & Jamieson, A. (2005). *Guidelines for online counselling and psychotherapy, including guidelines for online supervision* (2nd ed.). Rugby: BACP.

Anthony, K., & Goss, S. (2009). *Guidelines for online counselling and psychotherapy including guidelines for online supervision* (3rd ed.). Lutterworth: BACP.

Baltimore, M. (2000). Ethical considerations in the use of technology for marriage and family counselors. *Family Journal, 8*(4), 390–393.

Barak, A. (1999). Psychological applications on the Internet: A discipline on the threshold of a new millennium. *Applied and Preventive Psychology, 8*(4), 231–245.

Borders, L. D., & Brown, L. L. (2005). *The new handbook of counseling supervision.* Mahwah, NJ: Lahaska Press.

Chapman, R. A. (2005). Cybersupervision of entry level practicum supervisees: The effect on acquisition of counselor competence and confidence. *Journal of Technology in Counseling, 5*(1) [online]. [Accessed December 13, 2008]. Available from: http://jtc.colstate.edu/Vol5_1/Chapman.htm.

Coker, J. K., Jones, W. P., Staples, P. A., & Harbach, R. L. (2002). Cybersupervision in the first practicum: Implication for research and practice. *Journal of Guidance and Counseling, 18*(1), 33–38.

Corey, G., Corey, M. S., & Callanan, P. (2007). *Issues and ethics in the helping professions* (7th ed.). Pacific Grove, CA: Cengage Learning.

Coursol, D. H., & Lewis, J. (2000). Cyber-supervision: Close encounters in the new millennium. *Cybercounseling* [online]. [Accessed November 12, 2005]. Available from: http://cybercounseling.uncg.edu/manuscripts/cybersupervision.htm (Available upon request from authors).

Court, J. H., & Winwood, P. (2005). Seeing the light in cyberspace: A cautionary tale of developing a practical model for cyber-counseling and cybersupervision within the University of South Australia. *Journal of Technology in Counseling, 4*(1) [online]. [Accessed December 13, 2008]. Available from: http://jtc.colstate.edu/Vol4_1/Court/court.htm.

Greenwalt, B. C. (2001). Cybersupervision: Some ethical issues. [Electronic Version]. *AAMFT Supervision Bulletin* [online]. [Accessed January 4, 2009]. Available from: http://www.familytherapyresources.net/cgishl/twserver.exe/run:FTRUPD_2:TradeWinds_KEY=875.

Haynes, R., Corey, G., & Moulton, P. (2003). *Clinical supervision in the helping professions: A practical guide.* Pacific Grove, CA: Brooks/Cole.

The International Society for Mental Health Online. (2000). *Suggested principles for the online provision of mental health services* [online]. [Accessed December 13, 2008]. Available from: http://www.ismho.net/suggestions.asp.

Jerome, L. W., & Zaylor, C. (2000). Cyberspace: Creating a therapeutic environment for telehealth applications. *Professional Psychology: Research and Practice, 31*(5), 478–483.

Kanz, J. E. (2001). Clinical-supervision.com: Issues in the provision of online supervision. *Professional Psychology: Research and Practice, 32*(4), 415–420.

Lewis, J., Coursol, D., & Wahl, K. H. (2004). Researching the cybercounseling process: A study of the client and counselor experience. In J. W. Bloom & G. R. Walz (Eds.), *Cybercounseling and cyberlearning–An encore: Beginning and advanced strategies and resources.* Washington, DC: American Counseling Association.

Lewis, J., & Coursol, D. (2007). Addressing career issues online: The perception of counselor education professionals. *Journal of Employment Counseling, 44*(4), 146–154.

Loganbill, C., Hardy, E., & Delworth, U.

(1982). Supervision: A conceptual model. *Counseling Psychologist, 10*(1), 3–42.

Maples, M. F., & Han, S. (2008). Cyber-counseling in the United States and South Korea: Implications for counseling college students of the millennial generation and the networked generation. *Journal of Counseling and Development, 86*(2), 178–183.

Nagel, D. M., & Anthony, K. (2009). Ethical framework for the use of technology in mental health. *Online therapy institute* [online]. [Accessed December 4, 2009]. Available from: http://www.onlinetherapy institute.com/id43.html.

National Board of Certified Counselors. (1997). *Standards for the ethical practice of web counseling* [online]. [Accessed December 13, 2008]. Available from: http://www.nbcc.org/ethics/Default.aspx.

National Career Development Association. (1997). NCDA guidelines for the use of the Internet for provision of career information and planning services. *National Career Development Association* [online]. [Accessed December 3, 2009]. Available from: http://associationdatabase.com/aws/NCDA/pt/sp/guidelines_internet.

Paños, P. T., Paños, A., Cox, S. E., Roby, J. L., & Matheson, K. W. (2002). Ethical issues concerning the use of videoconferencing to supervise international social work field practicum students. *Journal of Social Work Education, 38*(3), 421–437.

Sampson, J. P., Kolodinsky, R. W., & Greeno, B. P. (1997). Counseling on the informa-tion highway: Future possibilities and potential problems. *Journal of Counseling and Development, 75*(3), 203–212.

Stoltenberg, C. D., & Delworth, U. (1987). *Supervising counselors and therapists: A developmental approach.* San Francisco: Jossey-Bass.

Storm, C. L., & Todd, T. C. (Eds.) (1997). *The reasonably complete systemic supervison resource guide.* Boston: Allyn and Bacon.

Trolley, B., & Silliker, A. (2005). The use of WebCT in the supervision of counseling interns. *Journal of Technology in Counseling, 4*(1) [online]. [Accessed December 13, 2008]. Available from: http://jtc.colstate.edu/Vol4_1/Trolley/Trolley.htm.

Vaccaro, N., & Lambie, G. W. (2007). Computer based counselor in training supervision: Ethical and practical implications for counselor educators and supervisors. *Counselor Education and Supervision, 47*(1), 46–57.

Watson, J. C. (2003). Computer-based supervision: Implementing computer technology into the delivery of counseling supervision. *Journal of Technology and Counseling, 3*(1) [online]. [Accessed December 3, 2009]. Available from: http://jtc.colstate.edu/vol3_1/Watson/Watson.htm.

Wood, J. A. V., Miller, T. W., & Hargrove, D. S. (2005). Clinical supervision in rural settings: A telehealth model. *Professional Psychology, Research and Practice, 36*(2), 173–179.

Chapter 29

ONLINE TRAINING FOR ONLINE MENTAL HEALTH

Nicole Gehl, Kate Anthony and DeeAnna Merz Nagel

INTRODUCTION

With the proliferation of online education available to students today, it is appropriate to discuss the various ways technology is being used to enhance counselor training. Text-based continuing education courses have existed for many years, before the Internet, in the form of correspondence courses. Now similar courses are offered online. The student is offered reading material and a multiple-choice test is usually given to establish proficiency.

But is that how we learn in the classroom? Mental health practitioners generally have at least some varying opportunity of experiential learning embedded within coursework that leads to a degree and post bachelor education usually requires a practicum or internship. Experiential processes and pedagogies can be incorporated into coursework by using synchronous and blended technology (Lehman & Berg, 2007).

TYPES OF ONLINE LEARNING ENVIRONMENTS

Whether the student is taking a college or university course along with other students that has a specific start time and continues for a period of several weeks, or the professional is taking a continuing education course that is the equivalent of one classroom hour, experiential processes can be offered to enhance the learning activities. Platforms such as Angel and Blackboard are being used in conventional colleges and university settings for technology-enhanced courses and stand-alone online courses as well. The systematic, structural design of the platform that allows for active and collaborative learning along with opportunities for communication is what makes technology-enhanced learning effective (Walker, 2007). This takes the standard online course that simply requires reading text and taking a test to a new level, utilizing Web 2.0 concepts (Ouyang et al., 2008). Within these learning platforms are features such as discussion boards or forums, wikis, blogs, email, instant message or chat, the ability to hear and view presentations that have been prerecorded and access to web links and uploaded documents. The platforms can be used to conduct both synchronous and asynchronous activities. With this plethora of technology-based learning tools, online learning can be an enriching experience for the student who is new to the field or for the practitioner who is seeking professional development.

Professionals who seek shorter instruction for the purposes of continuing education and ongoing professional development seek out opportunities to participate in group discussions online or via conference calls whether for peer consultation, clinical supervision or training and education. These teleseminars are usually cost-effective and well received by the participants (Edwards & Sofo, 1986). Teleseminars may be audio only or also allow for a visual component using an Internet meeting platform in which people can view a PowerPoint presentation or other documents. Webinars ranging in length from 15 minutes to hours are also becoming a popular way to learn material. Teleseminars and webinars may be offered live but can be made available to others as a downloadable purchase after their first broadcast. Other uses of technology include actual taping and recording of live events that are made available later to people who were unable to attend and the provision of podcasts that can be downloaded to an MP3 player or similar.

Counselor education options are broadened even further in virtual worlds. 3D virtual environments such as Second Life offer counselor educators the opportunity to provide immersive simulated environments for their students to develop and practice helping skills (Walker, 2009). While caution should be taken when utilizing role play in online environments, particularly virtual environments (Anthony & Nagel, 2010), education options in virtual worlds is another viable option for experiencing the work of the counselor and learning skills that will aid in the counselor's professional development.

With more and more user-friendly and cost-effective learning platforms now available, such as DigitalChalk, even the solo practitioner can offer group supervision and courses. Other professionals opt to create and customize a platform to conform to a particular course. One of the earliest examples of a platform designed around a course was www.online counsellors.co.uk, which was specifically tailored to mental health professionals who wished to work online via email and chat with their clients or service users. The philosophy behind the course was that when working with online clients, the experiential training required for this recreated the environment to be experienced in the future, i.e., without a physical or audio presence. Therefore, while communication was available to trainees to interact with each other and the facilitator, it was encouraged that this be done exclusively via text wherever possible on forums, chat and email.

The course offered a series of six modules taught asynchronously, self-paced, without deadlines to create flexibility for the trainee to fit the course around other commitments. The course was designed to be a progressive learning experience, from the first module on how relationships (nontherapeutic) develop and exist in Cyberspace, through theoretical models on the online therapeutic relationship and ethical considerations. The second part of the course was experiential, when trainees first responded to client emails and then observed client-therapist chat sessions (both based on actual anonymised material) while being asked to consider points of interest as the chat transcripts evolved. The final module was named "bringing it all together," where trainees wrote an essay (Personal Learning Statement) on everything they learned during the course, applying it to their own service and theoretical orientation and examining the ethical issues that they or their service would be likely to experience (or had experienced) in working online and how they would surmount them. Feedback was given throughout the course regarding skills such as using enhanced text (emoticons, netiquette, etc.), at the client email module and the final Personal Learning Statement.

Labardee (2009, p. 18) discusses training for online therapy further and Anthony and Goss (2009) underline its importance on behalf of the British Association for Counselling and Psychotherapy. In addition, the Association for Counselling and Psychotherapy Online (ACTO), based in the UK, now stipulate undertaking a training course to be eligible for membership. Jones and Stokes (2009) provide a useful discussion of training to be an online therapist and Anthony and Nagel (2010) dedicate an entire chapter to it.

Case Example–Personal Learning Statement

The following is an example of a Personal Learning Statement from the lead author of this chapter, a past-trainee of OnlineCounsellors.co.uk:

Outcome research in psychotherapies has revealed that there is not one psychotherapeutic methodology that produces consistently superior results to the others and that no one approach is clinically adequate for all problems, patients and situations. This observation has encouraged me to utilize perspectives across different orientations, under the premise that "the weakness of any one perspective might be complimented by another's strength" (Dryden and Norcross, 1991, p. 18). Much value can be derived from different methodologies, relevant to different patient's needs and presentation in therapy. Furthermore, different treatment methodologies may be beneficial for the same patient at different stages of treatment. I consider myself to be an existentially aware integrative psychotherapist. With each client in face-to-face settings, I develop a coherent theoretical structure and rationale for the interventions I choose and take care to give consideration to the underlying assumptions, goals and procedures from the therapies they draw. I commenced online therapy training with the intent of integrating online counseling techniques into my repertoire of work with clients. I have a keen interest in counseling at a distance and through Internet technology, as the use of computers and the Internet is already extremely integrated in my day-to-day life.

Prior to taking the online therapy training course, I was aware that it has been documented in numerous books and articles that online counseling is not a substitute for face-to-face psychotherapy and in reading the course material and going through the exercises I became better acquainted with the differences in communicating through these different mediums. A greater awareness of each one's differing opportunities and limitations has helped me to formulate my rationale for engaging with clients in both. In face-to-face therapy, we, as therapists have the advantage of all of our senses operating simultaneously, sending and receiving messages through the body as a pathway between our clients and ourselves. The body, according to Merleau-Ponty is "a series of lived through meanings," it is an active subject, never fixed (Merleau-Ponty, 1962, p. 153). The structure of the Internet provides options of communication with or without any visual or audio experience of the other, in the case of the former through video conferencing, in the case of the latter, through chat or email. Therapeutic interventions may be purely audio, such as telephone sessions, or through multimedia virtual reality avatars. My personal preference and what presently is the most common method of work at with clients online is through text, whether through synchronous online communication (internet relay chat) or asynchronous (Email.) With some clients with whom I have worked both face-to-face and online, I have found that inhibitions are lowered more than in face-to-face communications. I have found that I myself tend to be more impulsive using the written word. "Email therapy can be considered a sort of talking journal, where the individual can share his or her individual thoughts with the empathetic other" (Chechele & Stofle, 2003, p. 39).

Research has shown that clients who seek out online therapy may enter into a therapeutic relationship with a greater sense of ease, as in entering a virtual office, clients come into therapy

without the need to place attention on appearance or social norms. Some clients are more willing to explore sensitive issues online that they would be less apt to divulge in face-to-face setting, as "the cyberpsychological constructs of disinhibition and anonymity facilitate (at least initially) intimate connections" (Gillispie & Gackenbach, 2007, p. 91). In my work with clients over the Internet, I have utilized similes, metaphors and an assortment of tools to enhance communication and to avoid misinterpretation and to get closer to the inexpressible. "Lack of sensory input, when working with text, means that the words have to be supplemented with explanation, including adding the elements of netiquette that make up, in part, for lost sensory clues" (Goss & Anthony, 2003, p. 26). For example, hyptertext, pictures, graphics and video or sound files may be interjected into the communication all of which may become grist for the metaphorical mill.

[One section] on the online therapy course brought to my attention common techniques for enhancement of communication on the internet, most of which I had used before, but had given very little thought to the vast implications of, including the usage of emoticons, expressions within parenthesis or *asterisks* used to convey physical body language, the use of CAPS LOCK to indicate a raise in volume and intensity, the use of color or fonts and trailers which suggest a transition in dialogue. The translation of therapeutic skills to a medium that does not allow for nonverbal clues requires the therapist to consider how the body may be acted out through the text, to extrapolate from themes and read between the lines. "Writing affects the relationship and the relationship influences the quality of writing" (Suler, 2004, p. 4). I have come to appreciate that as a clinician in a unique relationship with each client it will remain an ongoing collaborative effort to find which combinations of text, sight, sound and virtual presence are therapeutic.

Language can never capture the complete truth and that language cannot be a packaged product carrying understanding in and of itself; however, the words we use may show something of the process in an embodied manner. I've learned that my presence online needs to facilitate my client in finding the felt sense of his or her experience as we co-create our relationship and my words bring into our communication a bodily sense of presence and hopefully an embodied understanding.

Another element of concern for me in translating face-to-face therapies into online versions is the consideration that on the Internet the therapeutic relationship is less spatially oriented than temporally oriented. Time is prior to space, according to Heidegger (1975), however time takes on different meanings within disembodied spaces.

In the simulated online chat between client and therapist and in my own experience working with clients online, I have found that in synchronous online communication some of the basic elements of conversation, such as turn taking and spontaneous expression of emotion, become challenging. That the client can experience the holding of simply being-with the therapist is not something that can be taken for granted in online text communications, there needs to be a more consistent "checking in" on the part of the therapist, as to whether or not his or her words are capturing what is intended by the communication. The tempo of the discourse is not easily gauged.

Before they become acquainted with each other's typing speed or ability neither the client nor the therapist can adequately anticipate response times nor can they necessarily distinguish what would be understood in face-to-face therapies as "working silences" from technical difficulties. I think that two simulated IRC sessions with the same client by different therapist in section 5 illustrated some of these challenges brilliantly. In my own practice, on several instances I have tentatively typed an intervention, while straddling the uncertainty of not wanting to interrupt the flow of my client's thought with my message and the potential of my client experiencing isolation due to my sitting in "virtual silence." I have also had the experience on more than one occasion of having begun to type a response to a client and then before sending, receiving another message from the client which then renders my current writing moot!

In asynchronous online communications, the aspect of temporality of our communication also plays significant and challenging role. The effects of the varied time delays in online communication, will impact the therapist and clinician alike. With words as my primary therapeutic tool, I enjoy the ability to take more time to carefully select the language used. In section 4, when reading and analyzing my correspondence with [the three clients], I almost forgot that they were not real clients! Additionally, as I crafted my intervention, the previous emails from these characters I had ready at hand. When I initially read these emails from these characters, I also considered the fact that I could not immediately imagine how long each had spent constructing their words, nor what time the messages were hypothetically sent and received, which also would have informed my replies to these clients.

Having completed the online therapy training course, I am keen to press forward with counseling clients over the internet. In order to provide the best possible services for my online clients, I will maintain memberships with organizations like ACTO and ISMHO in order to stay aware of current issues in the field. Additionally, I intend to seek out online supervision and perhaps at some point to commit to another series of online counseling sessions for personal self-development so that I can gain some more experience of online therapy from the client's perspective.

CONCLUSION

Experiential training using technology is already established and is only likely to grow and become more applicable to mobile devices in particular for a flexible training that can be undertaken on the move where appropriate, such as take-the-test trainings for CE (Continuing Education) and CPD Continuing Professional Development) credits. Caution should be exercised, however, in making sure the training offered does not attempt to, or imply that it can, train people to have the skills that are not actually provided, such as enabling students to carry out practical tasks without hands-on experience in doing so. It should also be noted that it can be a lonely environment, inviting lower motivation to attend or keep up unless full encouragement is given to utilize the Web 2.0 facets provided alongside a training, such as the forums, chatrooms and other technologically provided networking tools.

REFERENCES

Anthony, K., & Nagel, D. (2010). *Therapy online: [A practical guide].* London: Sage.

Anthony, K., & Goss. S. (2009). *Guidelines for online counselling and psychotherapy, including guidelines for online supervision* (3rd ed.). Rugby: BACP.

Chechele, P., & Stofle, G. (2003). Individual therapy online via email and Internet relay chat. In S. Goss & K. Anthony (Eds.), *Technology in counselling and psychotherapy, A practitioner's guide.* Basingstoke: Palgrave/Macmillan.

Dryden, W., & Norcross, J. (1991). *Dialogue with John Norcross: Toward integration (therapeutically speaking).* Maidenhead: Open University Press.

Edwards, P., & Sofo, F. (1986). Teleseminars and teacher education. *Research Report* [online]. [Accessed November 20, 2009]. Available from: http://www.eric.ed.gov/ERICWebPortal/custom/portlets/record Details/detailmini.jsp?_nfpb=true&_&ER ICExtSearch_SearchValue_0=ED276408 &ERICExtSearch_SearchType_0=no&ac cno=ED276408.

Gillispie, J. F., & Gackenbach, J. (2007). *Cyber rules: What you really need to know about the Internet. The essential guide for clinicians, educators and parents.* New York: Norton.

Goss, S., & Anthony, K. (Eds.) (2003). *Technology in counselling and psychotherapy, A practitioners guide.* Basingstoke: Palgrave/Macmillan.

Heidegger, M. (1975). *Poetry language, thought* (Trans. A. Hofetadter). New York: Harper and Row.

Jones, G., & Stokes, A. (2009). *Online counselling: A handbook for practitioners.* Basingstoke: Palgrave Macmillan.

Labardee, L. (2009). Online counseling crosses the chasm. *EAP Digest,* Summer, 12–20.

Lehman, R. M., & Berg, R. A. (2007) *147 Tips for synchronous and blended technology teaching and learning.* Madison, WI: Atwood.

Merleau-Ponty, M. (1962). *Phenomenology of perception* (Trans. C. Smith). New York: Humanities Press.

Ouyang, Y., Li, C., Li, H., Zhang, P., & Xiong, Z. (2008). A web 2.0 based computer knowledge learning platform. In *2008 International Conference on Computer Science and Software Engineering, Volume 5, 12/14 December 2008, Wuhan, China.* Washington: IEEE.

Suler, J. R. (2004). The psychology of text relationships. In R. Kraus, J. Zack & G. Strickler (Eds.), *Online counselling: A handbook for mental health professionals.* London: Elsevier.

Walker, J. D. (2007). Is technology-enhanced learning effective? Recent research and the "no significant difference" hypothesis. *University of Minnesota Digital Media Centre* [online]. [Accessed November 20, 2009]. Available from: http://dmc.umn.edu/spot light/tel-effectiveness.shtml.

Walker, V. L. (2009). 3D virtual learning in counselor education: Using Second Life in counselor skill development. *Journal of Virtual Worlds Research, 2*(1), 3–14.

Chapter 30

THE ROLE OF FILM AND
MEDIA IN MENTAL HEALTH

JEAN-ANNE SUTHERLAND

INTRODUCTION

"Oh My God, I think I Understand This"
(Albee, 1962, *Who's Afraid of Virginia Woolf?*)

For years two lovers have struggled against and with their passion for one another. Their lives are such that they can't say it out loud–can't claim one another in their day-to-day lives. Separated, their thoughts turn to one another. Together they know a passion, a connection and a love they've yet to find with another. When they can, the lovers sneak away and renew their love. Years go by. Time does not heal or eradicate their love. Jack is ready to claim the relationship in his life, but Ennis remains locked in fear. His angst concerning social condemnation ensnares him in denial. Jack, aware that he can't push Ennis to a place he is unwilling to go, is reduced to anger and tears. Tired of their separation, emotionally depleted by the hopelessness of their passion, Jack says to Ennis, "I wish I knew how to quit you"

That line, "I wish I knew how to quit you," has become a kind of iconic symbol of a gnashing and seemingly impossible love. The movie (Brokeback Mountain, 2005) and the line struck a chord with audiences–tapping into feelings of loss, hopelessness and contradiction. According to cinematherapist Birgit Wolz (cinematherapy.com),

> the main characters are incarnating the basic human needs for wholeness, fulfillment and a true love who accepts them as they really are. They struggle valiantly over the years to make their marriages, their children and their work sources of meaning, but neither man is able to fully engage with his life. Their story reveals the pain of living with hidden identities. (Wolz, 2009, p. 1)

Wolz then describes her work with Vince, a gay client who, after viewing the film, began an exploration into his life-long attempts to repudiate his homosexuality. Gay or straight, viewers of this film have the opportunity to come face to face with relationship dynamics, the integration of identities, feelings of loss, heartbreak and a visual representation of the price of fear.

FILM AND THERAPY

Films provide an opportunity for clients in a therapeutic setting to recognize, struggle with and potentially identify with deep seated conflicts. Increasingly, mental health professions have turned to film in the therapeutic setting. In 1944, in an article entitled *Psychodrama and Therapeutic Motion Pictures,* Moreno argued that films could reveal behaviors similar to those of clients. Moreno had in mind the production of films specifically drawing from therapy sessions in order to offer viewers a dose of realism. A bit ahead of his time, Moreno predated the critically acclaimed television show *In Treatment* by some 60 years. In this show, Gabriel Byrne plays a psychotherapist who, while working with a series of clients, struggles with his own insecurities and losses. Praised as much for what this show doesn't say as for what it does, *In Treatment* allows viewers to read between the lines. As Simons (2009) notes, "No one needs to fully, linguistically explain human pain and rebound: we spot it when we see it" (p. 1). Moreno had the same idea—use the power of film to illustrate psychodramatic material.

While Solomon (1995) claims the title "Father of Cinematherapy," it appears that therapists' ideas about the usefulness of this medium stem from the early days of film. Since the publication of Solomon's first book, films have become increasingly accessible. Besides the cinema itself, movies can be found at video stores, public libraries, through the mail (e.g., Netflix), on pay-for-view television and as computer downloads. As the techniques of filmmaking have advanced, making images and sounds more "real," so too has the accessibility of movies become more sophisticated.

While mental health and therapy is a favorite topic in Hollywood films, it is often depicted with humor and distortion. Whether the inappropriate therapist (e.g., *Running with Scissors,* 2006) or the over-the-top client (e.g., *Analyze This,* 1999), psychotherapy and mental illness are crowd pleasers. Occasionally, depictions of mental health issues give us pause such as the schizophrenic portrayed by Russell Crowe in *A Beautiful Mind* (2001). Sometimes a serious condition is made light as was Dudley Moore's loveable drunk in *Arthur* (1981). Considerably less funny was Nicolas Cage's performance as the writer who decides to drink himself to death in *Leaving Las Vegas* (1995). The question is, to what extent do these films matter? Can they "teach" us about our culture, ourselves, psychotherapy and mental health? Many argue that films are "just entertainment." However, louder is the argument that film, while a form of mass entertainment, instructs and informs audiences while both creating and reflecting culture (Giroux, 2002). Films are more than just entertainment; they can also be used to provide moral instruction or social observation, to offer a social context or to explore political judgment (Sutherland & Feltey, 2009).

Films tell stories. Myths once served to illustrate the beliefs, values and behaviors of its people. Today films provide us with glimpses into our culture. Like literature, movies instruct, entertain, offer principals and ideologies, values and life lessons. But, unlike literature, film does not rely on abstract symbols alone. Instead, films speak to us through images and sound (Boggs & Petrie, 2004). Films can both reinforce stereotypes and challenge viewers with new interpretations of old themes. Films show us the develop-

ment of individuals as they struggle with identity and self-esteem. In movies, we watch characters interact within the contexts of relationships. Films are a new kind of "text" through which we are provided stories, frames and representations of social life (Sutherland & Feltey, 2009). Just as mental health professionals have long integrated other media such as literature and music into counseling, films provide an opportunity for clients to view the representation of an otherwise abstract idea.

A REVIEW OF THE LITERATURE

The specifics of integrating film into therapy vary in the current literature. In their book, *Rent Two Films and Let's Talk in the Morning: Using Popular Movies in Psychotherapy,* Hesley and Hesley (2001) outline the benefits of film in counseling sessions. They call it "Video Work," a process whereby therapists and clients "discuss themes and characters in popular film that relate to core issues of ongoing therapy" (p. 4). The authors tell the story of a client struggling in her current relationship. Overeager to please her man, Hesley's client struggled with her own self-worth. Jan suggested she watch the movie *Singles* (1992). She asked her client to notice her emotions as she watched the film. Her client saw the connection between her struggles and the struggles of a woman in the film. Hesley notes that her client was also angry at having watched the film. What the client sees in a film often challenges personal constructions of reality. Helsey and Hesley stress that the use of films does not replace traditional therapy. Rather, this methodology ". . . emphasize[s] the partnership of conventional therapy and

film homework" (p. 5).

According to Hesley and Hesley, when a client is assigned a film to watch, seeds are planted for future sessions. Specifically, they assign a film, explaining to the client why that particular movie fits. Boundaries are established and clients are warned of offensive language or content. After a client views a film, the next session may or may not directly address it. Sometimes the client rejects the relevance of the movie, but still the session may take a turn that it otherwise would not. Hesley and Hesley do not suggest that films bring about change directly. Rather, having a client watch a particular film provides a focus and opens the possibility for self-understanding.

Other resources provide a "how-to" work with film and clients. In *Moving Therapy: Moving Therapy,* Ulus (2003) provides instructions to become a movie group therapist (he even offers suggestions regarding proper billing of clients for movie therapy). Ulus acknowledges the increased use of films by psychologists and educators, reviewing the concept of film use in group settings. In *Movies and Mental Illness: Using Films to Understand Psychopathology,* Wedding et al. (2005) regard films as the social mirror in which we are projected. The authors see films as significant teaching tools to augment students' understandings of psychopathology. Their book is organized by particular disorders, with suggested films that serve as illustrations. Both texts offer readers justification for the use of movies while providing a rich index of films to draw upon.

For a specific link between film and the psychoanalytic perspective, see Sabbadini's edited text, *Projected Shadows: Psychoanalytic Reflections on the Representation of Loss in European Cinema* (2007). In this work, film scholars and psychoanalysts explore film and Oedipal crises, representations of pathology, dreams and fantasies. Less a "how to" book than those previously noted, these essays provide a more academic grounding to the relationship between film and psychotherapy.

A visit to Wolz's website provides individuals with the tools for exploring one's inner life (emotionpicture.com; cinematherapy.com). At Wolz's site, one can skip the therapist and work alone. Wolz offers a list of films associated with particular struggles. After viewing, individuals are encouraged to ask themselves a number of questions such as: how did you feel when you observed . . . ; how and where in your life could you adopt this attitude . . . ; can you remember one situation in your life when you faced a fear . . . ? According to Wolz, movies can heal and help an individual in their "transformation." Wolz's model, outside of the context of therapy, lacks the give and take which stems from dialogue. As Hesley and Hesley note, the client may or may not make the immediate connec-

tion between the film and their personal lives. Certainly films can be viewed and explored by individuals outside of therapy with persons fully capable of reflection. However, oftentimes the temptation with film is to take literally that which can also be read symbolically. Dialogue with another provides the opportunity to steer clear of generalizations and arrive at meaningful connections.

Brown (2003) found that films were successful for use with female adolescent offenders. Acknowledging that films play an important role in the lives of adolescent girls, Brown developed a manual for use in treatment that centers on representations of sexism, racism, abuse/trauma, depression and substance abuse in film. In a full session, the girls watch a particular film. Subsequent sessions allow the adolescents to discuss relevant scenes. In this way, group leaders utilize film as a means of stimulating discussions of potentially difficult topics.

When discussed as a scene in a film, sensitive topics (e.g., abuse, depression) can feel more accessible to clients. After all, it is happening to someone else. Watching something "happen" to someone else can offer validation to clients who might have otherwise felt alone with their experiences. And subsequent discussions can allow clients to make connections between what they see as "film moments" and what they experience in their lives. That is, film has the potential to make clear the abstract–to bring into view what was otherwise distant and vague.

Also of significance is the body of literature addressing the usefulness of film in counselor student training. As Toman and Rak (2000) noted, "the use of motion pictures as a teaching tool can bring the personable and intimate study of human issues directly into the classroom, providing dialogue in the context of film characters' life circumstances." Between 1994 and 1998, Toman and Rak evaluated the use of film across four courses (teaching diagnosis, counseling theories, counseling interventions and ethics). Their overall results, based on the administration of a student survey, demonstrated positive responses from students. The use of film in classes was successful in "providing visual case examples for role plays, serving as catalysts for class discussions, bringing the tenets of theory to life, giving students the opportunity to rewrite ethical endings to replace unethical depictions and bringing dialogue and context into the classroom." The authors note concerns and considerations that must be addressed when using film in the classroom. Did the viewing of films actually increase knowledge of the material? To what extent are instructors offered a pedagogical tool for teaching with film?

As more therapists and course instructors integrate film into counseling and counseling training, the question of pedagogy becomes essential. Who is teaching us how to teach through film? While numerous works point out the advantages that film offers, fewer studies discuss the specifics of the pedagogical process. Higgins and Dermer (2001) go beyond a discussion of the advantages and offer detailed strategies for use in the classroom. These include: evaluating films from different theoretical orientations; evaluating films from different characters' perspectives; watching a film clip with no sound; analysis of student reactions; developing hypotheses and demonstrating how they were generated; development of treatment plans (for the characters in the film); evaluating development; film used as exam replacement or supplement. Part of building a film pedagogy involves thorough development of exercises and assessment of the effectiveness of such tools. Future work with film should consider not only the abundant advantages for the use of film, but also the intended objectives and outcomes.

CAUTIONS AND CONSIDERATIONS

A general caution must be considered when working with film. As we know, films, even when they look "real" and, even if they might be "inspired by a true story," are produced within the power structure of Hollywood or, at least, of a film production company. Problems can arise when films are accepted at face value without critical analysis. Issues of sexism, racism, classism, ageism (all of the "isms") are potentially missed without careful deliberation.

Unlike a novel which is usually the work of an individual, a film comes to us via a plethora of artists. The producers, screenwriters, directors, editors, cinematographer, sound crew and, of course, the actors all participate in the telling of the story. Each of those contributors brings something to the project. Each stands in a particular place that will impact the final story that we see and hear on the screen. Also, unlike works of literature, film production (particularly Hollywood films) almost always occurs under the umbrella of capitalism. Will the film profit financially? Will young men want to see it (movie makers know the importance of this demographic)? Thus, when a subject as sensitive as mental illness, or as complicated as human emotions, is approached in a film, it will take on drama and absurdities not necessarily "real." For example, when telling the tale of domestic violence, it is much more "interesting" to watch Jennifer Lopez pump iron so that her body is strong enough to beat the hell out her husband than to depict the usual methods by which a battered woman typically escapes (*Enough*, 2002). Issues of community, reliance on social networks—these are the resources needed for escaping an abusive home. But, that would make a boring film (or so Hollywood has trained us). Thus, while the film might motivate a woman to find some internal strength to "fight back," it is hopeful that the "fighting back" will seem as much symbolic as literal.

I am not suggesting that clients (or anyone for that matter) are passive participants in film viewing. While we once regarded audiences as sponge-like and vulnerable, we now understand that viewers participate in film viewing through processes of interpretation (Sutherland & Feltey, 2009). Even as we are inundated with movies, individuals sustain a kind of dialogue with films—dismissing parts that do not fit cognitively and embracing other parts. Even so, any discussion of film benefits by placing it into historical and social contexts. Consideration of the multiple layers of sexism, racism and classism allows us to see more clearly the perils the characters in this film face. Moreover, consideration of "isms" allow the film to speak to those layers of a

client's life. That is, for example, how might the outcomes of the character be different if she were African-American and not Caucasian? Or: what does this film *not* say in terms of social class limitations?

While we acknowledge that audiences are not passive, we also grant that movies tend to be utilized far more for escapism than for reflection. Miller (1999) noted that most moviegoers "see films as a means to get away from moral arguments, not to get into them" (p. 1). Most audience members are not searching a film for a theory or even a "lesson" for that matter—that is not how we are culturally oriented towards movies. Thus, while films stimulate dialogue and offer opportunities for contemplation, the "skill" for such musings is not necessarily intuitive. Guiding clients through a "reading" of film requires cognizance of film pedagogy. Giroux (2002) warns us against "textual essentialism," and the temptation to read films as sites of particular meanings and interpretations. Rather, when using film, we must remember to place our readings within the larger social contexts of dominant discourse, ideology and capitalism. *Who* has the power to tell the stories of love, loss, hopelessness, abuse, addiction and mental illness? From where did the dominant ideas of human struggling emerge? As we offer clients or students film in order to illustrate a concept, we must remember how representation itself works within the relations of power.

CONCLUSION

Increasingly, films are employed in therapy in order to illustrate behaviors, circumstances, disorders and distrac-

tions. Therapists know that people are more likely to view a movie about addiction than to read a text about the subject.

At present, there are multiple texts and websites for specific instruction concerning film and therapy. Resources range from the specific "how-to" to the theoretical. It follows that as access to films expands, use of film in therapeutic setting will increase. Important considerations involve appropriate "readings" of films—placing them within the larger social and historical context in which they are produced. While films strike at the heart of issues, they don't themselves capture the complexity of the issue. Films are an ideal tool for illustrating life, pain, loss and joy. The work of the therapist is to frame those representations in such as way as to provide meaningful analysis for the client. As Buddy (played by Kevin Spacey) reminds us in *Swimming with Sharks* (1994), "Life is not a movie. Good guys lose, everybody lies and love . . . does not conquer all."

REFERENCES

Albee, E. (1962). *Who's afraid of Virginia Woolf?* New York: Signet.

Boggs, J. M., & Petrie, D. W. (2004). *The art of watching films* (6th ed.). New York: McGraw-Hill.

Brown, T. K. S. (2003). *Therapeutic use of media with female adolescent offenders: A group treatment manual.* Thesis (Psy. D.). Alliant International University, California School of Professional Psychology, San Francisco Bay.

Giroux, H. (2002). *Breaking in to the movies.* Malden, MA: Blackwell.

Hesley, J. W., & Hesley, J. G. (2001). *Rent two films and let's talk in the morning: Using popular movies in psychotherapy.* New York: John Wiley and Sons.

Higgins, J. A., & Dermer, S. (2001). The use of film in marriage and family counselor education. *Counselor Education and Supervision, 40*(3), 182–193.

Miller, B. (1999). The work of interpretation: A theoretical defence of film theory and criticism. *Kinema: A journal for film and audiovisual media* [online]. [Accessed December 3, 2009]. Available from: http://www.kinema.uwaterloo.ca/article.php?id=209&feature.

Moreno, J. L. (1944). *Psychodrama and therapeutic motion pictures.* Sociometry. 7(2), 230–244.

Sabbadini, A. (2007). *Projected shadows: Psychoanalytic reflections on the representation of loss.* New York: Routledge Press.

Simons, I. (2009). HBO's 'In Treatment'. *Psychology Today* [online]. [Accessed December 3, 2009]. Available from: http://www.psychologytoday.com/blog/the-literary-mind/200904/hbos-in-treatment.

Soloman, G. (1995). *The motion picture prescription: Watch this movie and call me in the morning.* Santa Rosa, CA: Aslan.

Sutherland, J. A., & Feltey, K. (2009). *Cinematic sociology: Social life in film.* Pine Forge, CA: Sage.

Toman, S. M., & Rak, C. F. (2000). The use of cinema in the counselor education curriculum: Strategies and outcomes. *Counselor Education and Supervision, 40*(2), 105–115.

Ulus, F. (2003). *Moving therapy: Moving therapy.* Victoria, BC: Trafford.

Wedding, D., Boyd, M. A., &Niemec, R. M. (2005). *Movies and mental illness: Using films to understand psychopathology.* Göttingen: Hogrefe and Huber.

Wolz, B. (2009). Therapeutic movie review column. *Cinematherapy.com* [online]. [Accessed February 2, 2009]. Available from: http://www.cinematherapy.com/birgitarticles/brokeback-mountain.html.

CONCLUSION–INNOVATION AND THE FUTURE OF TECHNOLOGY IN MENTAL HEALTH

DeeAnna Merz Nagel and Kate Anthony

More and more people are reaching out through technology to educate themselves about mental health and to search for support in cyberspace. As technology advances and Web 2.0 concepts become integrated into our global culture, people will continue to find new and interesting ways to garner knowledge, join helpful communities and seek professional services. At the same time, mental health practitioners will be seeking new ways to attract and serve clients, adding technology delivery methods and using the Internet as a primary practice-building tool.

It is our hope that in distributing a book that presents such an expansive range of examples of how technology dovetails with mental health care, that this niche field will become more mainstream and considered less on the fringe of psychological and mental health studies. To that end, we have also founded the Online Therapy Institute (www.on linetherapyinstitute.com), offering training courses and educational materials as well as social networking and marketing opportunities for professionals. We have created various ethical frameworks that cut across cultural and geographical bar-

riers. Our frameworks are available to aid organizations, government agencies, certifying bodies and licensing boards in establishing codes or rules that may be applicable to a certain helping profession or locale. Our frameworks are designed to be modified as new technologies are developed.

We also seek new and innovative ways to approach therapy and educate therapists. In 2009, we contributed to The Future of Innovation, a project that the founders compare to a "Wikipedia" for innovation. At the time we contributed, The Future of Innovation website had already received hundreds of entries that have now been compiled into a book by the same title. In speaking about the future of innovation, von Stamm and Trifilova (2009) state eloquently:

> The future is not something that just happens to us; it is not inevitable or imposed on us and we are not simply puppets in someone else's play. We all make decisions, grasp or ignore opportunities, reject options. We can participate or avert our eyes. The future is our decision. If we choose to experiment and it fails, we can brush that failure

under the carpet or we can seek to learn from it. The future is in our hands. We need to take responsibility for it— and accept that our decisions come with risks. (von Stamm and Trifilova, 2009, p. 2)

While our entries are readily available at The Future of Innovation website (www.thefutureofinnovation.org), we felt our contributions to the project give a view into the future of innovation regarding the impact of technology on mental health. These essays also offer an edgy glimpse into future endeavors in which the editors are involved.

THE FUTURE OF INNOVATION IN TRAINING INNOVATIVE THERAPISTS

KATE ANTHONY

What does the future of innovation hold for the clients and providers of therapeutic services? As a trainer, I have used bespoke software to communicate, teach and consult with many therapists from all over the globe who want to use innovative methods of delivery to clients. Currently, this concentrates on service delivery via email and Internet Relay Chat and training delivery via forums, email, chat and a learning programme that is automatically delivered to the desktop. But what will my *future* training programs look like?

Let's start with SMS, or texting, via mobile phones. I am teaching therapists to communicate with clients in fewer than 160 characters, a need that is increasingly apparent as charities and similar mental health organisations offer this service to those in need. My current philosophy in training others to be a distance therapist is that in order to gain a truly experiential meaningful training, my trainees never experience me as a physical being, whether by photo on the web, meetings face-to-face or telephone calls. All communication is via text because—hey—that's how they will experience their clients once they have finished training. But how can I (and should

I) be training therapists to work in bursts of less than 160 characters?

Let's move on to being a Virtual Therapist in an environment such as Second Life and providing training for that. This is somehow easier than the SMS training dilemma—I will have a physical presence of sorts through my avatar and can meet in my virtual office or conference suite or institute to train them and use virtual tools. But we already have clients using such services and it is documented that such clients often attend sessions as different representations of the self—and sometimes even change avatars part way through a session. Should I use this fact as part of my training programme and illustrate this myself by appearing in one training session as KateElize Larnia, or as someone who looks completely different with a different name. Or even as a wolf or robot?

How about training therapists to use social and professional networking sites responsibly? Should I do this through Facebook or Twitter, for example? Facebook is hardly a training platform, but my trainees need an experiential platform. And if Twitter . . . can I train therapists in training sessions of under

140 characters–a task even more daunting than that of SMS!

And behind all of this lies the question of ethics. As an ethicist myself, I know the reality of keeping up with technological innovation in therapy and how the profession has been playing catch up with their uses for well over ten years now. I see a future of innovation in therapeutic interventions that will see me delivering training as a hologram, beaming myself to my trainees to train them in hologrammatic therapy. So maybe the future of innovation in therapy will bring us back round to traditional face-to-face methods after all. . . .

THE FUTURE OF INNOVATION: THE USE OF AVATARS IN PSYCHOTHERAPY

DeeAnna Merz Nagel

Avatar therapy is not new. The term has been discussed theoretically for nearly ten years. Now that virtual worlds have reached the mainstream and with the advent of gaming, many people understand the provocative power that exists with an avatar identity. People now live part of their lives virtually. Innovative uses of time both online and off mean that many of us live our lives in a mixed reality.

Three-dimensional, virtual world settings offer a level of sensory experience that enhances the therapeutic process. People now live innovatively by possessing both a physical life and a virtual life. Avatars allow for people to innovatively express identities as literal or metaphorical representations of self such as the inner child or the shadow. With innovative advances in technology and artificial intelligence, we now have the ability to simulate scenarios, manipulating outcomes and reframing experiences. Artificially intelligent avatars used in new and innovative forms of psychotherapy help a client heal from trauma, create a new ending to a dilemma, or work out unfinished business with a deceased loved one. These are but a few examples of how innovative avatar therapy simulations can enhance healing and promote good mental health.

Properly trained practitioners using innovative avatar therapy simulation have a clear understanding of more traditional approaches to distance therapy delivery methods. In addition, avatar therapists have adequate knowledge of the online disinhibition effect as well as trauma-related theories so that clients can be adequately prepared for avatar work. Avatar therapists understand the importance of titrating emotions and properly grounding the client using containment techniques. Keeping the client emotionally safe is paramount in a virtual environment because issues that would typically surface over several months or years often surface much more quickly in a virtual world setting.

Innovative avatar therapy simulation moves far beyond the therapist and client's avatar representations engaging in online traditional talk or text-based therapy. This innovation in psychotherapy combines artificial intelligence and distance technology with elements of traditional psychotherapeutic techniques. Training practitioners for this futuristic work brings innovation to the fields of psychotherapy and counselling education as we prepare practitioners to incorporate avatars and artificial intelligence across time zones thus bringing the art of psychotherapy to the global community.

Introducing innovative avatar therapy simulation to practitioners across all continents allows for many collaborative initiatives in counsellor education and mental health promotion providing for borderless interventions. People experience change with immediacy when virtual worlds, avatars and artificial intelligence are introduced into the psyche. The change is incorporated into their being, making the change permanent and not something to only be imagined.

As we move into the future, innovation and change is inevitable. Encompassing the many ways in which mental health will be impacted by technology will one day be a voluminous effort. We hope to bring updated content to the reader as new technologies and advancements begin to influence mental health.

REFERENCES

von Stamm, B., & Trifilova, A. (2009). *The future of innovation.* Farnham: Gower.

INDEX